Prophecy and Gnosis

Prophecy and Gnosis

ex APOCALYPTICISM
IN THE WAKE OF THE
LUTHERAN REFORMATION

Robin Bruce Barnes

ex 1988
Stanford University Press
Stanford, California

Stanford University Press
Stanford, California
©1988 by the Board of Trustees of the
Leland Stanford Junior University
Printed in the United States of America

CIP data appear at the end of the book

For Ann Lee

᨞ Acknowledgments

This study began as a doctoral dissertation at the University of Virginia. To my adviser, Professor H. C. Erik Midelfort, I owe the deepest debt a student can owe a mentor. His influence drew me to serious study in Reformation history, and he has continued to give unselfishly of his time and knowledge through the years I have worked on this book. His wisdom has both humbled and inspired me.

I am grateful to the Center for Reformation Research in St. Louis, and to the Director of the 1976 Summer Institute, Robert Kolb, for helping to launch my inquiry into sixteenth-century apocalypticism. I also wish to thank the directors and staffs of the British Library, the Württembergische Landesbibliothek in Stuttgart, the Bayerische Staatsbibliothek in Munich, and the Staats- und Universitätsbibliothek, Hamburg. I am particularly indebted to the staff of the Herzog August Bibliothek in Wolfenbüttel, whose patience and helpfulness greatly eased my research tasks.

The extensive revision and expansion of my dissertation that began in 1981 has been aided by grants from the German Academic Exchange Service, the American Council of Learned Societies, and Davidson College. I completed the manuscript in the near-perfect environment provided by the 1986 Folger Institute program "German Society: Its Forms and Sources 1450–1650," directed by Professor Tom Brady; my participation in the program was funded by the National Endowment for the Humanities. My thanks also go to the Duke Endowment for a grant to help cover publication costs.

I have benefited from comments on the manuscript by Mark Edwards, John Headley, and Lionel Rothkrug. Conversations with Miriam Chrisman, among other colleagues, have helped me develop whatever breadth of understanding lies behind this work. The editors at Stanford University Press have been models of efficiency and good judgment. Needless to say, I alone am responsible for whatever shortcomings remain.

To my teachers at Colby College and at the University of Virginia, including Clifford Berschneider, George Elison, Harold Raymond, Martin Havran, and Alexander Sedgwick, I owe thanks for nurturing in me an abiding love of the study of history. For informal but invaluable guidance in German language and culture I wish to thank Wolfram and Sighilt von Bleichert, and Frau Hannah Stamer.

To family I owe the most. My parents-in-law, Leo and Marion Bressler, have long indulged my ungodly work habits, while remaining steadfast in encouragement. My own parents, William A. and Shirley M. Barnes, gave me the best that parents can give: the loving discipline that ultimately frees the soul. To my spouse, Ann Lee Bressler, on whom I lean at every turn, I dedicate this book.

R.B.B.

Contents

Prophecy and Gnosis

Introduction

How many endings did the Middle Ages
have!   Michelet

In the year 1559, Philipp Melanchthon told hundreds of students
in a packed lecture hall that "there will occur in times to come great
and terrible changes and disorders. You young people are now yet
living in the golden time, but there will soon hereafter follow much
more horrible, more afflicted times, as is shown by the wonders that
happen and are seen daily, but that are ignored and made light of
with overwhelming confidence and stubborn malice." [1] The famed
theologian went on to describe some notable signs and wonders
that lately had been fulfilled. A strange lunar halo, accompanied by
a flaming lion and a wounded eagle in the heavens, had presaged
the death of Charles V. Another celestial wonder had foretold that
Prince John Frederick would return to rule in Saxony. Years before,
Martin Luther had seen signs telling of the great Reformation to
come. And now portents of all kinds abounded. There had been
several to indicate that the Turk would soon invade the West, and
Melanchthon sought to buttress the credibility of these signs. He
reminded his listeners that Johann Hilten, a fifteenth-century monk
widely reputed to have possessed prophetic powers, had predicted
that in 1600 the satanic forces of Gog and Magog would rule in
Germany. It was not long until then, and it was certain that "there
sit right here in this auditorium many among you who will experience it; may God then give you mercy." [2] Melanchthon described in
addition many signs and wonders that could only mean that the
end of the world was close at hand.

The students probably needed no reminders of these things. The society into which they had been born was thoroughly imbued with expectations of enormous upheaval and the end of the world. The Antichrist had been revealed; the truths of the Gospel had been recovered; the final acts of world history were now in progress. The sense of crisis that had so dominated the later Middle Ages had by no means dissolved; indeed, the Reformation had intensified and spread it. And as in earlier centuries, people faced the future with an outlook of combined hope, dread, and wonder. Clearly, the Last Day could not be far off; in fact it might be expected at any time. A passionate longing for deliverance competed with deep fear of the earthly trials still to come, and of the Judgment. All of these emotions inspired a restless curiosity about the future, about God's plan for mankind.

This feeling of crisis and imminent upheaval, so central in the history of the Western world, was one manifestation of the universal human desire to discover meaning through what Frank Kermode has called "the sense of an ending."[3] To see life, not just one's own life but that of the world as a whole, in relation to beginnings and ends is perhaps the most important need of the human psyche. This need is the starting place of eschatology. The history of eschatology lies at the heart of the history of culture and of civilization itself, for in beliefs concerning ends are reflected the most basic assumptions about meaning and purpose. The tendency to find the all-important end in an imminent crisis of the present world order and a decisive triumph of good over evil that is part of a divine plan may be termed "apocalypticism." Melanchthon's warning to his students was a typical expression of an apocalyptic sensibility that pervaded his culture and that had far-reaching significance.

The following chapters examine the nature and effects of this expectancy in Lutheran Germany during the century following the initial triumphs of the Reformation. My study seeks to show, in the first place, the continuing intensity of apocalyptic excitement among Luther's heirs. While I have not engaged in systematic comparisons, I do contend that in no other major confessional group of the sixteenth century did late medieval eschatological tensions remain so persistent and so broadly influential. Indeed, Luther's Reformation, in appropriating and imaginatively reconstructing the prophetic world-view, actually reinforced an inherited sense of expectancy, and helped to produce in sixteenth-century Germany a level of apocalyptic expectation that finds few parallels in Western history. Moreover, as the sixteenth century progressed, apocalyptic thinking in Lutheran areas tended to become more explicit, more reasoned, and more comprehensive.

There are, I will suggest, two essential elements in apocalyptic thought; I label these elements "prophetic" and "gnostic." These terms require careful definition (see Chapter 1), but they can be explained briefly as referring to the aspects of warning and consolation, on one hand, and discovery and insight, on the other. My central contention is that continuing prophetic excitement in the wake of the German Reformation prompted an ever expanding search for apocalyptic insight, a search that affected study of the Bible, of history, and of nature in fundamental ways. The study thus tries to make some of the more foreign preoccupations of that era more comprehensible by examining them in connection with a pervasive and evolving mood of expectancy. Finally, I have made an effort to understand the reasons for, and the implications of, the relatively sudden waning of this sensibility during the era of the Thirty Years' War.

The touchstone of the study is the assertion that Lutheranism was the only major confession of the Reformation era to give a clear, virtually doctrinal sanction to a powerful sense of eschatological expectancy. Neither the other main branches of Protestantism nor the prevailing traditions of Catholic piety were as thoroughly rooted as Lutheranism in a sense of nearing Judgment. The Wittenberger himself was largely responsible for stamping his movement with this apocalyptic character. For Luther, Christ stood poised to return, to deliver his own, and to deal the final blow to a corrupt world. The faithful could rejoice in the recovery of God's Word and the nearness of their salvation. Meanwhile they were called upon to steel themselves against the final ragings of Satan's powers on earth. The Antichrist had been discovered in the bosom of the Roman church. The Turk and other open enemies of the Gospel threatened to destroy Christendom. At times it appeared that biblical prophecy was coming closer to fulfillment every day. The proliferation of new sects and the waxing confusion over the true teachings of the Gospel gave further evidence that the Last Judgment drew near. Despite his own realization of the need for discretion in preaching on these matters—a realization aided by what he saw as the misuse of his ideas in the bloody Peasants' Revolt of

1525—Luther's personal expectancy was intense. There were times when his excitement seems to have crested, as in 1529–30 when he worked feverishly to understand current events, and particularly the onslaught of the Turk, in the context of his larger conception of history.[4] But he never abandoned this fundamental belief about the direction of history and its imminent end.

It needs to be emphasized that in Luther's eyes believers had every reason to rejoice over the nearness of Christ's return; in this respect he threw off the often morbid fear of punishment and destruction that had haunted the previous century. Yet with his insistence on the nearness of the end, Luther encouraged a high level of eschatological expectation among his followers; the anxious experience of looking forward and waiting remained. In fact, that experience was now given full and open sanction by the Reformer. While most of his predecessors and contemporaries took over common eschatological views more or less unconsciously, as inherited assumptions, Luther carefully sifted them and applied them with an unprecedented explicitness to the events of his day.[5] More important, the traditional views that he did accept were now incorporated into a potent vision, based on biblical imagery, that offered a coherent outlook on the world. More effectively than any previous interpreter, he gave a world-historical, indeed a world-transcending significance to contemporary events by placing them in an eschatological framework; everything pointed to the coming Day of Redemption. Luther found little or no comfort in contemplating the earthly future; hope lay in the discovery that his generation was witnessing and participating in the critical closing acts of history.

In the century after the break with Rome, Lutheran preachers and publicists hammered consistently on the theme of the Last Day and its nearness. As confessional lines hardened and the era of religious wars began, sermons and tracts emphasized more and more the need for immediate repentance and grew ever heavier with polemic against the enemies of the true church within and without Germany. Particularly with the outbreak of war against the emperor in 1546, a siege mentality began to grow within Lutheranism. As the century progressed, Lutherans felt increasingly threatened by a Catholic church bent on reconquest and by a militant, expanding Calvinism. Serious theological disputes split Luther's followers into bitterly opposed factions during the middle decades of the century; the divided house appeared weak and vulnerable. Despite the political victory of the Peace of Augsburg in 1555, there could be no sense of tranquility in the face of the Council of Trent and expanding Jesuit activity within the empire.[6] By 1600 a considerable number of well-publicized apostasies had intensified an already deep Lutheran defensiveness.

But beyond this, in the eyes of many Lutherans in the late sixteenth century, the entire social order appeared to be falling apart. Vice ran rampant as God's Word was ignored with more blatant impunity every day. The Germans, who had been blessed with the recovery and clear preaching of Christian truth, were proving themselves the most godless and ungrateful of peoples. What else could possibly be expected but a devastating outpouring of divine wrath upon Christ's enemies everywhere, and the Last Judgment itself?

The pervasiveness and the persistence of such views in Germany have rarely been acknowledged, especially among the many scholars who have studied English apocalypticism in the sixteenth and seventeenth centuries. Those who trace the development of the English apocalyptic tradition from Bale and Foxe in the sixteenth century through such later figures as Thomas Brightman and Joseph Mede must begin their works with lengthy references to the background of the Continental Reformation. But the usual implication of such studies is that apocalyptic prophecy found its fullest flowering in England. Typical is the assertion of Bryan Ball that "the seeds [of eschatological expectation] sown in the early spring of the Reformation were borne across the English Channel to take root in a climate favorable to their further development."[7] In fact, not only did the tradition of Reformation prophecy develop considerably later in England than it did in Germany; but the results of the present study suggest that throughout the sixteenth century and even later England saw only a weak reflection of the eschatological excitement that obtained among Lutherans. Most English interpreters were actually following in the footsteps of their German counterparts until well after 1600. The forms of expectation that did eventually find prominence in England were mostly the products of a confident Calvinist millenarianism, an outlook that was less intensely apocalyptic—so I will argue—than the prevailing Lutheran attitude.

Nor is there much evidence to suggest that other European lands were as deeply influenced as Lutheran Germany by apocalyptic thinking in the Reformation period. Where Catholicism was officially maintained, room for the airing of prophetic warnings or speculation appears to have narrowed considerably in this era of doctrinal tightening. To be sure, inherited prophetic traditions did not disappear. Hopes for a *renovatio mundi*, to be effected through a future angelic pope, or through a political figure such as the emperor Charles, persisted throughout the age, as did fears of the still expected Antichrist. Other expectations, such as those that allowed the Jesuits or the Franciscans an exalted role in a final great spreading of the faith, could also continue to flower. But such beliefs were not generally broadcast outside the groups of thinkers and the religious orders that tended to nurture them. Particularly in Italy and in Spain, the complex heritage of medieval and Renaissance prophecy was increasingly restricted by clerical hierarchies that sought to play down the implications of historical change for the role of the institutional church. While many apocalyptic ideas continued to circulate, it is difficult to avoid the impression that a general exclusion of such notions from both pulpit and press limited their overall currency.[8]

The same may be said for France, although here the tensions surrounding the Wars of Religion may have encouraged the adoption of apocalyptic attitudes among some groups. One French scholar has argued that the Catholic League of 1588–89 was a form of collective response to a sense of eschatological crisis.[9] It is striking to note, however, that many French apocalyptic works from this period were either translated from earlier German writings or based heavily on their ideas; it appears that French Catholic writers at this time drew freely from the stock of German Protestant apocalypticism, adapting its schemes and imagery to their need for consolation and for polemical ammunition in a situation of acute uncertainty. If it is true that the League was a response to a sense of crisis, this very fact helps to illustrate profound differences between French attitudes and the Lutheran apocalyptic posture. For as we will see, the consistent intensity of Lutheran expectations resulted at least partly from the assumption that a collective response to eschatological crisis was ultimately irrelevant. Individual repentance and watchfulness, not social action, were the only truly meaningful responses to God's Word in a crumbling world.

As the sixteenth century progressed, the main outlines of Luther's prophetic understanding proved to be consistently influential. But if his insights were not to become empty formulae, if faith forged in expectation was not to wane, there had to be a continual restatement, reinterpretation, and adjustment of those original positions. If the faithful were to persevere in the face of mounting troubles and dangers until the universal Judgment, they had to have a clear vision of what to expect during whatever time remained. Thus the search for prophetic understanding became ever more serious. The Lutheran emphasis on the direct encounter of every individual with God insured a continual ferment of interpretation as believers sought the guidance of the Holy Spirit in understanding prophetic matters. And if these were indeed the Last Days, it was to be expected that divine secrets should be uncovered, and that exciting revelations would be granted to persons of true faith. Especially because to many Lutherans the future appeared more and more threatening, the search for prophetic certainty often reached the stage of desperation.

Prophetic research blossomed in the later sixteenth century as professors, pastors, and laymen sought to achieve assurance in an increasingly confusing world. Searching more intently for signs that could bolster their eschatological faith, Luther's followers increasingly turned the intellectual methods of Renaissance humanism toward the goal of apocalyptic understanding. Evidence from history was used more and more to complement and support biblical prophecies, as ever more serious efforts were made to discern the outlines of the divine plan. Many other sources and methods could also serve this end. Astrologers, like preachers and theologians, were generally convinced that universal changes would soon occur, and many Lutherans sought eagerly after their forecasts. Mathematics and other nontheological tools were used with growing boldness in serious efforts to seek out clear answers to the mysteries of the Last Days. In addition, a wide variety of popular prophetic notions circulated freely, in large measure through the flood of books and pamphlets that rose continually during these decades. The printing press made available an ocean of ancient wisdom, occult lore, and magical theory. One current fed another as every new observation or speculation seemed to offer further hope of insight to true believers. By the late decades of the century a truly eclectic apocalypticism was emerging, in which the search for universal prophetic truth, for a saving knowledge or gnosis, knew virtually no bounds. Yet neither the pursuit nor the preaching of a supposed hidden wisdom ever entirely obscured the goal of prophetic warning and exhortation; concern for the salvation of souls did not disappear. This was still fundamentally a medieval apocalypticism, the expression of a religious sensibility that called sinners to repent before it was too late.

The high point of this interplay among eschatological teaching, popular notions, and other currents of thought came in the first years of the seventeenth century, before the outbreak of the Thirty Years' War. By that time, the search for prophetic truth had become something close to an obsession in Lutheran Germany. In their quest for clarity prophetic seekers had filled the air with cloudy speculations; the resulting aura of mystery only reinforced the pervasive sense of desperation. In this period, the wild proliferation of revelations and speculations began to draw bitter condemnation from an increasingly cautious church establishment. Orthodox leaders still shared a strong sense of eschatological expectancy. Nevertheless, as they began carefully to define the realm of legitimate prophecy, they denounced more and more harshly the effort to penetrate divine mysteries. The most avid seekers for prophetic truth, meanwhile, became alienated from what they saw as a blind and arid scholasticism. With these quarrels the common ground of apocalyptic consciousness was starting to break apart.

It may appear strange or questionable that the sort of speculative adventurousness we have described should be discovered in the Lutheran world of thought. One of Luther's most consistent themes, after all, was to condemn in no uncertain terms the pernicious effects of philosophy on faith; human cognition had nothing to do with salvation. Doctrinally, Lutheranism has always emphasized the utter impotence of unaided reason, and the period in which we are interested provides no exception. But there is another side to this story that seldom receives the emphasis it deserves. When Luther attacked reason, he meant only reason that "tyrannizes the conscience and puts itself in the place of God."[10] In its proper place, human reason was in fact a divine faculty. Reason illuminated by faith (*ratio fide illuminata*) was a necessary and wonderful gift of God. Indeed, faith demanded reason's support.[11] It was this sort of reason, an essentially intuitive rather than syllogistic approach to knowledge actually subverting the foundations of scholastic as well as humanist learning, that aided Luther in his prophetic interpretations and discoveries. Lutheran piety, as a child of this deeply intuitive reason, was by no means immune to the desire to see the world whole, or to comprehend the workings of God. A tensely eschatological faith demanded spiritual insight. It sought to understand all experience in terms of a single framework. The all-encompassing system of medieval Christianity had once afforded such a vision; but the universality of this vision had long been breaking down. Now Luther had subjected it to a fundamental reinterpretation, and his discoveries helped to shape new and pressing questions about the world.

Luther's Reformation was after all built upon discoveries. It was shaped not only by the rediscovery of essential insights into the meaning of faith and the Gospel, but also by the uncovering of prophetic truths from which believers thought they could recognize the meaning of the great events taking place around them. For Lutherans these two types of discovery were actually inseparable. To recognize truth was to give clear answers to some key prophetic questions. How, for instance, was one to be sure that the real Antichrist had been revealed, and what made it so certain that current events were ushering in the Day of Redemption? The virtual unanimity of Lutheran opinion on such matters was not a result of prophetic faith alone; it required a general acknowledgment that certain insights into scriptural prophecy were unquestionably true. These insights necessarily depended upon more than simple faith; they required proper understanding of God's plan for the world. But how and where did one draw the line between faith and understanding? This ancient problem was posed as acutely as ever in the prophetic thought of sixteenth-century Germany.

To be sure, many Lutherans resisted the notion that any prophetic certainty could be established beyond what Luther himself had discovered in Scripture. These believers kept the message of passages like Matthew 24:36 clearly in mind: "But of that day and hour [i.e. the time of the end] knoweth no man, no, not the angels of heaven, but my Father only."[12] Yet aside from the date of Christ's return there were many other pressing questions about the events of the Last Times; moreover Luther himself had made conjectures about the time of the end and related prophetic issues. Little wonder, then, that in the atmosphere of apprehension that grew up in late sixteenth-century Germany, Lutheran pastors and theologians were among those whose hopes and fears led them to speculate with a notable freedom. Among laymen there was still less hesitation. The proper attitude was one of watching and waiting. But how far could one wander in order to watch? Where and how far could one search for prophetic understanding? This issue was never clearly resolved, even among strict Lutherans, until the era of the Thirty Years' War. Strangely, that holocaust would help bring about a quite sudden collapse of apocalyptic expectancy in Germany, a collapse that marked as well as any change can the end of an age.

Although I have stressed the role of Lutheran piety, this is not intended to be a confessional study. It is rather an investigation of the ways in which prevalent religious assumptions both affected and reflected the intellectual patterns of a larger culture. The hopes, fears, and speculations to be investigated are primarily those of urban society—of pastors, teachers, and literate laymen in Lutheran cities and towns. The Protestant message was after all "pitched to the solid burgher," a fact that goes far to illuminate the successes and failures of the movement.[13] Among the literate and even the semiliterate members of burgher society, the message of Lutheran preachers and writers had its broadest and most lasting popular appeal. Whether we can appropriately use the term "popular" in this context is a matter of definition; these townsmen took part in a popular culture in the sense that they were open to influences from a number of different sources. They had some share in the learning of the educated elite. At the same time, they retained roots in inherited folk traditions. They were exposed to an ever expanding variety of religious ideas. They formed, finally, an increasingly articulate class, in which news, rumor, and propaganda could swiftly attain a broad currency. These various influences contributed to the formation of a powerful common sensibility that is now deceptively difficult to reconstruct.

This effort at reconstruction must avoid reducing the apocalyptic world-view either to a simple function of political, social, or economic forces, or to a purely subjective expression of religious experience. I have examined this sensibility both as it was shaped by external circumstances, and also as a complex of ideas with its own dynamic. But I have stressed the latter approach, partly out of a belief that the first responsibility of the historian must be to grapple with the minds of the past on their own terms. The world did not end in the sixteenth century, nor, so far as I am aware, has it ended since. To the extent that men expected some cosmic upheaval, they were clearly mistaken. The belief that the Last Judgment was imminent was part of a fiction people then used to make sense of their lives, a fiction most of us no longer find meaningful. But while we may see strong elements of naïveté in that picture of the world, we risk missing a great deal if we too quickly assume the condescending attitude of the enlightened analyst. As the medievalist Bernard McGinn has put it, "there is a wisdom and meaning in the symbols of apocalyptic spirituality that can easily be lost by the ham-handed application of the critical method." [14] We postmoderns have our own fictions, after all, and they are no less fundamental to our actions even though we may recognize them for what they are. Moreover, history simply refuses to be stuffed into today's categories of understanding, no matter how sophisticated and finely honed those categories may be. Our most important task must be to listen to the voices of the late Reformation era, to understand them in their own context before endeavoring to categorize or to explain.

On the other hand, to reject the sort of positivist reductionism that infects much of contemporary historical writing is not necessarily to embrace an equally untenable idealism. At best, this sort of debate in the philosophy of history results in an irresolvable chicken-and-egg riddle. Historical realities must be understood as social realities, in which material and mental conditions reflect and affect one another. The fullest possible understanding of any social world therefore requires that we examine it from both inside and outside, that is to say, both from the perspective of contemporaries and from our own. [15] Obviously, no effort to comprehend the atmosphere of tension and confusion in Germany during the late Reformation era can afford to ignore the sociopolitical circumstances to which the people of that time were reacting. At the same time, the deepest concerns of that society can never be adequately understood if we fail to see how thoroughly life was governed by inherited apocalyptic assumptions. Learned as well as common people continued to expect some enormous upheaval; with upheaval would come trial and judgment in one form or another.

Such a sensibility could affect thought and action in complex and obscure ways, and a great deal does indeed remain obscure about late Reformation culture. Despite the appearance of several studies that have improved our understanding of the intellectual climate of continental Europe in the later sixteenth and early seventeenth centuries, [16] scholars are still relatively unfamiliar with the nature and the context of German thought at that time. Some three-quarters of a century ago the period was described as the "terra incognita of

Lutheranism,"[17] and the phrase still applies, not only to Lutheranism *per se* but also to the world of ideas surrounding it. It applies especially to that shadowy realm of powerful but often only implicit beliefs, the discovery of which is so crucial to the understanding of any society, including our own.

1
⊷§ Apocalyptic Tradition and the Reformation

THE APOCALYPTIC OUTLOOK

The term "apocalypticism" allows of no clear and simple definition, for it refers to an extremely complex range of attitudes and ideas. In a general historical sense it designates a type of eschatological understanding that originated among the ancient Hebrews and that has influenced the Judeo-Christian tradition in varying degrees ever since. "Apocalypse" derives from a Greek word meaning "revelation," "discovery," or "disclosure." Jewish apocalypticism (c. 200 B.C. to 100 A.D.) showed an intense concern with imminent upheaval and a powerful desire to understand and illustrate the critical role of the present in the cosmic struggle between good and evil. Hope for the future of this world was generally abandoned, and attention was focused on an approaching judgment. Apocalyptic writings typically employed a highly dramatic form of presentation, using a bewildering variety of figurative devices to communicate the profound truths concerning this all-important crisis.[1] But such a listing of major characteristics will not take us very far. An introductory grasp of this form of understanding can best be gained if we consider it as incorporating elements that appeared in at least two other ancient forms of eschatological thought: prophecy and gnosticism.

"Prophecy" is most commonly understood as the prediction of future things; more generally and more properly, it refers to any spiritually inspired preaching or warning. A much more restricted meaning is often given to the term by Old Testament scholars who use it to designate the preaching of a definite period in Jewish his-

tory, beginning with Samuel and ending with Malachi. Prophecy in
this limited sense is opposed to "apocalyptic," which in biblical
studies denotes a later eschatological movement within Judaism.
Scholars have often tended to see the apocalyptic movement as no
more than a pale and twisted reflection of true prophecy, a crude
and uninspired sequel to the genuine vision and admonition of the
earlier age.

Thus the terms "prophetic" and "apocalyptic" have sometimes
been used in a larger sense as labels for what are taken to be healthy
and corrupt forms of eschatological understanding.[2] But historically the distinction is not so simple. Closer studies of the role of
apocalypticism in both Jewish and Christian thought have effectively rescued the movement from the charge of degenerate obscu-
rantism. Apocalyptic visions offered a kind of language which gave
meaning to the present in the context of a universal scheme. Although these visions were often esoteric in nature, they did include
an essentially prophetic message of promise and admonition.

Moreover, the origins of Christianity were intimately bound up
with the apocalyptic sensibility in Judaism, and in the history of the
Christian West, prophetic and apocalyptic forms of eschatology
have been so closely intertwined that it is difficult to make any clear
separation. Medieval prophecy was based upon a Christian conception of history that had inherent apocalyptic elements. For this reason, attempts to apply these categories to figures of premodern eras,
to distinguish the truly prophetic spirits from those who were ob-
sessed with mere apocalypticism, must be highly misleading. Such
a classification does violence to the thinking of people for whom
religious and moral issues could not be separated from prevailing
views on the meaning and direction of human history. The apocalypticism of the Middle Ages and the Reformation was genuinely
prophetic exhortation and consolation, notwithstanding our modern unwillingness to accept most of its forms.

This description has already hinted at the central role of discovery in the apocalyptic mentality—the importance of unveiling hidden truths. In this respect apocalypticism shares certain basic features with another strain of ancient religious thought: gnosticism.[3]
According to Walter Schmithals, apocalypticism and gnosticism
are "undoubtedly related mythological conceptions."[4] Both these
movements were characterized by radical pessimism toward the
present order of the world. In both, the current eon was destined

for dissolution. For apocalypticism God had preordained an end to this corrupt world when the righteous would be saved; for the gnostics the present cosmos, riddled with evil, would evaporate into nothingness once all the pneuma, or divine spirit, had been released from it. The two movements had in common the belief that a special class of persons—the chosen, the righteous, the spiritual ones—"do not share the fate of this eon that is passing away, but belong to the other, the higher, or the coming world."[5]

To be sure, there were key differences. In gnosis, for example, the division between the two eons was essentially spatial—the good was celestial, physically apart from evil—while in apocalyptic thought it was temporal. Yet this difference was not exclusive, since either form of understanding could and did make use of both spatial and temporal imagery.[6] Another difference was that the gnostic saw God as entirely separated from this evil world—his was an anticosmic dualism—while the apocalypticist, more closely tied to Jewish thought, continued to see the world as God's creation. Apocalypticism lamented not the world itself but rather the condition of the world. Yet a deeper similarity remains: the godly man belongs not to this world, but to the next; the present eon is held in contempt. Indeed the underlying links compelled Rudolf Otto to agree that "Gnosis is of the very spirit of apocalyptic teaching"; this is "a judgment," adds Schmithals, "which of course can be stated conversely as well."[7]

What we need to note particularly is that both the gnostic and the apocalypticist sought to understand, and to communicate to the worthy, an esoteric and all-important spiritual truth. For adherents of both movements this truth was once possessed, had somehow been lost, and was now being recovered. In gnosticism, the possessors of the divine sparks must come to awareness of their true origin and destiny; the gnostic must uncover a concealed reality. Comparably, apocalypticism almost always incorporates the notion that divine wisdom was granted to a few chosen men in times long past; this wisdom has since been obscured, and will be revealed again only in the Last Times.[8] The believer naturally desires this godly wisdom, though it is not quite the ultimate goal it is for the gnostic. As Christopher Rowland has written, "Knowing one's origins and destiny is just as much a concern of apocalyptic as [of] gnosticism, though in the former this knowledge has not yet become in itself a means of salvation."[9] As we will illustrate shortly, the quest for "gnosis," defined as a saving (or at least salvation-serving) knowledge of transcendent mysteries, would remain evident, if often quite muted, in later forms of Western apocalypticism.

The apocalyptic outlook on the world, then, may be understood as a strongly eschatological perspective or vision that incorporates elements of both prophetic preaching and gnostic seeking. But to refer to a single apocalyptic vision may be misleading; we are concerned rather with a complex of attitudes and beliefs that is bound to no particular conception of the divisions or limits of earthly history. The future might offer nothing but suffering until the end of the world, or it might hold the promise of salvation within time. Within Christian apocalypticism a great diversity of conceptions makes generalizations difficult. As Marjorie Reeves has written, "from its birth Christian thought held within it both a pessimistic and an optimistic expectation concerning history; its end could be conceived either as a mounting crescendo of evil or as the Millennium, a Messianic Age of Gold."[10]

Indeed Christian visions of the end often combined these expectations by anticipating a time of unimaginable suffering to be followed by the final triumph of the good. The prospects of trial, judgment, and deliverance were generally present together. Apocalyptic meditation thus "swings between terror and hope" as it surveys the landscape of the universal drama.[11] But again, the particulars of the dramatic conception could vary greatly from one scheme to another. In this connection it is also important to note that not every apocalyptic thinker waits in immediate anticipation of the final cosmic resolution. What is important is that the critical events of the Last Times have begun. While there may still be much to happen, the divine drama has reached a decisive stage.[12] To the extent that ignorance is suffering, the message is always urgent.

Recognizing this inherent urgency most easily in its more sensational manifestations, students of Western history in the medieval and early modern periods have traditionally tended to associate apocalyptic thought with outbursts of social radicalism or revolution. This tendency was epitomized by Norman Cohn's widely known *The Pursuit of the Millennium*, which sought to link the appearance of millenarian excitement in later medieval Europe with outbreaks of social and political revolt among the oppressed and dislocated.[13] Cohn's work saw millenarianism—the belief in the approaching realization of the Kingdom of God on Earth—as the most extreme and significant form of apocalypticism, which became a "dynamic social myth" only under conditions of severe social and psychological stress, as in the wake of famine, plague, or economic hardship. Cohn did recognize that conditions of social unrest cannot by themselves explain the appearance of millenarianism. Nonetheless his work helped to inspire a spate of more explicitly sociological studies that developed models to explain the conditions for millenarian seizures.[14]

More recent studies have shown that Cohn's approach was fundamentally flawed, and have supplied us with a fuller and more satisfactory understanding of the context of medieval millenarianism. Robert Lerner, for instance, has argued convincingly in a series of studies that chiliasm, or "the expectation of imminent, supernaturally inspired, radical betterment on earth before the Last Judgment,"[15] was by no means limited to religious fanatics and social revolutionaries; it was widespread and constant by the late Middle Ages. Such chiliastic conviction could be and sometimes was oriented toward revolutionary action, but it could equally well serve simply to "encourage perseverance in the face of persecution and bring hope in the face of trials."[16] It was in any case far more than a temporary psychological reaction to troubled times. Even a major disaster like the Black Death did not necessarily inspire any fundamentally new chiliastic schemes. Such major events could be and generally were understood in the context of a basically unchanging set of prophetic assumptions, which Lerner refers to as a mental "deep structure." This pattern of understanding lasted for centuries because it brought consolation, not just in times of exceptional suffering, but also in daily life.[17]

Other recent studies have emphasized that millenarianism needs to be seen as one variation of a broader apocalypticism in the Middle Ages, and that it is primarily this larger phenomenon that calls for understanding. Bernard McGinn has offered a helpful definition of apocalypticism which includes "first, a sense of the unity and structure of history conceived as a divinely predetermined totality; second, pessimism about the present and conviction of its imminent crisis; and third, belief in the proximate judgment of evil and triumph of the good, the element of vindication."[18] McGinn holds that while there is no one, clearly definable, "apocalyptic understanding of reality," the term can nonetheless stand usefully for a general pattern of beliefs about the meaning and direction of history. Considered in this way, medieval apocalypticism was often quite the opposite of a popular religious ideology with revolutionary implications. Apocalyptic schemes were a way of understanding political and social changes by integrating them into a transcendent scheme of meaning. As such, they could be used by clerics and other men of influence to support an established structure.

In fact, McGinn suggests that the influence of apocalyptic thought was predominantly conservative; the revolutionary use of apocalyptic ideas was the exception in the Middle Ages, not the rule. Current events could generally be fitted into an existing apocalyptic scheme, but at major historical turning points inherited schemes would be modified or expanded to account for these changes. McGinn finds three such turning points in medieval history that inspired bursts of apocalyptic creativity. These were "the conversion of the Roman empire, the onslaught of Islam, and the emergence of the high medieval papacy." [19] In each case, an apocalyptic understanding was developed that validated the new historical conditions and supported existing political structures. Far from being only an expression of protest or despair, apocalypticism was in fact a normal premodern way of making sense of present conditions.

It is true that insofar as apocalypticism shares the dualist emphasis of gnosticism, it always finds fault with present conditions. The current state of affairs always looks grim in comparison with the promise of the coming Kingdom or New Age. Yet this contrast between present woes and future peace does not automatically make the apocalyptic thinker a social or intellectual revolutionary. His message can be a call to contemplation rather than action, a comforting recognition that the events of the Last Times, like the entire structure of history, are in the hands of God. And if it is a call to action, this action may be in support of earthly rulers or institutions in their struggle against the forces of evil. Moreover, to the extent that apocalyptically inspired social action brings hopes or fears to realization, it may actually serve to reduce alienation and defuse expectancy. Neither did the quest for universal insight necessarily make apocalypticism revolutionary or heretical. Indeed the true division in Western history was never really between orthodoxy and gnosis, but rather between the gnosis that was accepted as true and the gnosis that was rejected as false.[20] The accepted gnosis was the one that could be domesticated and made to serve the needs of an establishment.

It is important to acknowledge, finally, that apocalypticism is "always more than a reaction to causal structures in existing reality."[21] Indeed apocalyptic assumptions themselves gave shape to "existing reality" for countless people over many centuries. To acknowledge that religious attitudes and expressions cannot be divorced from political and social circumstances is not to assert that they are at bottom governed by those circumstances; just as political and social developments force adjustments in patterns of thought, so too patterns of thought and belief are necessarily reflected in the way people act. As McGinn notes, "Perhaps the apocalypticist might be better described as one on the lookout for crisis, rather than one who merely reacts to it when it happens."[22] Such a "lookout" might be built on a prophetic "deep structure," but the potential for real creativity and originality within the apocalyptic world-view was nevertheless enormous. New conceptions, new insights into the divine plan and the Last Times could exercise a direct and lasting influence upon social realities. Thus, to glance ahead, Martin Luther's reimagining of the world in apocalyptic terms would create new social facts and new questions for his society, even though these facts and questions were still fundamentally the products of a medieval and prophetic world view.

Thus we will approach apocalypticism as a type of eschatological understanding that includes elements of both prophetic preaching and gnostic striving. Apocalypticism seeks to console and to warn by offering insight into the crucial role of the present in a cosmic struggle, the predetermined outcome of which is the approaching triumph of good over evil. It is inherently neither revolutionary nor quietist, but can appear in many different social contexts. And finally, it has the potential to shape social realities in original ways.

THE MEDIEVAL HERITAGE

The tensely expectant atmosphere of Reformation Germany was largely a continuation of tendencies that had been growing throughout the later Middle Ages. Yet apocalyptic assumptions and ideas had long been out of favor among the standard-bearers of Christian orthodoxy. From the time of Augustine down to the late Middle Ages, church doctrine had faced—or escaped—the prob-

lem of accounting for historical developments by playing down the
historical significance of the Last Things.[23] The Advent of Christ
had marked a new historical dispensation, but the promise of salvation to believers had nothing to do with the course of history
after Christ; indeed it had no true connection with historical progress at all. Rather, the church was the institutionalized means of
salvation, and no essential changes would take place in the present
order until the Second Coming, when history would end and the
Last Judgment would occur. For Augustine and the entire tradition
that followed him, the church itself represented Christ's reign on
earth. The Millennium, the rule of Christ with his saints, was interpreted figuratively as the whole period between the First and Second Advents. Although Augustine did think that he was living in
the sixth and last age of history, he emphasized those aspects of the
Final Judgment that applied to the individual soul, rather than
those that applied to history as a whole.[24] The church served its
own purposes by adopting this view, which deemphasized any notion of historical change, whether progress or decay. On these assumptions the time of the Second Advent could not be predicted at
all, and even the most general conjecture was utterly futile. The end
would be sudden and unexpected, and it would bring the final judgment of all history.

Strong as the hold of the Augustinian view became, however, it
could not eliminate the apocalyptic tendencies that had flourished
in the early church. Not only had there been widespread expectation of Christ's return to Judgment; some of the fathers, including
figures as important as Lactantius (c. 240–320), had taught of a
future golden age, a millennial kingdom on earth. By the fourth
and fifth centuries the church was beginning to discourage this sort
of explicit expectation, but a combination of traditions continued
to sustain fears and hopes for the historical future. Such traditions
were particularly strong in Byzantine Christianity, but they penetrated the West as well.[25] Thus for example an influential cluster of
prophecies concerning a great, last World Emperor grew out of the
Sibylline Oracles. These oracles were Christianized imitations of
the books of the Sibyls, Greek prophetesses famous throughout the
Hellenic world. They suggested that after a time of intense persecution and suffering a great ruler would lead the final crusade
against all enemies of Christendom, and would reign in glory before
the end of the world. Similar predictions were found in writings

attributed to the martyr-bishop Methodius (died c. 311); this Pseudo-Methodius was above all concerned with the enemies of Christ that would arise in the East before the end of the world, and with the chosen emperor who would oppose them. Such expectations remained alive, though very far from universal, throughout the early medieval period.

Other expressions of apocalyptic conviction continued despite the growing weight of Augustinian teachings. The figure of the Antichrist, the man of Satan who would come in the Last Days to persecute Christians and spread evil in the world, had already been feared by the end of the patristic period, and persistently haunted medieval believers. Pope Gregory the Great was hardly alone among early medieval churchmen in his conviction that the end was near.[26] As long as basic doctrines were not challenged and the taint of heretical speculation was avoided, a domesticated form of apocalypticism was allowed a place in Christian belief.

Around the turn of the millennium, however, apocalyptic expectation began to reemerge as a fully articulated feature of European Christianity. Although careful scholarship has long since punctured the notion that the year 1000 was a major focus of expectancy, it is possible that a waxing nervousness at the approach of that date contributed to a general trend toward belief in an approaching consummation.[27] But the growing influence of apocalyptic ideas needs to be understood against the background of a deeper shift in historical consciousness that was broadly in evidence by the twelfth century, a shift that reflected the accelerated pace of historical change itself.[28]

In writers like Rupert of Deutz (c. 1075–1129), Otto of Freising (d. 1158), Anselm of Havelberg (d. 1158), and Richard of St. Victor (d. 1173), the historical element was forcefully reasserted in Christian theology.[29] These thinkers contributed to the spread of efforts to correlate scriptural narratives and prophecies with actual historical events. Increasingly, the Bible was viewed as a special prophetic tool, a key to understanding the divine blueprint for universal history. Despite mounting discouragement from the defenders of scholastic orthodoxy, speculations and rumors concerning the appearance of Antichrist, the end of the world, and related themes became increasingly common during the twelfth and thirteenth centuries. Apocalyptic thought took on a greater variety of forms and served a greater variety of functions in an increasingly complex society. It could imply support for powerful rulers or institutions; conversely it could involve radical criticism of the church or secular authorities. Apocalyptic imagery became a key element in the polemical feuding between the popes and the Hohenstaufen, as each side discovered the forces of the Antichrist in the other. Although a good deal of apocalyptic expression was simply an adaptation of traditional schemes, there were many writers, for instance the visionary Hildegard of Bingen (d. 1179), who introduced highly original themes and imagery that enriched conceptions of the Last Times.

The most original prophetic thinker of the high medieval period was the Calabrian abbot Joachim of Fiore (1131–1202). Joachim's view of history and the future presented a radical challenge to the static construction inherited from Augustine. In his most influential writings, Joachim interpreted history through the Bible as a progressive unfolding of three stages, each of which was ruled over by one person of the Trinity. The Age of the Father, an age of fear and obedience under the Law, had been consummated in the coming of Christ. The Age of the Son was the present epoch of faith and tutelage under the Gospel. It would be followed in turn by the Age of the Holy Spirit, the fulfillment of spiritual freedom and love. This third and last historical stage, in which human history would be consummated, was already dawning in the late twelfth century; Joachim expected its full realization within a few generations after the year 1200. The divine truths of which he and his contemporaries had but glimpses would then be opened to constant contemplation. The progress of the spirit through the Old and the New Testaments would be completed.

These expectations represented a powerful sense of hope regarding the earthly future. The Age of the Spirit was to be an integral part of history, and it was in fact already dawning. Yet there was at the same time a strong streak of fearful apprehension in this scheme; the atrocities of the Antichrist and a general recrudescence of evil were still to precede the final age. Moreover, Joachim's thought did not represent a complete break with Augustinian assumptions, for the third and final stage would itself deteriorate. At its end would come tribulation and judgment; for Joachim too there could be no perfection before the actual end of the world.[30]

What was new in Joachim's thought was not simply a new sense of optimism or hope for the historical future. In speculations about the coming of Antichrist, apocalyptic hopes and fears had long complemented one another. The idea that the Antichrist's downfall would be followed by a golden time on earth before the end was a common one, and went back to no less an authority than St. Jerome. This final period was often seen as one of 45 days; the number was derived from Daniel 12: 11–12, where it was clear that the 1335 days the blessed would wait for their reward extended beyond the 1290 days of the "abomination of desolation." The days came to be interpreted as years according to a common exegetical principle; thus this final time could sometimes be viewed as the brief equivalent of an earthly Millennium. But the idea of such a mini-Millennium generally remained within the bounds of orthodoxy, since this period was usually expected to bring only a renewal and flowering of the New Testament, not a third dispensation.[31]

In medieval eyes, then, Joachim's main legacy lay not in an optimistic view of the Last Times, but in the potentially revolutionary implications of the idea that a wholly new historical dispensation was at hand. It was this line of thought that opened him to the charge of heresy; church leaders naturally abhorred the idea that their institution would soon be made irrelevant by the dawning of a new age. Joachim himself did not intend his writings to serve as a platform for church reform or dissent. But for many disaffected receivers of his thought, dissent and reform were natural steps. As early as the middle of the thirteenth century, elements of his apocalypticism were adopted by Franciscans who insisted on a rigorous observance of apostolic poverty, and who saw in the growing worldliness of the church the rise of oppressive anti-Christian forces before the arrival of the new age. This was only the beginning of what would become a long tradition of antiestablishment Joachimism. In retrospect, however, the largest significance of Joachim's work lay in his attempt to interpret the deepest mysteries of Scripture in historical terms. Though his writings were often extremely complex and obscure, filled as they were with esoteric reckonings and diagrams, it is nonetheless clear that his whole intellectual posture was bent toward a comprehensive understanding of history. By setting an example of research into scriptural secrets, his works gave a powerful impetus to the quest for apocalyptic insight. His ideas, though frequently misrepresented, became one of the sparks that led to a virtual explosion of eschatological expectation and predictive prophecy in the following centuries.

The times were ripe for this ground swell of apocalypticism in the later Middle Ages. The disasters and instability of the fourteenth and fifteenth centuries certainly helped to create a climate in which intense hopes and fears for the future flourished. But the reasons for the growth of an apocalyptic mood were as deep and complex as the entire history of that age. Social and intellectual change too swift to be understood helped to create a religious atmosphere in which the most intense piety could coexist with a deep sense of desperation. A spreading sense of historical crisis, of the senescence of the world, had already by the time of the Great Schism occasioned innumerable prophecies concerning profound troubles, the Second Advent, or a golden age soon to come. For every innovator like Joachim, there were a great many other commentators who stayed closer to traditional teachings while offering detailed schemes of prophetic interpretation based on the images, and especially the numbers, of Scripture. Increasingly the stewardship of apocalyptic ideas, like that of intellectual life in general, ceased to be a clerical monopoly and was taken up by members of an educated laity.[32] The new interests and aspirations of this class were reflected in prophecies such as those of Arnald of Villanova (d. 1311), who roundly denounced the "useless philosophical subtleties" of the Thomists, and predicted the advent of the Antichrist for 1378.[33] But many churchmen were equally moved by the growing desire for prophetic insight; even so exalted a cleric and philosopher as Nicholas of Cusa (d. 1464) engaged in complex scriptural reckoning, and developed a vision of the future persecution and final triumph of the church before the end of the world.

The main source of prophetic truth was of course the Bible. The main prophetic books, especially Daniel and Revelation, were searched with ever greater care for insights into the relationship of the present to both the past and the future. But a great many other authorities could be invoked, including the Church fathers, the Sibylline Oracles, the Pseudo-Methodius, Joachim, and such mysterious figures as Merlin, the legendary British prophet and magician of the fifth century. Anonymous texts such as the "Toledo Letter," which first appeared in 1184 and predicted the end of the world for 1186, were reissued many times in later centuries with dates and details changed to accord with contemporary speculations.[34] At the same time, inherited beliefs in signs and portents contributed to the general apocalyptic excitement of the age. Interpreters devoted enormous energies to determining which signs of the end had already occurred and which were still to come. Among the most widely disseminated prophetic legends was that of the Fifteen Signs before Doomsday, a series of portentous disasters that would occur on fifteen successive days directly before the Last Judgment. The tradition took a variety of forms; most were loose amalgamations from biblical apocrypha, but the legend was commonly attributed to the unimpeachable St. Jerome.[35] Interpreters combined and elaborated on the various inherited traditions, always discovering new ways to apply them to current circumstances. Thus for example the fervent Franciscan John of Rupescissa (died c. 1365), who was viewed with a combination of alarm and awe by high church authorities, drew upon a large number of prophetic texts to produce a violent scenario of coming events in which the king of France would play a heroic role and the corrupt clergy would be destroyed.[36]

Among both the learned and the people at large, hopes for radical change and world reformation were common throughout the later Middle Ages. Often, widely shared dreams for the future were expressed in the guise of infallible prediction. Visionaries like St. Birgitte of Sweden (d. 1373) and Brother Reinhard (d. 1503) could be cited as authorities to prove that the advent of a golden time or of a great prophet was not far off, even if enormous upheavals would have to be endured first. The reputations of such seers grew all the faster as their names appeared pseudonymously on numerous popular forecasts. Among the most widespread and powerful hopes, and one that had clear biblical support, was that which centered on the return of the prophets Enoch and Elijah. They would come in the Last Days to preach against the Antichrist, to convert the Jews, and to reform the church. Often the Last Elijah alone was referred to as the great messenger and tool of God before the end, for the Lord had told his people, "Behold, I will send you Elijah the prophet before the coming of the great and dreadful day of the Lord" (Malachi 4: 5).[37]

Closely associated with these hopes for a great prophet was the continuing tradition of predictions regarding the advent of a last World Emperor.[38] In Germany this legend gained new life in the wake of the struggles between the popes and the Hohenstaufen. Tales of the return of Frederick, ordained by God to restore the German-Roman monarchy and reform the church before the Last

Judgment, circulated throughout this period and continued right into Luther's time. No less influential before the Reformation were hopes for an angelic, wonder-working Pope who would come to reform the whole world.[39] Not a few of these hopeful prophecies reflected the influence of Joachimism. But there were many other prophetic traditions in circulation, and it would distort the picture to take any one of them as clearly predominant.

The various prophetic currents combined to produce a powerful tradition of reform sentiment, in which *Reformatio* in head and members was regarded as preparation for the coming union of Christ and his people.[40] Indeed, the fourteenth and fifteenth centuries saw a massive expansion in the use of prophecy as dissent against the political, social, and religious status quo. In Germany, for example, thoroughgoing disgust with the existing social order, along with religiously inspired hopes for reformation, was evident in writings such as the *Reformation of the Emperor Sigismund* (c. 1438). Countless other prophetic works predicting divine punishment of the clergy or of secular rulers, and radical changes to come, were clear mirrors of discontent. God's wrath would inevitably fall upon those responsible for present misery; his providence would bring the restoration of a lost order.[41]

Perhaps the most noteworthy example of the increasing use of prophecy in political polemic was the tendency to discover the Antichrist in the pope or in some other powerful ruler. Earlier medieval apocalypticism had not generally applied the legend in this polemical fashion; the significance of the Antichrist lay simply in the expectation of his advent as a sign of the Last Days. But it would be wrong to suggest that this multiplication of polemical interpretations indicates a dilution of true apocalyptic expectancy. As Richard Emmerson has clearly shown, the view of the Antichrist as a figure expected before doomsday remained common.[42] Moreover, the polemical use of the Antichrist idea did not exclude a sincere prophetic message or a genuine quest for saving insight, as even a cursory look at expectancy in the Wycliffite and Hussite movements would demonstrate.[43]

The insight for which apocalyptic thinkers strove often involved inquiry into nature, for the natural realm was included in God's plan for the world. It is not surprising that prophetic assumptions and goals lay behind the most ambitious medieval attempts to establish a universal science, such as that of the Franciscan Roger

Bacon (d. 1294). As Stewart Easton points out, Bacon ultimately "order[ed] his scientific work in such a way that the number of believers, candidates for salvation, will be increased, [and] that the understanding of existing believers will be deepened and their faith strengthened."[44] This program was the more urgently pursued because Bacon was steeped in the apocalyptic beliefs of his time. Whether or not he was actually a Joachimite,[45] it is certain that he was an ardent believer in apocalyptic prophecies, particularly the idea of the imminent approach of the Antichrist. His teachings were in the largest sense a means of preparing Christians for this test and for the end itself.

It further helps us to know that Bacon's quest for universal scientific insight was aimed at the revival of ancient wisdom; his goal was to recover truths that had been revealed to the ancients but later distorted and obscured. As a thinker in search of universal knowledge at once scientific and prophetic, Bacon differed greatly from the majority of scholastic thinkers, who followed Albertus Magnus and other famous teachers in a more modest and mundane view of the scientific enterprise. But although he was a maverick in his day, the friar's pursuit of mathematical and natural inquiry in the light of eschatological concerns would have many echoes in following centuries.

Among the methods Bacon used was astrology. The art had undergone a serious revival in Europe already by the twelfth century, and continued to grow in prestige throughout the high and late Middle Ages, as the desire grew to see into a highly uncertain future. Despite outright denunciations of the art by Augustine and a long list of only slightly lesser authorities, Christian practitioners rarely acknowledged any conflict between the tenets of faith and the deterministic implications of astrology. Moreover, during the trials and transformations that began after 1300, belief in prediction from the heavens was one of the few slender threads on which a sense of some tangible order could hang.

By the fifteenth century, astrology was enjoying a greater flowering and higher prestige than ever before. Especially after the advent of printing, astrological forecasts were eagerly sought by pious but curious townsfolk, and contributed directly both to apprehension over coming troubles and to dreams of future bliss. Typical were the predictions published by Johann Lichtenberger (d. 1503), a leading German stargazer, who forecast that the Turk would overrun Germany and lay siege to Cologne, but who also held out hopes for a great reforming prophet.[46] The importance of astrology in shaping the European prophetic mentality on the eve of the Reformation is not easy to overstate.

The rising interest in astrology was part of a broader Renaissance revival of ancient forms of prophecy and divination. Well before the Reformation, this revival, aided by the printing press, was exercising a subtle but definite influence on learned attitudes toward prophetic knowledge in general. Ancient divination rested on belief in the essential regularity of the universe; prediction was not a matter of divine revelation but of insight into universal patterns in nature and history. Humanist learning in these realms inevitably began to be applied in the area of prophetic inquiry, with the result that questions more precise than any before began to be asked about the meaning of natural signs and historical events.

In addition, however, essentially deterministic forms of divination, complemented by such classical motifs as the wheel of fortune—well known in the Middle Ages but increasingly popular in the Renaissance—encouraged a generally pessimistic sense of fatalism in the prophecy of the period.[47] In the often tense and morbid atmosphere of the fifteenth century, the influence of classical fatalism tended to strengthen prevalent fears of the future. The inevitability of future suffering became a constant theme of prophetic literature; fate or the workings of providence—the two were not often clearly distinguished—brought unavoidable decay and death to individuals, to society, indeed to the world as a whole. The dangers and troubles that lay ahead for Christendom were inescapable. In short, the classical revival did nothing to stem the apocalyptic apprehensions of the late Middle Ages. On the contrary, it supplied the means to articulate them.

Naturally, hopes for the earthly future also had a significant place in Renaissance prophecy. Older prophetic traditions looking forward to a time of deliverance could now find a complement in the expectations of a returning golden age that accompanied the new learning. The goal of recovering lost truth or spiritual insight appealed to zealous preachers and classical scholars alike. The pursuit of occult wisdom among Renaissance Platonists drew much of its inspiration from the sort of prophetic hope nourished by Joachimism and related trends. But as usual, there were two sides to this coin: although many Florentine intellectuals drank in Savonarola's promise of a *renovatio mundi*, they were equally moved by his terrifying warnings of divine chastisement.[48]

Scholars have begun to uncover the important role played by hopeful apocalyptic traditions in the great voyages of discovery. Christopher Columbus in particular appears to have been motivated by a conviction that he was called to help fulfill God's plan for the conversion of all lands and peoples to Christ before the end of the world. The *Imago mundi* of Pierre D'Ailly, an early-fifteenth-century compendium of ancient and medieval cosmology, geography, and prophetic teachings that drew heavily on the works of Roger Bacon, encouraged Columbus to visualize "a cosmos with a mathematically determinable beginning and end, unfolding in time and space according to divine plan," and to discover his own role in this cosmic drama.[49] We know too that Joachimism and related millennial beliefs helped to inspire the Franciscan missionary enterprise in the New World.[50] Much remains to be learned about the influence of apocalyptic mentalities in the whole enterprise of geographical discovery and expansion.

Although the various expressions of apocalyptic expectation were ultimately attempts to find meaning, hope, and assurance, the most common attitude toward the immediate future was one of dread. Generation after generation of late-medieval Christians lived in anticipation of terrible upheavals, and they unfailingly found the appropriate signs of the times. The fall of Constantinople to the Turks in 1453 appeared an especially ominous prelude to disaster for the entire Christian world. Fear of the infidel, often identified with the armies of the Antichrist or with Gog and Magog, the barbarian hordes that would sweep out of the East before the end, rose rapidly thereafter. Indeed in the decades preceding Luther's movement, the tone of prophecy became more and more one of pessimistic apprehension in the face of impending doom. An often morbid sense of decadence commonly led to a painful, guilt ridden fear of future punishment, of the *Dies irae*. The forces of decay and evil seemed to have taken over the world. The prevalence of this sensibility—in Northern and Central Europe at least—is evident from even a casual survey of the art and literature of the age. By the early sixteenth century it had spawned so many rumors and speculations that the Fifth Lateran Council (1512–17) issued a statement denouncing popular apocalyptic tendencies, and church authorities warned preachers against overzealous efforts to interpret biblical prophecies.[51] It was all threatening to get out of hand. But the general feeling remained; Geiler von Kaisersberg was merely repeating a common assumption when he warned that "there is no hope that things will go better for Christendom."[52] It seems arguable that such a highly charged prophetic atmosphere contributed to a mounting readiness for social and religious change, a prophetic undertow that helped to bring on the Reformation.[53]

Yet despite all that we have said about the growth of prophetic hopes and fears, late-medieval Christians had effective salves for their apprehensions in other forms of belief and practice. Although it would prove impossible for Luther, most medieval believers could to some extent assuage their fears of coming trials and judgment through confession, through good works, through personal communion with the saints, and through sensuous contact with the holy. If the future appeared uncertain or threatening, there was comfort to be had in the arms of Holy Mother Church and in the countless agencies that allowed a mediate contact between man and the divine. While Reformation theology may have brought a liberation from the more oppressive aspects of this spiritual bureaucracy, it also did away with the security these nonprophetic forms of piety afforded. Indeed from one perspective the medieval search for apocalyptic insight had its real flowering in the wake of Luther's Reformation, after the consciousness of world-historical crisis was legitimized, focused, and further intensified by the German Reformer.

REFORMATION ESCHATOLOGIES

The Reformation may be seen as the last great historical change of the Middle Ages to inspire new forms of apocalyptic understanding. As in earlier periods of significant change, the new schemes were in part adaptations, combinations, and extensions of the old. And as in earlier periods, these schemes could serve a variety of purposes. With the Reformation, however, far more than in any of the earlier medieval reorientations, a new apocalyptic understanding was inseparable from the events themselves; the new understanding lay very near the heart of the reform. In the case of Luther's Reformation especially, a reorientation of the apocalyptic imagination was essential to the self-definition and progress of the movement. An apocalyptic view of the struggle between the Gospel and its enemies was basic to the original Protestant message. The Protestant reformers, though deeply influenced by Augustine, departed from the Augustinian view of history by pointing to the vagaries that had faced the Word in the course of human history and to the prophetic significance of specific historical developments since the time of Christ. In this respect they legitimized the trend, continually growing throughout the high and late Middle Ages, toward the historical interpretation of prophecy. As we will emphasize further on, Luther was far more concerned with history in this sense than either Calvin or Zwingli; he more than any other major reformer was heir to the prophetic mentality of the preceding centuries. Yet all Protestants rejected in some measure the antihistorical view of the medieval church, and all saw their own age as a decisive one in the struggle between God and the Devil. The leaders of the reform did agree with Augustine that the Kingdom of God could never be a worldly kingdom; in this respect they repudiated the millenarian hopes that had weighed so heavily in medieval prophecy. But they and their followers were all affected by the sense of eschatological excitement that had been increasing before the Reformation.

This point has often been neglected in studies devoted to the Radical Reformation, and especially in works dealing with the outbreaks of social revolution in the early sixteenth century. The groups that made up the so-called "left wing" of the Reformation are thought to have shared "an eschatological mood far more intense than anything to be found in normative Protestantism or Catholicism,"[54] a mood reflected in hopes for an earthly millennium. Careful study has shown, however, that the most famous of all the Radical Reformers, Thomas Müntzer, did not in fact look to an earthly realization of the Kingdom of God. His eschatology was actually not very different from that of Luther, whose own expectancy was equally intense, though its implications for the worldly regiment were anything but radical. Both men expected the Last Judgment at any moment; they did not expect the establishment of an earthly paradise.[55] Their argument was less over the interpretation of God's plan for history than over the issue of man's role in bringing that plan to completion.

If apocalyptic excitement made a revolutionary, then this was a society of revolutionaries. It is true that the Peasants' War and troubles such as the debacle at Münster in 1535 appear to have dampened public airings of prophetic excitement among preachers of the reform. But these disturbances did not cause apocalyptic convictions to wane; nor did such convictions fade with the disappearance of revolutionary movements in Germany during the following decades. To appreciate the role of Reformation apocalypticism we must turn our attention to the widely shared Protestant expectations that continued throughout the era and that reflected the values of a larger culture.

Protestant piety in general directed the religious imagination away from the rituals of the medieval church and turned it toward prayer and prophecy.[56] In one sense this redirection narrowed the realm of the supernatural by restricting the possibilities for communion with the divine. Yet this narrowing was at the same time a focusing, for it concentrated the religious imagination upon the promise of salvation, upon a future-directed hope and the avenues by which it was revealed. Moreover, this focusing applied not only to religious belief strictly defined, but also to a broader realm of intellectual concerns. As R. J. W. Evans has suggested, "that part of the magical scheme of the Renaissance appropriated by Protestantism was the realm of prophecy, revelation, and predictability."[57] Here lies one possible answer to the recently posed question: "What are the markers for group identity and for social linkage and exclusion when processions and corporate ties around saints and relics have been eliminated?"[58] Shared prophetic myths certainly supplied some of the markers among Protestants.

But some Protestants were clearly more affected by prophetic concerns than others. Of the major reformers, Luther was by far the most strongly influenced by the apocalyptic sensibilities of his time. Indeed the contrast between Luther and Calvin in this regard is striking. For Luther there was a clear pattern of degeneration in world history.[59] Particularly for the centuries since the time of the early church, the record properly read showed little but a decline into corruption, and by correlating historical events with biblical prophecies Luther could announce the nearness of the final cataclysm—and deliverance for believers—with relative certainty.

Calvin, on the other hand, was far less concerned with the problem of history and its direction. He stayed closer to the Augustinian view than did any other reformer. His eschatology concentrated almost exclusively on personal salvation in death, and though he did speak often of the Judgment, his stress was above all on the hiddenness of the Last Day. The common apocalypticism of his age was thus mostly foreign to Calvin. Insofar as he was concerned with the prophetic meaning of history at all, his vision was suggestive of progressive growth rather than a sudden and drastic fulfillment of the scriptural prophecies of the end.[60] Although Calvin was far from any modern notion of historical betterment, he could nevertheless exhort his readers to a "zeal for daily progress" in the spreading of God's Kingdom before it attains fullness at the Last Day. Believers share in God's glory when "with ever-increasing splendor, he displays his light and truth, by which the darkness and falsehoods of Satan's kingdom vanish, are extinguished, and pass away."[61] Rarely did Luther show anything like such confidence in the earthly advance of the Kingdom.

Calvin did agree with Luther in emphatic rejection of chiliasm or millenarianism. The idea that Christ would return to rule on Earth for a thousand years, or that a truly godly kingdom could be established in his name, was a gross vulgarization in the eyes of both reformers. But far more clearly than the German Reformer, Calvin held out the possibility that God's plan allowed real hope for the earthly future. Indeed, despite Calvin's Augustinian avoidance of historically oriented eschatology, the hint of progressivism in his thought left the way open for the frank meliorism and chiliasm of many later Calvinist thinkers. Even though the Second Helvetic Confession of 1566 included an unequivocal rejection of millenarianism, hopes for some sort of godly kingdom on Earth were rarely far from the surface among later sixteenth-century Calvinists. By the early decades of the following century, the bold millenarianism of such men as Thomas Brightman in England and J. H. Alsted in Germany reflected the spread of an exuberant Calvinist conviction that God's plan to perfect the world was gradually coming to completion.[62] This sort of hopeful, forward-looking prophecy was very unlike the uneasy quest for assurance that characterized Lutheran apocalypticism.

To be sure, Calvinists, like Lutherans, had opportunities to feel endangered in the later sixteenth century and through much of the seventeenth. But Calvinists tended to react with greater confidence and aggressiveness to the threats facing them. Unlike the German Lutherans, who often identified the present plight of the Gospel with that of the internally torn and outwardly threatened "German nation," Calvinists most often saw themselves as part of a world-wide struggle against the forces of Satan. Moreover, in this struggle they would inevitably be victorious.[63] Perhaps partly as a result of this internationalism, sentiment for Protestant unity was common in Calvinism. In contrast, many Lutherans eyed Calvinists with extreme suspicion and hatred. To them this new creed smacked of shallow humanism, and was in some respects even more perfidious than the tyranny of Rome. And while Lutheran expansion had slowed considerably by the middle of the century, Calvinism was steadily gaining ground. The sort of confidence that inspired many Calvinists was alien to most Lutherans, who tended by this time to see deadly dangers everywhere.

Not only Calvin, but other key reformers as well, differed significantly from Luther's eschatological outlook. Like Calvin, Zwingli and Bucer were more deeply influenced by Erasmian humanism than was Luther; their reforming work, like Calvin's, was much concerned with the establishment of Christian discipline and thus with the formation of a truly Christian society. They did not share Luther's powerful sense of an imminent end, and hence devoted themselves with fewer reservations to the practical concerns of advancing the Kingdom on earth. It is true that in one sense for Zwingli, as well as for the other founders of the Reformed tradition, "the Kingdom of God is at hand."[64] But this eschatological orientation did not reveal itself in a firm conviction about the imminent end of history.

For Zwingli, the Kingdom of God extends into this world. It is not a wholly other Kingdom to be awaited, but rather impinges directly upon the *corpus christianum*. In his writings the Last Day often seems to recede behind the promise of a better world. As he wrote in the *Commentary on True and False Religion*, "Who can fail to see that the Day of the Lord is at hand?—not that last day on which the Lord will judge the whole world, but the day on which He is to correct the present condition of things."[65] In the entire *Commentary* there is but a single reference to Revelation and but one to Daniel; neither has anything to do with the prophecies of these books. Zwingli often addressed future generations in a tone of marked confidence, exhorting coming centuries to a zealous attention to Christian truth. "We pass on the torch," he wrote to posterity: "Live well!" Later Zwinglianism, however, under the leadership of men like Heinrich Bullinger and Rudolph Gwalther, would be significantly influenced by the sort of apocalyptic excitement that prevailed in Lutheran Germany.[66] The early differences between Lutheran and Zwinglian eschatology can be seen as one manifestation of a broader theological divergence between the Lutheran and Reformed movements, a divergence that Bernd Moeller convincingly linked to the continuing emphasis on the moral aspect of the community in the Upper German cities.[67] Humanist townsmen like Zwingli and Bucer had a "profound attachment to the urban structure," and thus a closer relationship to the medieval ideal of the city as "a miniature *corpus christianum*," than did Luther.[68] The latter's Reformation tended to dissolve this medieval sense of urban community, thus accelerating a process already farther advanced in the North. We can extrapolate as follows. For Zwingli and his early adherents, the community had a role to play in the advance of the Kingdom; this role assumed a historical future. But among Lutherans the promises and the judgments of God lost their communal significance; when the individual looked beyond himself, his only hope lay in resolution on a cosmic scale.[69]

Since Moeller's seminal essay appeared in 1962, scholars attempting to go farther in explaining differences among the various styles of reform have produced a stimulating array of conceptions. Most provocative of all has been the approach of Lionel Rothkrug. In a much-discussed work published in 1980, Rothkrug argued that the northern (or non-Romanized) parts of Germany, which were Christianized by force relatively late, never developed a religious belief in the mediating powers of saints and shrines. Since these shared means of penitential practice failed to develop, piety tended to remain highly individualized and personal. Penitence and redemption never became associated with corporate ethical values; hence the sacred and the social realms remained fundamentally separate for the people of this region. Luther's theology was a powerful expression of this native feeling of God's transcendence and the utter contingency of human life. From this perspective, Lutheran eschatology reflected a distinctive, inherited view of the world and redemption. Lutherans viewed the Last Day as the sudden dissolution of the present, for in most of Northern and Central Germany people had long discounted the value of earthly social reality. Reformed Protestants, on the other hand, tended to see the end as the culmination of a historical process involving the moral development of the community. Since elsewhere Europeans had traditionally come to assume a still fuller integration of the sacred and the social, piety in these areas was far less concerned with prophecy and a coming end.[70] To evaluate Rothkrug's larger thesis concerning regional mentalities is far beyond the scope of this work. Luther's eschatology may well have had roots in traditions of North German piety that went back many centuries. We can certainly acknowledge this possibility without also implying that his thinking was formed exclusively or essentially by local patterns of perception. In any case, Luther's apocalypticism, while firmly anchored in broader traditions of medieval thought, was also a powerfully imaginative and influential reconstruction of the prophetic world-view.

LUTHER'S EXPECTATION

Eschatological tension pervaded Luther's whole world-view. It is a characteristic that simply cannot be overlooked in any attempt to understand his life, his thought, or his historical significance. His expectancy needs to be considered in connection with the traditional spiritual preoccupations of the later Middle Ages, which shaped it in basic ways. Yet Will-Erich Peuckert certainly overstated the case when he asserted that "the entire eschatological stock of the Middle Ages lived on in Luther, and he himself lived thoroughly in it."[71] For Luther's attitudes and conceptions do show some original aspects. His was an imaginative reconstruction of the prophetic outlook, which reinforced and gave form to the inherited sense of expectancy. In fact, his views offered a key justification for the remarkably widespread and powerful apocalypticism that dominated German Protestantism through several generations.

Very near the heart of Luther's theology we find a longing for the Day of the Lord. In this life the believer has salvation only in faith, not yet in the fullness of experience. He has therefore to wait for the ultimate realization that will come with the eschaton. For the individual, this end is death. But just as the individual soul finds full salvation only after death, so the world as a whole is redeemed, and the Kingdom of God fully consummated, only with the Last Judgment and the end of this world. Thus far Luther agreed with the traditional conceptions of the Roman church. But a real theo-

logical departure lay in his understanding of the relationship between these two ends, death and final Judgment.

In the traditional Augustinian view, the death of an individual is
separated from the end of the world by an interval of time; the fate
of the soul during this interval needed to be explained. Death brings
the separation of body and soul. The soul may proceed to Heaven
or Hell (or, as the doctrine later developed, to Purgatory), and it
dwells in one of these states until the Last Day, when it is reunited
with the resurrected body and its final, eternal condition is established. There was something of a paradox here. While the disem-
bodied soul in heaven, for example, is blissfully enjoying salvation
in Christ, its condition is somehow less than perfect until it is reunited with the body.

For Luther, on the other hand, individual death and the Last
Judgment were both encounters with the same eternal moment.
From the limited perspective of time, the souls of the dead could be
pictured as falling into total unconsciousness, a deep, dreamless
sleep, until the end of the world. Within the world of time, there is
thus an interval between death and the Last Day. From the point of
view of the soul itself and of God, however, the final resurrection of
the whole man, and the Last Judgment itself, follow instantane-
ously upon death. To leave this world is no longer to experience
time. "For just as he does not know how it happens, who falls
asleep and comes to the morrow unexpectedly when he wakes, so
will we suddenly rise from the dead on the Last Day, not knowing
how we have been in and come through death." Outside this life, in
the world beyond, all time collapses into a single eternal instant.[72]

Luther's understanding of death and the Last Judgment provided
theological support for his heightened eschatological longing. In
the traditional view, the Last Judgment did little more than confirm
the status already granted to souls after death. The resurrection
became a rubber stamp for a judgment that was already mostly
complete. In Luther's scheme, though, at the end of the world and
the general resurrection, not only bodies but souls as well re-
awaken. Every man stands whole before the Judge. Thus all hope
and longing was focused on the Last Day. This difference in emphasis is manifest in other ways as well. For example, Luther did not
share the Augustinian notion of a *civitas Dei* on Earth. In the orthodox medieval view, the reign of Christ through the church was

a historical overlap between the present world and the future, eternal Kingdom of God.[73] Through the intermingling of time and eternity, the Kingdom could exist both in history and in the hereafter. Luther, however, tended to regard the eternal Kingdom as the antithesis of the world of time. The Christian lived outside of time through grace; he lived within time as a creature, as man. The Last Day brought the end of time in a fully literal sense.

Hence Luther's difference in outlook is also reflected in what we might call the metaphysics of the end. The Roman church had taught that Christ's coming would bring a final and profound transformation, but not complete annihilation, of the world. Only the form of the world would pass, not its nature or substance. Luther rejected the idea of a mere change in form; the world would change in essence, and the present order would be, in effect, utterly destroyed.[74] Again, the eschaton was to be a final event in the most radical sense. The new heaven and the new earth would be the setting for the incomprehensibly perfect Kingdom of God, in which the faithful would dwell eternally with Christ.

These theological views were not fully formulated until well after Luther had challenged the authority of Rome. They developed gradually and unsystematically during the Reformer's mature years, and had little immediate connection with his apocalyptic view of history, which is our main concern. Yet Luther's Christ-centered theology cannot be understood apart from his apocalyptic convictions. As Ulrich Asendorf has shown, Luther's theology is eschatological at its very heart, and apocalyptic elements were integral to his eschatological understanding. His revival of the New Testament hope included the expectation of an imminent end to history. Luther certainly recognized and often stressed the sense in which the Last Things began with the First Advent, the sense in which the whole New Testament epoch is the final hour of the world. But his consciousness was governed more directly by the sense of an evangelical breakthrough in his own time, at the center of which he found himself. The consciousness of that breakthrough was one with the conviction that judgment and deliverance were at hand. Luther's theology therefore cannot be "demythologized" without distortion.[75] Nor can it be labeled "prophetic" in a sense opposed to "apocalyptic."[76] It must be understood as the expression of a mind shaped—though not bound—by the assumptions and circumstances of that age.

Especially in the early stages of his reforming career, Luther showed a typically late-medieval combination of high hopes and despair for this world. Indeed many of the personality traits that have made Luther the object of detailed psychological speculation need to be understood as reflections of an apocalyptic vacillation between euphoric hope and deep despair, a vacillation extremely common in his age. This tendency was magnified in Luther because his was the sort of mind that cannot bear to remain in uncertainty.[77] He sought assurance; where it evaded him he became dejected and even morose. He could refer to his own era as a golden time in which the Gospel was preached with unprecedented force and clarity, a time of enormous promise. He never came close to millenarianism, yet he could on occasion show great hopes for whatever time was left to the world. He was not closed, for instance, to the traditional hope that the Gospel might spread among the Jews before the end. On the other hand, he could consider his age one of utter degeneracy, when people neglected the fates of their souls more blithely than ever. He was no stranger to that common feature of apocalyptic attitudes, the swinging between terror and hope.

In prophetic matters, as in all else, Luther's touchstone was Scripture. The interpretation of biblical prophecy was the key to his understanding of his movement and its significance in history. This use of Scripture was anything but new in Luther's day; he followed in the long tradition of commentators who had attempted to understand contemporary events in the context of biblical prophecy. In many respects his understanding was based upon traditional medieval exegesis. But on certain key points he broke fundamentally with inherited views, and his new interpretations became the foundation for the entire Protestant understanding of history. Luther's readings of the main prophetic books of the Bible are exemplary.

In the early years of the Reformation, Luther depended on the book of Daniel in developing his historical understanding.[78] He adopted the prevailing interpretation of the four world monarchies, which was based on Daniel's explanation of Nebuchadnezzar's dream (Daniel 2). The last of these monarchies was the Roman, and its final downfall was to coincide with the end of the world. The imagery of Daniel 2 clearly suggested historical decline, and as Luther's larger understanding developed, it reflected full agreement with this common medieval idea. He saw a broad pattern of degeneration in world history since the time of the patriarchs, which had ended with the flood. The decline included all of nature as well as human morality. It even extended to church history, for faith too had grown continually weaker.[79] Thus although Luther saw the end of the world as unequivocally an act of God, he was certainly influenced by the common late-medieval notion that the end would be a death of old age.[80]

Luther found the kingdoms of his own day represented in the ten horns of the fourth beast in Daniel 7. The "little horn" he usually identified with the Turk, the scourge of God, a punishment loosed against Christendom for its sin. According to Daniel, the little horn was to pluck out three of the ten horns—that is, to subdue three kingdoms—shortly before the Judgment. Because the Turk had already overrun the Latin kingdoms of Egypt, Greece, and Asia Minor, it was possible to suggest that these conquests were now at an end, and that all expectation should therefore be directed to the Last Day. On the basis of the prophecy against Gog in Ezekiel 39, however, Luther could predict that the fall of the Turk would precede the Judgment by a short time; this fall would then be yet another certain sign of the coming end.[81] In Daniel 11 he found a clear, detailed description of the papal Antichrist. He was thus sure that his own time was the "time of the end" referred to in chapter 12, when the meaning of these prophecies was to be revealed. Luther also found in Daniel general support for the idea of a final reformation in the church. While false teaching would seduce the majority of people in the Last Times, a great expansion of the Gospel, a final flowering of truth, would simultaneously occur.[82]

In his exposition of Daniel, Luther also engaged in some reckoning of prophetic periods such as the 70 weeks of chapter 9, the time granted to the Jews to put an end to sin. In a traditional vein, he interpreted the words to mean "weeks of years"; this period of 490 years began with Daniel's revelation and ended seven years after Christ's resurrection, when the apostles turned their preaching from the obstinate Jews to the pagans. In many similar ways Luther strove to establish precise correlations between the prophecies of the book and particular historical events. While he admitted that other interpreters could differ on such matters, Luther's passion for this sort of thing would help ensure the continued popularity of biblical time-reckoning among his followers. Above all he tried to show that the prophecies of Daniel had clearly come true, and that the prophet's vision of the end applied unambiguously to the present age. Indeed Luther's interpretation left no doubt at all about the character of his own time. "For my part," he concluded, "I am sure that the Day of Judgment is just around the corner. It doesn't matter that we don't know the precise day . . . perhaps someone else can figure it out. But it is certain that time is now at an end."[83]

The Revelation of John, on the other hand, confused Luther at first. It seemed so unclear that for a time he could even doubt its canonical authenticity. "My spirit cannot make its way into this book," he wrote in his first preface of 1522. Yet significantly, it was the one book he insisted should be illustrated in the early editions of the New Testament, a fact that implies respect for the power of the prophetic images of Revelation, as well as concern that they be properly understood.[84] While the upheavals of the mid-1520s and the arguments with the radicals may have led him to a temporary reticence about the book, by the end of the decade Luther had come to accept it as a genuine and important prophecy that nicely complemented Daniel. Despite the mysteries surrounding Revelation, he felt he could hardly afford to ignore it when current events were raising so many pressing questions that required answers from biblical prophecy. There were insights to be found here that were unobtainable anywhere else in the Scriptures. What particularly prodded Luther to formulate his interpretation of the Apocalypse was the Turkish menace, which came to a head in 1529 with the siege of Vienna; during this period of especially nervous apprehension he wrote his new and much fuller preface to the book.[85]

Luther's treatment of apocalyptic symbolism, here and elsewhere in the New Testament, remained at some points hesitant and uncomfortable. He occasionally had trouble conforming this rich and detailed symbolism to his own understanding.[86] Indeed at times his interpretations remained allegorical, for example when he discussed Antichrist imagery as referring to a type rather than to any particular historical institution.[87] But none of these facts should lead us to underestimate, as some have, the conviction with which Luther regarded the apocalyptic passages of the Bible as predictive prophecies with real, if often obscure, historical meaning. Nor should it blind us to the pivotal importance of Luther's views for the whole tradition of Protestant apocalypticism.[88]

In his 1530 preface to Revelation Luther described three sorts of prophecy that foretold events not otherwise mentioned in Scripture.[89] The first type used only plain words, no figures or images.

The second used both plain speech and images together; and the third used only images. The prophecies of Revelation were of this third type, and were thus most difficult to understand. "As long as this kind of prophecy remains without explanation and gets no sure interpretation, it is concealed and mute prophecy and has not yet come to the profit and fruit that it is to give to Christendom." Much of the meaning of Revelation was hidden, its interpretation unclear. Many stupid and dangerous things had been said of it. But since it was desirable to know surely the meaning of the book, Luther would "give other and higher minds something to consider" by presenting his own views.[90] He sought an interpretation that would be, if not certain, at least unobjectionable. Luther's treatments of Revelation and of other obscure parts of Scripture thus remained in many respects cautious and reserved. This very caution and reserve, however, helped to make his interpretations influential and provocative of further research.

In the early chapters of the book, Luther found the various afflictions that Christendom would have to suffer; the heresies and troubles of the early church in particular appeared as the seals opened by the angels in chapters 6 through 8. He also discovered that the two final abominations that Christians would have to bear, namely the papacy and the Turk, were clearly described here. The Mohammedan kingdom was indicated by Gog and Magog, whom Satan had sent to do battle against Christians once he had been loosed from his thousand-year bondage. The papacy was the whore of Babylon, the masterful perverter of the Gospel. Revelation also pictured the final propagation of the Gospel and the pouring out of God's wrath against the papacy through the seven angels and the seven vials (chapters 15 and 16). Here too was the most detailed biblical description of the Last Judgment; the believer could take comfort in this portrayal of the final destruction of all the enemies of Christ.

The crux of all that was new in Luther's reading of biblical prophecy, and the most influential of all his prophetic discoveries, was his identification of the Antichrist with the papacy at Rome. He had made the connection as early as 1518,[91] but the identification was not certain in his mind until about 1520, when he concluded that the whole structure of the Roman church was corrupt. Earlier critics of the church, for example John Hus and Savonarola, had identified the pope himself as the Antichrist. But these critics had based their charge mostly on moral considerations: the pope and his cardinals lived godless lives and ignored the spiritual needs of Christians; therefore they had to be doers of the devil's work. Luther's charge, on the other hand, was one of doctrine, of principle. The central teachings of the Roman church, the very presuppositions of the institution headed by the papacy, were leading people away from truth to idolatry, superstition, and ruin. It was no longer a matter of reforming the church leadership; it was one of rescuing the Word from the agents of Satan.[92] At times, especially early in his career, Luther could suggest that the Turk as well as the papacy shared in the character of the Antichrist. He could refer, for example, to the pope as the soul of the Antichrist, the Turk as the body; several medieval commentators had done so.[93] But Luther was finally unwilling to include the Turk under this name. The true Antichrist was the power that subverted Christendom from within, in the guise of Christ's vicar.[94]

The prevailing medieval view had been that the advent of the Antichrist was still in the future. On the basis of references in Revelation to a final oppression lasting 1260 days or 42 months (Revelation 11: 2–3), it was generally believed that the Antichrist would rule for only three and a half years. His reign would be a clear sign of the approaching Last Judgment. But for Luther and the entire early Protestant tradition, the Antichrist was not a person yet to appear but an institution that had already been active and gaining power for centuries. Thus in the place of medieval efforts to predict the biography of the Antichrist, Protestants stressed study of the history of the papacy.[95] Such study would make clear how the forces of evil had been able to pervert the church and to mislead believers for so long. It would also clarify the apocalyptic significance of the evangelical awakening now taking place.

To be sure, most early Reformation propaganda did not attempt to explain the history of the Antichrist in any detail, but rather emphasized the contrasts between the actions of the pope and the life of Christ. This was the intention, for instance, of Lucas Cranach's woodcuts of 1521 entitled *Passional Christi und Antichristi*. In this respect, as in many others, the new movement made use of long-established popular belief. It was also clear, on the other hand, that the revelation of the Antichrist was of central eschatological importance. It meant that the Last Days had arrived.[96] Through his discovery Luther clearly identified his own age as that of the final persecution of the true church.[97] Nothing more was to be expected before the end. The faithful had simply to bear the accumulation of atrocities on earth and wait for the joyful Day of Redemption. Meanwhile the faithless had everything to fear.

The image of the Antichrist, then, was central to Luther's eschatological understanding. Perhaps more than any other single idea, it gave shape to his vision of church history and of his own age. But too exclusive an emphasis on this idea obscures the importance of the nonpolemical elements in his thought about the Last Times. As Hans Preuss has shown, Luther was already convinced that the end was near well before he worked out his anti-Roman position.[98] His sense that universal judgment was imminent, a sense rooted in the expectancy of the late Middle Ages, preceded the development of his thinking on the Roman Antichrist. The discovery of the Antichrist was the dark complement to Luther's rediscovery of the Gospel; together these insights forced a newly clear prophetic understanding to crystallize in his thought, and, through this new understanding, late-medieval expectations received a fresh focus.

Indeed, while the revelation of the Antichrist was a key sign of the times, in Luther's eyes it was only one among many. Christ had announced clearly how things would go in the world as the end approached; he had intended believers to be able to tell when the day was at hand. Since signs had announced countless events of far lesser importance than the end of the world beforehand, it was clearly impossible that this final, complete transformation would go unheralded. To the faithful, the present signs could not have been more conclusive. Thus in a 1531 sermon on Luke 21, for example, Luther sought both to console and to strengthen believers against the frightening omens and evils that were ushering in the Day of Redemption.[99] By far the most terrible were the signs among men. People were plagued by the devil as never before. The Gospel was ignored. Vice, ingratitude, hate, and evil spread tangibly from day to day. The great enemies of Christ, the papacy and the Turk, raged violently against the Lord's followers, and this was not to mention the many sects that perverted the truth.

While there could hardly be any mistake about the meaning of such developments, there was yet more evidence in nature. Luther fully shared the common belief in natural signs and portents; he balked only at efforts to make study of such phenomena systematic, to discover a law of portents. Indeed, in Luther's eyes it was not even possible to distinguish God's signs from Satan's, since the supernatural causes of natural phenomena could not be directly perceived.[100] Yet it was not only possible but necessary to regard natural wonders as general signs of warning in these Last Times.

According to Luke 21: 25, Christ foretold that the first signs would be those in the heavens: in the sun, the moon, and the stars. As Matthew 24 showed, the sun and moon would lose their light, and the stars would fall. People would become fearful, not knowing which way to turn. There would follow many terrible disasters everywhere on the earth. Finally all creation would tremble: "heaven and earth will crack like an old house that is about to break up and collapse," leaving no doubt that the end had all but arrived. Luther left it to believers to judge if, and to what extent, these signs had already occurred. It was his "belief and certain hope," however, that most of them were already past; only a few were still to be awaited. If people wanted to believe, they had seen enough. How many great eclipses had been observed in only a few short years? The like had never before been seen. But those who did not believe in God's Word would not heed such signs even if the sun went dark daily and the stars fell in heaps. And although the astronomers (*Sternkündigen*) thought that these things occurred naturally, so that some could be predicted, yet even they did not deny that these were signs of something terrible, especially since they were now seen so frequently. There had in fact been countless signs that were clearly unnatural, such as several suns appearing at once. Disastrous storms, floods, and earthquakes were growing ever more frequent. To report all such signs would be to fill up a large book, wrote Luther. And yet the more these warnings multiplied, the less attention people paid. After all, this was how it had to be; otherwise these signs would not really be signs of the end.

While the signs were indeed terrible in their outward aspect, to the pious heart they were a source not of fear but of rejoicing. Without these announcements of the coming end, said Luther, the present generation would be the most miserable that ever lived upon the earth. The signs were truly signs of joy, for they meant that Christ was about to make good his promise. Whoever looked to the emperor as a savior did so in vain. Christ was the only savior, and if people rightly considered what his coming would mean they would daily fall on their knees and weep blood that it might happen soon. The Christian was not to despair if all went from bad to worse, for in the end evil would befall only his persecutors. As long as he knew that the Day of Redemption was about to arrive, the believer could gladly suffer all the evils of the world and the devil. It was necessary to bite into it all as into a sour apple, knowing that shortly everything would turn sweet. The wonderful, eternal summer promised in the image of the fig tree (Luke 21: 29–31) was about to begin. One had only to hope and to believe.

When human reason considered the world, wrote Luther, it saw nothing but trouble, pain, and death. But Christ spoke another language, and with it he could turn this miserable human prospect into one so lovely it exceeded comprehension. What was needed, then, was to learn "this art and new language" which would allow believers to regard the signs rightly, according to the Word.

For because we are to be new men [Christ] wants us also to have different and new thoughts, understanding, and sense; and to regard nothing according to reason, as it appears to the world, but rather as it appears in his eyes, and to direct ourselves to the future, invisible, new nature that we have to look forward to and that shall follow upon this unfortunate and miserable nature.[101]

Let them be terrified, wrote Luther, who look for nothing more than happy days on this earth. The true believer looked to a wholly different life in Christ.

Faith like Luther's has always posed a difficult and frustrating riddle to minds of a different cast. Erasmus was dismayed by Luther's unshakable certainty about saving faith and by his deep pessimism toward this world. He charged the Reformer with reviving the ancient heresies of Manichaean dualism and Gnosticism, accusations that some modern scholars find technically mistaken but nonetheless perceptive.[102] Heiko Oberman, while avoiding any open association between Luther and gnostic dualism, has emphasized how fully the Wittenberger lived in the conviction of all-encompassing conflict between God and the devil, a cosmic struggle from which there was no escape in this mortal existence. Luther did consistently try to overcome debilitating fear of the devil through an emphasis on the positive sustenance of faith. Yet because of Satan's constant activity, the normal state of this world was chaos. On the Last Day, God would make good the promise of deliverance from this chaos into eternity.[103]

Though the Bible was his main prophetic source, Luther was familiar with many other prophetic sources and traditions. His attitude was discriminating; in general, however, he was willing to accept prophecies that appeared to confirm or complement his own understanding. Naturally he rejected the visions of world reformation that much medieval prophecy had included. He likewise ignored some long-standing traditions, for example the Fifteen Signs before Doomsday, since they could not be adequately supported from Scripture. But he was quite ready to entertain a prediction reportedly made a century before the indulgence controversy by John Hus, that though a goose now burned, after a hundred years a swan would sing.[104] Likewise, for a time he could see in Frederick the Wise the fulfillment of pronouncements in the Sibylline Oracles about the emperor of the Last Days.[105] Again, while denying that he possessed special prophetic powers, he was not entirely opposed to the notion that he was the long-awaited prophet through whom God would effect the final reformation of the church.[106] Though unwilling to see himself—or anyone else—as the second Elijah sent explicitly to announce the return of Christ, he did believe that his role was a prophetic one, and he seems to have believed that a few predictions pertained to his own life. One was that of the Franciscan visionary Johann Hilten, who decades earlier had foreseen the rise of a great reformer.[107]

Clearly, such vaticinations had little or no effect on the inner spiritual development that led to Luther's evangelical breakthrough. Yet they should not be overlooked; they were elements of the climate in which his thinking developed. Once he had openly opposed the Church of Rome, prophecies of this sort could add their support to his belief that the Reformation marked the final act in the drama of world history. There can be no doubt, then, that many sources other than Scripture significantly influenced his prophetic consciousness.

For astrology and similar divinatory arts Luther had little use. But as Chapter 4 will emphasize, his opposition to such methods was a traditional Christian position that sought to defend God's freedom against any form of determinism; it had little in common with later forms of empirically based scepticism. Moreover, the rapid spread of astrological literature predicting imminent upheaval certainly contributed to the general sense of prophetic excitement, and surely helped to confirm Luther's sense that he was living in a climactic age.[108] When in 1527 he issued his own edition of Lichtenberger's prophecies, his aim was partly to counter what he saw as pagan superstition, but he also saw that much in these forecasts—including the hope of a great revival of the Gospel—could be interpreted in favor of his cause. Although the Reformer did ultimately reject astrology and other methods of divination presupposing pagan cosmology, he did not live in isolation from such Renaissance intellectual currents. Many of his colleagues and contemporaries were immersed in them, and Luther never threw the full weight of his reputation against them, or voiced disapproval in a way that could have had any lasting effect.[109]

Luther's prophetic outlook was also shaped by a sense of identification with German culture. To be sure, the Christian message was universal, and the current struggle to spread the Word involved all Christians. Any program of national betterment was rendered ultimately meaningless by the nearness of the end.[110] But Luther felt that the present crisis had particular significance for his German contemporaries. He adopted the medieval conception of a *translatio imperii*, a transfer of power and grace from one people to another, generally understood as involving a movement from East to West. Each people had its time of special grace from God, but in the history of the world few had ever seized the chance and lived up to what was offered them. It was now Germany's hour. Rarely had the Gospel been so clearly preached; rarely had any nation enjoyed such opportunities for learning and wisdom. If the Germans missed this chance it was gone forever.[111] Moreover, it was not simply the last chance for Germany. Since the Roman Empire was the last world monarchy, and Germany was the final bearer of the Roman imperium, this appeared to be the very last era of hope for the world. But as Luther watched, he thought he saw the time of grace passing quickly away. Just as the Jews had missed their great opportunity, so now Germany stood in great danger of losing what was offered.

Even in the heady early years of his movement, Luther had expressed dark forebodings of future punishment for the Germans. The "sin" of the Diet of Worms, he wrote in 1522, was in fact a sin of the whole German nation, which had at that assembly shown its scorn for divine truth.[112] But the Peasants' War clearly brought Luther's first deep disillusionment in his countrymen. He saw the war as a great punishment sent by God upon Germany. In the wake of that conflict, Luther warned that another and still more terrible outbreak was likely if the German people did not overcome their disdain for the Gospel. Yet the sins of his people seemed to grow ever more blatant and shocking in the Reformer's eyes.

It was no wonder that the Turk was threatening to sweep out of the East, where the Gospel was already extinguished, and to make Christendom swim in blood. Though Luther thought it most likely that the end would come before Gog overran Christendom, his warnings about the Turk served strongly to perpetuate the fifteenth-century nightmare of a scourging inflicted by the infidel.[113] He was amazed and scandalized at how quickly people fell back into their old *Sicherheit* once the immediate threat had receded. Already by 1530 he was complaining that Sodom and Gomorrah had not been a tenth so evil as Germany was now.[114] A heavy guilt lay upon the nation, and no state reform or virtuous ruler could erase it. In his later life Luther regularly uttered chilling prophecies about what would happen to Germany after his own death. The Gospel, he declared, would be driven underground. The devil would inspire murderous sects and deadly heresies. Famine, plague, and war would lay the land waste. It would be far worse for Germany than it had been for Jerusalem; for where the light of the Gospel had shone the brightest, there would the punishment fall heaviest for turning away.[115]

This growing disillusionment and pessimism applied not only to Germany but to worldly prospects in general. Open scorn for the truth was evident everywhere. Luther's later years saw the publication of violent and often vulgar polemics against all his enemies: Catholics, Turks, Jews, separatists, and other Protestants of almost every stripe. There is no question that the exuberance of the young Reformer became seriously dampened as the years passed; indeed hardly more than a decade after his break with Rome his expectations for the worldly future had become thoroughly bleak. He began a preface to a popular German work of 1533 with the lament that "the ungratefulness of the world is so overwhelmingly great, and it mounts so from day to day, that unless the Last Day comes we fear—or rather we must certainly predict and expect—God's horrible, frightful punishment and wrath, as he draws his light back unto himself and allows the darkness to come over all." Although the *Table Talk* is unreliable for making precise points about Luther's beliefs, the entries for the later years of his life show such a pervasive worldly pessimism and longing for the end that little doubt can remain about the strength of these attitudes. "I wish that

I and all my children were dead," he exclaimed. "For things are going to get still more awful in this world. Whoever remains alive will see that it will become worse and worse. That is why God is now taking away those who belong to him."[116] Since people turned further from God every day, they could expect nothing but catastrophe until the final cataclysm itself.

As Mark Edwards has made clear, Luther's growing pessimism and increasingly harsh indictments of his contemporaries cannot be explained by illness or his increasing age. They must be understood as expressions of frustration and disappointment in the face of the worldly struggle.[117] As Luther became more and more disillusioned, his hopes focused more and more exclusively on the nearness of deliverance. This change should not be regarded as fundamental, since his underlying eschatological orientation manifested itself throughout his career. But it is fair to say that the apocalyptic aspect of his thought became more pronounced as the years passed.

As to the time of the end, Luther was careful to warn that this could not be known. Yet he was not averse to a conjecture or two, and he frequently indulged in speculations as to how long the world could last. Often, as in the *Table Talk*, such speculation was casual and imprecise, without any pretense of calculation. The Last Day might come within five or six years, or within twenty, or within the lifetimes of people now living.[118] It was likely to occur in the springtime, around Easter, when once before Christ had renewed the world.[119] But elsewhere, as in his *Supputatio annorum mundi*,[120] he could undertake seriously to reckon the age of the world and to draw conclusions about the proximity of the end. This sort of concern does seem to have gained ground in Luther's mind as he grew older. It is not really necessary to decide whether this change should be construed positively, as an "increasing appreciation of the worth of chronology,"[121] or negatively, as a tendency to become "more and more calculating" as time passed.[122] In either case, this form of reckoning both reflected in Luther and reinforced in his followers an essentially apocalyptic view of history.

The *Supputatio annorum mundi*, Luther's major effort at world-historical calculation, shows better than any of his other writings how far he was from allegorizing the concept of the Last Day. The work typified the growing sixteenth-century concern for chronology, for discovering the exact outlines and pattern of world history since the Creation. It was based on a periodization that was far from new. The analogy between the six days of creation and the six thousand years of the world had originated in Jewish apocalyptic thought, with the idea that a thousand years are as a day in the eyes of the Lord. Around the time of Christ this scheme underwent a refinement in the Talmud; here the six thousand years were divided into three periods of two thousand years each. The first period predated the Law, the second was that of the Law, and the third was that of the Messiah. This scheme, which was attributed to the prophet Elias, was recognized by Augustine himself and had a persistent influence.

Luther may have encountered the idea first in a world history edited by Melanchthon, which appeared in 1531, the *Chronica* of Johann Carion. But he had shown general familiarity with such a triadic pattern much earlier than 1531; the scheme was common enough to make his prior acquaintance with it not unlikely.[123] He cited it at the very beginning of his *Supputatio*:

> Sex milibus annorum stabit mundus,
> Duobus milibus inane,
> Duobus milibus lex,
> Duobus milibus Messiah.[124]

A strict interpretation of the prophecy would, of course, have put the end of the world almost five hundred years away. But a few words from the New Testament explained away that possibility. The expectancy of the Reformation period ensured that a passage such as Matthew 24: 22 would become a central theme. Here Christ foretold that the days would be shortened for the sake of his elect, for "except those days should be shortened, there should no flesh be saved." Over fifteen hundred years of the last age had already elapsed. The end therefore had to be perilously close.

In form, the *Supputatio* was a lengthy chart of world history. Each page was divided into columns in which historical events were noted next to their appropriate dates. In the early sections of the work Luther sometimes displayed the history of the godly in one column and that of the godless in the other, but through the greater part no such distinctions were made. The chart began with the Creation and continued to 1540, which Luther reckoned as the year 5500 of the world. The chronology was derived above all from the Bible, but Luther did use other sources, including such ancients as Philo of Alexandria and such contemporary works as Melanch-

thon's edition of Carion's *Chronica*. He strove to improve the exactitude of earlier chronological works; his reckoning of the time
of Christ's birth, for example, differed from that of Carion by six
years.[125]

Such efforts at precision were clearly of secondary importance for
Luther. But he did hope by such means to afford greater insight into
the divine plan for history, and to support the conviction that the
Second Advent would occur sooner rather than later. Even discrep-
ancies in his calculations could serve this end. According to the
Supputatio the birth of Christ came in the year of the world 3960,
which did not quite match the prophecy of Elias. "Now this falls a
bit short of the four thousand," wrote Luther, "but the prophet
showed in this way that God will come sooner [than expected] and
will hasten to the end."[126] The Reformer was definitely not bound
by any one scheme of periodization. Yet his efforts at reckoning the
ages of world history clearly arose from a pressing desire for some
sort of prophetic assurance, a desire that came closer to the surface
as he experienced the trials of his later years. This deep need for
certainty in a universal order is so pronounced in Luther's thought
that it is not surprising that some have depicted the Reformer as
the preacher of a Stoic sense of necessity.[127] But one need not go this
far to acknowledge the central importance, for Luther, of trust in
God's promises.

While certain elements of his apocalypticism became more pronounced as Luther grew older, his eschatological outlook did not
change in any essential way once his differences with Rome had
become clear and his prophetic vision of history had begun to take
shape. He retained until the end of his life the apocalyptic beliefs
with which he had launched his movement. Although the tone of
his apocalyptic expression varied with time and circumstances, its
deeper premises did not. Luther continually emphasized that the
approach of the end was joyful news for every believer, while the
bad news from every earthly quarter merely confirmed his belief
that the Judgment was near. His prophecies for the time remaining,
particularly for Germany, became forecasts of darkest doom, but
they were still warnings to repentance for anyone who had ears
to hear.

Despite many claims to the contrary, Luther's Reformation did
not dissolve the extreme tension of the late Middle Ages. It actually
heightened the tense expectation by declaring inane all hopes for

the earthly future and by directing all hope to the imminent return of Christ. And Luther's style of expectancy, combined with his willingness to entertain various prophetic traditions and to speculate about the nearness of the end, could not but encourage further investigations into the unfolding truths of the Last Times.

APOCALYPTIC INSIGHT AND THE EVANGELICAL CAUSE

To what extent did the early evangelical movement as a whole share Luther's prophetic insights, and to what extent had he actually established the guidelines of a new prophetic vision? We need to explore these questions before going on to consider the development of Lutheran apocalypticism after the death of the Reformer himself.

There is abundant evidence that from the very beginning of the movement, among both the learned and the common folk, Luther's Reformation was thought to have apocalyptic significance. Indeed even before his beliefs had formed a movement, the controversy the Wittenberger stirred up appeared to some to imply eschatological upheaval. Among the earliest apocalyptic reactions to Luther was a pseudonymous work supposedly by the astronomer Jacob Pflaum of Ulm. Pflaum had considerable fame for his part in the publication of well-known astrological forecasts. He lived and wrote in the late fifteenth century and in the first few years of the sixteenth. This *Practica* was supposed to have been written in 1500, and it predicted events for 1520 perfectly, including the election of a new emperor and the appearance of one who would reveal and attack the corruption of the pope, the cardinals, and the priesthood. The work must have been composed about 1521, for around this time the correspondence of the predictions with what actually happened breaks down. The forecasts were an extremely confused mixture of medieval prophecies concerning the rise and defeat of the Antichrist, war, hunger, and pestilence, struggle against the Turk, and finally the dawn of an age of peace. The hazy conception of particulars, along with the general sense of earth-shaking changes to come, was typical of late-medieval prophecy. But the author left no doubt that Luther's argument with Rome "marked the beginning of an eschatological drama."[128]

Apocalyptic motifs were at least implicit in most early evangelical propaganda. These motifs reflected far more than an effective exploitation of popular beliefs; they were expressions of serious conviction. Huldreich Zwingli may not have intended a quite literal meaning when as early as 1519 he referred to the outspoken Augustinian as an Elias, a prophet sent to prepare the way of the Lord.[129] But Luther's followers soon ascribed to the Reformer an unequivocal status as a fulfiller of biblical prophecies. Early in 1522, for example, the Augustinian Michael Stifel, one of Luther's first highly vocal supporters, issued a popular work that identified the Reformer as the angel of Revelation 14: 6, who proclaims the eternal Gospel to every nation on earth, and who warns that the hour of God's judgment has come.[130] Although Luther heartily discouraged such efforts to establish his prophetic identity, a similarly apocalyptic tone would have a prominent place in subsequent popular propaganda. The idea that God was preparing for the final destruction of his enemies was rarely far from the surface, and was often explicit.

The apocalyptic emphasis of early Lutheranism tended to legitimize and to unburden the widespread popular expectancy of the time. For in countless sermons, pamphlets, and tracts, believers now found their feeling that their age was climactic forcefully confirmed, and confirmed in a way that freed them from the burden of guilt in these Last Days. Among those who already felt that the times were out of joint, apocalyptic Lutheran preaching struck a highly responsive key. Through its clear assertion that the final struggle had already begun, evangelical propaganda could only serve to reinforce, indeed to heighten, eschatological expectancy in Germany.[131]

In the main, the apocalyptic themes in early evangelical publications were heavily biblical. They derived from the well-known imagery of Daniel and Revelation, as well as from countless other passages of prophetic import from the Old and New Testaments. As we have seen, Luther attempted to put the expectancy of his age back into biblical focus, so that God's activity through history could be clearly recognized. The Reformation was not merely a revival of the Word, but a climactic revival clearly predicted in the Word itself, in Scripture. Biblical prophecy was the basis and the measure of all true prophecy; all hopes and expectations had ultimately to be judged by this standard. The Bible alone supplied full legitimacy for the great prophetic discoveries of the day.

Luther's interpretations of the apocalyptic imagery of the Bible were quickly and easily disseminated in the early Reformation. Early evangelical editions of the New Testament, for example, included woodcuts and commentary that clearly illustrated his view of the papal Antichrist, and that linked contemporary persons and places with specific passages in Revelation. The Apocalypse illustrations of the 1522 *Septembertestament* reflect Luther's understanding—worked out with the artist Lucas Cranach—of the history of the church, its persecution by the enemies of truth, and its ultimate triumph at the Last Day. The identification of the papacy with the whore of Babylon was here widely publicized through illustrations of the tiara-crowned whore riding upon the seven-headed beast (Revelation 17: 1–18), images that fairly bristled with apocalyptic implications. The city of Rome itself was equated with Babylon. The papacy could also be depicted as the beast from the bottomless pit (11: 7) or one of several other monsters mentioned in Revelation. An even greater sense of immediacy was probably conveyed in illustrations that showed political figures—Maximilian, Charles V, and the Archduke Ferdinand—adoring the beasts of the Apocalypse.[132] Luther and Melanchthon were concerned that this difficult text should be made accessible to the common man in a way that emphasized the Reformation as the rescue of God's Word from the forces of darkness, and that underlined how critical was the present strife. In nonpolemical ways, too, as in depictions of the pouring out of the vials of wrath, the Last Judgment, and the New Jerusalem, these woodcuts encouraged the Bible-beholding public to conceive in vivid mental images the literal fulfillment of scriptural prophecy.

The woodcuts from Cranach's shop show a new eschatological understanding, almost entirely different from the late-medieval conceptions reflected in Albrecht Dürer's now-famous Apocalypse cycle, on which they drew superficially. This new understanding, not Dürer's, would form the basis for later sixteenth-century illustrations of the Apocalypse, including those in the full German Bible of 1534. Indeed these woodcuts had an enormous influence, even though some of the symbolism may not have been clear to those who saw them. The Apocalypse illustrations quickly became inseparable from the text of the early German Bible; they were part of its appeal. Thus they appear to have been essentially successful in their attempt to disseminate Luther's prophetic discoveries. Their themes are echoed in scores of surviving broadsheets and popular woodcuts from the early decades of German Protestantism.[133]

Yet although Luther's biblical insights held a central importance for the self-definition of the early Reformation, the success of the movement also depended upon its ability to find support in long-standing popular prophetic traditions. Medieval prophetic notions did not by any means disappear altogether among Protestants; many of them lived on in the service of the Reform. We have seen that Luther himself accepted several popular prophecies that lent themselves to his cause. Similarly, evangelical propaganda in general was not averse to using nonbiblical sources and popular traditions when these squared with prevailing interpretations of biblical prophecy.

Thus a host of nonbiblical prophetic authorities continued to be cited by Lutherans who sought to show that their movement had long been foreseen among the inspired. In 1527, for example, Andreas Osiander updated and published an old Joachimist prophecy—not actually by Joachim himself—concerning the Antichrist and the papacy. Osiander had rather freely revised the work to emphasize Luther's role as an instrument of God who preached the Word and awakened people to the tyranny of the pope, and the message was made clearer by short verses supplied by Hans Sachs. To what extent Osiander saw the original as genuine prophecy is uncertain, but he did retain its essential elements, including the idea that the downfall of anti-Christian forces would be followed by a time of peace and virtue before the return of Christ. This *Wondrous Prophecy of the Papacy* is thus notable as an effort to adapt a Joachimite style of expectation to the evangelical cause.[134]

Along with the *Wondrous Prophecy*, Osiander also edited and published in 1527 a prophecy of Hildegard of Bingen that foresaw profound corruption throughout the world, followed by a recovery of the true church before the end.[135] In his preface Osiander cited both biblical prophecy and many other sources, including the predictions of various other spiritual men and women, the warnings of highly regarded clergymen and astronomers, signs in the heavens, and various visions, to show that the papacy's opposition to God's Word had been clearly announced.[136]

Another old source adopted by Lutherans was the so-called Magdeburg prophecy, which was a version of a long-lived medieval tradition known as the Tripoli prophecy. This was a rather cryptic prophetic message that foresaw, among other things, woe for the clergy, the tossing of the ship of Peter, famines, plagues, the annihilation of the mendicant orders, the subjection of the whole world by the "beast of the West" and the "lion of the East," a time of peace and fruitfulness, and the rise of the Antichrist. In 1531 or 1532, an unknown Lutheran adapted parts of the prophecy and merged them with another prediction he had discovered about a great emperor named Charles who would conquer all Europe, then reform both church and empire. The result appealed enormously to German Protestants. It was published in Wittenberg in 1532 as an appendix to the edition of the pseudo-Pflaum's *Practica* that appeared in that year, and it enjoyed lasting influence through its appearance in Carion's *Chronica*. Luther himself seems to have regarded it as confirmation that tremendous changes were imminent.[137]

Such appeals to extrabiblical prophecies and prophetic traditions were probably inevitable in light of their prevalence on the eve of the Reformation. A great collection of prophetic authority stood ready for evangelical publicists, and it was not likely to be ignored, since much of it predicted disasters for the church and the clergy and the hope of future reform. Frequently, extrabiblical sources complemented scriptural prophecy in popular works, as if a combination of authorities might help to convince the common man.[138] Since popular prophetic notions were often hazy and ambiguous, the process of adaptation was not generally difficult. Lutherans did not limit themselves to widely known traditions; they could also revive obscure visions or predictions when these seemed meaningful. Thus Luther could issue his own antipapal interpretation of the little-known vision of Brother Claus, a fifteenth-century Swiss hermit.[139] The Reformer felt he was dealing with a genuinely prophetic vision; properly to explain it could only further knowledge about the enemies of the Gospel.

Evangelical propagandists were somewhat less ready to accord equal status to astrological prophecy; in the first decades of the Reformation there were few direct appeals to astrological evidence among Lutheran publicists. Nonetheless, as we will see, the excitement aroused by astrological predictions certainly influenced the popular belief that current events were ushering in world-shaking changes, and in the burgeoning astrological literature of the time, explicit links were very often made between the heavenly signs and Luther's movement. Indeed, astrologers generally influenced people to think that the future promised yet greater changes and upheavals. The shoes of Lichtenberger and other influential astrologers of an earlier generation were now filled by such stargazers as Joseph Grünpeck, who, although a Catholic, predicted disaster for the Roman church; his work naturally appealed to Protestants.[140] Many Lutherans were not averse to citing astrological evidence if it could help to establish the prophetic significance of their movement.

Moreover, among Lutherans as with Luther himself, there was little hesitation to expound the significance of heavenly signs and other omens. Comets and other unusual events in the heavens were certain warning of coming troubles and of the end of the world. Publicists for the Reform eagerly cited all such signs, which had long been regarded with awe whether interpreted according to biblical prophecy or not. The printing press allowed propagandists of the Reform to exploit the sensational in the service of their cause. The signs included extraordinary events of every sort. The well-known pamphlet of Luther and Melanchthon interpreting the monstrous Monk-Calf and Papal Ass is but one example of the effort to find prophetic significance in freakish natural phenomena. The Monk-Calf, a grotesque misbirth with features suggesting clerical garb, was for Luther a revelation of the abomination of monkery, and was one more sign of warning as well as promise. The Papal Ass, interpreted somewhat more literally by Melanchthon, was a monster supposed to have been found dead in the Tiber at Rome in 1496. It revealed the nature of the papacy, its various repulsive parts symbolizing the supporters of the institution, its death pointing to the end of papal power. These monsters, like others described in popular literature, were perversions of the natural order and thus manifested in the particular the corruption of nature in general. God permitted them as signs of sin and disorder in the world.[141] The apocalyptic belief that this state of disorder had reached a crisis, and that resolution was imminent or already begun, was intimately connected with interest in signs and wonders.

Most Lutheran leaders shared the Reformer's own reluctance to be very precise in the interpretation of popular prophecies, visions, natural wonders, and the like. A cautious, spiritual interpretation was always more prudent. There was always the danger of popular misinterpretation, and this danger was hardly limited to rebellious peasants or Anabaptist sectarians. More than a few people—for example, the Nuremberg painter Paul Lautensack—were driven by the expectancy of the early Reform to chiliastic or otherwise unacceptable interpretations of the scriptural prophecy.[142] The perils of an imagination overheated by expectancy were obvious.

Yet it was difficult for prudence to outweigh conviction. Belief in portents and prophecies was strong among evangelical leaders; it was likely far less reserved among common burghers. As Robert Scribner has shown, the popular prophecies in evangelical propaganda were so highly effective largely because the propagandists themselves believed these prophecies.[143] The prophetic mood was so widely shared, and Luther's basic discoveries were so convincing, that almost any prophecy with antipapal or anticlerical overtones could be taken to support the reforming movement. It seems that any prophecy or method was accepted if it lent support to the evangelical cause. Thus, among early Lutherans there was no clear definition of acceptable prophetic insight, no clear limitation on what sources or methods could be used to clarify the significance of the movement. A variety of medieval prophecies, prophetic traditions, and prophetic methods were adapted to a new context, and contributed to the ground swell of excitement in the early Reformation.

Despite the continuance of these various traditions and their use in propaganda for the Reform, they were overshadowed, during the early decades of Luther's movement, by the heavy evangelical emphasis on biblical prophecy and on a few basic prophetic discoveries. The Reformation had a powerful momentum, and effected a sense of prophetic confidence. Lutheran apocalypticism had sanctioned, intensified, and focused the inherited prophetic expectancy mainly through a convincing interpretation of Scripture; the various extrabiblical traditions were useful but mostly incidental. Yet in the excitement of the early Reformation, no clear limits had been established, even by the recognized leaders of the movement, to the realm of acceptable prophecy or the criteria for genuine prophetic insight. The way was open for further apocalyptic speculation as time went on. By the troubled times of midcentury, the desire for prophetic certainty would motivate a widespread effort to exploit a broad range of prophetic traditions and methods more intensively.

2

⊷§ The Proliferation of the Last Things

THE LATER LAST TIMES

In the decades after Luther's death in 1546, the number of prophetic interpretations and apocalyptic warnings published in Lutheran centers rose rapidly and steadily. Popular summaries of Lutheran teaching about the Last Times, dire predictions for the future of Germany and of Christendom, and reports of signs of the coming end in the heavens and on earth flowed from the presses at a rate astonishing even by modern standards. Although these publications were extremely varied in style and content, they appear to have had a common goal: proclaiming and clarifying critical prophetic truths. A look at some of the causes and implications of this effort is needed to understand the excitement and confusion that were so prevalent in Germany in the late sixteenth century.

Several causes can be suggested for the desire of Lutherans to expound their eschatological teaching so forcefully. To begin with, Luther's own prophetic statements carried enormous weight. In his lifetime, innumerable admirers had called the Reformer a prophet, and after his death the designation became far more common still. He had earned the name as an inspired man of God, and he accepted it as long as it held no connotation of special revelation or spiritual status. But despite his own lively protests, Luther was regarded by many of his contemporaries as the second or third Elias, the prophet sent by God specifically to discover the Antichrist and announce the Gospel again in the Last Times. Such leaders as Melanchthon and Matthias Flacius often referred to him in this way, and many others followed suit, including preachers as influential as

Johannes Mathesius. Luther found even more inappropriate the common practice of identifying him with the prophetic angel of Revelation 14: 6, or with other biblical figures of eschatological import. Finally, there were occasional efforts virtually to deify the man. The physician Wolfgang Rychard of Ulm sought to begin a new calendar with Luther's advent, which appeared to him as the beginning of a new spiritual dispensation.[1] Such excesses were obviously the exception. Nevertheless among Lutherans throughout the sixteenth century his words were widely regarded as all but infallible; his predictions were rarely if ever challenged. And if Luther himself was no Christ figure, his Reformation was often compared directly to the first great flowering of the Gospel in the early church.[2]

At the same time, however, Luther's prophetic insights and warnings remained scattered throughout his voluminous writings; he had written nothing definitive or systematic on the theme of eschatology. His views had often remained implicit, and if we leave aside his commentaries on specific well-known biblical passages his thoughts in this realm were expressed almost randomly. Luther never wrote anything like a complete eschatological treatise, for the simple reason that his conviction about the nearness of deliverance underlay his whole work. Moreover, when he did publish formal expositions of the prophetic books of the Bible, his treatments tended to be cautious. Yet his own prophetic discoveries had developed important new meanings for these books. Thus later interpreters were naturally led to sift, summarize, and clarify the Reformer's ideas in the light of current events.

In the 1550s, collections of Luther's prophecies began to appear regularly. Some of these were brief pamphlets such as the *Several Prophetic Statements of Doctor Martin Luther, the Third Elias*, issued by a preacher of Nordhausen in 1552.[3] But Luther had much to say to worried times, and his dark warnings and forecasts could fill tomes. In 1557 Peter Glaser of Dresden published 120 of the Reformer's collected prophecies; by 1574 the number had grown to 200 in a work of well over 300 pages.[4] The first edition, explained Glaser in his preface to the 1574 edition, had long ago sold out and was now almost nowhere to be purchased. Many times he had been asked to reissue the work. Moreover several of Luther's writings had newly appeared in print, and many more prophecies were found in them. And since the Reformer's prophecies were proving more correct every day, the need to make them available was evident. Several other collections almost as large as Glaser's were also aimed at the mass market. Georg Walther explained that his edition was primarily for the benefit of those who could not afford the regular, larger editions of Luther's works. This sort of prophetic compendium remained popular well into the next century.

For every book devoted exclusively to Luther's predictions, there were many that referred to his fears and admonitions in one way or another. Scores of published sermons and short tracts included prefatory or concluding selections from the Reformer's warnings. Typical was the "Prophecy of Dr. Martin Luther, Written in Latin in His Own Hand, That God's Word Will Again Be Driven Out of Germany," which appeared on the back of the title page in a 1593 collection of sermons by Samuel Huber.[5] The tendency in such writings was to paint a uniformly dismal picture of worldly prospects, to emphasize that the last great prophet had retained no hope for this world and that he had longed for the coming of the Last Day.

Luther's own prophecies were supplemented by dozens of popular tracts in which Lutheran writers hammered away on the theme of the approaching Judgment Day. Many of these works were explicitly didactic, and sought to explain in the clearest possible terms the fundamental truths of these Last Times. Melchior Specker's *On the Glorious Coming of Jesus Christ to the Last Judgment*, for example, published in 1555, offered explanations of the basic New Testament passages on the Second Coming, the process of Judgment, and the glorious Kingdom that would follow.[6] Wolfgang Waldner, a preacher at Regensburg, carefully organized the subject under eleven chapter headings, the first of which was "That the Last Day Is Certain to Come, and That Another Life Will Follow It."[7] Hieronymus Menzel used the simplest language in his clear, step-by-step account of the Second Coming and the Last Judgment. His purpose was to present the scriptural evidence as straightforwardly as possible.[8] Johann Garcaeus concluded a tract intended for popular eschatological instruction with 30 questions and answers about the return of Christ. Since almost all of these questions had been addressed in the text, the purpose was simply to insure that the main points had been driven home. Why has the Last Judgment been announced beforehand? What proof do we have it will come? Why has God waited so long? What do the "Epicureans" think about this belief? Why did God keep the time of the end hidden from us? What signs do we have that the day is now approaching? What will follow the Judgment? How should we ready ourselves? Garcaeus clearly wished to make his teaching as unambiguous as possible, in order to offer his readers a solid prophetic certainty.[9] Naturally these tracts overflowed with denunciations of all the enemies of truth and with exhortations to perseverance in these supremely dangerous Last Times. The examples cited here are drawn from a host of such works.[10]

The systematization involved in all these efforts is no indication that the force of assumptions about the coming end was dwindling. On the contrary, the great proliferation of apocalyptic writings in the decades after Luther's death points to a confirmed, if somewhat grimmer conviction of the inevitability of future events. Many of Luther's early followers had awaited the return of Christ with ecstatic confidence, but the ecstasy wore off as the Reformation grew older. With the retrenching of the Roman church, the beginnings of strong and effective counter-Reformation measures, the war of the Protestant states against the emperor, the rapid spread of Calvinism and of numerous other sects, and finally just with the passage of time, the unpleasant realities of the worldly struggle loomed larger. The buoyant belief that had seen the Reformation as the last flash of the Gospel light was now beginning to feel the strain of events. But Lutherans reacted to this wavering of their early, sanguine hope with the emphatic reassertion of a common certainty: the Judgment was to be expected at any moment. Satan might be more active than ever before, but final justice was just around the corner. This was a crucial message for the faithful.

Indeed, events in this period seemed to bear out Luther's worst expectations. The Reformer's death in 1546 had left the evangelical churches without any single figure to whom all could look for inspiration. In the years that followed, the very wars, dissensions, and confusion he had predicted in fact appeared. He was dead but a few months when the War of the League of Schmalkalden broke out. The struggle seemed to many Lutherans the final act in the drama of world history. Despite the conviction that Christ himself would soon intervene, there were many truly terrified souls among those who stood to suffer the wrath of the emperor. For a time it looked as though the Reformation might very well be wiped out in the empire; this, then, would be the true test of oppressed believers. As it happened, however, Charles V failed to gain the support he needed to impose a religious settlement in Germany, and in 1555 Lutheranism was officially legalized through the Peace of Augsburg. But any interpretation that traces the beginnings of Lutheran complacency and torpor to this point is mistaken. Though the immediate menace had passed, the feeling that corruption was growing daily and that destruction was imminent certainly remained after 1555. Indeed the Last Judgment was preached more furiously than ever, for dangers were still perceived everywhere.

Luther had prophesied that after he died the Gospel would disappear, and many Lutherans, such as Nikolaus von Amsdorf, declared openly that the prophecy was being fulfilled.[11] Amsdorf had been a close friend of Luther since the early years of the Reformation, and was one of the natural leaders of the movement after Luther's death. But neither he, nor Melanchthon, nor anyone else had the prestige and authority to take the place of the Reformer. Disagreements over the interpretation of the Reformation message had already begun to divide Luther's followers in the 1530s and 1540s, and after 1546 the only unquestioned mediator was gone. Amsdorf became a leading light in one of the two major parties that emerged, whose members are generally termed Gnesio-Lutherans. Their less numerous opponents, known as Philippists, centered around Melanchthon.

Open factional dispute broke out first over the so-called "Interims" of 1548. After his defeat of the Protestant forces at Mühlberg in the preceding year, the emperor tried to wring concessions on issues of religious practice. The Augsburg Interim and later the Leipzig Interim were in essence compromises by which the Lutheran parties hoped to avert further imperial pressure. By agreeing to reintroduce Catholic practices in *adiaphora*, matters that made no difference in the issue of salvation, the Protestants hoped to maintain the core of their faith. But the documents proved to be sources of bitter controversy among Lutherans themselves. Melanchthon and his colleagues at Wittenberg, who had been responsible for the compromise embodied in the Leipzig Interim, were attacked by Amsdorf and others, who saw no possibility of constructive negotiation with Rome or her agents.[12] Far deeper differences of theological orientation underlay this dispute, and these soon became the focus of a conflict that continued for several decades. The main point at issue between the two groups was the role of good works in salvation. Oversimplifying, we may say that the

Gnesio-Lutherans maintained a radical solifidianism, asserting even that good works as such were detrimental to salvation, while the Philippists, who were somewhat readier to compromise and seek peace, argued that good works done in faith were helpful and perhaps even necessary to salvation.[13]

But here the theological issues can be safely ignored. What is important is that this sort of disagreement helped to fuel the apocalyptic sensibility that was already strong within Lutheranism. Countless other disputes between individuals and theological parties arose during the middle decades of the century, as Luther's heirs struggled to interpret his insights in the light of changing conditions. The resulting confusion only heightened the common expectation of imminent Judgment. Surely these troubled times after the passing of the last great prophet were nothing but the final convulsions of a hopelessly decadent world.

Even before the serious theological disputes had developed, the Interims were provoking apocalyptic reaction. Andreas Osiander thought he was witnessing, in the Augsburg Interim, God's final temptation before the end. On the basis of Revelation 11: 11, he expected the Interim to last three and a half years; he foresaw the pouring out of the vials of wrath during this time upon those who had deserted the Gospel. A final spreading of the Word over the world would then precede the defeat of the Antichrist and the Last Judgment.[14] The later Interim particularly became the target of harsh opposition; the arrangement was denounced as the work of the Antichrist, a final ruse by which the devil spread his poison. In the eyes of Andreas Musculus, it was the very sister of the Council of Trent. Clearly the world had been going rapidly from bad to worse since Luther's death; the only hope was that God would shorten the days for the sake of his elect.[15] But the subsequent theological squabbles were probably more demoralizing than the Interims themselves. Jacob Andreae had to explain that through these troubles God was testing his chosen before the end, just as gold and silver could only be separated from the dross through fire.[16]

Gnesio-Lutherans, Philippists, and other factions did not differ in their central eschatological teachings. All agreed that Christ would return in the flesh to judge mankind, that the Second Advent was not far off, that the Reformation was the final flowering of the Gospel, and that the current decadence of the worldly regiment was the result of Satan's last and greatest effort to win souls. If Amsdorf could charge that Melanchthon's views were undermining the Gospel in the Last Times, a Melanchthonian like Paul Eber could just as well see his opponents as a symptom of the madness of a corrupt, senile world approaching its end. Members of every theological faction, along with pastors and laymen who were members of no faction at all, shared in the popularization and intensification of Luther's expectations. The typical Lutheran pastor probably went about his work with little direct involvement in these quarrels, but was likely to take refuge from confusion in the comforting belief that the end was very near.[17]

Thus, during the 1550s and 1560s, the condition of the world appeared more and more hopeless to Lutheran observers. Rare was the religious treatise that did not give some expression to this feeling. Pastors railed against moral decadence and lack of faith with all the energy they could muster; lamentations over the rampant evil of the world grew into a full chorus. It was more than evocative rhetoric when Lutheran preachers bewailed the growing corruption of the world in this way. Nothing could have been more serious.

Georg Spalatin wondered how anyone might wish for a long life in such misery as now abounded. Caspar Cruciger thought that the complete suppression of the Gospel was not unlikely, and hoped for quick deliverance through the coming of the Last Day. Wolfgang Kaufman complained that to preach the Word was to be regarded as an ass; the godless wreaked their evil everywhere. Bartholomew Gerhard saw society coming apart at the seams: shameless vice rent the family, the church, and the schools. In Germany, wrote Josua Loner, Christian love had frozen to ice, and signs of the end were everywhere. According to Jacob Andreae, the Lutheran church was quickly degenerating into a moral wasteland. The prevailing confusion in religious teaching left no hope for David Chytraeus other than the coming Heavenly Kingdom.[18] Bartholomew Wolfhart, church superintendent at Hildesheim, was convinced that even the basic articles of faith were falling into oblivion, and his work *On the Last Day* was typical of scores of writings that undertook to remind the common man of the gravity of his plight.[19] We need not take seriously Wolfhart's charge that the Last Day had been practically forgotten; it was but one more expression of a widespread disappointment with the state of this world. When one preaches about the coming Judgment, he wrote, people complain that this is not the Gospel; they say the Gospel is not frightful but comforting to hear. Wolfhart evidently thought his hearers needed at least as much warning as comfort.

Such preachers were united in the belief that an ocean of indifference surrounded them. Andreas Musculus thought that most of the world simply mocked his heartfelt Christian warnings. Some people, he reported, said that even when they were young they had heard lots of talk about the Last Day, and that nothing much had changed since then. The beer tasted just as good as it always had, they joked, and as long as their money held out until the end they saw no reason to worry. For these poor sinners Musculus had nothing but pity and contempt.[20] As Wolfgang Waldner pointed out, St. Peter had predicted just such scorners in the Last Days; their appearance now helped to prove the crucial point.[21] The growing number of doubters was itself an indication that Judgment approached. Christ himself had often compared the corrupt times that had preceded the Flood with those that would come before the end. Since things were getting worse day by day, it was appropriate that Christians should think clearly about what awaited them.

Lutheran historians have argued that such pessimism must be distinguished from the essential convictions of early Lutheranism. Thus we are taught that the *Untergangsstimmung* of the sixteenth century, the conviction that the world was decaying and about to break up, was not the result of deeply felt experience, of a *Weltgefühl* or an *Urerlebnis*. Rather, such thinking was occasioned by particular events in the world and by a belief in signs and portents that was peripheral to the central aspects of religious experience. Underlying this position is the desire to distinguish between a faith unaffected by historical change and the many time-bound elements of the sixteenth-century world-picture. The upholders of this view remind us that Luther saw his own worldly melancholy as something to be overcome, as a tool of the devil. Pessimism, he thought, was something inborn in men, which must be driven out.[22]

But this distinction between faith and worldly pessimism should not obscure the depth of the latter in Lutheran thought. Pessimism toward earthly history was not merely a conclusion from signs and portents. It was an a priori assumption, part of an inherited world-picture that the signs merely supported. And it is far from simple to disentangle such assumptions from aspects of experience that were ostensibly more central. Luther's words and actions were all conditioned, however indirectly, by his belief that the world was sliding toward final destruction and Judgment. Virtually all of his colleagues and countless Lutheran preachers expressed the same conviction. Certainly the entire anthropology of early Lutheranism was not gloomy. Though the sorry prospects of this world were seldom forgotten, the coming of the Last Day also excited joyful expectation of resurrection and redemption, a new heaven and a new earth. Historical pessimism does not necessarily imply fatalism; it poses no obstacle to a life of faith active in love.

The heavy brunt of the pessimistic warning and denunciation that issued from the Lutheran chancel fell upon the Germans. Luther's own combination of high hopes and bitter disillusionment toward his countrymen continued to resound among his followers, but by the 1550s the forebodings of the Reformer's later years were clearly the dominant chord. In his collection of Luther's predictions, Peter Glaser offered a "Catalogue of the Sins on Account of Which Germany According to Luther's Prophecies Will Be Punished with Evil," followed by a similarly long list of the punishments themselves.[23] Amsdorf published "A Sermon Drawn from Luther's Writings on the Prophets, That Germany Will Be Destroyed and Laid Waste As Were Israel, Judaea, and Jerusalem."[24] Luther's own warning was echoed over and again: the punishments to precede the Last Day would fall the most heavily on those who had heard the Gospel most clearly preached, but who had remained most stubbornly deaf.

Andreas Musculus was sure that God had never showered any land with gifts as he had Germany during the preceding 40 or 50 years. But the Germans had utterly ignored and abused this grace. Paradoxically, before the Reformation people had considered future things with all zeal; many had done all they could to avoid future punishment, while the door to heaven was closed to them. But we, wrote Musculus, for whom that door has opened wide, no longer care about future things, about Heaven and Hell.[25] The vices of the Germans were already such that they could scarcely get any worse. "It is certain that we Germans, according to the words of our prophet [Luther], can expect not only God's punishment and wrath, but also a great and special misery."[26] The Rhine, the Elbe, the Oder, and the Danube would run blood-red before the end. For those who did not repent and change their ways immediately, what could be expected but inconceivably violent and horrible punishment before the Last Day?

Probably one major goal of such constant warning and exhortation to repentance was the promotion of moral and civil discipline. Might not the promise and threat of the apocalyptic struggle and the coming Last Day at least inspire moral reform, and thus contribute to social stability? After the upheavals of the early Reformation, peace and moral order were much-desired ends. The danger was clear that in such times as these the unwarranted hopes of the *Schwärmer* would infect the flock. The lesson of the revolutionary episode at Münster, where in 1534–35 a group of radical Anabaptists announced the advent of the New Jerusalem, had deeply impressed the Lutheran mind. One means of averting similar upheavals in the future was to make the true teachings on the coming end as clear and convincing as possible. Indeed, Lutheran preachers were not generally calling upon the common man to study biblical prophecy for himself, but to heed the warnings and teachings that were handed down to him from the pulpit, through the catechism, and in didactic tracts.[27] The polemical aspect of the apocalyptic message can be seen in the same light: a strong emphasis on defense of the besieged Gospel, along with zealous preaching against Rome and other enemies of truth in these Last Times, might have underlined the importance of peace and civil obedience among Christians.

Yet while these purposes probably did come into play, there is little evidence for the conclusion that the eschatological teachings of this era were prompted essentially by the need for social control, or that social control became their most important purpose. It is necessary to remember that these teachings were above all else the result of an existential certainty: the present, corrupt world would soon pass away. Lutheran expectation gave no encouragement to radical social or political activism primarily because it involved a deeply pessimistic view of whatever earthly future remained.[28] There was little hope that worldly conditions could improve before the end. All true believers were simply to guard themselves against the evils of the world, carrying on in the joyful faith that deliverance was near. Thus public morality and civil obedience were reflections of individual humility and repentance; the real concern was salvation. Most Lutheran preachers and writers were too worried about the fate of the Gospel to concern themselves with social discipline for its own sake.

As Gerald Strauss has shown, however, in at least one realm Lutherans did make vigorous efforts to improve conditions in the worldly regiment. Their program for human society, such as it was, focused on education and indoctrination of the young. Here we discover a major paradox in the Lutheran world-view. Through their educational efforts, the reformers planned, organized, and built as if to lay the groundwork for the future happiness of mankind. Yet what was the purpose if the end of the world was so close? "Why build so well if time was running out?"[29] There is no doubt of the sincerity of both the building efforts and the apocalyptic convictions. But the paradox was rarely consciously addressed. The general assumption was that the nearer the Last Judgment, the more urgent the need to prepare one's fellow men in every possible way. Still, reconciling these two beliefs posed spiritual and psychological difficulties; when their efforts fell short of success, Lutherans were prone to serious attacks of despair.[30]

We have seen evidence of this note of despair emerging by midcentury and later. Lutherans by no means abandoned their efforts to prepare their fellows for the final reckoning, but they more and more frequently expressed a sense of futility. Nothing could improve; it was all going down the drain. No one cared, no one listened. "People have weddings, they buy and sell, build and plant, as though they wanted to live forever; more so even than at the time of Noah and Lot," exclaimed the writer of one popular treatise.[31] This widespread *Sicherheit* was itself a sign of the end. The signs were everywhere for anyone who would see. There was still a chance that a few souls would hear the Word, see the danger, and repent in time to be saved. So the preaching went on, along with the effort to make known far and wide the incontrovertible evidence that the matter grew more critical by the day.

It was necessary to emphasize the limits of human understanding in these matters. Cautious Lutheran preachers and writers pointed out the importance of simple faith in the biblical promise. The fundamental truth that Christ would return to judge all mankind, if taken to heart, would lead to repentance. Beyond this believers were not required to go. Only the Holy Spirit could lead to insight into the otherwise unresearchable mysteries surrounding the Second Advent, and the Spirit did not reveal particulars of time or circumstance. Thus no one could know the time of the end, and to strive to know it was useless, even dangerous. The same was true of the details of the disastrous changes that would precede and accompany the end. These things were not revealed, nor was it necessary to know them. Such high things could not be understood in this life. For the present it was enough that people should in no way doubt the testimony of Scripture; they were to believe that the end would come very soon. The Lord had left the time of his return undisclosed for good reasons. Zealous attention would keep believers on their toes and ready for the Judgment.

Yet alongside the common acknowledgment that the end remained hidden stood the equally strong conviction that Jesus himself had clearly predicted the signs. He had instructed his followers to watch and wait. Moreover, careful as they were to warn the common man against imprudent inquiry into the mysteries of the Last Times, Lutheran writers were eager to support their convictions in every way they could. Since they maintained that their own age would unquestionably bring the end of the world, they needed evidence to distinguish the present from past epochs. A few decades earlier, Luther's basic discoveries and the Reformation itself had offered virtually complete proof that these were indeed the Last Times Christ had prophesied. The triumphant optimism of those first years had made it superfluous to search out more evidence; the end had arrived.

But in these later Last Times it became increasingly difficult for preachers to rely exclusively upon the original Reformation insights, and many threw themselves into a renewed search for specific testimonies to the coming Judgment. Believers began to discover new sources of prophetic witness and to rediscover old ones. They found signs of the coming end everywhere they looked, and they proceeded to report their findings with unprecedented thoroughness. The middle of the sixteenth century thus saw what might be called a proliferation of the Last Things—that is to say, a great increase in kind and amount of the evidence used to support apocalyptic convictions.

PROPHECY, HUMANISM, AND THE PRESS

Proofs of the coming end were sure to be found as soon as people looked for them. Apocalyptic conviction allowed virtually anything to be understood as part of the cosmic scheme now drawing to a close. To be sure, the expectancy of earlier eras had also sparked a

search for prophecies, miracles, and portents. But it was not until
the later Reformation that the search for apocalyptic evidence became both universal in scope and broadly popular.

Naturally, Luther's own expectancy was the primary authority
for the widening search. But by midcentury there were other influences at work. The serious troubles that began in the late 1540s
pointed out the need for certainty about the Reformation's place in
God's plan. The need became more and more pressing as Lutherans
felt the forces of historical change. The most important influence
on the search for prophetic evidence, however, was the spread of
what might be called popular humanism among an ever-growing
reading public. This kind of humanism was characterized above all
by interest in the natural sciences and in such studies as mathematics, astrology, and chronology. Its most famous representative was
Philipp Melanchthon.

Melanchthon was filled with curiosity about all the phenomena
of nature and human history; the same inquiring spirit was shared
by many of his colleagues and students, by a great many more Lutheran clergymen who had known the excitement of university life,
and by countless literate townsmen. Indeed the most avid intellectual interests of the *Praeceptor Germaniae* were genuinely popular,
insofar as his preoccupations were identical to those reflected in a
great deal of popular literature.[32] The eager curiosity shared by humanist academics and laymen alike virtually ensured that the *Praeceptor* and his associates at Wittenberg would have a weighty and
widespread influence on their culture. Although Melanchthon's so-
teriological arguments were never very widely accepted and were
eventually discredited in the Formula of Concord (1580), we need
not read very far in the popular literature of the later sixteenth century to realize that his intellectual methods had an extremely broad
appeal.[33] He was generally seen not as the remote symbol of an
oppressive orthodoxy, but rather as a great seeker of wisdom and
prophetic truth. His name was invoked in a surprising variety of
contexts in literature by urban clerics and the middle-class lay in-
telligentsia. Nevertheless, the spread of humanistic methods and interests should not be too closely associated with Melanchthon himself or with his circle at Wittenberg. The popularity of humanist
learning was a consequence of the ongoing spread of Renaissance
ideas in Germany; to this trend Melanchthon was merely one leading contributor.

Melanchthon's curiosity extended to prophecies and conjectures that applied to his own time and to the immediate future, and he often speculated freely about the course of future events, about the significance of omens and natural wonders, and about other matters that had little or nothing to do with formal theological teaching but that held the rapt attention of laymen. Luther himself had made innumerable predictions for the future of Germany and of Christendom, some of them fairly specific; moreover he could and did often refer to the prophetic significance of natural signs and wonders. But a more intense and more systematic interest in these matters helped to motivate prophetic speculation as the intellectual orientation exemplified by Melanchthon gained ground.

The Lutherans who shared most fully in this orientation were no less concerned than others with the ultimate importance of faith for salvation at the Last Judgment. But they were the quickest to seek for evidence of God's activity in a broad range of phenomena, including the phenomena of history and the natural world. They had a fairly flexible understanding of what constituted useful insight into the divine plan. Their humanistic interests made them ready to interpret nonbiblical prophecies, to search for signs in nature, and to employ astrology and similar arts in efforts to confirm basic prophetic truths. All these interests were at bottom expressions of a belief that God does not stand outside or above nature and history; he is *in* nature, not in a pantheistic sense, but as the creator and maintainer of all.[34] Hence knowledge of the world was inseparable from insight into God's purposes, and could only complement and strengthen faith. This intellectual orientation, typified by Melanchthon, was especially instrumental in effecting a proliferation of the Last Things in the second half of the sixteenth century.

The proliferation could never have occurred as it did, however, without the printed word. Although the flood of popular religious propaganda during the 1520s and the 1530s ebbed slightly in later decades, other sorts of publication continued to multiply; by the middle of the century a "mass literature," directed at everyone and accessible to nearly everyone, inundated Lutheran regions.[35] Moreover, by midcentury many printers had become considerably adept at catering to the interests of the reading public.

Publishers found those interests governed far less by the subtleties of theological argument than by practicality and curiosity. An enormous volume of popular literature was devoted to such subjects as health, diet, husbandry, and similar pragmatic concerns. But other forms of literature appealed more directly to popular curiosity: histories and chronologies, astrological predictions (beyond the weather forecasts found in simple almanacs), news of geographical discoveries and other notable events, and reports of wonders or miracles. If such forms of popular literature can be taken as a gauge of lay interests, the evidence suggests that the layman, while far from uninterested in theological truth, tended to seek for a knowledge of God that was somewhat different from that offered by the catechism and strict biblical preaching. Popular religious belief was based on a sense of God's all-encompassing power and of the presence of the spiritual behind all the workings of the everyday world.[36] The flood of popular literature provoked an ever-greater curiosity about these workings, and a growing desire to understand them as manifestations of God's purpose.

This burgeoning of popular literature had complex and far-reaching implications for the development of apocalyptic thinking. We have noted the great volume of prophetic literature Lutheran clergymen directed at the common man. Although Lutheran pastors and theologians continued to dominate the publication of prophetic literature, other voices were making themselves more often heard after 1550. It became clear that works of a prophetic or apocalyptic nature were always in demand. Indeed, in this age of spreading literacy, the publication of apocalyptic literature and the demand for it tended to reinforce one another, with a snowball effect.

More significantly, the spread of apocalyptic literature allowed a growing number of prophetic schemes and speculations to circulate. To the preachings and warnings of Lutheran clergymen were now more frequently added printed reports of other prophecies, both old and new. A variety of popular notions about the Last Times began to gain a truly widespread currency. One prophetic interpretation could now be compared with another, and the credibility of one weighed against that of another. Various traditions newly revived merged with expectations already current, or adapted to them. The printing press thus helped to stir up a ferment of prophetic interest that continued for many decades.

Indeed, printing effected a gradual transformation in the very nature of the apocalyptic sensibility. Inherited assumptions and patterns of thought were explored and expressed in a variety of new ways. They were reasoned out as never before, and made more explicit; their implications were analyzed. With the help of print, the thinking of German townsfolk became more autonomous and dynamic. But common assumptions about the character of the present age were not discarded; rather, they drew sharpened interest. Readers, by now generally accustomed to following a written argument or narrative, began to picture to themselves prophetic scenarios that were increasingly literal and precise. A more literal, historical approach to all prophecy was also probably encouraged by illustrations of past or predicted events with natural figures and backgrounds.[37] What before had been vivid but extremely pliant mental images, formed mostly on the basis of the spoken word, were now transformed into specific conceptions of what the future would bring, and of the meaning of the present.

But if in one respect printing could encourage more literal and precise mental images and prophetic scenarios, in another and more important way it could contribute to prophetic confusion. This sort of confusion was not limited to prophetic thought, but affected learning in general: as the printing press made available an increasing variety of sources, scholarship remained unfocused until the ability to discriminate among various intellectual traditions could catch up.[38] Among the people, printed literature represented learning and authority. A printed prophecy automatically carried weight. It was thus difficult to discard one prophecy in favor of another if differing scenarios were presented. One possible reaction to the dilemma was to allow a certain plausibility to every scheme, in the hope that further discoveries would soon resolve the uncertainty. Such haziness only reinforced the general curiosity and excitement and led to further speculation. But at the same time the assumption grew common that true prophetic knowledge was not easily come by, but was a high and hidden form of wisdom. This latter attitude became increasingly common in the Lutheran world of thought during the later sixteenth century. The tendency was by no means limited to the popular mind; it was also typical of the learned.

In several interrelated ways, then, the growing availability of printed literature contributed to the elaboration and even intensification of apocalyptic thinking. The prevailing political and religious confusion, the spread of popular humanist interests, and the booming printing industry acted together as leavening agents in the

already powerful apocalyptic thought of the age. Two general manifestations of this leavening process were the appeal to an increasing
variety of prophetic sources and traditions, and the expanding
search for signs of the end.

SOURCES OF WITNESS

The Scriptures were of course the ultimate prophetic authority.
Throughout the Reformation era they were mined, scoured, and
mined again for every glimmer of prophetic illumination they could
afford the present age. Moreover, all other prophecies and prophetic evidence had to be understood in the context of the Bible.
This requirement, however, put few strong constraints on the
search for additional testimony to the truths of the Last Times;
Scripture is highly accommodating in this respect. Next to the Bible
stood the better-known church fathers, and here again all the
sources were subjected to diligent scrutiny in the hope of finding
further support for the evangelical cause. Luther himself completed
the list of standard authorities among his followers; as we have
seen, his predictions and warnings were collected and edited with
commentaries showing how unimpeachable was his prophetic
insight.

Appeals to other ancient and medieval traditions had not died
out in the early decades of the Reformation. But in its earlier period
the movement had relatively little need for these additional sources
of prophetic confirmation; emphasis was overwhelmingly on the
new understanding of the Bible. As the century progressed, changing times saw a renewed search for witnesses to the truth. There
was a rich ancient and medieval heritage to draw on. Almost any
prophetic writer whose message included a stern warning to repentance, or who could be regarded as even vaguely anti-Roman, was
potential ammunition for Lutheran preachers and writers.

The greatest example of the search for prophetic truth through
the ages was the *Catalogus testium veritatis* of Matthias Flacius
Illyricus, published in 1556.[39] Flacius had gathered some 400 witnesses who had spoken against the papacy and its errors. Many of
these figures were obscure or entirely unknown to the sixteenth century before Flacius brought them to light again, but the work also
included such major writers as Joachim of Fiore. Flacius cited various supposed prophecies of Joachim that could be read as antipa-

pal, but he was apparently also willing to see Luther's movement as the fulfillment of Joachim's expected world Reformation.[40] Certainly Flacius entertained no thought of a new historical dispensation; he used only what suited his purposes. Yet his work did show remarkable openness to this and to many other sources that, without their prophetic character, would have been of little use to defenders of a biblical Protestantism.

Flacius was more concerned in his *Catalogus* with prophetic legitimation of the Reformation in the largest sense than with clarifying eschatological expectations. For a growing number of Luther's heirs, however, prophetic certainty meant discovering more precisely the character of their own times and what the future might yet hold in store before the end. For this purpose, prophetic witness meant not merely opposition to the papacy, but also an apocalyptic vision of what the Last Times would bring both for Christian believers and for anti-Christian powers. This was more the sort of witness that Melchior Ambach, preacher at Frankfurt am Main, had in mind when he issued a long, popular compendium of ancient and modern prophecies.[41] This work summarized in verse the thoughts of eighteen prophetic thinkers. Ambach claimed that the collection, which he titled *On the End of the World and the Coming of the Antichrist*, was the work of an unknown but clearly learned and God-fearing man who had lived at least a century earlier. The Lutheran preacher emphasized that such writings had never been more necessary to contemplate than at present. Although Holy Scripture was sufficient to inform believers of all that was necessary for salvation, wrote Ambach, God had awakened prophets in every age who had the special gift of interpreting the Bible to foretell the future. Their role was above all to warn mankind, and to prepare their hearers for the Judgment and for the shocking abominations that would precede it.

Ambach's prophets included important Old Testament characters, though Daniel was not among them. Other prophets classed among "Die Alten" included Sibylla Heraclea, St. John, and St. Paul. Those who lived after the apostolic age, "Die Jungen," included among others Methodius (that is, the Pseudo-Methodius), Joachim, Hildegard, and John of Rupescissa. All the prophecies included general warnings about future evils and the necessity of repentance, but several offered specific expectations that differed significantly from those commonly encouraged in Lutheran preaching.

The predictions attributed to Methodius, for example, suggested that, after a prescribed time of suffering, true Christians would enjoy a period of peace and security on earth, a final universal spread of Christian rule. The verses on John of Rupescissa stated that before the end all the peoples of the world would convert to Christ. The prophecies of Dieterich, a fifteenth-century monk, promised a great savior-emperor who would prepare the world for the Last Day. Indeed, the whole collection presented a kaleidoscope of prophecies, from which no one scheme emerged as definitive.

For Ambach himself the differences among the various predictions appear to have faded in the light of the general call to repentance. He did all he could to suggest that every one of these prophets was addressing the present age directly. In every case trouble and suffering were predicted for Christendom, and it was now clear that "the terrifying Day of the Lord and end of the world" was "at the door."[42] Readers found in Ambach's book a clear expression of the belief that prophets through the ages spoke directly and plainly to the present.

Ambach's work typified what amounted to a rush to discover old and venerable prophecies—venerable precisely because they were old, because they were testaments to ancient truths that, despite Luther's heroic efforts, were now ignored by an increasingly godless world. The Reformer had revived the wisdom that men of former ages had seen clearly, but that people now seemed all too willing to forget. The task was to teach again what was once known. The well of ancient wisdom stood ready, and offered to complement and clarify the prophetic lessons of Scripture.

The Prophecy of Elias, for example, did not appear in the Bible, but was clearly an important ancient truth that was useful for the understanding of God's Word. Melanchthon himself explained that this scheme of world history had been current among "the fathers and prophets," and that it was "perhaps passed down from the earliest fathers to Elias."[43] As Johann Garcaeus explained in his didactic tract of 1569, it was "an old cabalistic tradition or saying with the Jews, adorned with the name of Elias, that the world shall stand six thousand years: two thousand years without law, two thousand years with the Law, two thousand years shall the Messiah reign; but for the sake of the chosen the days will be shortened."[44] The scheme found its way into more and more popular literature after midcentury; most writers accepted it unhesitatingly and adduced it as though it were fully biblical. Ancient wisdom was hardly to be doubted.

Caspar Füger of Dresden found a message of warning and hope that likewise complemented Scripture in the writings of Lactantius, "a very learned man, who lived and wrote fully twelve hundred years ago, about three hundred years after the birth of Christ," and whose understanding of history was strongly apocalyptic. Since Lactantius himself had believed that testimonies of the truths of the coming end were not limited to canonical Scripture, he was an especially appropriate source for those who sought to complement their biblical understanding. In developing his own insights, he had made use of a remarkable range of sources, including the Sibyls, Hermetic literature, Jewish apocalypticism, and possibly even Zoroastrian texts.[45] Füger did not present passages that revealed Lactantius's millenarianism, but focused rather on his descriptions of the horrors that would befall mankind before the end. Füger's translation of these ancient predictions was issued at least twice. In another collection of prophetic writings Füger showed that the vaticinations of Lactantius were in agreement with the expectations of Johann Hilten and Luther among others; the insights of all these sages showed that the 1580s would bring universal cataclysm.[46]

Again, such sources as Lactantius and the Sibylline Oracles were revered mainly because they were old and they could be used to support current expectations. The Sibyls, as many writers believed, had correctly foreseen Christ's First Advent; hence it was folly to ignore their predictions for the Last Times. But a prophecy did not have to be very ancient to gain the credibility of age. As we saw above, any medieval prophetic vision that could be read as supporting the Reformation was grist for the mill. In 1577 Andreas Musculus pointed to the recent discovery and publication of several old vaticinations supporting the common assertion that the world could not last much longer. These forecasts had been written three or four hundred years earlier, according to Musculus, but they applied directly to the present age. They complemented the predictions of the astrologers—"our astrologers" he called them—who foresaw nothing but misery and affliction until 1580 or even 1588, unless the world came to an end before then.[47] Similarly, a highly popular collection of prophecies by Johann Carion, Paracelsus, and others included a "Prognosticon written some 300 years ago, found at Nuremberg, and sent by Veit Dietrich to Philipp Melanchthon."[48]

By the end of the century the effort to achieve prophetic clarity through old or ancient prophecies knew hardly any restraint. Popular prophetic writers frequently invoked Joachim, for example, to support expectations of imminent disaster and even to encourage hope for the speedy demise of the pope and a triumph of the Gospel before the end. Among the other important sources to which prophetic seekers could turn was the Fourth Book of Esdras (2 Esdras in English editions), an apocryphal Old Testament writing full of Jewish apocalypticism. Luther had regarded this book with ambivalence. He once referred to it as a prophecy for his own day that complemented the Apocalypse; at another time he wished that he could throw the "dreamer" who had written it into the Elbe.[49] But by the years around 1600 there were many students of prophecy who showed no such hesitation about ancient writings of this character.

Age was not the only virtue that lent authority to prophecies from outside the standard sources. There was a rapidly growing interest after about 1550 in forms of prophecy that were believed to depend on special prophetic methods or gifts. The most common prophetic method or art was astrology, which merits a separate chapter. Here we need to note in particular that, although claims to direct prophetic revelation were generally taboo among Lutherans, there was nonetheless a general eagerness to discover prophecies by people who possessed a "special prophetic spirit." Caspar Goldwurm attributed such a spirit to the fifteenth-century Italian astrologer Antonius Torquatus. The prophecies of Torquatus were heavily political. According to Goldwurm, he had clearly predicted the Reformation, the Peasants' War, the Turkish siege of Vienna, and other events of the sixteenth century. It was certain that there were still horrible calamities in store for Christendom before the end, and Goldwurm interpreted these warnings as a clear call to repentance.[50] Many other prophecies were similarly lent credibility with the claim that the author was specially inspired. According to the editor of prophecies attributed to John Capistrano, for instance, this "Silesian monk" had been "God-fearing and inspired, indeed a man blessed with a prophetic spirit."[51]

There was also after midcentury a waxing interest in the visions or revelations of obscure persons, whose insights could be interpreted constructively. Popular pamphlets were full of accounts of inspired warnings based upon the revelations of people otherwise unknown. Examples of widely publicized accounts of this sort could be cited almost without limit. One pamphlet recorded the utterances of two young girls who, deeply ill, spoke of terrible punishments to come for the godless at the Last Day; included was a "needful reminder by Doctor Martin Luther of sacred memory" concerning such occurrences.[52] In another short work, Johann Schütz commented on the prophecies of a "poor, simple, despised maiden about seventeen years old"; these were frenzied calls to repentance before this fallen world was destroyed.[53] In 1581 there appeared at Schweinfurt a "Newe Zeitung" reporting the vision of a nineteen-year-old boy to whom angels appeared as he was about to take the sacrament. They showed him the Last Judgment, the Resurrection, and the Heavenly Jerusalem. The local pastors took their cue, strongly exhorting readers and hearers to strengthen their faith.[54] Equally typical was Jacob Coler's report of a twelve-year-old girl, the daughter of upright and pious burghers in Berlin, to whom the angel Michael or Raphael appeared (she was so frightened she had forgotten which it was). The angel told her that Germany would incur a woeful punishment for unrestrained pride and arrogance, and instructed her to announce her vision far and wide. Coler described two similar admonitory wonders, and concluded with heavy apocalyptic preaching of his own.[55]

Somewhat more daring prophecies were attributed to a Wilhelm Friess or Friesen of Maastricht, who had recently died leaving written records of his visions and prophecies. According to one tract published at Nuremberg around 1558,[56] this man had foreseen "most strange and horrible changes," beyond the power of words to describe, for the five years preceding 1564. But after this the entire world would be quickly and miraculously reformed so that all men would live in perfect harmony and spiritual equality. Each man would then be filled with the Holy Spirit, and all the prophecies of Scripture would be understood. Still, no one would know the time of the Last Day. Wilhelm Friess died again in 1577; this time he left an account of a complex and obscure vision about the nations of Christendom. An appended prophecy foresaw great changes for the world in 1588, but called on every man to do penance immediately, since "no one knows when the Bridegroom will come." Published reports of such revelations and warnings became extremely common; these few examples must serve to illustrate what amounted to entire genres of popular prophetic literature.[57]

Again, despite the Lutheran proscription of claims to direct prophetic revelation, reports of inspired prophets roaming the towns and countryside inevitably reinforced the general expectancy. A pamphlet of 1586, for example, described the appearance of a new prophet before the town of Stettin. This handsome young man warned in a loud voice of disasters soon to come. First a great plague would sweep over the world, leaving only one in ten alive. The pope, the Turk, and the king of Poland would then bind together and overrun Germany, shedding blood among all who remained. Finally, however, God would raise up an unknown hero to lead the people; the pope and all his allies would be thrown into the fire. All this would happen before 1590. Readers were called upon to do penance in order to avoid God's eternal punishment.[58]

While such individual prophetic visions or revelations were common in popular literature, their importance was ultimately limited for a faith seeking universal comprehension. The extrabiblical sources of witness that became most influential were those that were validated by careful investigation of history or the natural world. What we need to note here, however, is that by the end of the sixteenth century, the sources of prophetic witness invoked by Luther's heirs were far more numerous and varied than they had been a few decades earlier. A great many voices now joined the standard authorities in announcing the truths of the Last Times. Among Lutherans, to be sure, any prophecy was valuable only as far as it served the message of the Gospel; "let us prophesy according to the proportion of faith" was Paul's rule (Romans 12: 6). But in practice the guidelines for interpretation were quite loose, and a rich variety of imagery and speculation was now being uncovered. Scripture did say, after all, that the Last Days would bring a pouring forth of the spirit. As the potential sources multiplied, the prophetic possibilities proliferated as never before. Whose interpretation was authoritative? The conscientious Bible reader was left to judge for himself. Perhaps, after considering the evidence, he might venture new insights of his own.

THE SIGNS

The clearest and most convincing complement to biblical prophecy was the signs of the times. Study of the signs became a many-sided preoccupation in the sixteenth century, for this study encompassed an enormous range of human experience. Academics like Melanchthon undertook to sort out the complexities by making a basic separation among three types of signs: unusual disorders in nature, political disturbances, and troubles in the church.[59] For our cruder, latter-day purposes we may simplify further with a division into two groups: the signs in human society and the signs in nature.

The signs in society had been almost all discovered by Luther himself; it was left for later generations merely to work out more explicit interpretations or, here and there, to perceive a new evil at work. Through most of the sixteenth century, interpreters maintained Luther's view that virtually all the signs had either already occurred or were now manifest. This was Nikolaus von Amsdorf's message in a popular tract on the signs that would precede the end.[60] First, the desertion from the faith which St. Paul had said must precede the Day of the Lord had taken place (2 Thessalonians 2 and 1 Timothy 4). The most obvious desertion had of course been that of the entire Church of Rome, but it is also clear that Amsdorf had his theological opponents, the Philippists or "Adiaphorists," in mind. Second, the Antichrist had been revealed by Martin Luther; this fact was so clear that no one could deny it. Third, the Roman kingdom, the last the earth would know according to Daniel, was on the verge of great changes. Since those changes could not bring a new order, they would bring the final cataclysm. Fourth, the pure teaching of the Gospel had been obscured by a layer of human traditions. This was happening not only among the papists but also among Lutherans; Amsdorf felt that human inventions were obtruding dangerously even in the evangelical camp. Finally, as John predicted in his Revelation, people worshipped the beast that called itself Christ. All these signs proved that the Last Day was close indeed.

Most discussions of the signs in society were no less biblical than Amsdorf's, but many attempted to compass more generally the degeneracy and lack of faith that writers typically saw everywhere. A number of listings circulated widely in popular literature. One such listing of 36 "Signs before the Last Day" originated in the *Geschichtbibel* (1531) of a Lutheran turned independent, Sebastian Franck. Franck's list was comprehensive, to say the least, though it laid heavy emphasis on the fulfillment of signs announced in the

Bible, on the drying up of faith, love, and truth, and on the prevalence of vice in the world. It was first adapted in 1549 by an anonymous editor for use in a collection of mostly astrological prophecies, but this was only the first in a series of adaptations and
reprintings through the sixteenth and early seventeenth centuries.[61]
In 1560 Franck's list was reworked by a Lutheran who emphasized
what he felt were the most blatant vices and troubles of his day,
including, for example, the rapid rise in prices that was causing
woeful suffering among the poor. Everywhere the misery of people
was increasing; avarice and covetousness gained the upper hand,
despite God's clear warnings. Men of sharp understanding pursued
worldly gain with undivided attention. Every sort of language,
learning, and new skill was applied selfishly for worldly welfare and
temporal happiness. In both worldly and spiritual affairs, perversity
reigned; error was the rule. Sects contradicted one another, twisting
the truth. Every man wished to be his own teacher and rejected true
doctrine. War and the cries of war were everywhere. People were
killing one another for their beliefs. Earthquakes, pestilence, and
natural disasters of every other form were spreading far and wide.
All was coming to a climax; it could not go on; the end would have
to come. One might dare hope for some improvement. "But every
day such grave disputes occur, so many dangers and all sorts of
affliction, that one neither can nor may establish an honest, wise,
and good order and Reformation. Therefore my writing and others
either are despised or will fall altogether into oblivion."[62] The faithful were to raise their heads and be always ready for the Judge.

   In contrast to this collection of 36 signs, the medieval tradition
of the fifteen signs almost never surfaced in Protestant writings.[63]
That Luther had passed them over is a partial explanation of this
absence, but even in the second half of the century the list is very
rarely encountered. Nicolaus Winckler of Schwäbisch Hall recognized it in a 1582 work devoted to possible scenarios of the end,
but the tradition never took hold in popular literature.[64] The reason
may lie partly in the exclusive focus of the fifteen signs on the future; they would occur on the last fifteen days before the end. Adherents of the Reform had little incentive to look forward to such a
series of signs; they believed that many important ones were already
to be seen, which proved that the Last Times were not merely close,
but had actually arrived.

The most sobering of these signs was the general moral degenera-tion to be seen everywhere. Arrogance and immorality grew more blatant by the day, warned Wolfgang Waldner, and would quickly increase in the short time before the Judgment.[65] The world was experiencing a violent upsurge of all kinds of evil, and the interpre-tation of the upsurge was a simple matter in light of biblical prophe-cies. As punishment for this spread of sin, the entire worldly regi-ment was certain to be afflicted by war, revolts, widespread hunger, and plague; indeed these evils were even now appearing.

Observers of the signs rarely failed to mention the tyranny of the Antichrist in these Last Times. But while Luther had finally decided that the true Antichrist was to be found only in the papacy, many of his later followers applied the term without hesitation to the Turk as well. The Turk and the Pope formed two "arms" of the Antichrist, or two separate Antichrists. Thus the two great enemies of the Gospel could be found at Rome and Constantinople. By the last decades of the century, some Lutheran commentators, such as Philipp Nicolai, could speak of many different Antichrists, the two great ones and many small ones, that were spreading evil in the world. Scriptural support for such a view could be found in 1 John 2: 18 and in 2 John 7, which spoke of many Antichrists. This was a more complex world than Luther had lived in, and it was no longer so easy to decide where the greatest danger to the spirit lay.[66]

It was natural to speak of two Antichrists in light of the continu-ing seriousness of the Ottoman threat. The Turk was the most ob-vious external enemy of Christendom; as preachers such as Jacob Andreae continued to make clear at length, the sins of those who called themselves Christians were likely to bring crushing punish-ment from this scourge of God before the end.[67] There was no clear consensus on this issue; Luther had sometimes read biblical proph-ecies to mean that Germany would not be conquered and that the Turk might even fall before the Last Day.[68] But a long tradition of medieval prophecies based on Ezekiel 38: 9 foresaw that Gog and Magog would overrun the people of God, and this notion retained great influence among Lutherans. The astrological predictions of Lichtenberger and the visions of Johann Hilten were frequently cited, and popular writings of all kinds forecast the very worst. Typical was Caspar Füger's popular poem, *A Prophecy of the Fu-ture Destruction of the German Land by the Turkish Emperor.*

Füger recited the sins that would bring a terrible fate upon Germany, and exhorted his countrymen to stand fast in faith as they waited for the Judgment.[69]

But again, for Füger and his contemporaries the Turk was only one of the evils that surrounded the faithful as signs of the times, especially in Germany. The sects were gaining the upper hand; the Gospel was being abandoned. In one place after another, cried Johann Lapaeus in 1578, the teachings of Calvin are accepted.[70] What else could be expected but the most horrible punishment? The rise of "Calvinists, Anabaptists, Enthusiasts, Antitrinitarians" and other perverted groups was a clear sign that the end was approaching. Yet the signs in society did, after all, point out more than bad news. It was widely recognized that a major sign of the end was the appearance of a second or last Elijah who would come to prepare the way of the Lord, and this prophecy had clearly been realized in Martin Luther. In the eyes of Andreas Musculus the signs included even the constant speaking and writing about the Last Day among his contemporaries. This sign was manifestly a gracious act of God meant to lead sinners to repentance.[71] Indeed the recognition of God's grace as a positive sign continued strongly in Lutheran preaching and writing. As Philipp Nicolai showed in 1606, since Dr. Luther's time the Gospel had been preached clearly and openly by a series of worthy servants.[72]

Nicolai's writings show that by around 1600 the notion that Luther himself had discovered all the signs had become somewhat less tenable, even among Lutheran clergymen. Major historical changes had taken place, which called for some evaluation in terms of biblical prophecy. According to Nicolai, for example, Scripture prophesied that before the Last Day many new lands would be discovered, and this had indeed happened. Indeed new continents and kingdoms had been found, of which even the greatest ancient geographers had been ignorant. Nicolai noted that the merchants and sailors of his native Hamburg, who sixty or eighty years earlier had hardly left the North Sea, now regularly travelled to Angola, to Brazil, and to many other distant lands. It was also well known that the Spaniards had ruthlessly killed thousands of American natives, and thus a prophecy of Ezekiel that God's wrath would fall upon the heathen had been fulfilled.[73] Still, such developments mainly served to show that the current state of things could not go on, that the world could not stand much longer.

Complementing the signs among men were those in the natural world. Collecting reports of natural wonders was, of course, hardly a new practice; it had found expression in print early on. An influential early collection was that of the Italian Gaspar Torella, published at Rome in 1507. Torella made traditional distinctions among the various sorts of wonders: "Portentum," "Prodigium," "Monstrum," "Ostentum," and the like. But these terms merely distinguished various types of one general phenomenon, namely signs sent by God to announce future troubles. In Germany, the astrologer Joseph Grünpeck had issued several works in the very early sixteenth century, in which predictions of terrible changes to come were based on the observation of wonders in the heavens and on earth.[74] We have seen that evangelical leaders regarded celestial and natural wonders as portents in the early Reformation; Luther believed they were proliferating in his own day. Although the Reformer and most of his colleagues had tried to be cautious in interpreting such phenomena, the religious upheaval in Germany spurred the whole concern to new orders of magnitude.

In 1532 the first true German wonder-books appeared; these were Latin works by Joachim Camerarius, a Lutheran, and Friederich Nausea, a Catholic cleric deeply engaged in the controversy of the early Reformation. The collection of Camerarius was graced by a preface in the form of a letter from Melanchthon to the Italian astrologer Lucas Gauricus. Both works expressed the belief that inexplicable natural wonders had to be divine signs of impending calamity and the end of the world. Neither book, however, was written for a popular audience, and their influence seems to have been quite limited.[75]

The caution that had marked early evangelical interpretations began quickly to evaporate in later decades. During the second half of the sixteenth century, German Lutherans found themselves surrounded by countless miracles and portents, many of which they regarded as unprecedented divine announcements and warnings. Indeed, by 1560 attention to the unusual in nature had become nothing less than an obsession. The discovery and interpretation of natural signs was an activity in which the best minds of the age took part. Melanchthon took deep interest in prodigies, monsters, unusual celestial phenomena, and the like, and he helped to encourage this interest in his students, colleagues, and literate contemporaries.[76] With this sort of encouragement and with printers awakening to the new opportunities, the rapid popularization of wonder literature began. Wonder-books were now produced in relatively inexpensive German editions for a mass market.

The best examples of typical German wonder literature are the works of Job Fincel, a professor of philosophy who had been among the inner circle of Melanchthon's students at Wittenberg. Between 1556 and 1567 Fincel published a series of three lengthy tracts on wonders or miraculous signs.[77] He linked the wonders directly to the course of ecclesiastical and secular history. Fincel could prove with countless examples that unnatural events portended disaster. Moreover, particular signs predicted particular evils. For example, a rain of blood was invariably followed by uprisings, rebellion, and the shedding of much human blood. Other conspicuous oddities foretold war, floods, earthquakes, and destructive fires. Among the signs that consistently announced outbreaks of plague in Germany was the birth of monsters; the wonder-books often described the most horrible of such births in vivid detail.

Hardly any tale of signs or disaster was beyond belief for Fincel. In fact it is probably fair to say that the more grotesque a report was, the better it served his purposes. Clearly there was an element of sensationalism here; it was part of the mass appeal of such works. Yet this characteristic did not undermine the assumptions and purposes of wonder literature. For the meaning of the signs was above all eschatological. Their recent massive multiplication could mean only one thing: the end of the world was at hand. The earth was overflowing with miraculous warnings of God's wrath.[78] Whoever scorned them was completely lost. Few ideas could be at once as serious and as sensational as this.

Unlike Luther, Fincel thought it both possible and necessary to distinguish clearly between portents from God and the workings of the devil. God performed his wonders directly, out of omnipotence, in order to bring people to the knowledge of him, while the devil worked mediately, through deceit, to confuse and corrupt. These standards may have been less than certain in practice, but Fincel was undaunted by such problems. After all, the most important signs were those clearly predicted by Christ in a few New Testament passages, for example Matthew 24. The direct correspondence between these biblical prophecies and the events of Fincel's own time put the meaning of the essential signs beyond all doubt. The Antichrist had been revealed; virtually all the other signs were manifest.

In fact, Fincel's apocalyptic assumptions were already so widely shared that he scarcely had to spell out the connections. His purpose was to show how closely God stood behind the workings of the world, and thus to warn and lead people to the betterment of their lives. He explained his role with a well-known passage from the book of Joel, which Luther himself had cited to justify predictive prophecy:

And it shall come to pass afterward, that I will pour out my spirit upon all flesh; and your sons and your daughters shall prophesy, your old men shall dream dreams, your young men shall see visions. . . . And i will shew wonders in the heavens and in the earth, blood, and fire, and pillars of smoke. The sun shall be turned into darkness, and the moon into blood, before the great and terrible day of the Lord come.[79]

These times had come. Fincel was hesitant to equate eclipses or the appearance of extra suns directly with the signs mentioned in this passage. He was generally content to leave to the astrologers the task of prediction on the evidence of celestial signs. Nonetheless he was certain that comets and heavenly visions meant future calamity, in accordance with all other testimony. Melanchthon himself was supposed to have correctly foreseen his own death from signs in the heavens, and Fincel carefully reported this incident.[80]

The prefaces to Fincel's works included violent polemic against the enemies of the Gospel, and he seems to have become increasingly strident in later editions, launching harsh attacks against the Jews and others who refused to see the truth as he saw it. His God was mainly an Old Testament image, manifesting himself through historical activity and threatening men with his wrath. It was above all Germany, the present-day Israel, that stood to suffer this wrath. "I believe," wrote Fincel, "that the affliction that will come over Germany will be quicker and greater than men can now believe or imagine, and this was also the opinion of Luther."[81] His certainty on this point was the greater because the portents were almost always ignored; the sins of the Germans knew no limit. Yet it was equally certain that believers would escape divine wrath, and that therefore they should take joy, instead of fright, from the signs.[82] Hence in his own way Fincel demonstrated the characteristic Lutheran tension between the human responses to divine wrath and divine love. He was not the only sixteenth-century Lutheran who, in warning of the coming Judgment, sometimes forgot about the other side of the message.

Fincel had little interest in history except insofar as it proved his theme. It was merely "a series of miraculous signs, whose accumulation points to the end of the world."[83] The renewed revelation of the Gospel through Luther and his Bible was one of the clearest indications that history was drawing to a close. Luther himself was accorded what amounted to quasi-messianic status in Fincel's writings. To heed the words of the Reformer was to be saved. Fincel followed Luther in carefully acknowledging the message of Matthew 24: 26; the time of the end was known to none but the Father. It is clear, however, that he went much further in the interpretation of portents than Luther himself, who had occasionally expressed doubt that a Christian needed to interpret signs at all beyond the simple demands of faith.[84]

Fincel's work is only one example of a genre that became common in the second half of the century. Wonder-books of various sorts appeared in growing numbers in the decades after 1560. Conrad Lycosthenes (Wolffhart) issued a major Latin collection at Basel in 1557; it was soon translated into German by the Lutheran publicist Johann Herold, and this edition enjoyed extreme popularity.[85] Lycosthenes listed among his sources not only Fincel, Luther, and Melanchthon, but also Sebastian Brant, Paracelsus, and many others. His work was, if possible, even more comprehensive than Fincel's; almost anything weird, unusual, or noteworthy could count as a wonder. Marcus Fritsch brought out a large Latin work in 1563 that focused on meteors, but also catalogued the prodigies and portents of recent history.[86] Caspar Goldwurm issued a book of *Wunderzeichen* in 1567 which came out in several subsequent editions.[87] Christopher Irenaeus, who had been a student of Melanchthon, published a long work on monstrous births, as well as a gloomy *Prognosticon* based on the comet of 1577.[88] The wonder collections continued to appear through the early seventeenth century, although the focus of interest seems to have shifted away from teratology and wondrous earthly events toward celestial omens, as in Johann Letzner's *Wunder-Spiegel* of 1604, which dealt with comets, new stars, and eclipses.[89] In all of these works, the assumption that God was sending his warnings to a stubborn mankind before the end was never far below the surface.

The wonder-books were generally organized in chronological fashion, and thus represented historical surveys of a sort. Lycosthenes' work covered wonders "from the beginning of the world," though the bulk of the work was naturally devoted to recent times. Goldwurm likewise began with the creation. Fincel's tomes began with 1517, reflecting the belief that Luther's discoveries marked the beginning of the end. The pervasive assumption in all these works was that God rules the whole world at all times, and that one could learn something about his rule by studying the divine activity over the course of time.

To facilitate such study, the authors of many wonder-books carefully cited and discussed the traditional distinctions among the various sorts of wonders. Thus Fincel, Lycosthenes, and others presented long definitions and explanations of the terms Torella used: "prodigium," "monstrum," "portentum," "ostentum," "miraculum," and so on. The signs could also be divided into those that came directly and miraculously from God, and those that had natural causes as well as supernatural. But some writers thought such complexities only obscured the essential lessons. Late in the century David Herlicius told the "common man" that he did not need to understand the academic distinctions often made among the various sorts of natural wonders; it was enough to understand Philipp Melanchthon's definition of a wonder as something very unusual in the course of nature. Herlicius emphasized the supernatural cause of bloody rain and other strange forms of precipitation, such as the raining of fire, oil, milk, earth, stones, chalk, hair, wool, wood, iron, meat, birds, frogs, fish, worms, bread, corn, and so on. Only the godless limit themselves to investigating the natural causes of such phenomena, he wrote. All men of understanding knew that these were signs of God's Judgment.[90]

The apocalyptic wonder-books were mainly a Protestant—and particularly a Lutheran—phenomenon.[91] It is no accident that the most influential of the wonder-hunters, Fincel, was a zealous Lutheran who had studied with Melanchthon. The combination of Lutheran expectancy with eager curiosity about the natural world led, in these writers, to an apocalyptic interpretation of unusual or noteworthy natural phenomena. Catholic opponents saw this Lutheran preoccupation as simply one more means by which people were led into heresy: a Catholic tract of 1581 asserted that the signs about which Lutherans were so excited were to be attributed to the devil and his agents.[92]

Naturally, attention to signs and wonders was not limited to these major collections. Each year dozens of popular works appeared in which the latest wonders were carefully noted and preached on. The description of unusual natural signs was also a central concern in illustrated broadsheets, which were extremely common by the middle of the century.[93] Lutheran sermons were likewise filled with references to natural omens. Christ's prophecies in Luke 21 and Matthew 24 were clearly coming to fulfillment, as more signs occurred every day. Preachers earnestly drew the attention of their hearers to the heavens and the earth, encouraging a vigilant watchfulness.

It seemed certain that nature was offering the clearest possible warnings. Terrible comets, amazing visions in the heavens, great winds and storms, floods, the birth of countless monsters, a sudden and mysterious thunderclap in the night: such events made inevitable comparisons between the present age and that of Noah—except that the coming destruction would be final. Andreas Musculus declared that more miraculous signs had occurred and been described in the past 40 years than in all previous ages of the world. When this evidence was considered in the light of biblical prophecy, what doubt could remain? "Woe to the land where signs occur," he warned his fellow Germans. "The greater and the more terrifying the miraculous signs, the greater the disaster to follow."[94] Such preaching encouraged continual watchfulness.

While there could be no doubt about a rain of fire or frogs, there was still some disagreement over precisely what occurrences qualified as wonders. Fincel denied that such natural events as eclipses and earthquakes were "wunderzeichen." Musculus agreed: too many preachers, he thought, obscured the meaning of the signs announced in the Bible. Those to which Luke 21 referred, for example, were not to be confused with the natural eclipses and other heavenly movements that could already be seen regularly every day. Many farmers and simple folk thought any unusual light or movement in the sky meant the stars were falling. Such beliefs were childish. When the sun and the moon finally went dark and the stars fell, the result would be the actual, final destruction of the world. The heavens and the earth would melt, crumble, and burn. Since all the stars and planets except the moon were much larger than the earth itself, their final falling would mean the sudden passing away of both earth and sky. The Son of Man would then appear in all his glory. It was likely that one great and unmistakable sign would precede the Second Advent; Musculus thought it might be an enor-

mous cross in the heavens, like the one Constantine had seen.
Biblical prophecies were not to be trivialized through overeager attempts to discover their fulfillment in everyday events. It was clear
enough that the end was close, but when the final signs appeared
even the doubters would understand.[95]

But despite such attempts to distinguish current signs from those
that would bring on the Judgment itself, the message of most of the
wonder literature was that all of creation demonstrated the nearness
of the end. Thus the signs were everywhere, and of all kinds. Toward the end of the century, a number of popular works dealt with
the mysterious writing found on several fish recently caught in the
Baltic. The writing was discovered to be a wondrous sign that allowed many of the deepest mysteries of Daniel and Revelation to be
unlocked in this dangerous Last Time.[96] As a preacher at Wettin
pointed out in 1594, the Lord himself had taught with the image of
the fig tree: when it sent out its shoots, one could know that summer was nigh. Even thus the signs throughout nature pointed to the
coming of the eternal summer. The more usual image was not one
of budding, however, but of weakness and decline. As Daniel
Schaller asserted, shortly after the creation men had lived a thousand years, while now 50 or 60 years brought old age and death.[97]
This inherited medieval belief could be found in most sixteenth-century thinkers; what was distinctive about the attitude of
Luther's heirs was the intensity and thoroughness of attempts to
support it with evidence.

By the last decades of the century the evidence from both history
and nature was regularly being collected into massive works that
left no sign or proof unexplored. Thus in 1595 Schaller produced a
long *Herald* offering 22 very full proofs that all biblical prophecies
had been completed and that the end stood "very near at the door."
Four years later Schaller followed this with an even longer work,
On the End of the World; and in 1604 the two works appeared
together as a huge *Theological Herald* which covered every conceivable question about the Last Judgment and its meaning for
mankind.[98] The signs of the end were so abundant that they filled
many such weighty tomes.

PROPHECY AND DISCOVERY

The proliferation of the Last Things was part of a broader effort
to maintain prophetic certainty in the face of new conditions. The

belief that the events of the Last Times had begun took on an increasingly important role among Luther's heirs; indeed the imminence of cosmic upheaval and the Last Judgment became, for the generations after Luther's death, a principle or framework by which all human experience could be organized. Because it was such an all-embracing assumption, any new observations about the world could fit into it immediately; every event fell into the wide net of biblical prophecy and its supporting traditions. Preachers and writers often emphasized that universal experience proved the nearness of the end, and in fact this was true, since there was hardly an experience that could not be used to prove the assumption.

It was, of course, not really a matter of proof at all; those who were convinced that the Judgment was coming were merely confirmed in their beliefs by these arguments, while those who ignored them were not likely to change. For the greater number of literate Lutherans, however, the apocalyptic world view did not merely persist. It became more comprehensive and more explicit in literature of the sort we have examined. The overall result was no greater clarity in the popular understanding of the Last Things, but rather a growing desire to probe the cloud of mystery that inevitably hung over these matters. Thus the question of what constituted proper prophetic insight became more and more pressing.

Luther, as we learned earlier, usually treated worldly prophecy as no more than a secondary tool in the all-important prophetic calling. In his eyes, universal religious prophecy did not concern itself with particulars. Nevertheless, Luther did make a fair number of specific predictions. And when he answered the demand for prophetic insight through the interpretation of Scripture, some general scenario inevitably emerged. But what made one interpretation credible, another doubtful or worthless? Luther usually adduced faith or the presence of the Holy Spirit as the criterion of credible prophecy. But if this was the highest of standards, it was also the vaguest and the most difficult to apply. The only article of faith with direct prophetic implications was that Christ would return for the Judgment;[99] all other prophetic understanding was ultimately a matter of interpretation or conjecture. The problem, though, was not only one of choosing among a variety of possible interpretations. An equally if not more difficult question was how far one might take the investigation.

Closely linked with this issue was a separate problem that Luther had not resolved, and that his thought actually made more pressing. Were there hidden truths in the Bible that required special gifts, skills, or methods to discover? While both the Catholic church and the radical reformers had asserted the obscurity of the Scriptures as a whole, Luther maintained that the Bible possessed a self-interpreting clarity.[100] Despite his insistence on its clarity and sufficiency, Luther did acknowledge that Scripture contained many passages that were in themselves obscure. He taught that the meaning of such passages always agreed with the larger sense of Scripture, but this principle was not enough to illuminate the mysterious passages fully. Indeed, Luther openly acknowledged that simple faith was not sufficient to understand some parts of Scripture when he wrote that "he who cannot understand the dark [passages] must stay in the light."[101] His own attitude toward such "dark" passages, combined with his many prophetic utterances, only heightened the desire of later generations to fill out Luther's insights, to realize in prophetic terms the clarity he had always propounded.

God had completed his revelation; of this there could be no question among Augustinian Protestants. Lutherans conceived of the Reformation not as an unveiling of new truths but as a return to old ones. The essence of divine revelation, once preached openly, had been obscured for centuries; Luther had simply rediscovered it. Yet by the same token, the question now arose whether this recovery could blossom in further prophetic clarity among the faithful. After all, the belief that prophetic secrets would be revealed before the end had been central to Luther's own discoveries. The great prophet Daniel, for example, had himself not understood the words he was told to write; rather they were "closed up and sealed till the time of the end" (Daniel 12: 9). The Reformation had begun that time of revelation.

Although many saw Luther's findings as the last word, beyond which it was unnecessary to seek, Luther himself did not claim to have exhausted the search for prophetic truth. Since he had insisted that he possessed no special gift other than the guidance of the Holy Spirit, there was no clear reason to believe that others could not gain further, and equally valid, insights. This idea did not, of course, justify claims to direct revelation independent of Scripture; Luther had opposed Thomas Müntzer and the other radicals on just this issue. Nor did it give free rein to imaginative interpretation

of biblical prophecies, for Luther had established the basic principles of Reformation prophecy. It did, however, acknowledge that
in a decisive time for the church and the world, the Bible offered
the inspired student truths yet unsuspected. Indeed, the Reformation built on the principle that prophetic truth was the exclusive
property of no one age. And since Luther had had his forerunners
in men like Hus, there was certainly no cause to believe that his
followers could not carry this process of discovery a bit further
during the short time remaining to the world.

Throughout the sixteenth century, the striving for further prophetic clarity contended with the desire to absolutize Luther's Reformation, to make the Reformer's word the last. Prophetic striving
should not be confused with the relativizing approach to the early
reformers and their accomplishments that became common among
Calvinist thinkers by 1600.[102] In this view, Luther had begun the
process of rebuilding the true church; it was up to later believers to
proceed further with this work of reconstruction and cleansing.
This outlook might be better described as meliorist than apocalyptic, for it stressed the possibility of gradual development in the
church and in Christian society before the end. The Lutheran striving for additional prophetic clarity was not founded on the hope
for moral improvement or progress. It was purely a matter of contemplating God's promises and their imminent fulfillment. Ultimately, even the wildest prophetic schemes that emerged among
Luther's heirs—and some were wild indeed—looked not to any
gradual working out of God's plan, but to some sudden, cosmic
transformation. They were attempts to maintain the sort of apocalyptic certainty and intensity for which the Reformer himself had
stood.

For a task of such importance, believers were tempted to use
whatever tools were at hand. To understand the most common Lutheran attitudes toward various prophetic methods, we can do no
better than again to invoke Philipp Melanchthon. In his essential
understanding of religious prophecy and of biblical interpretation
the *Praeceptor Germaniae* was at one with Luther. On the other
hand, he was readier than his older colleague to approve "natural"
or worldly prophecy, if it was not abused. Melanchthon could
enthusiastically encourage astrological prediction, because he believed the art was based on the discovery of natural causes in the
divine order.

Melanchthon's high appreciation of special prophetic gifts had the same general basis. Like many of his contemporaries, he believed that some people had a greater gift than others for seeing into the future. But he made a special effort to give rational support to this belief. Just as one man had more aptitude for music or singing, another more for mathematics and the art of number-reckoning, so some people had more natural ability for prophecy. They had some "secret insight or otherwise hidden sense" that allowed them to foresee future events. These souls often received their revelations in prophetic dreams. Such dreams were unusual in that they arose not out of the elements or constitution of the human body, but rather were caused by the special power and influence of the stars, "through which the inborn and natural prophetic power hidden in men is awakened and excited to such an extent as to announce future things." Melanchthon could cite numerous examples of prophetic dreams that had been fulfilled.[103]

At the same time, the *Praeceptor* believed that knowledge of the future for its own sake was worse than useless, and he warned against the indiscriminate use of God's gifts. In a preface to an exposition of Revelation by Johannes Funck,[104] he distinguished two motives for prophecies of future things. One was vain curiosity,[105] the other comfort or consolation. Curiosity was to be avoided; it grew out of man's corrupt nature, which seeks unnecessary knowledge. Moreover, to muse over what God has not revealed to us, as for example "who will be victorious, France or Burgundy," was simply futile. On the other hand, God had indeed announced some important facts about what lay ahead. That the true church would be small and persecuted, that many dissensions and false teachings would arise, that this miserable life would end with a glorious resurrection and a Judgment for eternity—these prophecies and others like them brought strength and comfort, and were anything but vain. "To inquire about future things out of these motives, and in the measure that God has revealed them, is right and pleasing to God," Melanchthon wrote.

God had revealed some earthly events of the greatest magnitude, asserted the professor. Abraham was told, for example, that his children would suffer persecution for four hundred years in Egypt. Without such knowledge, his people would have suffered blindly, without consolation. Many equally great things were foretold to the prophet Daniel. Through him the progression of the world kingdoms was announced; and from this progression one could gain understanding of why Christ came when he did, as well as some insight into the circumstances of his return. This sort of thing God revealed simply and clearly for the consolation of all believers. Since he had forewarned that in the Last Times errors and terrors of all sorts would appear, the pope, the Turk, and other contemporary evils could be recognized for what they were. These persecutions were clearly foretold by the prophets and the apostles; the faithful were called upon to hold fast to the true Gospel.

But there were many more specific prophecies, for example in Revelation, that were somewhat unclear. They had to do, for instance, with the specific times of various upheavals, or with the reigns of particular kings. One did not need to know these things as long as one was aware of the general teachings on the Last Day and what was expected of the Christian. It was useful, though, to have some learned instruction in these matters so that one might better appreciate God's plan. Such instruction was to be had from men like Methodius, who in the early Middle Ages had clearly prophesied the rise of Moslem power and the resulting persecution of Christendom. Similarly the monk Johann Hilten had prophesied that in 1516 a great reformation of the church would begin. Since Hilten had hit so close to the mark, "his other prophecies are not to be scorned." Among these was the prediction that Gog and Magog—or the Turk—would in 1600 rule powerfully over Germany and Italy, and that about that time a tremendous persecution of the true Christian church would take place. Many people laughed at such threats and thought they were fables. But that was all the more reason to watch carefully and pray to God for the protection of the fatherland and of believing souls.[106]

Thus Melanchthon thought that to understand prophetic mysteries one ought to listen to those with a prophetic gift or special learning. But this was really to beg the question: just who did possess this gift or this learning? How could one know whom to trust? Melanchthon's own scattered statements on such points suggest a certain ambiguity. He was not quite clear on how prophetic gifts were related to the workings of the Holy Spirit. Saving faith did not need to understand high and difficult mysteries. Yet those who did understand certainly shared something valuable. In a time of confusion and expectancy, it is not surprising that this elusive understanding of the mysteries was sought more and more desperately.

But the quest for certainty was to result in still greater confusion, for it was easy to identify this hidden and difficult knowledge with the saving knowledge of faith.

Among academics, whose very profession was the making of distinctions, there was evident desire to maintain the separation between natural gifts and spiritual insight. The Wittenberg professor Caspar Peucer was, like his father-in-law Melanchthon, concerned to draw the line between legitimate and illegitimate means of searching into the future. He issued a major work on the various forms of divination, the popularity of which is attested by the great frequency with which it was republished after its initial appearance in 1553.[107] Here astrology and many of the more common forms of divination by natural magic were approved. Methods with spiritual overtones, such as the Cabala, were generally rejected; others were reviled as diabolical. Yet the grounds upon which Peucer judged certain means to be superstitious or dangerous are not always clear. Moreover, the sorts of natural divination that he condoned were sometimes referred to as though they were universal prophetic methods. The professor himself, then, had trouble maintaining his own distinctions. On the whole, the work must have given powerful support to the practice of divination; it encouraged people to discover what awaited them in the future by whatever approved method they could. This sort of encouragement was hardly needed.

It would be easy but misleading to point to Melanchthon, his colleagues, and his students as culprits who promoted an irresponsible and pernicious trend toward the investigation of prophetic mysteries. Melanchthon and Peucer should be viewed only as examples, not necessarily as major initiators, of the quest for prophetic insight through the methods we have been discussing. They are important because they demonstrate so well the link that was forming between apocalyptic assumptions and intellectual fashions during the later Reformation period. It is true that Melanchthonians were often quick and enthusiastic seekers after intellectual certainty, but they were by no means alone in these apprehensive times. The tools of prophetic discovery could be used by all. And if a religious and intellectual leader like Melanchthon could show ambiguity on the nature of prophetic gifts and insight, one can only guess how much greater the confusion must have been among tens of thousands of earnest and apprehensive German burghers.

3
✍ Time, History, and Reckoning

THE SENSE OF TIME AND HISTORY

The apocalyptic outlook involves an interpretation of the past as well as a view of the future. Reformation apocalyptic assumptions were inseparable from contemporary approaches to history; changes in one realm would inevitably be reflected in the other. A growing historical awareness underlay increasingly explicit Lutheran conceptions of the Last Things in the middle and late decades of the sixteenth century. Just as people were learning to see the past as a more or less distant realm about which there was much to discover, so they imagined future events and the eschaton itself more and more as discrete occurrences in a preordained plan, about which people could learn through careful, divinely guided research. This tendency was not unique to Germany, but since the sense of eschatological struggle was so highly developed in German Lutheranism, here the interplay between apocalyptic excitement and a growing concern with historical change was especially strong.[1]

To the premodern mind, history was more than merely a succession of events in time that are rendered understandable through the discovery of their causal relations. Past, present, and future were not conceived primarily as points or segments in a linear development. Rather, past and future shared a larger meaning that bound them together with the present and that could make them, in a sense, immediate. In this "figural" view of history, as it is often called, events were linked to one another not temporally by causality, but rather atemporally by a higher meaning. For the medieval Christian, this higher meaning lay entirely in God's lessons for sinful mankind. The key source of these lessons was naturally the Scriptures. Scriptural events were valued less as unique historical occurrences than as moral examples that pointed beyond themselves. Thus the events of the Old Testament prefigured those of the New Testament, New Testament events fulfilled those of the Old, and together the Old and New Testaments pointed beyond history to God's eternal and unchanging plan.[2] Moreover, the figural view was not limited to biblical interpretation. It was a way of understanding all of reality. What mattered about particular historical occurrences was the way they reflected unchanging truths.

This sense of history closely complemented the assumption of timeless cosmic structure that the medieval church encouraged. But it would be wrong to associate the figural sense of history exclusively with Christianity, or even with the Judeo-Christian tradition. It was part of a sensibility that did not take time as an objective standard of reality, part of a mentality for which the spoken or preached word could lend reality to any historical scene.[3] Thus for the medieval Christian, the great acts of the divine drama, from the Creation to the Last Judgment, were impressed on the mind as contemporary realities, images and forces ever present.

During the Renaissance, however, this figural view of history was met by the growth of a new, more literal, linear conception. Central to this developing historical understanding was the sense of anachronism, of historical perspective. Renaissance thinkers learned to see the past as qualitatively different from the present. A sense of the distance separating the present from all past societies began to emerge. The literal and figural views were not, of course, mutually exclusive ways of viewing the world; they have coexisted in some measure throughout Western history. But during the Renaissance the sense of historical time was clearly becoming dominant among the literate, frequently turning into a genuine obsession. Associated not only with change but often directly with life itself, time was omnipotent, and could be virtually deified, as what causes life to come into being and to end.[4]

The Protestant revolt certainly contributed to the spread of a concern with time and history. The Reformation was built on "the rediscovery of the living God of the Bible, who actively intervenes in the affairs of men, the Lord and Judge of history."[5] As John Headley notes, although Luther did on occasion employ a figural or typological approach, "his belief in Christ's abiding presence at all moments of history serves to spring the typological system." Luther "allows the events of the Old Testament to assume their own worth outside of a typological system." The effect was to put greater value on the individual historical event.[6] Moreover, through its very rejection of the spiritual authority of the Eternal City, the Reform sparked historical inquiry on many fronts.

The abolition of tradition as justification for belief left the historian freer to investigate the past on its own terms, and encouraged the establishment of history as an autonomous discipline. It is no accident that several Lutheran universities, following a proposal made by Luther himself, introduced separate chairs of history as early as the 1540s and 1550s.[7] In addition, the violent polemics of the age spurred the awareness of historical change and the search for historical evidence that could support various theological positions; we have already seen, for example, how energetically Lutherans sought prophetic evidence from the past. The new medium of print was probably also an influence on Reformation conceptions of time and history. Throughout the sixteenth century, printing would help to intensify and disseminate clear mental images both of past events and of future possibilities.

Clearly, however, the Reformation belief in the importance of time and history was qualified in a fundamental way. For those who lived with a deep sense of divine power and action in the world, time could never be the ultimate referent. It could not be considered apart from the created world, outside of which stood God as the only absolute. In the Reformation mind, time was always subject to the will of God, never an abstract power in and of itself. For example, in a popular tract entitled *Of the World and Time*, Valentin Engelhart defined time as "the duration of the whole world, created by God for the sake of men, and so ordered that it necessarily began together with the world, and will ever be measured out through the movement of the Heavens, which it also measures in turn, until it ceases and has an end together with the world on the day when God will change it."[8] Johann Garcaeus, in a learned Latin work on all the ways of measuring time, similarly stressed its place in the divine order, and concluded with many pages of evidence about the end of time and conjectures about when it would come.[9] The will of God was understood as operating through a plan for the world, which gave clear outlines to the seeming chaos of time. In this way the sense of time as sweeping, arbitrary power was kept under control.

The Reformation in Germany thus revealed both a preoccupation with the vagaries of temporal change and a desire to reduce time to a comprehensible order. Not insignificantly, this cultural environment saw the high point of the clock as a symbol of the universe, and of the clockmaking art as an expression of a world-view.[10] The clock not only measured time; it was the embodiment of precision, order, and control. Many of the highly elaborate German clocks of the century after 1550 were in effect efforts to understand and to illustrate the divine governance of the world. The same goal is manifest in the Reformation concern with universal history. Time was not an absolute measure, but it was at least a measure of all earthly things. By discovering its order, divisions, and limits, people could better understand their worldly fate, and better appreciate the promise that lay beyond. Desire for this sort of understanding became especially intense among German Lutherans, for whom the events of the Reformation produced a sense of ultimate historical crisis.

Luther's own apocalyptic expectations were inseparable from his understanding of the past. His sense of history and the sense that came to pervade early Lutheranism were thoroughly eschatological: every question about the past had implications for the overall pattern of world history, and hence for the present and future as well. Indeed, the past was studied for its testimony to the truth of Scripture and for the prophetic insights it could afford. Apocalyptic expectancy and a growing interest in history were thus two sides of the same coin. The Lutheran sense of history reflected a rising awareness of temporal change and of the value of historical study, but it ultimately included a forceful reassertion of the medieval Christian conception of history as the great theater of the divine will, and an apocalyptic vision of the triumphant cosmic order to come with the end of time.

STUDIUM CHRONOLOGICUM

In his *Liber chronicarum* of 1493, the Nuremberg physician Hartmann Schedel used the traditional pattern of six ages to organize world history between the Creation and the Last Judgment. His work owes part of its minor fame to Schedel's imaginative device of leaving several blank folio pages between the end of his historical record and the concluding description of the Last Judgment. The blank pages were obviously an invitation for readers to figure out how current events fitted into the divine plan by which history was coming to completion, and to take stock of their own lives as the Day approached. Schedel was influenced by humanist historical writing only superficially; in its general character his work was hardly different from scores of high and late medieval universal chronicles.[11]

The same, in fact, could be said for the bulk of German Protestant historical writing for fully a century after the Lutheran revolt, particularly for the world chronologies that reflected the larger historical consciousness of the vast majority of literate people. The massive corpus of such works appears from one perspective to have perpetuated the medieval effort to understand history in terms of preordained patterns. The schemes of historical periodization that dominated sixteenth-century historical thought were the four monarchies of Daniel and the triadic "prophecy of Elias." Melanchthon adopted the latter scheme in preference to the traditional notion of the six ages, which he believed had caused "more a disordering than an ordering" of historical understanding.[12] The prophecy of Elias offered a simpler and more definite outline that would prove more conducive to historical reckoning, but the purposes it served were not essentially new. Similarly, in their use of the idea of the four monarchies, the reformers were hardly making innovations. Rather they were actually reasserting the thoroughly medieval and even antihumanist belief in the continuation of the Roman Empire.[13] What was new in the sixteenth century was that such schemes and methods of periodization were applied more systematically and precisely than ever, and that under the influence of Reformation thought they first became truly popular tools of understanding.

The Elias scheme, involving the partition of history into the age before the Law, the age of the Law, and the age of the Messiah, was generally applied to sacred history, the scheme of the four monarchies to political history. Sacred and profane history were not, however, regarded as separate disciplines; they were complementary means to an overall eschatological conception of universal history. Indeed, both schemes of periodization confirmed that world history was nearing its end. Such conceptions thus worked against attitudes toward history and historical evidence that could be called characteristically modern.[14] These schemes inevitably inhibited the search for causes in history, since they allowed every event a place in a preordained plan, a limitation and ordering of events between the Creation and the Last Judgment. The same was true of another highly influential method of finding order in history: astrology. Not a few medieval historical writers had used astrological patterns to complement the established biblical schemes,[15] and despite the confusion of the effort to make the various reckonings fit together, astrological evidence would become increasingly important in sixteenth-century chronologies. The historical writing of sixteenth-century Germany was thus largely *studium chronologicum*; the most popular and influential sort of inquiry into the past was one that sought to identify the place of events precisely in an a priori scheme. A complex world of speculation and debate arose within the bounds of this effort.

While universal history continued to dominate the historical consciousness of the age, other forms of historical writing were emerging. But the appearance of these new forms did not necessarily reflect any waning of the prophetic outlook. The most famous early Protestant historical work, the *Magdeburg Centuries* of Matthias Flacius and others, was church history, not world history, and covered only the first thirteen centuries after Christ.[16] In this work history served to legitimize the Reformation as a return to the true church. Flacius and his colleagues sought mainly to show that the Reformation was anything but the institution of a new order, a break with divinely approved tradition. Rather it was the Roman church that had introduced innovations in ritual and doctrine, thereby perverting the Word. The somewhat awkward division of church history into centuries resulted at least in part from the lack of a clear scheme of periodization for the Christian era; the prevalent universal schemes were not particularly helpful in illuminating changes within this period. Thus the goals and scope of the work were such that the theme of Judgment, and the vision of the Reformation as the final earthly struggle against darkness, were left mostly implicit. But eschatological thought was not foreign to the work as a whole.[17] The *Magdeburg Centuries* did not represent a rejection of prophetic history or the apocalyptic vision of the Reformation. Indeed, such a work could not have been written without a strong consciousness of decisive struggle. The *Centuries* had, in any case, a limited impact on the preaching of the late Reformation, partly because the work was too large to be suited for university instruction.[18]

The real prime mover of historical study in Lutheran Germany was Melanchthon. The *Praeceptor Germaniae* enthusiastically encouraged and promoted virtually all learning about the past. Under his influence, generations of Lutheran pastors were exposed to world history as part of their training. For Melanchthon, history was the record of God's work. To read it was to gain a better understanding of the Scriptures. Indeed, next to the Bible itself, there was nothing one could study with greater benefit.[19] History supplied examples of every virtue and vice, but at the same time it taught that God alone was responsible for the rise and fall of all kingdoms and powers on earth. God controlled past, present, and future; all occurred according to his will.

Despite its seeming straightforwardness, a certain tension characterized this understanding of history. On the one hand, Melanchthon saw God as the direct ruler of all life, willing and governing the course of history at all times. On the other hand, he was more than ready to discover historical laws at work, patterns by which the entire complex and variegated course of human events became comprehensible. For Melanchthon and those who shared his conceptions, the common ground of these views was the belief that the rule of God was effected through his promises and prophecies. The hope of discovering how these promises and prophecies were manifest in the world was the main inspiration for the study of history.

Melanchthon's most noteworthy historical effort was the *Chronica Carionis*, a work of universal history that became a standard reference in Lutheran Germany and enjoyed considerable popularity elsewhere as well. Johann Carion had been a schoolmate of Melanchthon at Tübingen. Famed as a heavy drinker, he was also well known for his astrological prophecies, which he issued regularly as court astrologer to the elector of Brandenburg. Around 1530 he submitted a long chronicle of world history to Melanchthon for revision and publication. The Wittenberg professor was so convinced of the value of such undertakings that he rewrote the *Chronica* and published it in an enlarged German edition in 1532, retaining Carion's name on the title page. The work was subsequently revised and reissued in no fewer than fifteen German edi-

tions before 1564; a Latin translation of 1537 facilitated its translation into other vernaculars and brought it great popularity
outside Germany as well.[20]

The *Chronica* made use of both the four monarchies and the
prophecy of Elias, and thus became the main vehicle for the entry
of the latter scheme into Reformation thought. Melanchthon had
probably learned of the prophecy of Elias in a translation of the
Talmud by his great-granduncle Johann Reuchlin, and was no
doubt eager to put it to good use in a popular world history.[21] In
his introduction to the 1532 edition, he left little doubt about the
implications of the scheme. The third and last age would certainly
be cut short, as Matthew 24 made clear. The prophecy was a mar-
velous chronological confirmation of other biblical forecasts as
well, and all of them showed that the end of the world was not far
off. The four monarchies showed exactly the same thing: the German emperor represented the last head of the Roman kingdom, and
"the Holy Scripture comforts us and teaches us clearly that the last
day shall come soon after the destruction of this German kingdom."[22] Not surprisingly in light of Carion's profession and the
preoccupations of his editor, the *Chronica* also made some use of
astrology in making sense of the tangle of worldly events, for example in explaining the "fortune and misfortune" of Emperor
Maximilian.[23] Celestial motions were part of the pattern of history;
they could help to shed light on the larger meaning of events.

Although the *Chronica* distinguished sacred from profane history, it suggested that through the gift of prophecy to the church
these two realms could be understood as a unity. Prophecy made
the outer progression of worldly events comprehensible in terms of
God's plan.[24] The effect of this understanding was to underline the
inseparability of faith from a particular conception of past and
present events, and from the expectation of certain future events. It
could not be denied that historical changes had a certain dynamic
of their own, that they could be interpreted as particular causes and
effects, and the *Chronica* did not ignore this sort of explanation.
But true understanding of world history required a search for
deeper causes. As Caspar Peucer wrote in his preface to the 1573
edition of the work, the mighty worldly kingdoms had all lasted
about five hundred years. Their collapse after this period might be
attributable partly to the gradual corruption of morals. But it was
equally apparent that it pleased God to sustain kingdoms only this

long and no longer. It so happened that nearly five hundred years
had passed since Germany had assumed the Roman imperium. At
the same time, all the present signs and the prophecies of Scripture
indicated that the last days of the world were fast approaching. But
God's mercy knew no bounds, and he might delay punishment long
enough for a few sinners yet to repent.[25]

In the text of the *Chronica*, the longest sections were devoted to
the third age of the Elias scheme, the time after Christ. While the
Bible itself could be consulted by anyone interested in the history
of earlier eras, its prophetic illumination of the postapostolic age
could now be more fully grasped with this popular survey. The
Chronica offered a mine of information for research into issues such
as the origin of the Roman Antichrist or the recent persecution of
believers. Again, there was no question about the character of the
present age. The corruption of human affairs grew uglier from day
to day; history was now at the brink of its final disasters. Some
heavy hints were dropped to make the meaning still clearer. The
Jewish rule (*Judischen Policey*), for instance, lasted 1582 years from
the Exodus until its final destruction. Readers were to take careful
note of this number, and to remind themselves that "the time is not
far off when the Son of God will again take human form, and will
exterminate all godless kingdoms."[26] Altogether there could hardly
have been a work better calculated to inspire investigation into prophetic epochs and the approach of the Last Day.

A large number of similar chronologies appeared in Germany
during the sixteenth century, almost all of them reflecting the same
basic view of history. The *Geschichtbibel* of the spiritualist Sebastian Franck, for example, despite its many differences from more
orthodox Lutheran positions, helped to popularize attitudes closely
related to Luther's own about God's rule in history and the imminent end of the world. Franck's work circulated widely among Lutherans, and we have seen that his list of "Signs before the Last
Day" was well known.[27] We have also noted Luther's own contribution to the study of chronology, the *Supputatio annorum mundi*.
In fact, Luther's work may have supplied a more important model
than even the *Chronica Carionis* for the dozens of later writings that
tried to establish the exact prophetic outlines of history since the
Creation.

The first part of a large and widely read chronology by Johann
Funck was published in Nuremberg in 1544; the completed work,

which covered world history from the Creation to the present day and used the four monarchies for periodization, has the appearance of a greatly expanded version of Luther's *Supputatio*. It was re-issued several times at Wittenberg.[28] Funck was one of several stu-dents of chronology whose work led them to make serious efforts to predict what was yet to come before the end of the world. Even in this work, he claimed he had cleared up the mysteries of chro-nology in Revelation and other biblical prophecies. Like other stu-dents of the subject, he supported his chronological findings with astronomical (or astrological) evidence.

Abraham Bucholzer, whose father was a close friend of Melanch-thon and who studied at Wittenberg, built upon Funck's accom-plishments in even larger chartings of world chronology, which became popular in Germany.[29] Bucholzer's works reflect a mind fascinated with the measurement, computation, and correct order-ing of historical time. Another long charting of world history, an elaborate and detailed analysis of the statue in Nebuchadnezzar's dream (Daniel 2), came from the pen of Laurentius Faustus in 1586; Heinrich Bünting issued a similar work at Zerbst in 1590. In 1600 the Jena professor Elias Reusner produced a study entitled *Isagoges historicae libri duo* that was cited frequently by other stu-dents of chronology. This is to cite only a few of the larger and better-known works.[30]

Numerous volumes of lesser bulk but similar aims appear to have been intended for university students. The famous historian of the Schmalkaldic League, Johannes Sleidan, wrote a brief but highly regarded world chronicle, based on the four monarchies of Daniel, that found use in the schools.[31] Its approach was familiar: the cur-rent empire was the last and its end was near; the expected calami-ties were to be endured in the certainty that all the prophecies of Scripture were soon to be realized. David Chytraeus may have been inspired partly by Sleidan to publish his own somewhat abbreviated but similar version of a world chronology in 1573. In his *Compen-dium chronicarum* of 1586, another relatively short work intended for students, Michael Neander emphasized the direct connection between ancient Rome and the current empire. Considering the threat from the Turk, he saw Rome still under seige by the barbari-ans. It was thus clear that the fall of the last world empire was still to come.[32] The themes of the major chronologies were also popu-larized in far shorter and simpler works, some of them designed to be read aloud. Conrad Baur, for instance, wrote a *Compendiolvm Chronologicvm* that presented the history of the world from the Creation to 1606 in rhymed couplets.[33]

Since large portions of these works were often devoted to detailed investigations of specific chronological problems, they were not always entirely explicit about eschatological themes. Yet more often than not, there could be no mistaking the assumptions that lay behind all the highly involved arguments and reckonings. In his *Reckoning and Time-Register*, for example, Georg Nigrinus stressed that the hour had come for all preachers to preach nothing but immediate repentance. Moses and the other prophets were to be read with all diligence, for these men had not only recorded the most important events among their own people, they had also foretold what would happen, and when, right up to the end of the world. There were several great contemporaries who, according to Nigrinus, performed the same prophetic function; one of them was Philipp Melanchthon. Hoping to follow the example of these great men, Nigrinus had tried his own hand at a reckoning of world history. His goal was that men "might rightly view the beginning, middle, and end of this world."[34] His main framework was the prophecy of Elias. Noting that his own estimate of the age of the world (5,540 years in 1570) differed from the figures arrived at by Funck and others, Nigrinus showed a typical Lutheran stubbornness: "Let him doubt who will, let anyone believe what he will; I have no doubts about this reckoning." And even if the calculation could be argued with, "still it is certain and undeniably true that we are in the last minutes of the world."[35] Shortly after the publication of his *Reckoning* Nigrinus was preaching at length on Daniel and Revelation.[36]

Nigrinus received support for his calculation of the world's age from Leonard Krentzheim, superintendent of the church at Liegnitz and a product of Melanchthonian schooling. Krentzheim's *Chronologia* is a good example of the blossoming *studium chronologicum* in the late sixteenth century. It is a massive work of some eight hundred folio pages that traces the history of the world in detail from its beginning to 1576. To produce a work of such proportions, Krentzheim depended heavily on earlier chronologies of the same sort; he referred to those of Melanchthon (the *Chronica Carionis*), Funck, Bullinger, David Chytraeus, and Nigrinus, among others. The study of the past as these men had pursued it was highly useful and taught lessons of profound importance. But in case history did not speak for itself, Krentzheim reminded his readers that the world would "not remain eternally in its present condition, but at a certain time have an end, and there will follow another life, and a complete renewal of all creatures."[37]

In typical fashion, Krentzheim's work assumed the four monarchies as an organizing principle. The work was also similar to other world chronologies of its time in providing much more lengthy and detailed treatment for recent centuries than for earlier ages. Moreover, especially in the narrative for the period after 1517, long descriptions of political and religious events were supplemented by reports of wonders, disasters, and ominous signs. Tales of horrible persecution of true believers by the pope were frequent, and the Turk took his usual place as the other main enemy of the Gospel. The *Chronologia* also made extensive use of astrological calculations. Planetary conjunctions and other celestial signs were more often simply reported than actually used for reckoning, but even so the work made clear that such signs had a definite relation to worldly events. Krentzheim regarded 1574 as a year worthy of particular notice, because of the many important conjunctions that had occurred then. In addition, he found that 1574 marked the end of several prophetically significant periods that were divisible by seven and nine. It was left to the reader to discover the full significance of these somewhat arcane correlations, but apparently for Krentzheim they confirmed that 1574 was some sort of climax for portents, and a key year for reckoning the last stages of history. The *Chronologia* was not published until 1577, but its author continued to record signs of divine wrath until he sent the manuscript to the printer.

Although Krentzheim's estimate of the age of the world agreed with that of Nigrinus, agreement of reckonings was increasingly tenuous and scarce. Debate could become intense, even among researchers who limited their evidence to the historical and prophetic books of the Bible. Careful inquiries devoted exclusively to discovering the exact age of the world became common in the later sixteenth century. Michael Aitzinger, a Catholic nobleman who issued some notoriously un-Catholic writings, used scriptural evidence in a long series of charts to prove that in 1566 the world was exactly 5,526 years old. A matter so important had to be investigated with precision. Almost every other reckoning had been wrong: Melanchthon had been off by two years, Funck by three. Nostradamus, Pico della Mirandola, Carion, Brenz, and many others had erred as well. The correct reckoning would help people understand precisely how one age had followed another, and how near the Last Day was.[38] Among Lutherans the issue became hotter by the year. The number of points on which differences could arise was almost endless. For example, Bucholzer's estimate of the period from the Creation to the destruction of the Temple differed from Funck's by nine years. As both preachers and laymen became more and more involved in establishing a precise world chronology, new questions and issues arose to complicate the task of finding the exact age of the creation.

The study of chronology took on new urgency, and learned investigations were pushed to a new level of sophistication, with the promulgation of the Gregorian calendar in 1582. Even though learned students of chronology all over Europe were aware that the old Julian system was inaccurate, Protestants showed remarkable solidarity in refusing to accept the change. Since the new calendar had been ordered by the pope, it was rejected on principle. Among German Lutherans the response was particularly fierce. The Antichrist had announced the alteration in order to confuse and weaken believers. Even granting that the old calendar had faults, there was still no good reason for the change, since all calendars would be obsolete as soon as Christ appeared. The papacy was acting as though the world would go on forever, for it dared to call the new system "perpetual."

Most aspects of the long debate over the calendar reform need not concern us.[39] But the change inspired still more intense study of chronology and its implications for the current eschatological struggle. The typical Lutheran view was that this devious and dangerous innovation harked back to the first appearance of the Antichrist at the time of the Nicene Council, when a change was made in the traditional means of calculating the date of Easter. The dating of Easter was extremely important, not only because Easter was the most sacred of anniversaries, but also because it established the keystone of the entire church calendar. Luther's own criticism of the Nicene Council and its arrogation of legislative authority on such matters was reissued in popular form in 1584; a commentary by an anonymous editor declared that the Reformer's words were an ominous prophetic judgment upon this latest calendar change.

The Lutheran position was abundantly detailed in such writings as a *Brief Consideration of the Emendation of the Year*, by Lambertus Floridus Plieninger.[40] The changes made by the Council, wrote Plieninger, were directly associated with the introduction of false worship. Research into biblical prophecy showed clearly that the pope's new "reform" was a final effort to deceive believers. It was calculated to break up the religious peace, to weaken Germany so that the Roman tyranny might be reestablished there. If the principles of outward toleration were not maintained, Germany would soon swim in blood. A bloodbath seemed all too likely both from the threatening signs now seen everywhere, and from a careful study of history and prophecy. Plieninger drew support from the prophecy of Elias, from the history of empires, from astrological patterns, and above all from Daniel and Revelation, to argue that the last "woe" (Revelation 11) had begun. For Plieninger the "science of time" was absolutely necessary, and inseparable from the study of biblical prophecy.

The historical reckonings prompted by the new calendar were many and varied. The highly respected professor of mathematics Michael Maestlin was among those who recognized the errors in the old system but nevertheless opposed the new one. Maestlin supported his position with many technical and pragmatic considerations, but he insisted also that no new calendar was needed on account of the closeness of the Last Day.[41] Although the prophecy of Elias might not be certain, since it was not found in the Bible, it was nonetheless clear that the end was near. All the evidence of chronological study bore out this conclusion. Although time in itself was essentially incomprehensible, Maestlin argued, God had given mankind the tools and the ability to understand something about its order. For this famous teacher the revelations of faith and the art of time-reckoning were perfectly complementary. Maestlin's work on this issue, addressed in German to a lay audience, spurred many readers to reckonings of their own; later popular literature cited him frequently.

By the close of the sixteenth century, the study of world chronology had become an extremely complex and sophisticated field, in which learned scholars debated over countless questions of exact dating. Such issues as the correct date of Christ's birth, for instance, were vigorously argued by major chronologists like Elias Reusner and Sethus Calvisius, as well as by astrologers and astronomers like Helisaeus Roeslin and Johann Kepler.[42] Problems of this sort were never again regarded with such gravity as they were during this era, when they seemed to many observers to bear directly on the interpretation of all-important prophetic matters.

It is true that by 1600 many of the concerns we have noted had been rendered obsolete by new methods of inquiry that originated outside the Lutheran realm. The French jurist Jean Bodin had effectively begun the dissolution of the prevailing world-historical schemes by allowing an independent concentration on human actions in society. Bodin had openly rejected the notion that the Roman Empire lived on among the Germans; he also dismissed eschatological speculation as irrelevant to the understanding of history. The great classical scholar Joseph Scaliger had initiated a revolution in chronology by studying various ancient systems of timekeeping, which allowed him, as Francis Haber wrote, "to compile for the first time in the modern period a sound—though sometimes erroneous—universal chronology of profane history, as distinguished from the uncritical and somewhat mythological sacred history of traditional Christianity."[43] Nevertheless, the new methods and approaches were all but totally ignored in Germany, especially in areas dominated by the prophetic faith of Lutheranism. Although there were signs of change as early as the opening of the seventeenth century, several decades passed before the hold of prophetic history was significantly weakened.[44]

The multiplication of world chronologies by Lutheran authors in the late Reformation suggests a strong desire to retain a sense of assurance in the midst of historical change. The shift in historical thinking that Bodin represented found few friends in the Lutheran world of thought, where apocalyptic assumptions helped to maintain, in somewhat altered form, the medieval tradition of the universal chronicle. To the chroniclers the vicissitudes of time appeared to be reaching an inevitable limit. They drew a mental map of the entire course of world history, and saw themselves as moving very quickly toward the edge. Their journey along this course was preordained, and each moment was necessary in a quite definite way for the completion of the whole. A rigorous subjection of all time to visual analogy reduced the dizzying confusion of historical change to a kind of order. It was emphasized that God continually involved himself in history, rewarding and punishing, and that his ways were ultimately unfathomable to the human mind. He was bound by no schedule. But his promises would be kept, and it was clear from these that he was about to bring the whole action to a close. The growing confusion and debate over details hardly touched the underlying conviction. The possibilities of chronological and prophetic interpretation multiplied, but the underlying attitude did not change.

PROPHETIC POSSIBILITIES

When Lutherans thought about the prospects for whatever short time was left to the world, they most often adopted the views that Luther had helped to establish. On one hand, no further significant changes were to be expected. Since the Reformation marked the beginning of the Last Days, believers did not need to speculate about what still awaited them. The end might come at any moment and would in any case occur very soon; it was the only prospect that mattered. On the other hand, since one could not know just how close the time was, one had to face the possibility that some years or even decades remained. In this case, the Lutheran view of historical degeneration predominated. There would be wars and social upheaval; the forces of evil would rage more and more violently; the decay of nature would continue. In either case, faithful patience was all that was needed. Countless sermons and tracts urged believers to look beyond this vale of tears to the eternal Kingdom. False hope for this world was to be avoided at all costs.

Throughout the sixteenth century and later, this idea of the future remained at the heart of the Lutheran sensibility. Toward the end of the century, Martin Mirus expressed the common conception when he explained in a sermon how the learned divided history into three ages. The age of reason and wisdom had lasted until the time of Abraham. Learning and the arts had flourished, as peace held the upper hand. In the second age, which lasted to the time of Augustus, the heart had reigned; men strove bravely for honor and glory, and were drawn into great and terrible wars. In the third and last age, the human belly held sway; men lived like beasts, seeking neither honor nor virtue. Surely the devil had his way in the world at present, wrote Mirus. The only hope lay in the promise of the Last Day.[45]

Still, the potential sources of prophetic witness were many. If, as time passed, it began to look as though the Lord might hold off for a few years, the desire to fill in the picture in a slightly fuller and more satisfying way became more and more irresistible. Increasingly, Lutheran preachers and writers began exploring prophetic possibilities, either weighing old ones to see which conformed best to evangelical beliefs, or offering new scenarios of their own based directly on biblical evidence and the observation of current events. This proliferation of prophetic possibilities occurred because of, not despite, the general Lutheran agreement that the Last Things had already begun.

Andreas Osiander was among those Lutherans who quite early in the Reformation had drawn on such medieval prophets as Joachim and Hildegard. What he had produced were not speculative prophetic works; rather they were broad, general attacks on Rome. But Osiander did make a major contribution to speculative literature with his *Conjectures on the Last Days and the End of the World*, issued in Latin in 1544 and in German a year later.[46] Here the downfall of the Antichrist was projected for 1672. A period of some sixteen years would follow during which the Gospel would be preached throughout the world. At the end of this time, just as people began to think that all was well and they could live as they pleased, a terrible punishment would befall them and the Lord would come like a thief in the night. To be sure, this uncommon conjecture merely reflected Osiander's thinking during one short period of his life. His reaction to the Augsburg Interim, only three years after the publication of the *Conjectures*, showed a much more imminent and somewhat different sense of God's impending wrath, the final spread of the Word, the destruction of the Antichrist, and the Last Judgment. Yet both of these scenarios from the middle to the late 1540s included the hope that the future would bring a sudden and glorious expansion of the Gospel.

Similarly limited hopes for the Last Times are encountered ever more often among Lutheran commentators in the late sixteenth century. The traditional medieval conception of a short triumph of the true church after the defeat of the Antichrist was too attractive to remain unexplored. Even among Luther's heirs, it was difficult to sever eschatological expectations entirely from worldly hopes. Ultimately all agreed that attention should focus on the final and eternal union with Christ. But that focus did not necessarily exclude the possibility that a short time of peace, like the calm before a storm, might precede his coming.

In the Lutheran world of thought, such hope for worldly triumph generally remained tentative and conjectural. It had nothing to do with the articles of faith, and it could always turn out to be mistaken. Moreover, as a purely speculative hope, it was definitely not a call to action. If such a victory did come about, it would be entirely the work of God; nothing but faith was required from the believer. Finally, this limited spiritual triumph was not to be confused with the patently heretical idea of a Kingdom of God on earth. The victory would be incomplete; the enemies of Christ would not be destroyed altogether. And it would be short, in most descriptions lasting no more than the 45 years suggested by Daniel 12. In these respects, those who foresaw a brief recovery before the Judgment were making no radical departure from the prevailing Lutheran outlook.

What was most different here from Luther's usual view was the sense that the Reformation by itself had not quite fulfilled the divine plan for history. Predictions like Osiander's of a future worldwide spread of the Gospel were among the first clear expressions of waning confidence among Lutherans. In fact, by placing the expected date of the Last Day decades in the future, some Lutherans in the late sixteenth century betrayed their heightened pessimism about what Christians would have to suffer in the years just ahead. If history was indeed the working out of a divine plan, the current disappointing state of affairs seemed sometimes to suggest that it could not be coming to a close just yet. Indeed, in his later years Luther himself had occasionally hinted that the end might be as much as a couple of hundred years off; he also foresaw a bleak future for Germany. So it was not difficult for some to conclude that further important events would have to occur before the Judgment. In this case the most natural scenario, and the easiest to support with scriptural evidence, was that the persecution of the true church would continue to grow while Luther's glorious message brought comfort to believers. At last the Antichrist would be struck down, and the Gospel would enjoy its truly final hour. It is important to recognize that such schemes did not destroy the high expectation characteristic of the early Reformation. While these scenarios acknowledged that the end might yet be some way off, at the same time they insisted that the final worldly struggle had begun, and that great and terrible changes could be anticipated at any time.

It was clear from biblical prophecy that there would be a great advance of the Gospel before the end. Generally the Reformation itself was seen as this advance. Yet even among rigorously orthodox Lutherans, there was leeway for a variety of notions on such matters. Andreas Musculus thought this great advance of the Gospel might be understood in one of three ways. First, it could mean the spread of the Word from its very announcement in Zion or Jerusalem. It could also be seen, though, as the expansion of Christian teaching within a few recent decades to many different places where it had been previously unknown. Though the expansion had mostly been accomplished by Papists, it could not be denied that there were many simple, believing Christians among foreign peoples who would be saved through their baptism and faith. Third, Musculus thought it conceivable, though not likely, that a final spread of the Gospel might yet occur just before the end of the world. The Word might gain ground through a quick push out of the North and West toward the East. The kingdoms of Mohammed might fall, and the Jews might even convert before the return of Christ, as Luther had hoped. While Musculus was hesitant about this last interpretation, he left the matter to "the judgment of God."[47]

Many writers were far less hesitant to conjecture. In a collection of sermons on Ezekiel 38 and 39, for example, Heinrich Efferhen preached confidently that before the end of the world Gog and Magog—the Turk—would conquer and oppress Christendom. Then God in his mercy would overthrow this terrible enemy, and his face would no longer be hidden to his people. Indeed all the peoples of the world, seeing this great triumph, would contract a zeal for holiness and convert to the true belief. This time would be the period of the 45 days mentioned in Daniel 12, when believers would be free not only from worldly enemies but from death itself. But although it would seem for a time that God's people were truly adhering to his Word, they would be unable to free themselves of sin. Soon, then, the Lord would come with his Judgment lest his people should sink back into their old ways. It was not clear just how soon all of this was to be expected, but it would surely not be long, since the Last Times had already begun.[48]

No less remarkable were the forecasts for coming years found in a prophecy by a Lutheran layman from about 1560. Paul Sever claimed that his predictions were made on the basis of eclipses and conjunctions in the heavens, though no reference to astrological evidence appeared anywhere outside the title of his tract.[49] The decade before 1570 would see a complete breakdown in the world, but true Christians, it seems, were to draw together into Saxony. The extent of the coming suffering through war, anarchy, and general disaster was difficult to describe. Then in 1570 a "new reformation" would begin in both the worldly and spiritual regiments. A great and pious emperor would come to power, Hungary and Constantinople would return to Christian rule, and Switzerland would again be part of the empire. A final time of peace and glory would begin.

Sever's work is just one example of renewed interest in the old tradition of messianic emperor prophecies among German Protestants during the later sixteenth century. One Catholic critic of Lutheran prophecies noted with dismay that the old beliefs in a sleeping potentate who would awake and return to reform the world were understood by "almost everyone" to apply to the present age.[50] According to Theodore Ursinus of Nuremberg, old chronicles said that the Emperor Frederick II had never died, but rather "sits in a very old, ruined castle, as if sleeping. And he simply shall not be able to die before the holy city of Jerusalem and that beloved land are again taken from the Turkish tyrants, and the Turk himself is subdued by the Roman Empire."[51] Such thoughts had been generally muted among the first generation of Protestants, but the period between 1555 and the opening of the Thirty Years' War saw a flowering of speculations regarding a Protestant imperium, a trend that had close links with the inheritance of dreams about a last World Emperor.[52] While most Lutheran apocalypticism remained more purely spiritual than the tradition of emperor prophecies, the appearance of such hopes in popular literature is further evidence that many prophetic scenarios were being revived and considered.

A good illustration of interest in a broad variety of prophetic possibilities is afforded by Nicholaus Winckler's *Considerations on Future Changes in Worldly Rule and the End of the World*, published at Augsburg in 1582. Here the major opinions concerning the Last Times were carefully surveyed. Winckler thought such a survey would be valuable, for he did not doubt "that in this coming year, as previously, the astronomers as well as the theologians will write, as is incumbent upon them, many and various sorts of considerations of future changes, troubles, dangers, and perhaps also of the end of the world, which is approaching."[53] In fact he was

interested almost exclusively in one point from the opinions he had
gathered: when would the Judgment occur? His own thoughts, he
realized, would not please everyone. All sorts of ideas were in the
air, and it had to be recognized that "nothing certain can be discerned *in specie de tempore iudicii finalis.*"[54] His aim was merely to
present opinions, not to attack false beliefs. Each reader was free to
hold to his own view on the time of the end, although among believers its nearness was not to be doubted.

By far the most important evidence was to be found in Scripture
and in the writings of the fathers. One old and respectable opinion,
attributed to Aquinas among others, was that the world would
stand as long after the birth of Christ as it had before. Scriptural
support for this idea could be found in Habakkuk 3: 2 and elsewhere.[55] But most interpreters believed that this view offered no
basis for exact calculation: the First Advent was merely a general
dividing point in world history; on this evidence one could make
virtually no predictions of the date of the end. A somewhat similar
opinion was that of Augustine, who held that the present age fell
within the millennium, but that the millennium had to be construed
as a symbolic period. It was thus impossible to predict when the
Antichrist would appear. Winckler, who was writing with the support of the emperor and probably wanted to avoid arousing his
patron's ire with inflammatory anti-Romanism, had no comment on
this point. Rather he turned directly to a consideration of the view
that the thousand years of Satan's bondage had long since passed.
If this view were accepted, just when had the thousand years ended?
What, according to Scripture, was to follow it? Warming to his
implicitly Protestant theme, Winckler lost himself in the job of sort-
ing out the various scenarios and calculations that bore directly on
his own age. One long section was devoted to the spreading expectations for tremendous changes and perhaps the Last Judgment itself in 1588. Could these be defended on the basis of Scripture, and
not just the "dead letter" of nature? Winckler thought so. He
showed that between 328—an ostensibly significant year in the
time of Constantine and Pope Sylvester—and 1588, there lay exactly 1260 years. That number appeared in Revelation 12: 6, as the
number of days (interpreted as years) that the woman clothed with
the sun (the church) was protected from the dragon (Satan).

In the second part of his work, Winckler examined the complementary evidence in nature. The signs for 1588 promised un-

imagined horrors, including worldwide religious upheaval and a bloodbath inflicted on Christendom. Altogether, though human reasoning could never get beyond conjecture, the testimony of the natural world fairly clinched the main argument: the terrible last days of the world were at hand. Yet Winckler too ended on a note of hope. "After great upheaval," he wrote, "the clergy will obtain the upper hand through the power of God Almighty; for God's Word must by the power of Enoch and Elijah be preached again after great persecution and misery, before the coming of the great Day of the Lord."[56] His reference to the clergy was deliberately ambiguous, but Winckler probably had in mind the ministers of reformed Christendom.

An enormous *Prognosticon Theologicvm* written about 1584 helps to show how such predictions of final triumph could emerge within Lutheran apocalypticism.[57] Adam Nachenmoser was a zealous Lutheran, completely absorbed in prophetic hopes and speculations. He intended the *Prognosticon* to be "an interpretation of all the prophecies of the Old and the New Testaments"; it would serve to sort out recent predictions for 1588 and the years to follow, and to show which of them had value. The magnitude of the task begins to explain the bewildering complexity and enormous length of the work.

One of the keys to Nachenmoser's research was the "spiritual desolation" (*geistliche Wüste*) that Scripture predicted for the time after Christ. This period of darkness had begun with the Council of Nicaea in 326 or 327 and would last no more than 1260 years. It would therefore end, or at least begin its disappearance, in 1586 or 1587. The desolation was none other than the kingdom of Antichrist, whose members were the pope and the Turk. The Roman arm had been dealt a heavy blow by Luther and the Reformation, but before it was destroyed it would oppress believers—meaning above all Germany—as never before. The destruction of the Roman tyranny was to come from the Turk, who would overrun Italy and Germany in 1587 or 1588. The sufferings of Christians would be at their worst during this time of testing. Not long afterward, the Turk too would be defeated, though this would come about not through human but through heavenly power. In 1590 the Gospel would be preached to all nations and a wonderful unity would be achieved. The revived German-Roman monarchy would purge the Christian church of all evils, and a golden time would follow for the whole world. The Last Day would then be close at hand. Nachenmoser offered numerous conjectures of the date; 1635 seemed most likely, since this would end the final 45 years. But many speculations were possible, and none was perfectly certain. Shortly before the end, though, most people would again fall away from the Gospel, and the whole world would suffer terrors and punishments beyond comprehension. Nachenmoser described the Last Judgment itself in good Lutheran fashion.

Despite the attractions of the future evangelical triumph and of the glorious Last Day itself, these were not the focus of attention for the author of the *Prognosticon*. Rather, the time from 1584 to 1590, the six years of the immediate future, received his most lengthy and careful investigation. These years would parallel the decisive early years of the Reformation from 1524 to 1530. Just as 1525 saw widespread rebellion and bloodshed, for example, so would 1585 and the years to follow. As in 1528 (actually 1529) the Turks besieged Vienna and threatened to overrun all Germany, in 1588 a similar attack would be successful. The year 1529 was deeply troubled and tense for the early reformers, but in 1530 the Augsburg Confession marked a wonderful triumph. So in 1589 the Germans would stand in desperate straits, but in 1590 they would be reunified and through them the Gospel would be preached to all nations. For Nachenmoser, then, Luther's Reformation was a preview of the final reformation to come.

These elaborate conjectures were firmly rooted in the Lutheran world of thought. The *Prognosticon* exhibited an extremely strong sense of German identity and suffering. The pope and the Turk were the greatest enemies of the true church. Biblical prophecies applied clearly to the events of the past, the present, and the immediate future. The evils of the world would have to come to a climax before the end, but the way of the Christian was straight and clear. The future misfortunes of Germany had to be foretold, wrote Nachenmoser, "that you may better reconcile yourself to the future Cross, and may know that this pleases God our Heavenly Father, and that he will hereby see who will be true and constant to his Word, persevere to his final end, and triumphantly carry away the unfaded crown."[58] Even the short golden time before the end was to be above all a time of watching, waiting, and praying for the return of Christ. The fervent hope for a final reformation that Nachenmoser disguised as prophecy was becoming increasingly common in Germany.

That hope appeared, for example, in Philipp Nicolai's *History of the Kingdom of Christ.*[59] Nicolai, a leading preacher and theologian at Hamburg, thought it likely that a new but final persecution of the true church by the pope would begin in 1625. It would be the last of the three "hours" or times of trouble predicted for the church in the Last Times. The first of these had begun with Luther's death in 1546; bloody wars and much confusion had followed. The second had come in 1588 and immediately afterward. This "hour" was the time of the Armada, and it was also marked by unusual persecution of Christians by the church of Rome. Nicolai thus ensured retrospective validity for hundreds of dire predictions for 1588. The third and last period of severe persecution would begin in 1625. All of these dates arose from long and laborious juggling of figures from Scripture. The idea of three persecutions was traditional. Luther had used it, but in a very different way.[60] Nicolai had given it a new relevance likely to appeal to his nervous contemporaries in Germany.

The last tyranny of the pope would last only four and a half years, until 1629. Then the final, heavenly hour of the church on earth would begin. In the decades before 1670, the Gospel would wax more powerful than ever before. Believers would gain the upper hand all over the world; it would be a time of great rejoicing and happiness for Christians. The ten kingdoms previously persecuted by the pope would all renounce his authority and bind themselves together. They would fall upon Italy as a single force, and burn the city of Rome. The true church would enjoy a golden time of peace before the Last Day. This would be the consummation of the "triumphant joyful song of the church here on earth" that had begun with Luther, the mighty angel of Revelation 10. The enemies of Christ would finally be defeated on earth, but they would not be thrown into Hell until the Judgment itself.[61]

At the end of his work Nicolai acknowledged that in fact all might happen very differently. He echoed a prophecy of Luther that the true Gospel might be driven underground, so that it could be preached only in a few, distant, arctic places and in a few private homes. Gog and the power of Rome might see more worldly success. But at the Last Day all evil powers would be destroyed, and the essence of these predictions would be fulfilled. In the last analysis it did not matter to Nicolai if his specific predictions failed, for with the final appearance of Christ all would be set right. Yet all his biblical interpretation and prophetic calculation supported Nicolai's hope for a final earthly triumph of the church; this triumph was the wonderful secret he thought he had discovered.

The same sort of hopes Nachenmoser and Nicolai voiced can be found in a large number of writings by Lutheran preachers, teachers, and publicists. Elias Reusner, for instance, whose chronological works were mentioned above, offered a reckoning of world history and biblical prophecy similar to Nicolai's; he determined that the year 335 had seen the beginning of the abomination of desolation. The end of the 1290 years preordained for that abomination (Daniel 12: 11) would come in 1625, and the end of the world would come after 1335 years, in 1670.[62] The Saxon court preacher Matthias Hoe devoted a section of his long commentary on the Apocalypse to arguing that Rome would be destroyed and the Roman Antichrist would fall before the Last Day. Hoe did not make clear what sort of conditions would follow the Antichrist's fall, but he was convinced that this was what Revelation meant when it spoke of the "triumph of the Lamb."[63] Sometimes the hope of a brief earthly triumph before the end was expressed indirectly or ambiguously, but Luther's followers were clearly open to it.

In fact, some of those followers proved to be open to far more daring conceptions. A tract of 1620 on world chronology by Nicolaus Hartprecht, felicitously entitled *Tuba Temporis*, combined many of the characteristics of traditional Lutheran chronological reckoning and apocalyptic preaching with explicit hopes for a coming third age.[64] Hartprecht's calculations of the world ages were based heavily on the traditional biblical passages, but he also made reference to prophecies by Paracelsus. He seems also to have been influenced to some extent by Joachimism and by certain forms of number-mysticism. He paid special attention to the time when the Antichrist, the Turk, and other unbelievers would be crushed, apparently by 1625. It remained unclear how long the third age would last, but Hartprecht seems to have imagined that the Last Judgment itself was quite close. Despite unorthodox elements, Hartprecht's book was in many respects a traditionally Lutheran inquiry into the divine plan for history. A later chapter will show that the same combination of unorthodox expectations and a traditional Lutheran quest for prophetic certainty characterized even the "new prophets"—like Paul Nagel and Paul Felgenhauer—who by 1620 became open enemies of the Lutheran establishment. Not long after Hartprecht's tract appeared, a certain Gottlieb Heylandt attempted to summarize the chronological and prophetic discoveries of past decades. In a work entitled *Examen Chronologicum* he stressed the importance of understanding the meaning of the present age.[65] Heylandt cited many learned men, including Melanchthon, Funck, Krentzheim, and Kepler, all of whom had devoted great effort to chronological study. On the other hand, numerous recent writings stood on shaky foundations and had to be read with caution. Here Heylandt pointed to works by Jacob Tilner, Paul Nagel, Nicolaus Hartprecht, Paul Felgenhauer, "and others of the like." Heylandt's discussion left no doubt that he had taken great pains to compare a large number of speculations and to establish what he felt was the best possible understanding of world chronology. Authoritative findings showed that the world might have existed for as long as 5,948 years, and Heylandt accepted as certain the six-thousand-year limit that the prophecy of Elias set.

Heylandt supplemented the findings of chronological research with evidence from the heavens, reviewing important celestial signs and taking note of the many warnings about their meaning. He took as a near certainty Kepler's speculation that the new star of 1604 might portend the sudden conversion of the Jews and other non-Christians before the Last Day. All his evidence, in short, pointed to the nearness of Christ's return, and there were strong indications that this might come in 1623, the very next year. Despite his reservations about certain recent investigations, Heylandt drew support from anyone whose work confirmed his general conclusion. Thus he could approvingly cite Paul Nagel, whose elaborate speculations about a coming third age were scorned by many Lutherans, in the same pages that referred the reader to Georg Rost, Nagel's archenemy. He could suggest a triumph of the true church after the fall of Rome, while engaging in highly typical Lutheran eschatological preaching. Heylandt had not really weighed the various authors against one another; he had given some legitimacy to them all.

In 1623 Heylandt published a long analysis of the Apocalypse, prefaced with a selection from Luther's introduction to the book, in which he showed more clearly his eclectic tendencies. His treatment began with a discussion of prophecies that had been already fulfilled. These referred above all to the Lutheran Reformation, which was of central prophetic importance. In a more detailed treatment of things yet to come, Heylandt drew on a remarkable variety of chronologists and prophetic writers, including Paracelsus and the English millenarian Thomas Brightman. He was selective in what he took from many of his sources; his references to Brightman, for example, were often critical. When forced to take a stand, Heylandt expressed straightforwardly Lutheran judgments. Thus for example he concluded a long discussion of the New Jerusalem and how it was to be understood by acknowledging that the position of those who adhered to the Augsburg Confession was "without any doubt the best, and fits most properly with our context."[66] Although such passages appear to reflect unfeigned confessional loyalty, Heylandt nevertheless showed an extremely broad appreciation for the insights of apocalyptic thinkers of every kind. His writings demonstrate that among some Lutherans in the early seventeenth century the prophetic possibilities had become numerous indeed.

When it came to prophetic speculation, there had never been a well-defined orthodox position among Lutherans. Osiander's speculations may have appeared silly in Luther's eyes, but they did not constitute outright error. Among intellectually cautious Lutherans, attempts to construct precise scenarios for the time remaining before the end were seen more as foolish than as dangerous. While the standard prediction remained simply that the end was very close, there was nothing to prevent the multiplication of prophetic scenarios as the quest for assurance and insight went on.

THE ART OF RECKONING

Conjectures about prophetic possibilities were often supported with careful arithmetical reckonings. The reckoning of prophetic epochs on the basis of Scripture was a well-established medieval practice; a long line of interpreters was inspired by the assumption that believers could gain insight into God's plan for history by correlating scriptural narratives and prophecies with past and present events.

One such interpreter whose work proved influential in Germany was Nicholas of Cusa, who wrote his *Conjectures of the Last Days* about 1452.[67] Cusa warned against seeking knowledge of the future out of mere curiosity, but he thought that through the Scriptures a limited and comforting revelation of things to come was possible. Indeed he presented a strong defense of biblical reckoning, writing, "If we put aside all arrogance, and consider in the fear of God what serves the edification of the Christian church, it is in my view not to be censured if pious Christians engage in conjecture of future things through the Holy Scripture, and seek therein comfort and refreshment in the vale of tears and pilgrimage of this wretched life."[68] Cusa's Platonic leanings encouraged him to see periods or cycles in history; he believed that before the end of the world, the church would suffer an oppression far more terrible than any known before, and would then begin "to strive toward eternal peace" before the end.[69] This pattern was the pattern of Christ's life writ large: a final, horrible persecution, followed by a resurrection before the end.

Nicholas of Cusa thus shared the common medieval belief in a final triumph of the true church, but supported it in an unusual way. In some of his conjectures, for example, he used the idea of "jubilee years," periods of 50 years in church history.[70] Since Christ had lived 34 years on earth, it was probable that his Second Advent would occur after the 34th jubilee year of the church, most likely between 1700 and 1734. According to Cusa this calculation agreed closely with that of Daniel, who had foretold in 559 B.C. that the church would be cleansed after 2300 years. These thoughts seem to have reflected their author's larger conception of "the conjectural art," which stressed the inherent limitations of the human mind, but also recognized the ability of man to make within these limitations "a conjectural universe in the likeness of the real one."[71]

Luther's Reformation could, for a time, make efforts to reckon historical time appear all but irrelevant. The end had arrived; calculations were not needed. Indeed many Lutherans remained deeply distrustful of the entire practice of prophetic reckoning. Amsdorf, for example, was unrelenting in his condemnation of specific predictions, for he had learned to associate them with other, more serious errors. As early as 1528 he had engaged in a dispute with the Anabaptist leader Melchior Hoffmann over the possibility of predicting the time of the Second Coming.[72] Throughout his long life Amsdorf remained on his guard against the sort of prediction he had opposed in Hoffmann.

In this Amsdorf represented the attitude of a large number of theologians and preachers who, though fully sharing the general excitement, regarded attempts at precise prediction as generally self-defeating. As the preacher David Meder emphasized, God had good reasons for keeping the time of the end hidden from men. It was hidden, first of all, so that the godless would always be encouraged to repent, while the godly would always watch and be ready. Then too it was hidden so that poor sinners would never despair of turning back to God, thinking that it was too late. It was hidden, third, so that Christians would suffer patiently all the time, and so that they would always be concerned for their eternal salvation. What would it serve to know the time anyway? Such knowledge would be worse than useless; it would lead many people to get away with whatever they could before it was time to repent.[73]

The desire for prophetic assurance, however, produced numerous efforts to achieve more definite insight. Already in the 1530s Luther and his colleagues had had to deal with an advocate of exact reckoning among their own ranks in the case of Michael Stifel (see chapter 5). In later decades, as worldly conditions appeared to degenerate, followers of Luther hardly imagined they were doing anything illegitimate when their sense of chronology led them to speculate about the future. Had not the Reformer himself done the same? For the many embattled preachers convinced that faith was fast disappearing, prophetic conjectures based on history and the Bible were immediately useful, indeed necessary, as ammunition in the struggle of the Last Days. Even Lutherans who eschewed precise forecasts could and did draw regularly on a standard repertory of general historical reckonings, such as the one that established the closeness of the end from the prophecy of Elias.

But such standard and general reckonings could hardly answer the need for concrete prophetic insight. Typical of the waxing desire for a measure of precision, as well as the willingness to consider new prophetic scenarios, was Osiander's *Conjectures on the Last Days*. The title and some of the main ideas of this work seem to have been borrowed from Nicholas of Cusa's tract of 1452.[74] Osiander had also been influenced by the Neoplatonic and cabalistic teachings of Giovanni Pico della Mirandola, partly through the humanist Johann Reuchlin and his circle; a lost work of Pico, a *Tractatus de vera temporum supputatione*, may have affected the organization of the *Conjectures*. An ardent student of mathematics, astronomy, and history, Osiander was also learned in Hebrew.[75] He was therefore well prepared to seek out answers to some of the otherwise hidden mysteries of Scripture.

The *Conjectures* were issued to honor a request by Melanchthon, who, after finishing his own commentary on Daniel,[76] sought a more definite reckoning of the eras mentioned in that prophetic book. Osiander stressed that, although no man could know the exact time of Christ's coming, true Christians might comprehend its closeness within certain limits. It might be possible to know the year, "or conjecture very nigh it."[77] The Lord had said only that the day and hour could not be known. In fact he had commanded men to research the time of the end, for this knowledge was a great comfort to believers. Both the common man and the learned had responsibilities in observing the signs and reckoning the time.

Osiander offered four conjectures. The first was a general calculation based on the prophecy of Elias; it was sure that the last two thousand years would be cut short. This prophetic scheme, Osiander noted approvingly, had been used in conjunction with the Cabala by Pico. More specific were the reckoning that 1656 years had come between Adam and the Flood, and the analogy with the age after the appearance of the Second Adam; Osiander seems to have been a major popularizer of this idea among Lutherans. The third conjecture depended on Nicholas of Cusa's idea of the jubilee year and the number of years Christ lived on earth: the church would have its end in the 34th jubilee, and 33 times 50 gives 1650. The fourth conjecture was by far the most important and the most involved. Osiander judged from Daniel that Rome was to attain world dominance twice. By an unusual interpretation he saw the "little horn" of Daniel 7 as neither the Turk nor the pope but as Julius Caesar, and he thought the destruction of the beast in Daniel referred not to the Last Judgment but to the end of the first Roman rule. The second domination was described not in Daniel but in Revelation. The name and number of the beast of Revelation 13 had to be analyzed in Hebrew, wrote Osiander, since in that tongue every name was also a number, and this knowledge could lead to the discovery of important secrets. The Hebrew letters for the number of the beast yielded "römisch"—this was one secret that was already out.

Osiander's prediction of the downfall of the Roman Antichrist also depended on some original reckoning. Referring to the prophecies of 2 Thessalonians 2 and Revelation, he argued that since the

Gospel had to be spread throughout the world before the Second Advent, the pope would have to fall some time before the end. The second tyranny of Rome was to last 1260 years. It would have made a pleasing reckoning to begin this period with the time of Constantine; the papacy's demise would then fall around 1576. But Lorenzo Valla and others had shown the Donation of Constantine to be false; hence that emperor's reign could not mark the beginning of the reign of Antichrist in the Latin church. Osiander was forced to look for another date, and he came up with 412 A.D., when (according to his belief) the city of Rome was plundered and burned, and the first Roman rule came to an end. Simple arithmetic thus put the collapse of the papacy in 1672. How Osiander reached the calculation of sixteen years for the final period of open preaching but false security remains something of a mystery. He closed by stating that these were merely conjectures, but they could not be far wrong if his senses did not deceive him.[78]

Soon after the appearance of the *Conjectures*, Osiander's son-in-law, Johannes Funck, made some similar efforts in a commentary on Revelation. Funck insisted that the number of the beast, 666, was more than simply an indication of the Roman Antichrist; something else was still hidden in the number. He concluded that it had to refer to years. The tyranny of the papacy began in 885; thus its end would be due around 1550. Readers were not to imagine that the collapse would happen all at once. It would take time, just as a house must crack before it falls. Further reckoning on the evidence of Daniel established that 1550 also marked the end of the 1290 days of the "abomination of desolation" which had begun in the year 261 (how this abomination differed from the pope's tyranny was not made clear). If the 45 years through which the faithful would have to wait for their reward were now added, the end could be expected in 1595. The writer assured his readers that these were his own fallible insights, but added, "I hold to it, that after the downfall of the Antichrist, that is, after his name, honor, and power in both kingdoms are taken away, there will be no more than 45 years remaining to this world."[79]

The influence of Osiander's work was more than a family affair; indeed it seems to have established something of a tradition of such conjectures among Lutherans. Cunman Flinsbach, for example, a kinsman and student of Melanchthon, followed with his own work titled *Conjecturae extremorum temporum*, in which several of

Osiander's methods were followed, but which was somewhat more reserved about specifying dates.[80] Flinsbach was certain that the world would not stand long past the time of the "Reverend Father Doctor Luther." Far fuller reckonings of the final time were presented in Leonard Krentzheim's *Christian Conjectures on Future Conditions*, which appeared in a German translation by Marcus Rullus in 1583.[81] The *Christian Conjectures*, which could be taken as a natural complement to Krentzheim's massive *Chronologia*, were full of the conviction that current troubles were only the beginning of a great wave of punishments and miseries that would come like a flood over all of Christendom. Enormous upsets were to be expected in both the church and the worldly regiment. Krentzheim protested strongly that he had no intention of researching the secrets of God, which had to remain hidden. He sought only to spread further the light that Nicholas of Cusa had revealed a century earlier, and that Andreas Osiander and Cunman Flinsbach had shown more recently. Krentzheim's hope was that his work would lead readers to repentance.

Krentzheim's research had obviously been extensive. He seems to have been familiar with virtually all the current methods of reckoning. He examined in detail many analogies between the periods of the Old and New Testaments, with much attention to the "wonder year" 1588. Other reckonings supported the forecast of the monk Johann Hilten that in 1600 Europe would be overrun by a terrible tyrant. The number 1600, which appears in an obscure context in Revelation 14: 20, marked many critical spans in world history; it was one of several key periods or cycles (Krentzheim used the term *Jahrcirckel*) that were regarded as basic measures of time. Through a long parallel between the first world monarchy—that of the Ninevites—with the last—the present Roman imperium— Krentzheim hoped to warn fellow Germans against future calamity; according to the book of Jonah, the Ninevites had escaped the wrath of God by sudden and sincere repentance. Krentzheim contended that the books of Daniel and Revelation "actually describe and demonstrate the final downfall, last times, and end of the Roman monarchy and church," as well as of the Turk. More importantly, they also told "where one should begin to count [the years prescribed for these anti-Christian powers], even if somewhat obscurely, nevertheless in such a way that it can in some measure be researched and grasped, by those who understand, through the aid and illumination of the Holy Spirit."[82] The spirit led Krentzheim to calculate that the end of persecution under the Antichrist would probably come around 1592, and that the 45 years following that date would see the beginnings of recovery in the Christian church.[83]

All this barely scratches the surface of Krentzheim's highly complex reckonings. He offered a myriad of interpretations to show that the downfall of the Antichrist and the end of the world would both occur no later than 1630, the hundredth anniversary of the Augsburg Confession (also 1600 years after Jesus began to preach, 1500 years after the "last Jewish war," 42 years after the wonder year 1588, and so on—all these numbers had biblical significance). Krentzheim based several conjectures on the prophecy of Elias, others on comparisons between the age before the Flood and his own day, still others on astrological observations. He referred to a major planetary conjunction expected in 1584 and to scores of other signs, including the new star of 1572, the comet of 1577, and proliferating wonders in the heavens, on earth, and in human society. Repeatedly, Krentzheim protested that he was not trying to investigate God's secrets. It must not be supposed, he told his readers, that God was compelled to act at any particular time. In the last analysis, all was in God's hands. But without a doubt the time to turn back to him had come.

His emphasis on prophetic cycles or periods and his hope for a return to peace before the end show Krentzheim's debts to Nicholas of Cusa and to the larger tradition of medieval reckoning. In fact, appended to his own bulky work was another set of conjectures based on the reckonings of Cusa.[84] This was an effort to show how the prophecies of the famous cardinal were being fulfilled. Luther was the second Elias, and the Reformation was the wonderful beginning of the Last Times. Krentzheim quoted Cusa as predicting that "the number of believers will increase continually, and the longer the light of true doctrine continues the more it will spread, up until the fourth jubilee year (that is 150 years), and through it will occur all sorts of signs and wonders." Knowledge of Christ would spread over the whole world. Then would come the last great persecution of believers, followed by the downfall of the Antichrist. Before the end, the church would begin to strive toward eternal peace. Although the dates forecast by Cusa differed slightly from his own—the cardinal had calculated as late as 1734 for the Last Day—Krentzheim found general support in these prophecies for his own hope that the true church would triumph before the end. If an exalted prophet of the Reformation had reckoned in this way, then certainly such investigations were of use to the faithful.[85]

Krentzheim's work was published in 1583, too early to take into account the apocalyptic implications of the new calendar of 1582. The appearance of the calendar provoked a spate of bold apocalyptic speculations. Eustachius Poyssel, for example, went off on a series of deep quests for insight as a result of the change. Along with such other Lutheran commentators as Plieninger, Poyssel thought the Nicene Council had perverted original Christian practices by introducing an arbitrary method to determine the date of Easter. Between the year of that change (323 according to Poyssel) and 1583, when the new calendar was published by the pope, lay a span of 1260 years. The first change took place under the emperor Constantine; the second under Rudolph. In these two names, constantinvs and rvdolphvs, were found letters that gave the number 666, the number of the beast. Hence this period of 1260 years had been the preordained time of the Antichrist. Poyssel then argued that, as the destruction of Jerusalem had come 40 years after the first Christian Easter, it was likely that the end of the world would come 40 years after the last calendar change, or in 1623. This was only one among scores of calculations he offered to show that 1623 would in all probability bring the Judgment. He figured, for instance, that the Israelite kingdom had lasted a total of 1590 years. By starting with 1590 A.D. and adding the 33 years of Christ's life on earth, one obtained 1623—and further certainty as to the time of the end.[86] This description hardly hints at the complexity and richness of Poyssel's apocalyptic reckonings in a series of tracts issued over several years; we will return to his prophetic methods (see chapter 5).

Although the calendar change continued to concern seekers of apocalyptic insight, it was only one source of preoccupation among many as the turn of the century approached. The Turkish menace, for instance, also inspired increasingly careful and detailed reckoning. David Herlicius, a polyhistor and teacher of mathematics at Greifswald, was convinced that evidence from Scripture, history, and the heavens proved the imminent collapse of the giant enemy kingdom in the East. In his *Tractatus Theologastronomistoricus* Herlicius mustered all possible support for this expectation and for the conviction that the end of the world would quickly follow.[87]

Mohammed himself had predicted that his downfall would come
after a thousand years; if he was born in 597, the end would be due
in 1597. The monk Johann Hilten, though, who had correctly predicted Luther's Reformation, foresaw that in 1600 a tyrant would
rule over all Europe; this prediction might mean a last expansion
of the Turkish power before its overthrow. Like Krentzheim, Herlicius referred to 1600 as a remarkable *Jahrcirckel*; significant periods of 1600 years had been common in history, so something of
great import was naturally awaited. Herlicius used the prophecy of
Elias, as well as the four monarchies and various mathematical
analogies, as evidence that the year 1600 would mark the completion of several important historical terms. Much weighty evidence
was associated with periods of 1000 and 500 years; the latter was
a "numerus mysticus & climacterius" derived from the 70 weeks of
years of Daniel 9. In some of his reckonings Herlicius made careful
adjustments in his figures to account for the difference between
Arabic and Julian years; these adjustments implied that the downfall of the Turk might come even earlier than otherwise expected.
He drew heavily on the major Lutheran chronologies for detailed
support for his calculations. Reckonings of planetary conjunctions
and other heavenly movements also drew Herlicius's careful attention; some of the most respected astrologers predicted earthshaking
changes for the Turkish kingdom.[88] These future prospects offered
the ultimate warning and the greatest possible promise.

Even more highly involved reckonings of this sort appeared in
the second book of Philipp Nicolai's *History of the Kingdom of
Christ*, which investigated the preordained times of the Kingdom
and its enemies. Like many engaged in such research, Nicolai interpreted the words of the angel in Daniel 12 to mean that the mysteries of the end would be revealed in the Last Days to those blessed
with understanding. The Lord had commanded not only that believers should watch closely for all the signs of the end, but also that
they should be diligent to learn the times allotted to the enemies of
the church. Nicolai wrote that he had worked long and assiduously
on these calculations, and he hoped that other learned men would
do their part to clear up the mysteries of these Last Times.

His inquiry began with an all-important question: how long
would the Christian church endure? The number 1600 from Revelation 14 was crucial. Like Krentzheim, Herlicius, and others,
Nicolai took it to signify a term of years; this was among the im-

portant hidden meanings in Scripture. The period of 1600 years was a "key to all chronological treasures, which many have sought with great effort and reflection."[89] To this figure was then added 41½ years, the "hour" of "spiritual harvest." This figure seems to have been based partly on the time (or hour) of punishment for the Jews, which lasted from the 29th year of Christ—when the ministry of John the Baptist began—to A.D. 70. The sum of 1641½ years marked the time that God had granted to the Christian church on earth. This time began in A.D. 29 and would end in 1670. In that year great things beyond the power of human thought would surely occur. Through detailed calculations the Hamburg preacher found several ways to support this finding.

Nicolai carefully denied that any final necessity attached to his calculations. The Last Day might come sooner for the sake of the elect, or it might be delayed on account of God's infinite patience and mercy. These computations were not articles of faith but efforts at understanding. Yet although Nicolai admitted he might be in error about the year of the end, he stoutly maintained that such divine mysteries were ultimately discoverable. He was, moreover, fairly confident that his reckonings were correct. He had done nothing more than make explicit what had lain hidden in Scripture. Often he referred without qualification to "the discovered universal end of all time, namely the year 1670."[90] This reckoning of the end of time was only the beginning. Pages and pages of complex calculations showed that almost any major phenomenon or period had its indication in the Bible. God ruled over history according to a measure that lay hidden in Scripture.

Thus in the years around 1600, interest in historical reckoning was reaching a high peak in Lutheran Germany. Some hint of the intensity of this interest can be seen in the debate sparked by a work first issued in 1596 by Nicolas Reymers (Raimarus Ursus), a court astronomer for the emperor Rudolph at Prague.[91] This was a *Chronological, Certain, and Irrefutable Proof, from the Holy Scripture and Fathers, That the World Will Perish and the Last Day Will Come within 77 Years.* Many books were being published, wrote Reymers, that cried out unanimously that the end of the world was near. "But how near or how far, says none of them; much less does any of them show anything demonstratively on the true and unfailing basis of holy divine Scripture." He maintained that before him no chronologist had achieved an accurate reckoning of world history. Of the many who had tried to calculate the true age of the world, some had come close, but none had hit the right figure exactly. Therefore Reymers had "necessarily, and for the betterment of the Christian community," taken the task upon himself.[92] When the work was done properly, the proof mentioned in the title would be established. Reymers's proof had two parts. The first was to show that the world could not last longer than six thousand years; the second was that in 1596 the world was 5,923 years old. Scripture and the fathers together showed the first part beyond doubt. The idea of the six ages, the prophecy of Elias (admittedly found in the Talmud, not the Bible, but a venerable prophecy nonetheless), and the declaration of Matthew and Mark that the time would be shortened left no question here. To demonstrate his second point, Reymers presented a detailed but on the whole typical chart reckoning the age of the world from biblical evidence.

This *Irrefutable Proof* had a wide readership in Germany, but a common reaction to the calculation of Reymers was that it allowed too much time before the Last Day. Jacob Tilner of Halle was thus inspired to introduce his own *Chronological Time-Reckoning and Certain Proof from Holy Scripture That the World Will Shortly Perish and the Last Day Will Come within 44 Years*. Citing the recent spate of thick books dealing with the end of the world, Tilner parroted the words of the Prague astronomer: "But how near or how far says none of them; much less does any of them show anything demonstratively on the true and unfailing basis of holy divine Scripture."[93] In order to further Christian understanding, Tilner had undertaken to set the matter straight. But in contrast to the almost academic tone of Reymers's work, a passionate call to repentance in these utterly corrupt Last Times resounded through Tilner's work. God was preparing to punish this evil world; he had already shown great patience. Tilner warned that since his words were based directly on Scripture, they could be ignored only at the greatest peril. His reckoning of world history was exactly that of Reymers. If the world were to stand for a full six thousand years, the end would come in 1673. But since the days would be shortened, the Judgment was certain to come before then, and Tilner settled on the year 1656. Those who listened to him, and to others who spoke the truth, would be prepared.

Even if tremendous upheavals were to precede 1656, that date was still several decades away, and the delay made an unsatisfying prospect to some minds. Luther himself had consistently stressed that the Judgment was quite close, and he had gone through periods of extremely high expectation when he doubted that the world could last more than a year or two longer. Albert Hitfeld of Magdeburg must have been in a similar state of mind when he responded to Tilner's work in a *Counterproof That the World Cannot Stand for Another 42 Years.*[94] Hitfeld was sure that Tilner had not read the Scriptures, particularly Daniel, closely enough. Had he read more carefully, he would have seen that the end of the Roman empire would coincide with the end of the world. The time prescribed for Rome was 1656 years. This period almost certainly began in 43 B.C. with the official inception of the reign of Caesar. It would therefore end in 1613, the very year in which Hitfeld's pamphlet was published. On this reckoning the end was imminent indeed, and Hitfeld was convinced that all evidence supported his conclusion. The letters of IVDICIVM added up to 1613, but this was the least important of his proofs. In fact, Hitfeld thought he could determine the very day. He settled on September 8, which he took for the date of the end of the Jewish polity at the hands of Rome. Though he refused, in light of the biblical warnings, to affirm that day as necessarily the time of the end, he was nonetheless quite sure that "this must be the correct understanding of Daniel. This and none other."

The tracts of Tilner and Hitfeld were examples of the least sophisticated voices in a wide-ranging debate. There were much more learned responses to such speculations as those of Reymers. The *Chronologia* of Johann Wolther, for example, demonstrated an extraordinarily broad acquaintance with all sorts of chronological and astrological studies. Wolther, a pastor at Lichtenhagen in Saxony, complained that Reymers had not lived up to his promise. Though his enterprise had been laudable, he had not figured properly after all. In some cases Reymers's conclusions were directly contrary to Scripture, and his proofs were very poorly established. Wolther was sure that theologians, historians, and astrologers would find great value in his own work.

Several attempts had recently been made, he wrote, to establish a concordance among the testimonies of astronomy, theology, and history from the beginning of the world to the present. The results had been woefully inadequate, and the *Chronologia* would demonstrate the proper approach. Wolther took issue not only with the calculations of Reymers, but also with the best known chronologists of the preceding century, including Funck, Bucholzer, and Calvisius. He engaged in long and involved reckonings, both biblical and astronomical, to show that the world had existed longer than was commonly supposed. Wolther's main concern, however, hardly depended on such precise figuring, for above all he sought to show that, though corruption already penetrated to every corner of the world, shocking miseries were still in store before the end. Wolther preached in violent tones against corrupters of the Word, including Zwinglians and Calvinists and all others who ignored what he found most important. His tract was a comprehensive collection of evidence that the final, desperate persecution at the hands of the Antichrist was imminent, and that nature was nearing the end of its course.[95] The time would certainly be shortened for the sake of the elect; the hour to repent was at hand. In the mind of this Lutheran pastor, the details of calculation were important only insofar as they inspired hope and fear.

The sorts of reckoning we have explored were a most sober and serious pursuit. The task of reading these works, not to mention writing them, must have consumed many a hard hour. Adam Nachenmoser's *Prognosticon*, for example, pursued the details of prophetic reckoning to lengths that must have tried the patience of the most avid readers. The reasoning behind each calculation was exhaustively explained in the hope that no question would be left unanswered. Nachenmoser's most important tools were numbers; his investigation was essentially a matter of juggling and interpreting numbers drawn from the Bible, history, the heavens, or from thin air. Such careful interpretation and calculation, he stressed, was in no way sinful if put to proper use. In a similar passage, Nicolaus Hartprecht, the author of *Tuba Temporis*, wrote that no one doubted that chronological reckoning was a necessary task. Since the time of Luther, many learned men had investigated the age of the world and had sought to discover how long it would last. Philipp Melanchthon was among those who recommended chronological study. Without doubt it was difficult work and no task for one man; mistakes were very easily made. The secrets of the Last Time had remained hidden for good reason, but now the time approached when the meaning of all the prophetic numbers would be uncovered. Had God made announcements about the future through his prophecies in Scripture only to have these things remain forever hidden under a veil of mystery? On the contrary; he intended the mysteries to be revealed so that people might be saved. Even if the world remained wrapped up in its ungodly concerns, the message would not be lost on true Christians.[96]

Prophetic speculation with biblical and historical evidence was thus an integral part of the early Lutheran tradition. From the early years of the Reformation until well into the seventeenth century, efforts multiplied to discover objective truths about the proximity of the Judgment and about the nature and order of events to precede it. We have seen a good deal of inconsistency and disagreement among the various scenarios and reckonings. As time passed and the variety of conjectures and calculations expanded, some of Luther's heirs became absorbed in simply considering the possibilities. But so many possibilities could lead to mounting uncertainty and confusion, even desperation. It is no wonder, then, that in the decades around 1600 there were fewer and fewer "conjectures," more and more "proofs" about the Last Times.

HISTORY AND SALVATION

The conjectures and reckonings presented in this chapter are only some more explicit examples of tendencies that were extremely common in the late Reformation. They provide evidence that the historical interpretation of prophecy among Lutherans during this era was not limited to any one approach. The strong belief that history was the working out of a divine plan gave rise to a variety of speculations about what was still to come, including the vision of an earthly triumph for the true church after a period of violent persecution. Although some Lutherans attempted to discourage all but the most reserved interpretations of biblical prophecy as it applied to the past, the present, and especially the future, no boundaries were established to distinguish pious from impious reckonings and conjectures. Hence as time passed, prophetic investigation tended to seek more openly for certainty and precision.

The effort to correlate history and prophecy, which seems to have reached a peak in Germany in the decades around 1600, cannot be interpreted merely as a symptom of loss of insight into the real meaning of the Second Advent, or as a decline into superstition after the earlier inspiration had faded. From the beginning, Luther had looked to an imminent, objective end of history. As his sixteenth-century followers learned to picture history more and more as a process of irreversible change, their hopes and fears became linked still more closely to the coming of the Last Day. Increasingly conscious of the historical dimension, they put a limit to its significance by predicting its imminent end. They hoped above all to retain trust in God's promises. The promise of the Reformation was that deliverance was near in an explicit, historical sense. If the original expectation had been a little hasty, it was natural to make some minor readjustments and to continue in the same apocalyptic faith. Thus medieval preconceptions were perpetuated in the altered framework of Lutheran historical assumptions.

Nothing could have been further from a critical conception of history based on the weighing of evidence and the analysis of causes and effects. For Reformation Lutherans, the lessons of history were spiritual. The past as well as the future called out a promise to believers and threatened the faithless with eternal punishment. History was a grand universal drama, with clearly indentifiable acts and a predictable final curtain. The audience might have some questions about what the director had in mind for the final act, but the outline of the plot was clear. Only later, during the upheavals of the seventeenth century, did the intense eschatological expectation inimical to a modern sense of history disappear in Germany.

4
⇜ Apocalyptic Astrology

ASTROLOGY AND REFORMATION

The sixteenth century was a golden age for astrological prophecy. The blossoming of Renaissance magic gave a new impetus to the ancient art, and in Germany as elsewhere the spread of printing helped arouse and feed a growing popular interest in this and other forms of divination. In the decades just prior to the Reformation, astrological predictions for popular consumption were already very common. The art flowered throughout the sixteenth century despite the well-known attacks of Pico della Mirandola and others and despite continual doctrinal disapproval. Calvin flatly opposed astrology; Catholicism had long frowned officially, though ineffectively, upon it. Luther regarded it neutrally at best, and often discounted it as a practice full of superstitions, errors, and potential abuses. Yet later in the sixteenth century, Lutheran Germany was probably more fully given over to the study than any other part of Europe; there was at least no place where astrological interest was greater. Lutheran churchmen became highly tolerant and even supportive of the art, in contrast, for instance, to the French clergy, who repeatedly sought to limit or control astrological prediction. Indeed, astrologers fully shared the apprehension and excitement characteristic of Reformation Germany, and contributed to it as well. Since these points have not gone unnoticed, it is surprising that more attention has not been paid to the close links between astrological prophecy and the apocalyptic sensibility Lutheranism encouraged.[1]

There is rich evidence for the influence of astrological prediction at the time of Luther's struggle with Rome; in fact, one nineteenth-century interpretation saw astrology as an important underlying cause of both the Reformation and the Peasants' War.[2] Astrology was in any case the predictive method par excellence, and it had an important role in shaping people's hopes and fears for the future. Several types of celestial prediction were respectable as well as popular. Among these was the practice of reckoning individual nativities and horoscopes. Literate burghers and humbler folk, who could not always afford such personal extravagance, consulted annual *practica* or almanacs. These contained predictions for everything, from the weather and favorable planting dates to princely deaths expected in the coming year. The most sensational and most widely discussed predictions were those that looked years or decades into the future of a nation, or of the whole world. As so many others were at that time, astrologers were generally convinced that enormous changes and upsets would soon occur; their works were full of the common feeling of impending disaster.

One of the most famous German stargazers was Johann Lichtenberger, whose prophecies were reissued regularly throughout the sixteenth century and into the seventeenth. His major work, the *Prognosticatio*, which first appeared in Latin in 1488, reflects the mixture of hope and dread that was characteristic of the late Middle Ages.[3] It was actually copied in large measure from an earlier work by Paul of Middelburg, a professor at Padua, who in turn had depended heavily on the Arab writer Albumazar.[4] On the evidence of an ominous planetary conjunction in 1484, Middelburg had foreseen great changes in both church and state. Lichtenberger, adding to the earlier tract, produced a veritable grab-bag of medieval apocalypticism, a work that was influential because it was open to widely differing interpretations. Profound troubles and suffering were sure to come, but the *Prognosticatio* permitted the hope of an age of peace. Lichtenberger blended astrology together with old prophecies of doom and victory to form a new and potent mixture.

Probably equally influential were the writings of Joseph Grünpeck, a court scholar for Emperor Maximilian and one of the most prolific astrological writers of the early sixteenth century. Grünpeck issued several prophecies that predicted great dangers for the ship of St. Peter and for the entire social order.[5] Astrology also figured heavily in other types of popular prophecy. An anonymous and undated early sixteenth-century prophetic tract based on the Sibyls, Birgitte, Cyril of Jerusalem (d. 386), Joachim, Methodius, and Brother Reinhard included also an explicit appeal to the evidence of the heavens, and a strong defense of astrology as a divinely ordained means of human understanding. The evidence of the stars complemented the forecasts of the prophets in foretelling a time of terrible troubles, to be followed by a great reformation that would free the Germans from Roman tyranny and last until 1581, when presumably the world would end.[6]

A notable example of the sort of expectation that flourished in Germany at this time is the common forecast of a universal deluge in 1524.[7] The exact origin of this prediction is uncertain, but it probably derived from excessively eager reading of a work originally published in 1499 by Johann Stoeffler of Justingen (d. 1531) with the help of Jacob Pflaum.[8] Stoeffler had accurately foretold that in February of 1524 no fewer than twenty planetary conjunctions would occur, sixteen of which would occupy a "watery" sign (Cancer, Scorpio, or Pisces). It was not long before a virtual flood of popular astrological predictions appeared in order to warn Christendom of the approaching deluge. Though many learned observers rejected predictions of a flood, most agreed that some horrible experience was forthcoming. The pervasiveness of the conviction is attested by numerous writings from that time. Among the better-known writings that contributed to expectation was a 1523 *practica* by Leonhard Reinmann, which predicted not only a flood but a general uprising of the peasants and common people to institute a regime of social justice and equality.[9] Apprehension increased from year to year; here is a perfect example of the sort of gloomy foreboding that had been so prevalent before the Reformation. Johann Carion, the court astrologer at Brandenburg and later the author of the *Chronica*, even set a precise date for the disaster: July 15, 1525. According to legend, on that day the elector and his wife took refuge on a mountain. Around the same time Albrecht Dürer reported a vivid dream in which an immense downpour engulfed the earth. Among astrologers who favored the spreading evangelical cause, alarmist forecasts may have served as religious propaganda by emphasizing that a critical hour of decision had arrived. But whether this purpose was intended or not, the proliferation of such dire predictions could only encourage a movement urging immediate reform and repentance.[10]

We have seen how powerfully Martin Luther was affected by the sense of crisis that dominated the early sixteenth century. But his expectancy was highly biblical and carefully focused; he was somewhat cautious about other prophecies. He did interpret contemporary signs in the heavens as portents of the Last Day, but was usually wary of precise forecasts. He had only ridicule for those astrologers who had predicted a great flood for 1524 but had said nothing about a peasant rebellion in the following year. For him, as for the medieval church, astrology was suspect whenever it claimed to provide a systematic means of foretelling future events. Such a claim implicitly challenged the authority of God, as it seemed to bind him to the laws of nature. But this line of argument never led Luther to an open and categorical rejection of astrology as it was understood in his day. On balance he must certainly be seen as an enemy of astrological prediction, but his attitude posed no obstacle to the unprecedented popularity of the art in late Reformation Germany.

In Lutheran writings of the early Reformation, the heavy evangelical emphasis on biblical prophecy overshadowed astrology, as well as other nonscriptural prophetic methods and traditions. Nevertheless the appetite for astrological prediction seems to have remained strong among the people. The predictions of Johann Carion provide good examples of the predictions that continued to circulate widely in this period. Carion published many different kinds of forecasts,[11] but during these decades he was best known for prognostications that ran ten to twenty years into the future. He wrote one to cover the years from 1527 or 1528 to 1540; it was apparently updated several times for later periods, for example 1536 to 1550.[12] His predictions were wide-ranging; they included pronouncements on various matters of church and state, predictions of the weather, announcements of unusual natural phenomena, and much obscure prophecy on general changes to come. Although Carion rarely implied that the end of the world was very close, he did often dwell on the evils that the near future would bring. Often, too, he wrote in a churchly style that lent an air of great significance to his words. During his own lifetime and long afterwards, Carion was criticized for failing to base his prophecies on purely astrological grounds, though the astrologer himself insisted that they were so based. Since his reasoning was vague, his prophecies were easily adaptable by later purveyors of prophetic wisdom. They were reedited and reissued many times in the decades after his death in 1536.

Carion wrote for a Lutheran audience, and his later prophecies may have been attractive to Lutherans partly because they reflected the general Lutheran pessimism about the secular future. Increasingly, however, other kinds of astrological prophecy circulated in Lutheran areas. By the 1530s, for example, predictions by the famous Paracelsus were becoming known. In a work published at Augsburg in 1536, Paracelsus foretold the coming of the end in 1560, an expectation that may have contributed to the multiplication of tense warnings around midcentury.[13] More frequently reprinted in later decades was an anonymously edited collection of prophecies by Paracelsus, Lichtenberger, Grünpeck, Carion, the Sibyls, "and others," which first appeared in 1549.[14] These prophecies offered a variety of schemes and imagery that emphasized the criticalness of recent events and suggested still greater changes to come. Several of the prophecies were obscurely allegorical; most were clearly anti-Roman in tone and contained dark warnings about the future. Those of Lichtenberger and Grünpeck applied to political as well as to religious affairs, and held out hope for a universal reformation to come. In almost all these prophecies, there was some ambiguity about what had already been fulfilled and what was yet to occur. The publication of the anthology in 1549 again suggests that by midcentury a search for extrabiblical prophetic authorities was in progress.

Not until after about 1550 did astrologers and preachers really begin to develop a mutual accommodation in Lutheran Germany. Before that time, there had been considerable obstacles to cooperation. Luther's opinions, for example, could not be easily ignored or reinterpreted until some years after his death. It was perhaps not quite accidental that Melanchthon's famous lectures on astrology were delivered and published only after the death of Luther.[15] Moreover, it was not until the middle of the century that a fresh generation of Protestant students, fully imbued with both Lutheran theology and the desire for other kinds of learning, really came into its own. Astrologers of the early Reformation were perhaps still governed by assumptions alien to the Lutheran world of thought. In the second half of the century, however, the words of German astrologers enjoyed serious respect among all classes, and came increasingly to express common Lutheran attitudes.

FAITH AND THEORY

Astrology, as one noted scholar has put it, was "a fundamental component in the philosophy of an internally related cosmos." [16] The art was part of a larger outlook that presupposed a universal structure or plan, in which every object and event had its place. In theory, this insistence on universal order could lead to cosmic determinism and fatalism. As practiced by the ancients, astrology and all similar arts were ultimately in conflict with the Judeo-Christian conception of a God who is absolutely free and who works his will directly in the world. Yet during the Middle Ages and Renaissance the potential conflict between astrology and theology often went unrealized. This was the case particularly in Reformation Germany, where despite Luther's reservations the art became a widespread preoccupation by the later decades of the sixteenth century. Indeed, as a result of shared attitudes and assumptions, astrology and theology could and did cooperate during this age to sustain and elaborate an apocalyptic world-picture.

Luther tried to explain what believers ought to think about prediction from the stars. Partly to oppose what he saw as the astrological excesses of his day, he published his own edition of Lichtenberger's prophecies at Wittenberg in 1527. [17] He added a preface that spelled out his own position. True prophecy, he wrote, comes through the Holy Spirit. False prophecy is inspired by Satan, and works to prevent and destroy true faith. But Lichtenberger's prophecies were neither true nor false in this sense, for they were not spiritual at all. They were grounded in the natural action of the stars. Lichtenberger appealed neither to faith nor to conscience; his words neither consoled nor warned. He spoke merely of corporeal things, of external phenomena. Astrology was an old heathen art, already common among the Chaldeans. To what extent, asked the Reformer, were such arts to be trusted?

Perhaps they were not to be scorned altogether, he wrote, since Lichtenberger had hit some things right. But God alone knew and ruled over the future. Often he did give portents of evils to come—even the ancients were aware of such portents, though ignorant of their cause. God effected directly such signs as comets, darkenings of the sun and moon, and unusual heavenly phenomena. He worked similar wonders on earth, for example when freaks were born among animals and men. These signs had but one purpose: to warn and threaten the godless. The faithful had nothing to fear, indeed nothing to do with such warnings. But what then of these prophecies? Luther concluded that though heavenly portents were certainly abundant, to attempt to make an art of reading these signs was fundamentally mistaken. No system of interpretation was possible, for God could make interpretations fail or succeed. Christians, then, did not need to be concerned with prophecies like Lichtenberger's, for such predictions were not reliable. The godless were to heed them not because of the art upon which they were supposedly grounded, but because of the warning signs to which they referred. Luther distrusted astrology to the extent that it drew attention away from genuinely spiritual concerns. But he did not oppose careful observation and interpretation of signs in the heavens.

Luther's cold shoulder for the science of astrology is often contrasted with Melanchthon's enthusiasm, not infrequently to imply that Melanchthon was therefore more superstitious than his older colleague. Clearly, Luther's attitude toward his friend's involvement in such studies was one of opposition in principle but strained toleration in practice. Yet it has rightly been noted that Luther's opposition to the art was inherited from medieval thinking, and did not bring him any closer to a modern view of the matter. At the same time, Melanchthon's interest in astrology was in fact moving toward the humanization and secularization of the sciences.[18]

Melanchthon's search for order in celestial influences actually derived from the very impulse that led him to propound prophetic schemes for history with such insistence. In both realms he sought to investigate the divine plan. His desire had consequences that were manifest in small matters as well as large. Thus for instance it helped to convince Melanchthon, along with many of his astrologer colleagues, that Luther must have been born in 1484, for this was the year of the great conjunction that had announced profound religious changes. A minor controversy arose over the issue, for other evidence pointed to 1483. Melanchthon claimed to have consulted Luther's mother, who agreed that 1484 was probably the correct year. The dispute was trivial, but it shows how consistently Melanchthon pursued the goal of an orderly correlation of celestial phenomena with historical events.[19]

Students of Melanchthon's thought have disagreed as to whether the *Praeceptor Germaniae* was actually under the sway of the fatalism inherent in ancient cosmology. Some scholars see in his astrological concerns, which were shared by so many of his German contemporaries, a strong attraction to the notion of destiny, which has had a profound though often obscure influence in German culture. His astrology, according to this argument, manifests a Hellenistic, anti-Christian train in his thought.[20] Other historians, however, insist that Melanchthon clearly distinguished between a Stoic, or fatalistic, view of natural causation and the Aristotelian conception to which he subscribed. In the latter conception, nature is no purely mechanistic construction set in motion by God. God does not simply stand outside or above nature; he is *in* nature, not in a pantheistic sense, but as the Creator and Maintainer of all.[21] Nature is the realm of secondary causes, whereas God is the primary cause. With this understanding there is room both for the free action of God and for the subordinate freedom of choice granted to men. In this second view, then, Melanchthon's astrological interests, rightly understood, in no way contradicted the message of the Gospel. Clearly this debate does not end with Melanchthon himself, but extends to the implications of astrology in sixteenth-century Germany.

It would be satisfying to judge decisively, but it appears that both views are partly right. Pursued consistently, astrology necessarily implies fatalism. Melanchthon is said to have thought that stargazers like Carion went too far in predicting particular events; astrology was not so precise an art.[22] But Melanchthon did assume that some degree of consistency was possible; moreover, many of his students and followers were more convinced than their master of the potential exactitude of divination from the stars. Caspar Peucer, in his tract on the various sorts of divination, expressed hope for the eventual perfection of the discipline.[23] He was not alone in this hope, for in the second half of the century efforts to improve astrology, to make it more scientific and dependable, became frequent. Attempts were made to gather data more systematically, and through induction to formulate more dependable rules of prediction.[24] Any such effort to achieve consistency and exactitude in astrological prediction tended implicitly to bind God to his laws. At the same time, however, the Melanchthonian conception of astrology simply perpetuated a paradox central to Lutheran, indeed to Christian teaching: the coexistence of human responsibility and God's preordination. This existential paradox is a cornerstone of every theistic faith, but when carried over into the realm of natural science it inevitably becomes the source of open contradictions.

Either God has established a consistent order in nature, or he has not. Thus either natural events and worldly occurrences are in theory predictable, or they are not.

Credible astrology depended on the assumption that phenomena are predictable. Lutheran practitioners often used the phrase "astra inclinant, sed non necessitant" to suggest that natural forces were important but secondary to the workings of the spirit. Sidereal fatalism, by implication, applied only to unbelievers; only the godless world was subject to the laws of nature. But these words, often added as a pious afterthought to the ends of works that offered precise forecasts, do not explain how astrologers avoided the fatalistic implications of their art as it was actually practiced. To achieve consistency, they had to assume that believers as well as unbelievers were subject to the workings of the stars.

A full explanation needs to take into account the prophetic assumptions that surrounded all learning in that era. Lutheran astrologers construed sidereal fatalism as divine purpose, and they could do this primarily because their vision of the future was informed by the coming end. The dangers of historical fatalism were more than offset by the promise of redemption, a promise that took historical form as the Second Coming. Astrology was an art concerned with natural causes; since God worked through those causes, the art could also help confirm the biblical prophecy of the inevitable end of history. Melanchthon and most other Lutheran astrologers maintained unfailingly that the time of the end and the other mysteries of the Last Days were known only to God. Nevertheless, since biblical prophecy could be correlated with history, astrological insight into the future could not fail to have prophetic implications. In fact, astrological prophecy in the later sixteenth century became more than ever a kind of preaching. It contained indeed an element of fatalism about this world, but the sense that this old creation was in its final throes worked against despair, causing astrological writings to be filled with warnings and exhortations to repentance. The effort to discover manifestations of divine order was so intensely pursued because insight into that order revealed a prophetic message of great urgency.

Strictly speaking, astrology concerned the regular celestial motions and events, such as conjunctions, oppositions, and eclipses, and their effects on the natural realm on earth. It did not include comets, new stars, and other unusual events in the skies, which sixteenth-century observers tended to regard as portents. Again in a strict sense, portents were direct acts of God meant to warn the godless and perhaps to console believers. This was of course a concept sanctioned by Scripture, and it had full support from Luther. A portent was a sign and nothing more; if punishment or disaster followed, this too was a direct result of divine action.

Nevertheless, observers of the heavens had a natural interest in everything they saw in the realm above the earth, and the study of astrology broadly conceived had to take all heavenly changes and motions into account. Many of the popular astrological writings of the period showed a tendency to blur the distinction between astrology proper and a concern with portents, and this blurring helped to further the close association of astrological prophecies with theological expectations. Eclipses, for example, which sixteenth-century astronomers were learning to predict with some accuracy, were often discussed as signs of the Last Time, especially since the evidence suggested that they were occurring more and more frequently. Conversely, comets were sometimes analyzed not merely as divine signs, but as exercising natural influence as well. Thus, especially in popular writings, astrology became the study of celestial phenomena in general and their significance for mankind. God worked both directly and through secondary causes, governing and warning at the same time. Understood in this larger sense, astrology could more easily become a spiritual art, used to complement biblical apocalypticism.

Even when strictly conceived, the art had apocalyptic implications. Attention to them is clearly evident in the theoretical justifications for their work that Lutheran astrologers offered. For example, the highly respected Bohemian mathematician and astrologer Cyprian Leowitz, who had strong Lutheran leanings and connections and was an admirer of Melanchthon, argued that although the time of the Second Advent was hidden, no reasonable person could fail to recognize that the Creator had intended mankind to understand many future things. Such understanding could be gained from the created world. "For surely God has wished to place the changing of time before our eyes like a clock or an hourglass. Therefore no one of right understanding can despise this art [astrology], which from certain and provable causes and arguments derives universal conjectures and occasional conclusions."[25] Of course, the art was not to be used in any way that might reduce

God's honor or glory. He was in no way bound by his creatures, and he could end the world as easily under one sign as under another. But it was also true that he would not lightly unsettle the order he had established. Since that order had lasted from the beginning of the world, it would doubtless continue to the end. The best astrological conjectures agreed with the prophecies of Scripture: the eternal Kingdom was close at hand.

Open assertions of the prophetic value of astrology became more common and more strident as the century progressed. Lutheran practitioners offered spirited arguments in favor of the "astronomical art" as a good and Christian means of prediction that ought to lead to the betterment of lives by means of the warnings it afforded. It was a gift of God to mankind, by which people might and should learn to fear the Lord's wrath. Even the pagans had learned to regard heavenly signs as threatening portents.

In a *practica* for 1575 the pastor Georg Caesius made explicit what many others only implied: a knowledge of the art of *astronomia* was positively necessary for right understanding of Scripture. Many biblical passages could not be properly interpreted without such knowledge. Adam, Seth, Enoch, and the other early men had themselves been excellent mathematicians. Acts 7 showed that Moses was learned in the wisdom of the Egyptians; what further proof was needed that astrology was an excellent and legitimate tool for predicting the future? The whole art was not to be rejected on account of misuse, for by that reasoning it would be necessary to do away with all the arts, indeed with Holy Scripture itself. Luther was not of a contrary opinion, wrote Caesius, for he too had held that heavenly conjunctions and eclipses were signs of God's wrath and future punishment. Caesius issued other annual predictions that similarly praised astrology, efforts to reckon the age of the world, and the like.[26] In a forecast for 1581 he made note of Melanchthon's love for astrology, and referred to him as "vnser aller Praeceptor in doctrina Physica."[27] He also emphasized that he himself studied both astrology and theology. Several years later Caesius opposed the changes made in the old Roman calendar; they were unnecessary, since the end was so close.

Caesius's son, Georg Friederich, also a pastor-astrologer, continued in these assumptions. In his annual *prognosticon* for 1603, he wrote that "any man of understanding can learn from the stars, which God has printed and put in the heavens like letters in a book, what great doings and signs of wrath he sends to threaten us sinful men." This task was essential as the Last Day drew near. It was, Caesius emphasized, important to avoid the superstitious uses of astrology of which the Chaldeans and Egyptians had been guilty, but the proper and ancient art was not to be questioned.[28] Another popular writer, Adam Ursinus, pointed out that Adam and the first generations had been graced with high understanding of astronomy and the other natural arts, and had used them as steps to godly wisdom. This wisdom had been lost through human weakness, sin, and ungratefulness, the results of which were evident everywhere.[29]

Against this background one may understand the conception of astrology propounded by the well-known Lutheran Johann Arndt. In book 2 of his famous *Four Books on True Christianity*, Arndt discussed the place of astrology in the Christian view of the world.[30] He agreed with the enemies of the art that it was often badly mis-used. Any practice that led people away from belief to superstition and idolatry was to be opposed. The holy prophets had reviled the astrologers among the Jews, for God spoke in ways to which such natural methods were deaf. Similarly, under the New Testament, Christ himself was to be the great moving force among believers. But Arndt questioned whether this meant that celestial motions had no effect in human affairs. In terms that remind us of Melanch-thon's, he suggested that God worked through natural means: "For through the course of the heavens he orders time and the year, and has composed and established all our affairs by certain time and number."[31]

The Lord himself, moreover, had told of signs in the heavens, in the sun, moon, and stars. Thus the heavens were a great mirror, in which a wise man could learn of future happenings on earth. Arndt cited Scripture repeatedly as proof of this notion. Experience showed that eclipses, comets, and other such events portended great changes and troubles. Most human illness, too, was a result of as-tral influences, "as the true doctors know."[32] In fact a human being was the firmament writ small, a microcosm of the creation. The forces of the heavens were also the natural forces at work within the individual. The mistake of the Jewish astrologers was to try to discover in nature the part of God's work that was unresearchable. To do so was impossible, but it was not what the true astrologer was attempting in studying the creation. The true astrologer under-stood, moreover, that one who lived in faith was no longer a child of Saturn, Mars, or the Moon, but a child of God. The believer thereby escaped the fate of all natural things. All the powers of the firmament were subordinate to faith, and the believer ruled over nature. All things were possible to him. Here and elsewhere, Arndt emphasized that he wrote as an ardent and sincere upholder of the Augsburg Confession and the Formula of Concord.

Though Arndt recognized the supremacy of faith, it was more common to emphasize the positive alliance between faith and astrology properly pursued. Lorentz Eichstadt, for example, divided all prophecy into three types: supernatural, unnatural, and natural. The first came directly from the Holy Spirit, as had the prophecies of Daniel. Unnatural prophecies were those pursued by forbidden and demonic means: all witchcraft, necromancy, and black magic were of this sort. Natural prophecy, finally, was what was read from the book of nature, and it was a good and useful Christian art. Astrology, according to Eichstadt, was a branch of natural magic that observed and investigated the influence of the higher spheres upon the lower elements. It could not contradict spiritual prophecy, but rather complemented it. Indeed, by 1600 the notion that there was a perfect concordance between true astrology and biblical prophecy was widespread.[33]

Not many outright attacks on astrology appeared in Germany during this era, and the few that did appear were met among Lutherans either with general denunciation or with a deaf ear. Proponents of prediction from the stars adduced arguments from authority, from experience, from reason, from nature, and from Scripture to show that astrology was a fully Christian study and practice. In the early seventeenth century Melchior Schaerer, a pastor at Mentzingen, stoutly defended the art against recent attacks by Philipp Fesel. Schaerer quoted a work of Heinrich Bünting that undertook to explain Luther's attitude. The Reformer had struggled against a world of learning in which not only was theology perverted, but all the liberal arts were corrupted by falsehood and superstition. Thus he had had to attack some arts and sciences, such as astrology, much more sharply than he would have liked, since the times called for it. Now that theology had been purified and the arts set upon a new foundation, the two could flourish and complement one another. When one rightly considered Luther's judgment of astrology, added Schaerer, it was clear that he had rejected only the abuse of the art, not its proper use.[34]

The attacks of Fesel and others fanned the embers of the debate over astrology in Germany, but the defenders were a formidable majority. Kepler warned those who rightfully opposed astrological superstition "not to throw the baby out with the bath."[35] Many ardent defenders of the art, like the pastor Christopher Cnoll, a deacon at Sprottau, felt obliged to expound on its profound necessity in this last age of the world. For Cnoll, astrology in a broad sense meant more than the art of learning to predict natural events from heavenly phenomena; it also involved understanding the larger spiritual meaning of such phenomena. The latter sort of understanding was not systematic; it was based on the Word.

There were those, Cnoll explained, who insisted that eclipses and other common astronomical events were not the signs Christ had foretold, for when these latter, terrible signs occurred, the end would follow immediately. Cnoll agreed that natural occurrences were not signs of the end, but he argued that in fact strange, incomprehensible, and frightening things were now seen daily. The sun and the moon took strange shapes and sometimes multiplied. The weird new stars and giant comets were anything but usual. Fiery visions in the skies grew more common. As Luther had written, to list all such signs would fill many large books. Cnoll went on for many chapters detailing the meanings of various astrological events, both regular and irregular. It was beyond doubt that the stars had strong natural influence over events on earth. Not only did all the greatest philosophers and doctors believe so, but even simple people would look at anyone who denied this as a fool—as if one could possibly ignore the influence of the heavens in planting, in sailing, and so on. It was equally certain that "one must not exclude God from the workings of the stars."[36] He controlled these things as he did all others. He had initiated a regular order that he generally maintained, and from this order one could make reasonably certain predictions. To be sure, one had to avoid the excesses of which the ancient heathen astrologers were guilty. The Christian was not to fear the signs in themselves, for this was to attribute too much power to them. He was to pay attention to what God, who stood behind all heavenly signs and movements, was saying to man. Above all, one needed to heed the prophecies of Christ himself and to be ready for his return.

The distinctive Lutheran attitude toward astrology arose from the need to retain prophetic certainty in a time when the whole evangelical heritage seemed increasingly threatened. Luther's heirs sought comfort in the idea that every event, no matter how upsetting, was necessary for the completion of the divine plan. While Catholics emphasized freedom of the will, Protestants insisted that God controlled all of history at every moment, and that man was utterly helpless. But whereas Calvinism developed an aggressive creed and adopted prophecies that encouraged worldly confidence, Lutherans, increasingly on the defensive, tended to cultivate prophetic methods that assumed a fixed divine scheme and that assured believers of final triumph. Astrologers as well as preachers harped on the need for patience and stoic perseverance through the trials to come. Lutheran astrology implied, to be sure, a kind of fatalism, but fatalism with an important qualification. The call to repentance never ceased; the prediction of future evils was really a kind of preaching meant to bring souls to God.

THE PREACHING OF THE STARS

Since stargazers tried to establish consistent rules for their study, astrological research was tied very closely to the study of chronology. The astrologer was concerned to show how the movements of the heavens were correlated with historical patterns. Hence at least the more respectable forms of astrological prophecy overlapped with the kind of historical reckoning and speculation discussed in Chapter 3. Carion's *Chronica* used astrological evidence, and other chronologists like Leonard Krentzheim made careful note of celestial phenomena in their histories of the world. At the same time, astrologers trying to achieve consistency in their art drew heavily on world chronologies to show the larger correlations on which they sought to base their judgments. But even more clearly than the chronological studies, astrological writings from the Lutheran realm were filled with apocalyptic warnings and preaching. In principle, of course, the evidence of the heavens was there for anyone to see, but astrologers implicitly claimed a special training or understanding that made them preachers of prophetic truth.

Relatively scholarly writers, like Krentzheim, took pains to make their astrological reasoning as explicit as possible. Like a host of other investigators, Krentzheim came to see deep significance in a great celestial conjunction expected in 1584. All the planets would come together in the fiery trigon, the triangle defined by the "fiery" signs of Aries, Leo, and Sagittarius. According to the nearly unanimous opinion of the more sophisticated sixteenth-century stargazers, such an event had come to pass only six times in the history of the world, at regular intervals of about 795 years.[37] Similar conjunctions had occurred in the times of Enoch, Noah, Moses, Elijah, Christ, and Charlemagne; each time enormous changes had followed. In some reckonings the period was exact indeed: Johann Wolther figured that 794 years and 214 days separated each occurrence. The ancient notion of the cosmic week contributed to the conviction that the seventh great conjunction, that of 1584, would be the last of its kind, and would herald the end of the world. As God had created the world in six days and had rested on the seventh, the coming conjunction was sometimes referred to as the great Sabbath conjunction. According to some investigators, the same configuration had obtained when God created the world; if one counted this way the last would be the eighth. In either case the prophecy of Elias had to be reckoned with. If the world were to last long enough for yet another great conjunction in the fiery trigon, it would be well over six thousand years old. Since this prospect was highly doubtful, the conclusion was clear. Although Krentzheim and other observers repeatedly stressed that the time of the end was in the hands of God, they found it difficult to argue against such evidence. The lesson of the great conjunction, and the admonitions that invariably accompanied it, found their way into sermons and apocalyptic tracts of all sorts.[38]

More comprehensive efforts to strengthen astrological prophecy with the evidence of chronology also multiplied in the later sixteenth century. During a long career Cyprian Leowitz published many astrological works, among them his *Historical Account of the Great Planetary Conjunctions, Eclipses of the Sun, and Comets, and Their Effects in the Fourth Monarchy, with a Prognostication from 1564 Through the Following Twenty Years.*[39] Leowitz carefully detailed all the important signs since the beginning of the Roman monarchy, taking particular note of those that had preceded significant events—the birth of Christ, the outbreak of great wars. Leowitz's correlation of signs and events continued right down to the sixteenth century, through many pages. In the latest decades hardly a year passed without mention of some major heavenly sign and the events that followed, but it was hardly surprising that signs should multiply toward the end of the last monarchy. Even though this historical catalogue filled three quarters of the work, it was in large measure only background for the prognostication that followed.[40] Leowitz began with the "terrifying eclipse of the sun" observed in Cancer on June 20, 1563. Together with the planetary configurations at that time, the eclipse announced a gruesome series of events, including devastating storms and the demise of many rulers. Here and throughout his *Prognosticon*, Leowitz justified his predictions by referring to what had followed similar celestial patterns in the past. Eclipses in Cancer had preceded many of the greatest misfortunes in history. Leowitz expressed particular fears for France and Bohemia, but most of the signs were universal, and the astrologer left little doubt about his own opinion of their meaning. His writing often read like a sermon, as in his exhortation to "awake, oh kings and princes of both classes; appeal, cry, and sigh from the heart to God, and turn to him with humble, penitent, and contrite hearts. . . . For verily, verily, God who is righteous will severely afflict you and punish you all for these [your] sins."[41] Leowitz predicted a great war that would divide the rulers of the Roman kingdom into two camps: those who stood with the emperor and those who opposed him. Since Leowitz's work seems to have been composed at the request of the emperor,[42] the need for this sort of prediction, and for the expression of hope that a mighty prince might yet restore order and virtue, is easily understandable. But such hopes were hardly encouraged by the signs themselves, for according to these the twenty years ahead would see little comfort and much misery.

The last pages of the *Prognosticon* contained a forecast of the end of the world. Although few happy signs would appear in the years before 1584, in that year a conjunction of nearly all the planets in Aries, an eclipse of the sun in Taurus, a great comet, and many additional celestial portents would together signify an upset of the very greatest magnitude. Indeed, they would probably herald the Second Coming. Leowitz admitted that similar signs had occurred shortly before the birth of Christ, as they had in the time of Charlemagne, but the world had not ended then. The reason was that in the time of Charlemagne the world was not even five thousand years old, while a "holy prophecy" foretold that the world would stand for six thousand years. In 1584 the age of the world would be approaching that figure; since the days would be shortened for the sake of the elect, the end was surely at hand. It would be another eight hundred years before such signs appeared again, and that the world should last so long was "directly contrary to the prophecy."[43] This reasoning supported the central message of the *Prognosticon*: an exhortation to do penance and to turn to God while there was still time. For Leowitz, the attempt to improve the precision and dependability of astrological prediction and to rid it of superstition did not eliminate the prophetic implications of the art.

Few of the more popular *practica* and *prognostica* of the period contained much detailed astrological reasoning. They were content to describe some of the signs and the consequent outlook for the years to come. So earnest were many astrologers about their interpretations of celestial signs that their writings contained more preaching than anything else. Thus for instance Johann Hebenstreit, a physician at Erfurt, warned loudly and repeatedly of coming dangers. Among his productions was a *Prognosticon Historicvm vnd Physicvm* for 1566.[44] This work did try to show how certain signs had been consistently followed by troubles and plagues, but its emphasis lay heavily on the current signs, which made the outlook for the immediate future particularly gloomy. Above all, Hebenstreit's attention seems to have been on Rome and the papacy; the real terror would fall there, as the prophecies of Savonarola and others helped to show. But the entire Roman kingdom faced terrible tumult. Hebenstreit hinted at hopes that, after the downfall of the enemies of the Gospel, things might get better. Yet none of his hints was very clear. The work left the reader with a general sense of culminating eschatological struggle and sounded the cry for immediate repentance. A significant feature of this *Prognosticon* and others like it was that weighty, world-historical matters were juxtaposed with straightforward, informative predictions about the weather, prospects for health, and so on. The common reader to whom such works were addressed necessarily had more than the approaching end of the world on his mind; the closeness of the end, however, was one of the assumptions that governed daily life.

Similarly, the *Ivdicivm Astrologicvm* of Nicolaus Orphanus had all the characteristics of a sermon calling for repentance.[45] The *Ivdi-*

civm, published in 1573, covered the years from 1574 to 1578, about which Orphanus had very little hopeful to say. There were one or two cheerful prospects, such as an "amicable agreement and union concerning religion"—he must have had an inkling of the Formula of Concord. But generally wars, disease, and unrest would worsen and spread. In 1577 and 1578, the effects of several eclipses in earlier years would overlap with frightening results. Europe would be engulfed in conflict; the Turk would attack with devastating success; natural and unnatural disasters of all sorts would be everyday occurrences. The picture was, on the whole, bloodcurdling. Orphanus painted it again in even darker colors a few years later, in an updated version focusing on 1577 and 1578. Evil, suffering, death, and complete breakdown were coming. The only hope lay in turning immediately and fully to God, for "the time is near and hard by the door, and the golden age is over."[46]

For their predictions Orphanus and many of his fellow astrologers used planetary conjunctions, oppositions, and eclipses of the sun and moon as listed in the famous *Prutenic Tables* of Erasmus Reinhold, a professor at Wittenberg. These tables were based on the observations of Copernicus. Like many early upholders of Copernicus, Reinhold was convinced that the heavenly events he so carefully charted indicated future changes; indeed, he had spoken of "a great impending alteration of all empires."[47] Orphanus and dozens of popular astrologers like him were thus taking a natural step when they used the signs as a support for a strong call to repentance.

These few brief descriptions hardly scratch the surface of the genre of popular astrological works. The clearest characteristic of such writings was pessimism for the years ahead, a dwelling on the divine punishment that was inevitably coming. Sometimes they held out the hope that quick and sincere repentance would persuade God to withhold the worst of his wrath. Often, too, they implied that true believers would escape most or even all of the suffering. Yet almost always the prospect for years or decades to come was thoroughly bleak, and only the end of the time of trial could bring the Last Day or a final return to earthly peace. To the extent that such writings suggested the need for perseverance, they may have reflected a Stoic trend in late sixteenth-century attitudes. Indeed, Lutheran writers were fond of citing Seneca to help emphasize the need for patient suffering through earthly trials.

Usually, though, the Christian element was much stronger than the Stoic. There was more than a trace of sermonizing even in the everyday astrological calendars and almanacs. Such writers as Georg Henisch, a physician and teacher of mathematical sciences at Augsburg, produced scores of astrological almanacs and prophecies filled with speculations about the changes and dangers to come. Henisch was a man of broad learning and varied intellectual interests who seems to have been as convinced as his neighbors that the world was in its dotage.[48] Tobias Moller found in the heavens evidence that God stood ready to punish the sins of Germany above all. Nicolaus Winckler, whose speculations on future possibilities were discussed in chapter 3, was a regular writer of astrological *practica*, most of which painted a bleak picture of coming years and warned Christians to prepare.[49] And if astrologers often sounded like preachers, it was equally common for Lutheran pastors to practice astrology and to use the results in their calling. A large proportion of popular astrological writing was in fact from the hands of Lutheran clergymen. Georg Caesius was only one of many pastors who issued series of prophecies, all of which were in essence calls to repentance before the day of wrath. All the signs pointed to wrath and punishment and to the approach of the Last Day.[50]

Naturally, not all readers took the predictions of the astrologers seriously. A number of satirical imitations of typical astrological prophecies appeared during the first half of the sixteenth century; the genre grew larger and its tone more biting in the later decades. The most widely known satire was Johann Fischart's *Aller Practick Grossmutter* of 1572–74, but several others were almost as successful. Such works offered silly platitudes about things that might always be expected: there would be great darkness at midnight, it would be cold in the winter, a good many old people would die, and so on. The satires made fun of the terminology and calculations used in popular prophecies and held the pretensions of the writers up to ridicule.[51] But this kind of satire attests mostly to the popularity of what it attacked. Neither mocking humor nor serious attack could break the virtual spell cast by the astrologers. To refer to a writer as a great astronomer or mathematician was enough to give his words instant authority. Thus for example Caspar Goldwurm attributed several editions of general political prophecies that contained no explicit astrology at all to "the highly renowned astronomer . . . Antonius Torquatus," a name unfamiliar to most Germans.[52] Lutheran astrologers themselves sometimes criticized what they believed to be excesses in attempts at prediction. The prophecies of the Brandenburg physician Leonhardt Thurneisser, for example, drew fire from many astrologers for their too precise and imprudent political forecasting, and for abandoning "the old observations, precepts, and experience."[53] But most outright critics of the combination of astrological prediction with apocalyptic prophecy were Catholic stargazers who hoped to keep their art free from the taint of heresy and the threat of ridicule. Catholic astrologers like Johann Rasch tried to discredit the prophecies of Protestants in various ways. In 1584 Rasch issued a *Gegenpractic* that attacked the prophecies of imminent doom and revelation that had been appearing in rapidly growing numbers. The recent would-be prophets, he wrote, had made astrology look laughable with their absurd predictions. Neither the end of the world nor the fall of great ruling houses, such as that of Austria, was to be expected soon. Rasch pointed out that the prophecies current among Protestants often contradicted one another, and he ridiculed the common forecasts for 1588. Astrology, he argued, taught nothing at all about the time of the Last Day.[54] In a later work he made additional criticisms: the preacher-astrologers argued that punishment could be avoided through repentance, but philosophical practitioners of the art knew that the workings of the heavens had nothing to do with sin. Nevertheless, this Catholic astrologer was by no means averse to daring predictions so long as they served his own ends.[55]

Another Catholic critic, Johann Nas (under the pseudonym Jonas Philognysius), was equally contemptuous of the Lutheran tendency to theologize astrology. The "Leovitzisch" or "Hebenstreytisch" fashion was mere foolery, for in every year there was some evil and misfortune, just as there were eclipses and other such phenomena. Astrological prophecy had led to many kinds of heresy through the centuries; Luther himself had written against it, as had Johann Eck. But it was clear to what nonsense Luther's teachings had led. Now his heretical followers, armed with their mathematical follies, were seeing "if for a while longer they can dupe the people, proving from the constellations that Luther's doctrine is right and steady, and will last until the end of the world, which they say will come in 1588."[56]

The evangelical pastors were drunk with such things. Their day was over; new heretics (Calvinists) were taking over.

Lutheran sermons from the late sixteenth and early seventeenth centuries rarely show anything but complete agreement with the common astrological forecasts. It became fully routine for preachers to correlate the heavenly signs Christ foretold with recent natural phenomena. Around 1570 Simon Pauli of Rostock preached a sermon on Luke 21: 25–37 that made as explicit as possible the connections between the words of the Bible and contemporary heavenly appearances. Although recent eclipses had their causes in nature, they also signified great punishments and suffering. What could be more ominous than the two or three suns seen at once in 1566?[57] Lucas Pollio likewise carefully noted the heavenly signs and conjunctions in a sermon on the Last Day, drawing attention particularly to the seventh and last great conjunction in the fiery trigon, expected in 1584. In another explication of Luke 21, Martin Mirus divided the signs of the end into three types, of which those in the heavens formed one. More signs had been seen in the last thirty years than in the previous five hundred. It was time to prepare for the Judge, said Mirus. Such examples could easily be multiplied.[58]

Even Lutherans who avoided making the common claims for astrology knew how to take advantage of the popular interest in the art. Astrological terms could be used in titles, for instance, and throughout texts, so as to attract the reading public to a work that contained no real astrology at all, but only biblical teaching. Thus Jacob Andreae published sermons "set forth according to the course of the earthly planets, from which every simple Christian may see what sort of happiness or misery now awaits Germany."[59] Andreae began by referring to "a great, terrifying eclipse of the sun" that occurred in 1567, and the misery it portended. But predictions of this kind, he insisted, were never exact or certain, "for the art of our astrologers is in principle nothing other (at its best) than a diligent observation of the course of the heavens, and a comparison of this with earthly events," from which comparison certain general rules were derived. Such rules did have some practical uses, but they could not ensure accurate prediction of the future. The most famous mathematician in Germany, Andreae assured his readers, agreed with this point. Christians were therefore urged to pay attention to the real signs of the Last Day that Christ himself had foretold. These were the signs in human affairs, which constituted a practica that could not fail. To heed these warning signs required no art, for the "earthly planets" were human sins. Andreae clearly hoped to turn the popular obsession with portents and prediction to a better end. With the same end in view, Michael Eichler wrote a "Biblical Calendar" that sought to teach the lessons of the "most certain astronomy of the Holy Scripture." It was a selection of scriptural readings for every day in the year.[60]

In the early Reformation astrological terminology had occasionally been used metaphorically to preach the evangelical message,[61] and this practice continued in later decades as a means of capitalizing on the familiar astrological notions. Heinrich Winand wrote a poem, "The Imperial Diet of the Seven Heavenly Princes," in which the rulers of the firmament, the planets, complained about earthly corruption and discussed the punishment soon to come from God.[62] Caspar Stiller produced a *Geistliche Practica Astrologica* that used astrological forces and events to explain spiritual matters by analogy.[63] Thus Christ was the spiritual sun, whose eclipse had harmful effects on earth, and so on. These works, all by Lutheran pastors, showed a clear conviction of impending divine punishment; their less than literal use of astrological imagery did not at all imply a weakening expectation. Indeed, Lutherans who opposed astrology were likely to regard its growing popularity as another sign of universal degeneration. Moreover, for every preacher who used astrology allegorically, many more never missed a printed word from the better-known German astrologers.

The predictions of the astrologers were the most direct cause of the widespread belief that 1588 would see violent alterations in the world order, if not the end itself. The origins of the famous expectation for that year are obscure, but it was popularly expressed in a quatrain:

> So man wirt zelen achtzig acht
> Das ist das Jar, das ich betracht,
> Gehet dann die Welt nicht unter
> So geschieht doch sonst gross Wunder.

The many slight variations on the verse may attest to its strength in oral tradition.[64] In any case it is rarely seen in print before 1570. Most commonly it was attributed to the famous German astronomer Regiomontanus (d. 1476), who was thought to have composed it over a hundred years before 1570, but sometimes the honor was granted to another astronomer, such as Johann Stoeffler, or to a supposed astronomer of special prophetic ability, like Johann Hilten. Occasionally the words were traced to Melanchthon, and one preacher even held that Luther himself was fond of repeating them.[65]

Most observers thought that well before 1588 there would be major signs, impossible to ignore. Many stargazers focused on the great conjunction of 1584, arguing that the full force of this sign would not be felt until four years later. That conjunction was only a small piece of the astrological evidence pointing to enormous changes, troubles, and cosmic upheaval. Nicholaus Winckler offered a three-page list of signs that would occur between 1583 and 1588. Taken together, these implied dangers the like of which had not been seen for over a thousand years. Among the portents was a major eclipse of the sun in April, 1584, which suggested savage attacks on Christendom by its earthly enemies. Though preachers and theologians were generally more reserved about making precise forecasts, their apocalyptic preaching could only intensify the effect of such astrological pronouncements.

Among those deeply concerned with the dangers expected by 1588 was Nicolaus Weiss, a mathematician, who lectured his readers on the perils of ungratefulness to God. In one sense Weiss called for an almost Stoic perseverance; he cited Seneca to emphasize the risks of unthankfulness. At the same time, he stressed God's active involvement in human affairs. In a *Prognosticon astrologicum* for the years from 1572 to 1588, he announced that his purpose was to foretell the punishments that would certainly befall God's people unless they returned to obedience. Only if they turned back to God might the chastisements, which included persecution by the "Turkish dog" and other un-Christian peoples, be turned away. These predictions, supposedly astrological, were offered without any explanation of the reasoning behind them. Weiss updated the *Prognosticon* in 1578 and reissued it as a *Practica for Ten Years*.[66] The revised version emphasized even more strongly that astrological signs, especially the great conjunction to come in 1584, indicated the near fulfillment of all biblical prophecies. In Weiss's view hardly a bright spot remained before 1588; much of what was to come was too terrible to contemplate. He continued to publish similar predictions telling of future "misery and affliction in Germany" and encouraging repentance.[67]

Weiss was only one of the scores of astrologers and preachers who put 1588 at the center of prophetic attention. The common Lutheran expectations for that year drew further criticism and ridicule from Catholic astrologers. In 1587 Johann Rasch issued a practica for the following "great, wondrous leap year."[68] In this book he catalogued and sought to debunk a long series of prophecies predicting doom for 1588; naturally, almost all his targets were Lutherans. He tried to show how little was to be feared, since countless other Protestant prophecies of this sort had failed to come true.

Since expectations for 1588 became so strong and widely shared, one might expect that their disappointment discouraged prophetic interest and excitement. If anything, the opposite was true.[69] The 1590s certainly saw no lapse of predictions and prophecies for earthshaking change, and astrological assumptions were very far from losing their power over both learned and popular minds. To those concerned with the salvation of souls, the danger seemed to be that people might think the time of crisis was past, might lapse into yet ranker faithlessness and immorality. Such was the fear, for example, of Daniel Schaller, preacher at Stendal. Schaller wrote a *New Theological Prognosticon for 1589 and Following Years* to oppose the notion that people could now relax.[70] The tract was aimed at those who believed that "with the year '88 they are over the mountain of anguish." Contrary to all the hope and faith of believers, wrote Schaller, the Lord had provided for a rather peaceful, healthy, and fruitful year. But he had done so only because of his infinite patience and mercy. It was blind and foolish to assume that such earthly good fortune meant the Day of the Lord no longer threatened.

The peaceful passing of 1588 in Germany did not lead Schaller to doubt the value of reckonings and predictions in general. He began his work with praise for *studium chronologicum* and the contemplation of God's promises. The prophecies for 1588 had been made because eclipses and the whole aspect of the heavens had indicated future upheaval and terrible change. The signs had not been misinterpreted; rather God had suddenly and miraculously halted the threatening punishment. Now it was to be feared that the world would misinterpret God's act of mercy. Where, people would ask, were the evils the theologians and the astronomers had predicted? The simple truth, according to Schaller, was that they were still to come. He referred his readers to the "prognostications of the learned" if they wished to be thoroughly convinced that the celestial signs were all bad. To be sure, some of those who studied the stars had gone too far in claiming that their forecasts were absolutely certain. One had to recognize that everything was the work of God and that nothing could bind him. But it would still be a great mistake to scorn what the learned and experienced astronomers announced on the evidence of celestial configurations. The Bible itself instructed believers to heed the signs in the sun, moon, and stars. "Our faithful Eckhart" spoke of preachers in the heavens. In fact, wrote Schaller, if people would only open their eyes and take a good look around they would see that the predictions for 1588 were neither all wrong, nor in vain. In every land scarcity, disunity, upheaval, sickness, and destruction had the upper hand, and there was no hope for anything better.

Nevertheless, since astrological predictions sometimes failed, one had to look at Scripture for proof that the last hour of the world had arrived. The prophets and apostles referred to the time after Christ as the evening of the world; the Gospel was a supper after which the world had to go to bed. The world seemed in every respect like a weak, old body ready to collapse, and scriptural prophecy led one to expect nothing else. Further, the Bible showed that nothing good would precede the end. The Gospels, St. Paul, and Revelation all taught that utter misery would prevail before the Second Advent. "The ancient mathematician Moses" also foretold that God would send curses upon his people. Yet as if to spite all such prophecies and warnings, people were more confident than ever. The peace and security of the past year were only further signs that the Judgment was at hand, for it would come when it was least expected. The only way to continue in God's mercy was to lay away the old Adam and become new creatures in Christ. Thus, though the messages of biblical and astrological prophecy were much the same, only the Gospel offered hope. In his *Herald* of 1595, Schaller emphasized again that the signs in the heavens were multiplying as never before. Although eclipses, comets, and the like did have natural causes, the Scriptures warned explicitly that such phenomena would appear with great frequency before the end.

Numerous other popular writings had the same purpose as Schaller's work of 1589. A pamphlet of that year extended the popular quatrain to claim that the prophecy about 1588 had in fact been correct: "wonders" of all sorts had occurred throughout Christendom, and the end was still coming.[71] The preacher Thomas Hartmann recalled in 1605 how before 1588 many people had waited and watched carefully, piously regulating their lives. But now "many of these same people dream and imagine that from now on nothing but sheer golden years and times will follow until the end of the world, in which one will be able to walk as on roses, dancing, singing, and leaping. Thus too they begin to free themselves again, eating, drinking, carousing, wasting, building, dealing, doing business, as if now they lived only for such things, and the end of the world were still a long way off."[72] Such confidence was nothing but an epicurean dream. It was directly contrary not only to the Word and to Luther's teachings, but even to daily experience. Terrible divine punishments were coming; things had been getting worse and worse since 1588, and evil would soon reign everywhere. Other writings by both astrologers and pastors after 1588 indicate that apocalyptic expectation and faith in astrology were both perhaps stronger than ever before. The pastor Michael Babst, to take but one example, wrote a treatise to show that the influence of the seven planets was particularly dangerous in these last, corrupt times. There was nothing left but to throw oneself on the mercy of God.[73]

It would be wrong, however, to single out any one year, or even several key years, as all-important in astrological and apocalyptic expectation. In the numerous reckonings of the era, great significance could be found for almost any date. The year 1600 was regarded with particular attention, because of the appearance of that number in Revelation 14. The astrologers probably awaited 1604 with greater anticipation, for a major planetary conjunction was foreseen then. The new star of that year helped to ensure that the general expectation of some universal alteration continued to be high. If any one year after 1588 can be singled out as evoking similar expectations and calculations, especially among the astrologically minded, it was 1623. Attention to this date apparently began in the writings of Eustachius Poyssel on the new calendar, which appeared in a series of editions during the late 1580s and 1590s. By the second decade of the new century, Poyssel's predictions were

taken up by numerous astrological writers, who lent them new support. Expectations for 1623 were greatly intensified by the comet
of 1618 (to be discussed more fully further on), and by the political
crisis in the empire that began the Thirty Years' War. Many astrologers, like Isaac Habrecht of Strassburg, saw the comet of 1618 as a
sign referring to a major planetary conjunction foreseen for the
later year.[74]

Lorentz Eichstadt, a doctor of philosophy and medicine from
Pomerania, was among those who paid close attention to the conjunction of 1623, which would see Saturn and Jupiter together in
the fiery trigon. Proceeding mostly by induction from what had
followed similar conjunctions in the past, he left no doubt that
something very special, terrifying, and wonderful would occur soon
afterward. Biblical prophecy suggested that this would be the Last
Judgment. Eichstadt held out hope that even as the miseries of the
Last Time grew worse, a great final expansion of the Christian faith
might occur. But his own last message was, "Do penance; watch."[75]

To be sure, numerous astrological observers continued to look
beyond 1623. In 1622, for instance, a writer calling himself Valesius Minymus, "an especially sympathetic lover of the oppressed,
right-believing church," argued at length that prediction from the
stars was a good and useful art, and paid special attention to the
major heavenly conjunctions of the previous 50 years (since 1572,
when a highly portentous new star had appeared). Taken together,
all the conjunctions pointed to the final downfall of the papal Antichrist between 1623 and 1628. The Jews would be converted
thereafter, and a better time for the church and the world would
follow. An enormous host of prophetic authorities, as diverse as
Joachim, Nicholas of Cusa, Cunman Flinsbach, and Tycho Brahe,
could be cited to support this vision. The time of the end itself,
however, was hidden to all creatures, even to the angels.[76] Despite
such writings, though, 1623 was, as we will see, the last focus of
truly widespread astrological expectancy in Germany.[77]

THE FALLING SKY

As mentioned earlier, for many Lutherans astrology meant not
only the science of prediction from the regular heavenly movements, but the study of the heavens in general. During the later
sixteenth century, as wave after wave of popular astrological litera-

ture swept over Germany, attention turned increasingly to the skies for whatever prophetic insight could be gained. When one took into account not only the movements of stars and planets but the whole aspect of the heavens, it was certain that some unprecedented alteration was imminent. This certainty is most evident in the reaction of Lutheran observers to new stars, comets, and other unpredictable events. Luther had declared that such appearances were certainly signs of God's wrath. He added that the faithful could ignore them, since only the godless had anything to fear, but avid stargazers and earnest pastors were not about to let pass the opportunities opened by these signs. For many centuries such events had been interpreted as portents of danger, suffering, and evil; the idea went back at least as far as Ptolemy.[78] In Lutheran Germany, where evidence of a decline into corruption was proof of the nearness of deliverance, these new spectacles were seized upon and publicized with unprecedented avidity.

In tracts devoted to eschatological teaching, such phenomena received increasingly explicit discussion. One example is a popular work of 1562 by Johann Pfeffinger, a Wittenberg professor. Pfeffinger found little but decadence in the world as a whole, and he preached as strongly as any of his fellow Lutherans on the need for immediate repentance. But he gave particular importance to some special signs of the coming Judgment. Daily one could see in the heavens "eclipses of the sun and moon, various types of meteors, comets, and the like, red and blood-colored clouds, besides all sorts of unusual and terrifying shapes and visions."[79] A recent celestial sign Pfeffinger considered particularly worthy of note was a pattern of brilliant white beams in the sky, shining down to the horizon in all directions. This event and similar signs indicated the preaching of the Gospel in places where it had never before been heard. These signs also warned that the great majority of people continually ignored the teachings of the Bible. Unusual heavenly appearances were one more proof that mankind would soon suffer either the Last Day itself, or a horrible convulsion of all classes and the entire world order, as God vented his wrath over the sins of mankind. Pfeffinger claimed that he had presented only the simplest and most important interpretations. He strongly recommended that mathematicians and astronomers should continue to observe and interpret the signs in the heavens, taking care that their interpretations were conformable to faith and that they served the betterment of lives.

The major new stars appeared in 1572 and 1604, the most noteworthy comets in 1577, 1596, 1607, and 1618. There were several other novae and comets during our period; none failed to attract attention. In the history of science, the new stars in particular are granted central importance in the breakdown of Aristotelian cosmology; they showed that the heavens were not, in fact, unchanging and incorruptible. But even this shift in attitude, limited to a handful of learned astronomers, was not inconsistent with the idea that such phenomena were cosmic portents. Indeed, if the heavens were corrupt it was because the entire creation was about to break up. Changes in the firmament underlined the transience of the entire natural world, and thus, at least for a time, reinforced the belief that the end was near. Our interest here is not in the rise of new attitudes, but rather in the intensification of old ones on the meaning of such celestial appearances. The number of tracts published in response to them was enormous.

The writings issued by astrologers and pastors were often strikingly similar, for all shared interest in the details of the phenomena as well as in their meaning for a degenerate world. To be sure, serious professional astronomers were more interested than others in determining the precise natural characteristics of these objects, and certainly by 1618 there were a few who thought it unprofitable to speculate about the comet's supernatural significance. But it should not surprise us that, at least for a time, Tycho Brahe thought the star of 1572 was a creation of God that he now "exhibited to a world hastening to its end."[80] Brahe engaged in correspondence on the subject with the theologian David Chytraeus, who had written on both the new star of 1572 and the comet of 1577.[81] Michael Maestlin, Kepler's teacher at Tübingen, also declared the new star a divine creation that escaped all human understanding in these Last Times. Referring to the comet of 1577, he argued that generations of experience proved such signs were precursors of misfortune that should warn Christians to turn to God.[82]

Other professional stargazers were much more forceful in expounding the bad news these events announced. Countless astrological predictions foresaw pestilence, drought, famine, war, political breakdown, and anarchy from such portents. Preachers like Sigismund Schwabe were quick to take their cue. As the end of the world drew near, it was more important than ever to watch for these warning signs, wrote Schwabe, but they were ignored more and more callously even as they multiplied. This neglect of the obvious was another sign of the times, and all the more reason for sincere repentance.[83] In a tract on the 1577 comet, the theologian Christoph Irenaeus invoked Luther's grim predictions for Germany, and a thorough catalogue of the signs in the heavens and on earth left no doubt that now was the last chance for repentance.[84] Jacob Heerbrand published a short tract in verse to drive home to the common man the comet's message: sin would soon be punished and all creation brought to an end.[85] The same comet inspired other Lutheran preachers and astrologers to write analyses of such phenomena and their effects throughout history. Comets were always warnings, but this one, regarded in the harsh light of the times, had particular significance.[86]

Interest in such phenomena continued to grow as popular literature increasingly reported noteworthy celestial events. According to one report, there were more comets in 1585, 1593, and 1596, and another new star in 1602. Perhaps because numerous prophecies had looked to 1600 as a highly significant turning point, and because 1604 saw another major planetary conjunction, the surprising new star of September, 1604, evoked a host of especially frenzied apocalyptic interpretations.[87] Almost every astrologer, amateur or professional, issued some declaration on the apocalyptic significance of this amazing appearance. Christ's injunction to believers to hold their heads high and watch was taken even more seriously, if this was possible, than it had been half a century earlier. Among the tracts that seem to have circulated most widely was one by David Herlicius, which analyzed the new star not only as a sign but also to discover what its natural influence might be. It was likely to effect disaster; it signalled the coming end.[88] In 1607 yet another comet set off a further wave of warnings and interpretations.

Few observers as yet questioned the assumption that these events were harbingers of misfortune or of the Last Day. One astronomer who began to raise questions was Johann Kepler. In a tract on the new star of 1604, Kepler wrote sarcastically about the great commotion that would result at the printing shops as every pretender to learning rushed to get his interpretation into print.[89] But Kepler was still virtually alone in his nascent scepticism. He was soon engaged in debate on the matter by Helisaeus Roeslin, a mathemati-

cian and physician in the Palatinate. The two were good friends and
wrote with respect for one another, but their differences were significant.[90] Roeslin argued that Kepler, who was still a young man,
lacked experience in these matters. The sober truth was that "there
will be war and cries of war until the Last Day, and thus too there
will be comets and other terrible signs, of which Christ also said
that when we see them we should be warned and made to understand that our deliverance is near."[91] Roeslin offered a more original interpretation of new stars: comets were harbingers of disaster,
but the brilliant appearances of novae meant not bad but good
news. The good news was "not to be understood as outward good-
ness or as outward [earthly] peace, but as spiritual gifts, spiritual
peace, spiritual light, and as the truth that will penetrate the whole
world and will yet enlighten Jews, pagans, and Turks before the
Last Day, as Kepler also holds."[92] Thus the spreading good news
before the Last Day was indicated by the new stars, the mounting
terror and suffering by the comets. Here was Lutheran teaching in
a novel form, but the message was familiar: the seventh and last
angel of Revelation was about to sound the final blast of the
trumpet.

   Roeslin engaged in a detailed study of both sorts of portents,
with special attention to the comet of 1607. He cited Tycho Brahe,
Michael Maestlin, Kepler, and other well-known astronomers to
support his own argument that "the firmament or heavens are not
immutable, as Aristotle held, but mutable, or at least not entirely
immutable." This point was shown clearly enough by the remarkable phenomena of the past 40 years, since 1572. Indeed, to understand the significance of the comet of 1607, one had to go back
even farther, at least to the comet of 1556, which Roeslin claimed
to have seen as a youth. A survey of all the signs since then led him
to the conclusion that nothing of any significance ever happened in
the world that was not foretold by signs from God, "both in the
heavens and on earth, in the upper and lower worlds, in the great
world as well as the small, the microcosm of man, as daily experience shows."[93] Roeslin also undertook to defend the art of astrology against its most famous opponents, including Pico.

   The trends we have been following reached their climax with the
highly visible comet of 1618, which provoked an unprecedented
number of responses. David Herlicius began a relatively typical
work on the comet by declaring that two developments were im-

minent. One was the violent upsetting of all earthly order and the retreat of true worship to a few isolated places, "as Master Luther prophesied." The other was the Last Judgment, when God would put an end to this desperate world. Both the Word of God and natural conjectures made this prediction obvious. That there was no longer any good in the world was evident. That more misery was to come was certain. In the meantime, God filled the heavens and the earth with miraculous signs to console and to warn. The task of astronomers, no less than of preachers of God's Word, was to warn the fallen world about these signs, and for this reason Herlicius had paid heed to the works of "high masters" like Kepler, David Fabricius, and Peter Crüger.

Herlicius described the comet with care, and then considered various opinions on its nature. Aristotle had ascribed such things to purely physical causes, and some contemporary astronomers held a similar view. But other highly learned men, Brahe for one, insisted that the origin of comets was supernatural: they were direct works of God. Fabricius too had explained that such signs were created from nothing along with the rest of the world, and that their appearance announced extraordinary events. According to Herlicius this opinion was old and respected, and Johann Kepler was among its defenders. Still to be mentioned was the true, spiritual cause of comets, which was unquestionably the most important. This was human sin, which grew worse from day to day. Comets were indicators of the fiery wrath of God, warnings to repentance. Herlicius offered historical examples, going back as far as 1301, to show that comets in the sign of Scorpio were particularly ominous, often bringing bloody wars in their wake. Beyond dispute all comets meant bad news in both the natural and spiritual realms. Doctor Luther had warned of the coming divine wrath; now the latest news sheets told of more signs in every quarter. God in his great mercy was still working to convert recalcitrant souls, but there was not long to wait.[94]

We noted earlier that Eustachius Poyssel's expectations for 1623 gained great popularity, especially after the comet of 1618. Albert Hitfeld, who had so confidently predicted the end for September 8, 1613, on chronological evidence, was among the many popular writers who thought the comet pointed unquestionably to the coming of the Judgment in 1623.[95] Equally excited was Erasmus Schmidt, dean of the philosophical faculty at Wittenberg. Schmidt focused his attention on the planetary conjunction expected in 1623; he made explicit references to Poyssel's calculations based on the calendar change. He was unsure whether 1623 would bring the end of the world or a devastating blow to the enemies of the Gospel, particularly to the Roman Antichrist. Since the latter possibility was a real one in Schmidt's eyes, he held at least an implicit hope for a flowering of the true church before the end. The professor made it clear that the comet of 1618 was only the most recent in a series of celestial signs since 1572 that had announced great religious changes.[96]

The comets and new stars, then, may have aided the breakdown of the Aristotelian cosmos, but for those who shared the assumptions of Lutheran apocalypticism, this breakdown was also the most convincing evidence that the world was coming to an end. In fact, the soaring interest in proofs of celestial mutability was more and more accompanied by the conviction that the firmament was literally contracting: yet more evidence that the world was growing old and weak. This notion, like so many elements of Lutheran prophetic belief, was not new in late Reformation Germany, but it was argued with mounting frequency, and it now had virtually endless support in all the other signs of the times. Philipp Melanchthon gave the idea his stamp of approval in a sermon on Luke 21; the sun had sunk nearly ten thousand German miles closer to the earth since the time of Ptolemy.[97] Johann Garcaeus emphasized that the sun was not only closer; it had also become weaker. The sun was like a feeble old man, losing strength from day to day. All the powers of the heavens, wrote Daniel Schaller, prepared for their demise; the firmament had already descended 9,976 miles. The sun hung lower, showing that soon it would be replaced altogether by the Son of Righteousness as the whole edifice of nature collapsed. The point became a commonplace in Lutheran preaching on the signs of the end. In 1613 Valerius Herberger declared in a sermon that the firmament had by now contracted some 26,000 miles. But one did not need to be an astronomer to know that nature was preparing for some enormous change. Simple country folk could testify that nature was going haywire. The old house was indeed cracking up.[98]

Throughout the Reformation, assumptions of degeneration were expressed in countless reports of strange heavenly appearances. By the early seventeenth century, such phenomena far outnumbered natural wonders on earth. In fact, merely earthly wonders seem to have been forgotten nearly altogether. Perhaps they were not forgotten, but simply taken for granted as eyes turned heavenward for signs of coming cosmic change. Reports on multiple suns, for example the three suns seen at once at Strassburg in 1622, seem to have become especially common. Isaac Habrecht issued a work treating this strange phenomenon as one of many signs warning men to repent, and clergymen in Strassburg published their own admonitory reports.⁹⁹ In 1625 Lorentz Eichstadt wrote even more forcefully about the appearance of five suns at once near Stettin. So amazing a phenomenon warranted careful investigation. After giving a detailed account of what was seen and of various theories to explain it, Eichstadt concluded that four of the suns were merely images or reflections that could be explained by cloud formations and the like. The false suns probably originated two or three German miles above the earth, whereas the real sun was over a million miles away. Yet as the heathen philosophers understood, nothing ever happened to the sun that had no significance for men.

That this sign could have certain natural consequences was clear from past experience. Eichstadt cited Luther, Melanchthon, Peucer, Herlicius, and other authorities to make the point that it also had a supernatural meaning. The false suns meant false prophets, who perverted evangelical teaching. Also portended were terrible wars and a decline into anarchy, as Luther had predicted. All these things together made it certain that the Last Day was near. That would be the glorious Day of Resurrection, when the misery and suffering of this world would end forever and the wonderful eternal Kingdom would be realized.¹⁰⁰

We will see that by the opening of the Thirty Years' War the first serious questioning of the beliefs that nature was decaying, and that comets and other heavenly appearances were divine warning signs, had begun. By 1618, though, the tide had not yet turned; it was just cresting. The alliance between prophetic faith and celestial observation was just reaching its full potential.

MACROCOSM, MICROCOSM, AND RENEWAL

The fundamental assumption of astrology is that hidden natural influences tie the cosmos together as if it were an organism. For this reason astrology has been called the key and the basis to all magic.¹⁰¹ The Melanchthonian understanding of nature discussed earlier was one expression of an essentially magical world-picture, in which correspondences and influences among the various parts of creation were open to investigation. Most evangelical believers felt little need to balk at such an understanding. To be sure, human reason was weak and fallen. But as long as Lutherans acknowledged that God and the human soul were ultimately distinct from the realm of secondary causes, and that therefore the understanding of nature offered no hope for any fundamental alteration of the human condition, there was nothing to prevent the use of an art like astrology to assist in the contemplation of God's promises and the need for repentance.

Astrology had close links with the notion that man, the microcosm, was a reflection of the world as a whole, the macrocosm. This Renaissance idea of natural conformity was espoused even by such strictly orthodox theologians as Jacob Heerbrand.[102] For such thinkers God's creation could be investigated, admired, and to a certain extent understood, but the fate of the world and of every soul remained in God's hands. There was, however, only a rather vague boundary between this conception and the form of sixteenth-century nature mysticism found in such thinkers as Paracelsus. The late Reformation followers of this famous physician, very many of whom considered themselves good Lutherans, took the theory of man as microcosm a step further. If man reflected the larger world, and if that larger world was in fact the embodiment of God's plan, then man could find the key to universal secrets not only within nature but within his own being. Further, since nothing happened in the soul that was not reflected in God's universal construct, salvation could be seen not only as a gift of grace but as the result of the inner transformation of the individual through imaginative power.[103] This Paracelsian understanding, involving as it did the fuller integration of the human mind and soul into the cosmos, actually demanded inner transformation as a prerequisite to the renewal of the world. There was a more pronounced mystical element here than there was in the Melanchthonian conception of nature.

Even though in some respects these Paracelsian ideas were radically opposed to the principles of Lutheranism, they had a growing influence among Luther's heirs. Indeed, on the whole they probably had a warmer reception among Lutherans than anywhere else. A major reason for their popularity was that the Paracelsian view was also characterized by certain eschatological assumptions that complemented the pervasive Lutheran apocalypticism. The thought of Paracelsus was rife with eschatological themes and implications. He subscribed to a fully teleological cosmology that reflected his Christian understanding of time.[104] His conception of history and the eschaton had real similarities to the dominant conception among Lutheran thinkers. German Paracelsians generally felt that universal change was imminent. Paracelsian astrology, in keeping with the larger, magical world-view, strove to realize a universal transformation, or at least some return to peace and harmony, before the end of the world. Outwardly similar if more limited hopes were not foreign to Lutherans. The notion that the history of the world represented a single cosmic cycle implied for many Lutherans one last and sudden triumph of truth before the end; God's people would then be able to contemplate the universal plan in peace. Virtually all Lutherans held that the Last Times had begun and that the end of the world was near. Although the principles may have been different, Paracelsian astrology shared with Lutheranism belief in the imminent, sudden, and spiritually effected transformation of the world. In the tense, confused decades preceding the outbreak of the Thirty Years' War, conditions were right in Lutheran Germany for the adoption of any philosophical system that promised great, future change.[105]

The Paracelsian understanding of astrology influenced a late sixteenth-century work often attributed to the famous mystic and secret dissenter against official Lutheranism, Valentin Weigel. This is the tract *Astrology Theologized (Astrologia theologizata)*.[106] While its attribution to Weigel has been cast into strong doubt, it is safe to assume that the work originated in a Lutheran context. The tract gives an explicit description of the relationship between macrocosm and microcosm, and at the same time lays "great stress on the providential action of God throughout His created universe— both in the stellar realm and in man himself."[107] Here too the hope for universal transformation combined with the dedication to contemplation that typified Lutheran apocalyptic astrology.

To explore such themes more fully, we will focus on a writer who exemplifies still better the union of Lutheran prophetic consciousness with a striving for magical insight through astrology. It should be kept in mind that many others, to one degree or another, exhibited the same tendencies. Paul Nagel of Leipzig, reviled by the hardening theological establishment as a fanatical chiliast, a Rosicrucian, and a false prophet, directly equated the message of biblical prophecy to that of the heavens. His writings, which were extremely popular, showed the strong influence of Paracelsus and the eruption of theosophic mysticism in Germany. But they were also grounded squarely in the tradition of Lutheran apocalypticism and astrological prediction, apart from which the wild magical schemes and dreams of this period can hardly be understood.[108]

Nagel had not yet developed his elaborate prophetic insights when he published his treatise on the new star of 1604; he began his efforts at apocalyptic interpretation as a typically excited Lutheran observer.[109] The star was a sign of great punishment, of the Last Judgment, and of deliverance. Nagel warned readers of God's wrath at sin, and railed in typical Lutheran fashion against the pope, the Jesuits, and the epicureans who scorned God's Word. Nor had Nagel gone a great deal farther in his *Catoptromantia Physica* of 1610. Here he simply asserted the prophetic value of astrology, and stressed the idea of man the microcosm, referring directly to Paracelsus. At the same time, he strongly defended the absolute freedom of God, and pointed out the limits of astrological knowledge. He also emphasized that the true astrologer had to be extremely knowledgeable in many fields. He had to know mathematics and medicine and be thoroughly versed in the Scriptures, particularly in the Prophets and the Apocalypse. Nagel gave a further hint of the future direction of his thought when he mentioned that the most important constellation was an "apocalyptic constellation."[110]

The great comet of 1618 helped to crystallize Nagel's thoughts. By 1619 he had developed a comprehensive apocalyptic vision in which astrology played a central role, and during the brief period before his death (probably in 1621), a remarkable stream of intensely excited writings flowed from his pen. These tracts constitute a truly rich and impressive amalgam of traditional Lutheran eschatological imagery, chronological study, numerology, and astrological calculation.

Nagel believed that the right observation of nature held the same lessons that could be learned from Revelation. The book of nature and this prophetic book of Scripture were in a deep and important sense identical. But a proper reading required spiritual insight. The ordinary astronomer or astrologer could never hope to predict anything with certainty; his successes were merely by chance. It was no surprise, then, that the learned stargazers had failed to foresee recent events. The true astrologer, on the other hand, was aided by divine wisdom, and saw in the book of nature the true secrets of Revelation. Hence Nagel distinguished his own true astronomy, the "Astronomy of Grace," from the "heathen astronomy" (*astronomiam gentilem*), common since the time of the Babylonians, that had its famous latter-day representatives in men like Brahe, Kepler, Roeslin, and Herlicius. Their heathen astronomy was not founded on God's Word but on error and superstition.

The true Astronomy of Grace could be grasped by anyone who opened his eyes and looked with enlightened understanding. Whether one used the book of Revelation or the firmament, one needed only to read as a child of the new birth. In this way the holy patriarchs and many other wise men, including the oriental magi, Moses, Solomon, and Hermes, had read in the book of the heavens, even before Scripture was written and gathered together. Those who understood "apocalyptic astronomy" and its heavenly secrets were the saved. They would likewise be able to follow and take delight in Nagel's highly involved and lengthy reckonings on coming earthly disasters, the "third age" or golden time to follow, and the end of the world and Last Judgment, which according to some of his works would come in 1666.

Nagel's vaticinations were saturated with theosophical mysticism; once a man had seen with true spiritual vision, all the complex calculations and the parallels between the Apocalypse and the heavens would be perfectly clear to him. In a *Prognosticon Astrologo-Cabalisticum* for 1620, in which Nagel referred to himself as a "theologian and astronomer," he combined detailed analysis of astrological signs with heavy biblical preaching. The magical element was strongly in evidence. God had created the world as a sphere, and hence all creation moved in spheres or circles. As it had begun in perfection, so it must end in perfection, and therefore there had to be a "third age." The final age would be quite short, beginning around 1624 and lasting for only 42 years. Moreover, the final paradise had to be understood primarily as a paradise within people's hearts, as they became filled with the Holy Spirit.[111] In later works, Nagel's astrological apocalypticism developed and expanded into an all-encompassing vision, transcending historical considerations, which holds the interest of the modern reader if only because of its deep sincerity and childlike faith in man's spiritual gifts. Despite his astrology and his mysticism, however, Nagel did not ignore the role of Christ in salvation; his thought showed the direct influence of his Lutheran background and environment.

The new and more radical uses of astrology typified by Nagel, which appeared primarily in the early seventeenth century, were clearly heretical from the Lutheran point of view. But we are in a far better position to understand them after examining the Lutheran use of astrology through the sixteenth century, for there are certainly continuities to be seen here as well as breaks. Nagel shared with the other astrologers we have discussed not only his powerful sense of eschatological excitement, but also his desire to gain from the natural world a visual confirmation of religious prophecy. For both the heretic and the orthodox, such confirmation meant seeing with the eyes of faith, seeing more than natural images in the heavens. Nagel thus presents an extreme development of the common tendency to use astrology to confirm biblical prophecy. Although by about 1620 Nagel was in conscious reaction against the prevailing systematic astrology and the rise of an orthodox or "school" theology, in his own mind he was also carrying on what was best in Luther's teaching and in the quest for astrological insight that had developed among Luther's heirs. Luther himself had questioned the value of the "heathen art" as it was practiced by Lichtenberger and others; it was only natural, at a time when all eyes turned to the heavens, for Nagel to insist that another sort of astrology, one that required looking with the eyes of the spirit, was necessary.

By the time of Nagel's death, the use of astrology for apocalyptic investigation had reached its peak, and the most eager proponents of astrological prediction were thrown on the defensive, as orthodox theologians set about to exclude them from the realm of legitimate prophecy. Throughout the century following the Reformation, to be sure, some Lutherans had been enemies of all such prediction, especially of any attempt to use it for religious prophecy. For decades their voices were hardly heard, as evangelical believers sought more and more intently to support their spiritual hopes with visual evidence from the natural world. But by 1620 the use of astrology in apocalyptic speculation had begun to take on a different aspect. In writers like Nagel, the combination of astrology and theology was accompanied by outright heresy. Astrology was increasingly associated with a broad range of magical and occult beliefs that orthodox Lutherans regarded with rapidly growing suspicion.

Another chapter will examine the Lutheran reaction against the eschatological use of astrology. Here we must simply note that, though the art certainly continued to thrive in Germany throughout the seventeenth century and beyond, as a form of prophetic gnosis astrology had seen its greatest flowering in the decades before the Thirty Years' War.

5

✒ Paths to a Hidden Wisdom

Nihil enim est opertum quod non revela-
bitur, et occultum, quod non scietur
Matthew 10: 26

A SEEKER IN WITTENBERG

In 1588 the magician Giordano Bruno left Wittenberg after a visit of two years. This period, during which Bruno had taught at the university, was apparently one of extraordinary intensity and creativity in his mental world. From all indications it was one of the happiest and most productive times in the life of that seeker after universal wisdom.[1]

Part of the evidence for Bruno's enjoyment of Wittenberg is the farewell speech he delivered to the faculty. The speech is an extended panegyric to Minerva, or wisdom, as the object most worthy of human striving. "For God loves no one unless he clings to Wisdom," he proclaimed, citing Solomon. "It shines forth more gloriously than the sun and the stars, and compared with light it is far more important."[2] Though absolute wisdom was unattainable in this life, awareness of the voice of wisdom in the created world and in one's own spirit was the true goal of man. But Bruno did not limit his praise to wisdom itself; he eulogized the Germans as its present guardians and cultivators. The ancient inheritance that had first appeared among the Egyptians and the Assyrians had found its latest home in the land of Cusa, Copernicus, and Paracelsus, the land of the great Reformer himself.

It was inevitable that laudatory lines about Luther would appear in a valediction to the Wittenberg faculty. Yet Bruno's words suggest that he was interested in more than the fulfillment of a formal obligation. He saw Luther as the great liberator of the human mind and spirit from tyranny and superstition. Had the Reformer perhaps only begun this magnificent work? he asked rhetorically, hinting at enlightenments yet to come. Luther was in any case the great hero who had done more than any other to establish Germany as the dwelling-place of wisdom. Apparently the friendly reception and the encouragement he had received from the Lutherans had made a strong impression on Bruno, and he seems to have believed that Germany provided the most promising ground for a yet greater flowering of wisdom among men. His references to Germany reflect at least a genuine admiration for the atmosphere he had found there.[3]

How is it that such a profoundly unorthodox thinker could spend two years at the very center of Lutheran Germany, and later express nothing but admiration and gratitude? According to one interpretation, positive tolerance was not what allowed Bruno to remain peacefully at Wittenberg, but rather the unsettled and directionless heterodoxy that resulted from disunity among the advisers of the Saxon elector Christian I during that period. Once their disunity was resolved, Bruno was forced to leave.[4] This view hardly explains the genuine warmth, gratitude, and admiration Bruno expressed in his address. Before his stay in Wittenberg, he had been harshly critical of Germany and its people.[5] But here he enthusiastically adapted the idea of the *translatio imperii* to the progress of wisdom in the world: Germany now enjoyed the full blessings of the inheritance. Indeed if the Germans fully realized the power of their genius and applied it in higher studies, they could achieve a kind of divine status. These were not the opinions of one who had been more or less accidentally accommodated. If the professors at Wittenberg had reports of his lectures or were familiar with Bruno's work at all, they were certainly aware that he pursued a profoundly magical form of thinking. Yet the magician himself made it clear that he had found here far more polite attention and a much kinder reception than he had received at French and English universities.[6]

Not all German Protestants, let alone Catholics, were equally likely to indulge such a thinker. Earlier at Marburg, the Hessian university, the rector had denied Bruno permission to lecture; just why is not known. It is known that during his peaceful stay at Wittenberg, the theological faculty included conservative Lutherans like Georg Mylius and Polycarp Leyser, both of whom expressed a strong sense of apocalyptic struggle and impending judgment.

Bruno's anti-Roman propaganda, if nothing more, must have appealed to theologians of this brand. It is far from certain that he was forced to leave; he seems to have departed without animosity. Apparently the change in atmosphere resulting from a shakeup of the faculty was enough to provoke the flight of this restless spirit.[7] In any case, after a few months in Prague, Bruno enjoyed another comparatively peaceful stay at the Lutheran university of Helmstedt, until early 1590. It is therefore not enough to invoke a freakish state of political and ideological confusion to explain the attitude he expressed toward Luther and the Germans. We are still left with the fact that a man notorious in many parts of Europe for his heterodox speculations spent two happy and productive years at the hub of the Lutheran world.

Part of the explanation surely lies in the general spirit of toleration that Melanchthonian humanism had established in some Lutheran universities. The tight adherence to Aristotle common at Oxford, Geneva, and elsewhere had been at least partially loosened, and Protestant scholasticism had not yet hardened into a closed system of dialectics. Yet it would appear that more than mere tolerance was at work in Bruno's reception among the Lutherans; there is evidence to suggest wide-ranging curiosity, even adventurousness. We have seen elements of the same curiosity in our examinations of historical reckoning and astrological prophecy, and we have discovered that a central driving force behind such explorations was the conviction that the Last Times had arrived, that cosmic upheaval and judgment were imminent. This sense of apocalyptic excitement could push the search for intellectual understanding of divine truths still further. Indeed, the broadly-based Lutheran expectancy contributed strongly to the magical and occult strivings so characteristic of German thought in the decades around 1600. Bruno felt at home in Wittenberg at least partly because German Lutherans were themselves engaged in the search for universal, prophetic truth in the Last Times.

Like most other German universities at this time, Wittenberg subscribed quite fully to the revival of antiquity. Belief in the superiority of ancient wisdom was well-nigh universal. In one sense, the Renaissance notion of an ancient wisdom was at odds with the confessional understanding of truth held by devoted Lutherans. The ancient wisdom was so highly valued by Renaissance seekers partly because it was obscure, and it was obscure because it seemed a core of divine knowledge that lay behind and united all religious and philosophical doctrines. The underlying implication that all creeds should be tolerated could not have been more foreign to Lutheran confessionalism. Yet the notion of ancient wisdom could also be interpreted in a properly Lutheran sense. All that was necessary was to insist that a certain doctrinal insight was not merely another outer wrapping of the deeper truth, but an essential, or even the essential, piece of that truth. Precisely this view allowed partisans of Luther's Reformation to be, at the same time, avid pursuers of ancient or hidden knowledge.

In the search for further learning at the fount of ancient wisdom, the Renaissance magus, who claimed to be reviving and carrying on this very tradition, could become a highly admired figure.[8] Among those Lutherans for whom the search for prophetic insight was central, a magus like Bruno could represent the hope of prophetic clarity despite the profound unorthodoxy of his thought. Indeed, the more elusive the secrets of the Last Day became, the more attractive the bold speculations of the magi appeared. Martin Luther had recovered the essential core of saving knowledge, as Bruno acknowledged, but for many Lutherans the Reformer's own discoveries did not make further insight impossible. The pastor Christopher Cnoll was venting a common Lutheran sentiment when he wrote in 1616 that "*inventuris non obstant inventa*, [that is] although many things have been discovered, this does not prevent the discovery of yet more."[9] Such a hope was by no means monopolized by Philippists or crypto-Calvinists; in fact among those who favored ongoing humanist reform, the desire for revelations about sudden cosmic transformations to come was likely to be relatively subdued. It was rather among the Lutherans who identified most closely with the heritage of Luther himself that the need for continuing prophetic assurance was greatest.

To cite magical and occult strivings is to enter a virtually limitless field of inquiry. The phrase is meant only to supply a common denominator for a wide variety of intellectual pursuits that were spurred on by high expectancy during the later sixteenth and early seventeenth centuries. Besides astrology, which has already been discussed, a great many other paths were open to the magical pilgrim. All of these paths lay within a larger magical world-view characterized by a striving for gnosis, for saving knowledge, and thus ultimately religious in nature. Thus the term "magic" in this chapter does not primarily denote the effort to control occult forces for practical ends. Although this effort was central to popular magic, as well as to some major traditions passed down from the ancient world, in the Renaissance a more purely spiritual magic also gained ground. Spiritual magic was essentially a mystical orientation seeking universal comprehension. This magical quest for universal understanding did not develop solely from eschatological expectation. Renaissance magic as a search for gnosis had many sources: the revival of Platonism, the recovery of ancient texts, and others still. Many elements of German magical thought had originally been imported from Italy, where interest in this realm was stimulated largely by general enthusiasm for the ancients. But the magical striving for occult wisdom flourished in late Reformation Germany mainly because it was encouraged by the larger desire to understand the meaning of the present in a universal spiritual scheme.

Whether or not in the era around 1600 denizens of the Lutheran areas of the Empire were more deeply immersed in magical enterprises than were those of predominantly Catholic or Calvinist areas must remain an open question. R. J. W. Evans has admirably demonstrated how great a role the magical world-view played at the court of Rudolph II in Prague and in the general development of the Habsburg monarchy,[10] though in the intellectual world of Prague in particular the strong influence of Lutheran apocalypticism ought to be taken into account. It does seem likely, however, that in areas influenced by Lutheran expectancy, intellectual and contemplative forms of magic were less the prerogative of the educated nobility and more the common possession of burgher culture. A close look at the relationship between apocalyptic expectancy and various magical preoccupations in the Lutheran world can lend support to this suggestion.

What follows will focus first on the most universal tool of prophetic insight, numbers. We have already encountered a good deal of number-reckoning in chronology and astrology, but Lutherans often found a much more direct significance for numbers in their quest for understanding. It will also help to consider how various forms of nature mysticism and other magical trends may have been related to the general expectancy. A later section will explore more fully the notion of hidden knowledge in order to find out what the purveyors of occult truth in late Reformation Germany thought they were doing. Finally, we shall try to see how all these strivings for prophetic, saving knowledge were related to the hope for a new reformation, a spiritual transformation and triumph of wisdom, as that hope arose especially in the early years of the seventeenth century.

MICHAEL STIFEL'S STEPCHILDREN

Among the most ancient and potent tools that could be applied to prophetic interpretation was the art of reckoning with numbers. In Jewish apocalyptic literature numbers had already played an important though somewhat obscure role, and through the entire Christian era the knowledge of numbers was generally viewed as indispensable to full appreciation of prophetic mysteries. Augustine wrote that "many . . . numbers and patterns of numbers are placed by way of similitudes in the sacred books as secrets which are often closed to readers because of ignorance of numbers."[11] For premodern thinkers generally the importance of numbers was symbolic and qualitative as well as objective and quantitative. It was especially characteristic of the late medieval and early modern periods that the two uses merged: measurement was often at the same time a search for meaning.[12]

For Luther, as for many of his contemporaries, the primary and perhaps even sole application of numbers to prophecy lay in the realm of chronology. The figures in the Bible referred to prophetic eras, the discovery of which was a task that absorbed vast energies. But a deeper significance was often sought for numbers. They could appear in a Pythagorean light as elements in the structure of creation. All numbers, not just those found in the Bible, were reflections of the underlying universal truths. They were real, and visible things were not. God had ordered the world according to numerical measure; hence through a knowledge of number one could see directly into the workings of nature. Such a conception of numbers was central to the magical world-view, but it was by no means therefore taboo among Lutherans. In fact, mathematics could be an extremely useful tool for those who sought for prophetic certainty in a highly expectant society. No very clear separation could be made between the use of scriptural numbers to reckon prophetic eras and the interpretation of numbers as symbols of the structure of creation. The two uses could appear to be simply different emphases in a common effort to illuminate faith with understanding. It is hardly surprising, then, that through the magical use of number some strict and faithful spirits should have sought to discover hidden truths.

One such spirit was the pastor and mathematician Michael Stifel. Stifel was one of Luther's earliest supporters and a close friend of the Reformer. He had been an Augustinian monk at Esslingen in 1520 when he heard about Luther's differences with Rome. Struggling with his conscience, he finally became convinced by Revelation 13 that Pope Leo X had to be the beast of the Apocalypse, and he proved this to his own satisfaction by a reckoning of the number of the beast: leo x decimvs rendered 666 if the m was discounted as standing for *mysterium*. "From that time on," wrote Stifel, "I have always loved the Revelation of John, and held it to be a godly thing."[13]

Stifel's love for the Apocalypse seems to have continued for the rest of his life. His thought was dominated by images from the book, and he sought signs of the coming Last Day everywhere. Above all, he was fascinated with the numbers found in this and other prophetic books of the Bible. While active as a preacher, he began to reckon the exact day of the approaching end from Daniel and Revelation. He developed his own method of calculation, using Latin letters and a system of "pyramidal" numbers; these ideas will be discussed further on. Becoming more and more certain of his insights, he framed them in 22 "articles," and took these to Luther for comment. Luther warned him that nothing of the sort could be certain, and that his efforts could be misleading. For several years thereafter Stifel refrained from apocalyptic calculations, though his zeal for numbers and mathematics never flagged. He became active and effective in spreading the Reformation message, and Luther sent him as far as Austria for this purpose. During this time Stifel gained the admiration and friendship of Melanchthon, though in later years, during the theological disputes between Melanchthonians and their theological opponents, Stifel was a strong supporter of the latter camp.

The combination in his personality of apocalyptic excitement and mathematical talent made it almost inevitable that Stifel would again take up his biblical reckonings, and this he did. Inspired partly by Luther's preface of 1530 to the Book of Revelation, he produced in 1532 a work entitled *Rechenbüchlein Vom End Christi. Apocalypsis in Apocalypsim.*[14] Here he maintained that the time of the Last Day had indeed been hidden through the centuries. But according to Daniel 12: 9 this secret was to be revealed in the Last Time, which had now arrived. Applying his arithmetical methods to biblical prophecies, he reckoned that the end would definitely come in 1533. In the early months of that year he felt he could become more precise, setting not only the day but the very hour: eight o'clock in the morning on St. Luke's Day (October 19). So certain was he that he announced his discovery from the pulpit of his church at Lochau, a village near Wittenberg. A local uproar followed, as many of his hearers left off work and sold their belongings. Ignoring the repeated warnings of colleagues, Stifel gathered up an excited congregation and prayed earnestly with them right up to the very hour he had predicted for the final cataclysm. When the time passed and nothing happened, the people drove Stifel out of his church.[15] Only the defense of Luther himself saved him from outright condemnation by the commission that looked into the matter. Luther, though hurt by bitter words from Stifel, played down his friend's error: "Michael has had a bit of a temptation, but it will do him no harm; it will rather be of help to him, thank God."[16] Through the good offices of Melanchthon, Stifel was soon reassigned to another pastorate at nearby Holzdorf.

Despite a certain notoriety gained from this incident, Stifel became a respected mathematician. By 1541 he was teaching mathematics at Wittenberg. In 1544 he published his *magnum opus*, the *Arithmetica integra*. This was a Latin work of over three hundred folio pages, and it is Stifel's main claim to fame in the history of mathematics. In it he made some significant contributions to the development of logarithms and to early forms of algebra.[17] The work was quite strictly academic, with no application of numbers to contemporary events or biblical mysteries. It did deal at length, though, with "pyramidal numbers," on which his earlier apocalyptic computations had been based, and which he would use again for that purpose. The *Arithmetica* included a preface by Melanchthon, who had high praise for Stifel's mathematical studies. Stifel's *Deutsche Arithmetica* of 1545 likewise avoided controversial calculations; in this work he concerned himself with reckoning historical periods and dates in the church calendar.[18]

In the troubled times after Luther's death, Stifel was again drawn to the explication of biblical prophecies through numbers. He was still calculating in 1553, when he published *A Very Wonderful*

Word-Reckoning. Here, on the basis of a complex numerology and much obscure juggling of names and figures, he interpreted most of the major scriptural prophecies. Although he foretold no date explicitly for the Last Day, Stifel probably intended the diligent reader to be able to come to some conclusion on this point. The work discusses some interesting aspects of the reckoning art as Stifel conceived it. For example, every number had a substance, while its representation in figures consisted merely of "accidents" or a "disguise." Hence, one was ultimately able to investigate biblical mysteries no matter what language one employed. There were, however, reasons to use Latin rather than Greek or any other language. First, the secrets of the beast had been fulfilled in the Latin, not the Greek, church. Also, since they had been discovered from within that church, they had to be explained with Latin. Thirdly, reckonings in the Latin language would serve many more people than would reckonings in Greek. Lastly, Latin had a more consistent orthography than Greek. Probably the most important reason for Stifel's defense of reckoning in Latin was that he knew no Greek or Hebrew—though he failed to mention this.

Stifel prefaced his investigation of the mysteries of Daniel by explaining that the prophet himself had not fully understood the divine words addressed to him. The deepest truths were concealed in a secret language of number, in which they would eventually be revealed. Stifel engaged in a good deal of fairly standard chronological reckoning using the numbers of the book; for several dates he cited Luther's *Supputatio annorum mundi.* Thus the year in which the "worldly papacy" began, 852, plus the number of the beast, 666, rendered 1518, the year in which the papal tyranny was overthrown. Stifel's most important method involved the correlation of "pyramidal" numbers with 23 letters of the alphabet, omitting J, U, and W, which were variations of I and V. To each letter was assigned a value, so that if A is 1, B is 3, C is 6, D is 10, and so on in pyramidal fashion to Z, the value of which is thus 276. The sum of these numbers is 2300, which number was but a "preface" to the other important numbers of Daniel and Revelation. Stifel attributed especially great significance to the numbers 2300, 1290, 1260, 1335, and 666, all of which he found in those books. Through the use of these numbers and his special methods—the details of which remain obscure—Stifel claimed to have clarified the basic biblical mysteries. He denied that God was granting to the

church of the end-time knowledge that had been kept from the
early Christians; his work was simply a way of gaining clearer insights
into ancient Christian truths that had been recovered by Doctor
Luther.[19] Yet beyond the identification of the pope with the beast
and the revelation that the Last Times had arrived, his conclusions
are anything but clear to modern eyes.

Nonetheless we can gain some insight into the style of Stifel's
number-mysticism through his final diagram, which must have presented a formidable puzzle to many of his readers.

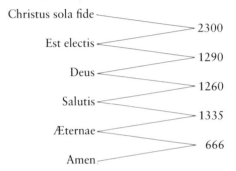

The attentive and enterprising student would first note the simple
Protestant message of the words on the left: "By faith alone, Christ
is for the elect the God of eternal salvation. Amen." Next, reckoning the numerical value of those words by the method outlined
above, he could obtain the following:

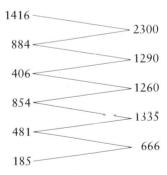

By adding each pair of numbers on the left (e.g. 1416 + 884, 884
+ 406, etc.) one would obtain the apocalyptic numbers on the
right. The major prophetic numbers of Scripture, then, had hidden
within them this message of joy and comfort to believers.

No doubt many other hidden numerical meanings could be discovered. Stifel was not about to be rebuked again for overstepping the limits of legitimate questioning. Yet if he now refrained from explicit predictions, it was not because he thought them impossible. He defended the calculations of his word-reckoning with an argument that would become more common later in the century. It is true, he wrote, that according to Scripture a thousand years is like a day in the eyes of the Lord, but nowhere do we read that this is the case for man. "When the Scripture deals with the last days of the world it speaks of them not as the time is for God, but rather as it is for us."[20] Otherwise, according to Stifel, Christ would have described the signs of the end in vain. In other words, believers were intended to learn about the time of Christ's return. Stifel offered several other arguments to show that the Last Day could not be allegorized away, and that it was an event about which one needed to learn.

It was no coincidence that the most notorious case of enthusiastic reckoning in Lutheranism involved a man who was as much a mathematician as he was a pastor. As did other branches of learning undergoing revival in the sixteenth century, "arithmetical art" appeared to be a tool that might finally unravel cosmic mysteries. It is not known where Stifel learned to reckon as he did with numbers and letters. The Jewish Cabala involved similar practices, and it is possible that Stifel learned about them through the works of Johann Reuchlin, specifically *De arte cabalistica*, or through those of Agrippa of Nettesheim. Agrippa in particular had propounded ideas that were thoroughly Pythagorean and cabalistic: numbers were the outward reflections of the spiritual elements that comprised the world. More definite influence can be attributed to an algebraic work by Christoff Rudolph, a professor of mathematics at Vienna, which had appeared in print as early as 1524 and which Stifel later reissued in revised form.[21] Rudolph's work was the first to introduce algebraic techniques in Germany, and it was the very first to use the symbols for addition ($+$), subtraction ($-$), and square and cube roots as they are used today. It was not merely a textbook, however; it was a work for the number-lover, offering even a puzzle involving reckoning with letters and numbers.[22]

Whatever his sources, Stifel was no charlatan and was not trying to delude anyone. He was convinced that everything happened according to number; therefore through numbers and their relations one could discover God's plans for the world. Since the Creator had supplied such wonderful arithmetical instruments with which the meaning of biblical prophecies could be investigated, he must have intended them to be used. Stifel's enthusiasm, however, became too much even for those otherwise favorable toward prophetic research: Andreas Osiander wrote that Stifel's delirious reckonings were enough to make him throw up.[23] This from one who only a few years later was himself reckoning the number of the beast and the time of the end through cabalistic and similar methods.

Stifel's profound interest in numbers and their significance was largely personal, but it also reflects the general expansion of interest in mathematics during the sixteenth century. The use of Arabic numerals became common in Europe only in the late fifteenth century, and the Reformation coincided with a rapid development of mathematics and related studies. Several prominent Lutherans, including Melanchthon, were among the enthusiastic advocates of mathematical learning. Melanchthon lectured on the importance of the subject, and in a preface to Stifel's highly respected *Arithmetica integra* he had high praise for the art of number-reckoning. It cultivated the understanding and accustomed one to take pleasure in truth and certainty.[24] Although Melanchthon himself was no mathematician, and although he did not approve the sort of numerological reckoning that had made Stifel notorious, he was nonetheless highly conscious of the significance of numbers. His general enthusiasm for mathematics helped spread the notion that numerology could give insight into universal mysteries. This notion could be, and often was, supported with scriptural passages like Wisdom 11: 20: "thou [God] hast ordered all things according to measure, number, and weight." The mind seeking the preordained limits of history and the inner workings of the divine plan gained welcome encouragement from such words.

Stifel's ill-fated effort at exact prediction was often held up among Lutherans as a warning. God had chosen not to reveal the time of the end, and for good reason. Yet the desire for certainty about the Last Times could not be simply ordered away. As long as sweeping changes were tensely awaited, there would be strong temptation to make calculations and forecasts. Lutheran piety was naturally drawn to illuminate the realm of expectation. Through Stifel's disgrace the results of overly avid curiosity had been condemned. Nevertheless, the impulse behind his reckoning was widespread, and could not be easily laid to rest. Moreover, no certain boundary separated pious conjecture from dangerous, unwarranted calculation.

Already by midcentury it was common for Lutherans to offer "cabalistic" support for the belief that the Reformation had begun the Last Times. Typical was Georg Walther's proof that St. Augustine must have foreseen the advent of Luther. He found the prophecy hidden in a line from the *Te Deum laudamus*: "Tibi cherubin & seraphin incessabili voce proclamant." Adding up the value of the Roman numerals, MCCCCLLVVIIIIIII, rendered 1517.[25] A growing number of investigators would follow Andreas Osiander in defending specific predictions using such methods as mere conjectures, not to be confused with faith, but nonetheless of great value to the faithful. Yet something more than conjecture was sought.

We can here consider only a small sampling of the encouragement given to number-reckoning. In 1567 Nicolas Selnecker published a long exegetical work on *The Prophet Daniel and the Revelation of John*.[26] Selnecker was a long-term student of Melanchthon who nevertheless refused, after his teacher's death in 1560, to join either the Philippists or their enemies. He was among the many of that era who saw in Germany little but ignorance, corruption, and scorn for the Gospel. The last hour of the world had arrived, he asserted, as Luther had often preached and written. The calculations and reckonings Selnecker presented were mostly historical, but his attitude would hardly have discouraged anyone who planned further research into prophetic mysteries. He considered various interpretations of the number of the beast, and cited Osiander on the topic. He referred with frank admiration to the methods of Stifel, explaining the idea of pyramidal numbers and their application to biblical prophecies. More than once he employed simple numerological techniques in his own exposition. He seems to have agreed with Stifel and many others that number-reckoning demonstrated exact agreement between the prophecies of Daniel and Revelation.

Selnecker admitted that one had to be cautious in such weighty matters. Although Stifel's style of calculation was "lovely and wonderful, and certainly not to be censured," it was "nevertheless somewhat difficult, and perhaps too high for the common man." Therefore Selnecker chose not to pursue it, but rather to "save it for another time and opportunity." As to what more might be indicated by such means, we will let that stand as well. Indeed, we cannot understand everything; that is how it reasonably ought to be. We have much to learn and experience from day to day, until we enter into the just and high school of the highest schoolmaster, Jesus Christ, who will reveal everything to us, and teach us what here we cannot know—and also perhaps should not know.[27]

What, on balance, was Selnecker saying? He seems to have expressed his own uncertainty as to the limits of human understanding. Just how much more remained to be said on prophetic matters? If such research was "too high for the common man," then what sort of adept was qualified to pursue it? Readers of this long and involved apocalyptic tract might well have concluded that, given tools like Stifel's, much indeed might be learned "from day to day."

"The common man," moreover, was very much interested in these high matters, and other writers catered to the popular appetite for such learning. Sigismund Schwabe seems to have done this in his *Arithmetica historica* of 1593. Schwabe, another sometime student of Melanchthon, was one of the most original and noteworthy preachers of the second half of the sixteenth century. He hoped to prepare souls for the coming Last Judgment by bridging the gap between biblical teaching and everyday experience. In the *Arithmetica* he avoided explicit apocalyptic reckoning, yet few other writings could have been as encouraging to that enterprise. For Schwabe, the importance of the "praiseworthy art of reckoning" was that through it one could learn to recognize "the divine creation and ordering of all things." Among its specific uses was the calculation of historical time. It could also be employed "to investigate many beautiful mysteries and secrets of Holy Scripture." Arithmetical art was an extremely practical tool as well. It could resolve all sorts of difficult everyday problems. Schwabe also warned against "misuse" of the reckoning art, but did not spell out what he meant.[28]

The *Arithmetica* deftly combined arithmetical instruction with biblical teaching. It illustrated various number operations and rules with scriptural examples. Thus the first operation, simple counting, was demonstrated by numbering the years from the Creation to the birth of Christ, 3,970. In another example Schwabe counted up the cost of Solomon's temple. The number seven had a particular significance. It appeared often in the Scriptures, and it applied to many mysteries and wonders in the natural world. Schwabe concluded that the number seven "signifies both time and eternity," for it equalled six plus one. Six was the number of "work days" the world would last, that is, six thousand years. This period was the time of struggle and travail on earth. Christ had promised that on the seventh day he would return to rule eternally.

Schwabe used hundreds of biblical stories and moral lessons to illustrate addition, subtraction, multiplication, division, geometrical progression, the rules of proportion, and so on. His approach aimed to promote both biblical and mathematical learning. At the same time, it surely helped to make popular the notion that numbers and calculation provided a potential key to every problem, and that proper reckoning could produce godly wisdom. In one section, Schwabe gave instructions for reckoning historical dates with numbers and letters: the methods of Stifel were now being disseminated as tools for everyman. Schwabe argued, for example, that the year Martin Luther began to preach and write for the true Gospel, 1516, was indicated in the words "Ecce florent valles cum evangelio." [29] This example was only the beginning of a long list, covering many historical events both great and small. Schwabe gave the impression that nothing could not be calculated in this way. He reckoned the number of miles travelled by the apostle Paul and interpreted the significance of this figure. His own birthdate was indicated in his Latinized name: SigisMunDus SueuUs (MDVVVVVII = 1527). Despite the apparent banality of these exercises, Schwabe was no naive enthusiast; his writing shows broad acquaintance with humanistic and theological learning. For him, the simplest number operations seem to have been demonstrations that God had supplied powerful methods of investigating the world.

With the help of writings like Schwabe's, mathematical reckoning was becoming one of the popular passions of the age, very often linked to the search for prophetic truth. The importance of numbers in prophecy was so great that Moses himself was commonly regarded as the original mathematical genius, whose insights were now being recovered. Astrologers almost always considered their own art inseparable from mathematical understanding. According to the Silesian pastor and astronomer Christopher Cnoll, the task of interpreting the signs of the times fell especially to theologians who had studied mathematics. Indeed, Cnoll admonished every Christian to take care that he did not show himself a heathen in these matters; some understanding of mathematical method was positively necessary.[30] Again, while numbers were most commonly employed in chronology, their value went far beyond that of a neutral or objective measure. The sense of numbers as universal qualities remained strong.

Once a reader of such works became convinced of the power of numerology and related methods, he was not likely to be satisfied until he had turned this power toward the largest questions. This desire underlay the unprecedented expansion of research into biblical and universal mysteries during the late sixteenth century. The more often believers used mathematics, astrology, and related tools to reveal truths in the world around them, the surer they became that great divine mysteries remained to be solved. Moreover, the use of such tools raised new questions that begged for further investigation. The ever more common application of such methods did not, of course, bring people any closer to the discovery of divine secrets. Instead, it made the problems of prophetic interpretation more and more complex, until to some seekers wisdom appeared obtainable only through special revelation, or through a long series of occult operations, or by some combination of the two.

A craving to understand the mysteries of numbers became the major characteristic of the search for occult prophetic wisdom at the end of the century. Increasingly the mystical value of numbers was emphasized. Works such as David Herlicius's *De mysteriis numerorum* served to fuel interest, but hardly helped to clear up the mysteries.[31] Methods such as Stifel's were more and more commonly applied by seekers after prophetic knowledge. Among the amazing tracts of Eustachius Poyssel, for example, is one entitled *The Key of David*, which adopted Stifel's system of reckoning and expanded it. Stifel's method had been to assign each Latin letter a number value, in pyramidal fashion, from A (1) to Z (276); Poyssel now discovered the "cabalistic" secret that if one also reversed the correlations, assigning 276 to A and 1 to Z, at least twice as many mysteries could be discovered. By using the two methods in a complementary way, he offered reckonings to show that virtually every current condition or event could be understood with this wonderful key, which he called the Cabala. Poyssel's prophetic attention was mostly on the recent effort to drive Luther's teaching out of Saxony—in other words the attempt of Elector Christian I to introduce a second reformation along Calvinist lines. Poyssel showed in detail with his method that this terrible turn of events was a neces-

sary part of the divine scheme, as was the return to Lutheran truth
by 1592. Precise number-reckoning also showed that the accession
as count palatine of the young Frederick IV, who appeared to be
leading a Lutheran revival in that state as well, heralded great things
in these Last Times.[32]

The mystical value of numbers meant that the measurement of
time and the measurement of space were full of analogies and parallels. In another tract Poyssel analyzed in great detail the dimensions of the New Jerusalem as described in Revelation 21 and 22.
These dimensions were also the prophetic dimensions of history,
and they indicated that the Second Advent would come in 1623.[33]
The same general principles were applied on a much more grandi-
ose scale in Simon Studion's enormous prophetic tract "Naometria," completed in 1604.[34] Studion was a learned schoolmaster in
Württemberg who had studied mathematics at Tübingen. As early
as 1594 it was rumored that he had penetrated some of the most
important divine secrets, had seen their meaning for his age, and
was at work on a book that would make these discoveries known.
Although the "Naometria" was never published, it seems to have
circulated widely in manuscript form. The "new measurement" of
the title was a measurement of the entire cosmos; the dimensions
of Solomon's temple and many other numbers found in Scripture
revealed the outlines of universal history. The "Naometria" shows
the influence of Poyssel: Studion researched the mysteries with "the
key of David" and took over many of Poyssel's reckonings, including the dating of the Second Advent in 1623.

Similar assumptions about numbers and measurement were common in the Lutheran world of thought. They were expressed with
deep biblical learning by the Tübingen doctor of theology Matthias
Hafenreffer in his enormous *Templum Ezechielis*. Hafenreffer understood the temple described in the last nine chapters of Ezekiel as
a complete prophetic image of the New Testament church; its mea-
surements were a summary of prophetic truth.[35] In the 1620s Paul
Nagel made the magical correspondence of temporal and spatial
measurement as explicit as it would ever get: the circumference of
the earth was equal to the number of years the earth would stand,
and the figure for both, 5614, was the sum of the key prophetic
numbers of the Bible.[36]

The idea that numbers could lead to the ultimate gnosis lay at the
heart of the magical apocalypticism of the early seventeenth cen-

tury. As an influential apocalyptic tract of 1612 by Johann Dobricius stated, "numbers are godly, secret things, godly characters— the entire Holy Scripture uses them; thus everything else in nature is set in its proportion and measure through the will of the Almighty who creates it."[37] What lent this inherited medieval assumption of the divinity of numbers such power in late Reformation Germany was the combination in many minds of intense expectation and Renaissance learning.

The mathematician Johann Faulhaber of Ulm combined real mathematical talent with eschatological fervor to a degree rarely matched, even in his own age. Faulhaber closely resembled Stifel in his undeniable ability, sincerity, and enthusiasm for seeking out the prophetic truths of Scripture. But he had a larger following in his own time than Stifel had enjoyed decades before. Students came from all over Germany and Switzerland to his school for instruction in arithmetical arts. He was a friend of Michael Maestlin and other respected academics.[38] Between 1604 and about 1632 Faulhaber published at least 25 mathematical writings, most of which dealt in one way or another with the eschatological mysteries of the Bible. Adopting the usual position of those who would discover these mysteries, Faulhaber held that the Almighty had promised to reveal profound secrets in the Last Times. Yet not just anyone might learn these things. God revealed his wisdom only through the gift of grace to the believer. He had granted this gift abundantly to Faulhaber, who had been able to see many wonderful arts and secrets in the Bible. These discoveries had depended as well on deep study in arithmetical science. Certain truths, it seems, were granted directly to the sincere believer. But understanding the deeper ones required gifts of mathematical ability as well as of grace. A passage from Esdras helped to make this point. The Lord tells Ezra, "some things you shall make public, and some you shall deliver in secret to the wise" (2 Esdras 14: 26). The notion that there was a select number of the wise or specially gifted, through whom prophetic secrets might be revealed, was gaining considerable currency by the first decades of the seventeenth century.

The gifts of faith, wisdom, and understanding were often virtually indistinguishable in Faulhaber's writings. Although the ancient revelatory mediums of Urim and Thummim were lost,[39] he told readers, so that no mortal man could understand divine operations without special revelation, "nevertheless it has pleased the Holy

Spirit to conceal several magical arts [*Wunderkünsten*] in the biblical numbers, which he gives to his own to reveal and recognize according to his measure, for comfort in the Last Times."[40] Was the understanding of these arts open to the simple believer, or only to the believing adept? It is not easy to decide what Faulhaber meant here. Faulhaber himself had no doubt, at any rate, that he had discovered "cabalistic, mathematical, and philosophical arts" that had lain hidden for many ages. To him who received understanding of these, "a door will be opened through which he will be unfailingly introduced into the arcana and secrets of godly wisdom, and will learn to understand and observe great hidden things."[41] Faulhaber was certain no true believer would scorn what he had to say.

The believer was in a difficult position if he was not accomplished in algebra and in mathematics generally, for Faulhaber lived in a world of numbers. All nature was proportioned by number through the will of God. Were there not numerical references throughout the Bible? And did not Revelation say of 666, "Here is wisdom"? Faulhaber took over Stifel's "pyramidal numbers" and used them to discover a deep significance in several biblical numbers. In their purely mathematical aspect, his demonstrations were no doubt clear to at least some readers. But what he was getting at in most of his complex operations is not easy to grasp. Faulhaber preferred to make his readers work, to discover for themselves the secrets he had found. Thus he could fill pages with questions that demanded algebraic calculation; whoever worked through them with assiduity and understanding deserved the pearl of wisdom that Faulhaber had helped him find. That wisdom might concern the character of Gog and Magog, or the time left to the world before its end. The *New Cabalistic Art and Magical Reckoning on Gog and Magog*, for example, was nothing but a long and extremely involved puzzle, the solution of which was supposed to be a twelve-word sentence in German that would explain the scriptural prophecies about these anti-Christian forces.[42] The author of this little exercise in discovery was careful to emphasize that human reason was in no way sufficient for searching out prophetic truth. The Holy Spirit had to inspire one; if one was driven by mere curiosity, the effort would be in vain. Faulhaber hoped only to share wisdom and consolation with the worthy, with those who understood, in the Last Days of the world.

Faulhaber maintained that his mathematical and cabalistic methods had led him to predict the great comet of 1618. Once the comet had appeared, he issued a short work full of complex, apocalyptic, "cabalistic" calculations to explain its meaning.[43] It seems doubtful that anyone actually learned anything from his equations and symbols, but one message was clear: the comet announced divine miracles and pointed to the return of Christ. There was perhaps still time for the godless to repent and turn to him. As for those who loved God, perhaps they would be encouraged to reach for yet higher learning; such aspiration was after all expected in these Last Times.[44]

Faulhaber was only one of many investigators who employed magical number-reckoning in the full blossoming of prophetic speculation after 1600.[45] Stifel's assumptions about the value of numbers were now growing widespread; so was confidence that the deepest secrets of the Bible might finally be understood. Stifel's inheritance became an orgy of magical, cabalistic, and apocalyptic speculation in such writings as those of Johann Hörner, "burgher of Heilbronn." Hörner had read the works of Stifel, and gave him credit for "the origin of the Latin Cabala." But Hörner's own work, published in 1619, was infinitely more wide-ranging; he was heir to a century of apocalyptic speculation, and he was convinced that now the deepest truths could be fully uncovered through mathematical analysis of Scripture. The revelation was in any case bulky: the second book of Hörner's work alone contained some 285 pages of incredibly obscure reckoning. But there is no doubt that he was fully in the Lutheran tradition. He engaged in the typical apotheosis of Luther, intense polemic against the Roman Antichrist, and the like, and presented theological arguments that showed a genuine understanding of Reformation teachings. For Hörner as for countless others at that time, the true teachings of the Gospel and the true art of number-reckoning were one.[46]

Paul Nagel, whose works were heavily mathematical as well as astrological, echoed Hörner in explaining that Stifel and others before him had been unable to solve such mysteries as the time of the Last Day because the proper tools had not yet been available. Now that the time was at hand, the meaning of the "mystical numbers" was no longer concealed. Thus hundreds of seekers set pen to paper in order to contribute to the great work. Every created thing had its appointed beginning and end; the task was to discover the great events that would necessarily happen according to the heavenly clockwork. But the task implied no merely mechanistic sensibility, for the measure of the heavens and the earth was also a measure of truth, a revelation of the living Word of God.

APOCALYPSE, NATURE MYSTICISM, AND MAGIC

Numerology was only one of the methods that seemed to offer the promise of prophetic discovery in an increasingly confusing world. The broad search for hidden, saving knowledge was inspired by a deep desire to discover universal meaning in the present. The present, in this context, must be understood to mean not only current events, but more generally and more literally what is present to the senses, or what is perceived. The search for eschatological meaning in the present thus included the investigation of nature, as it had in the thought of the medieval magus Roger Bacon.

The notion that the Reformation in general and Lutheranism in particular were hostile to natural science is—to be brief and blunt—mistaken. Luther and the tradition that followed him saw Christ himself as "substantially present everywhere, in and through all creatures, in all their parts and places."[47] Although Luther's view did not necessarily imply anything about the metaphysics of divine action in the world,[48] it was the heart of a positive attitude toward the investigation of nature. Sixteenth-century Lutherans often exhibited unusual curiosity about the workings of the created world. Luther could say that "we are now at the dawn of a new life, for we are beginning to regain a knowledge of the creation, a knowledge we had forfeited by the fall of Adam. . . . In God's creation we recognize the power of his Word." Luther attributed this new appreciation of nature directly to the evangelical understanding of the Word; he chided Erasmus as one who looked at the created world "as a cow stares at a new gate."[49] We should not forget that Lutherans subsidized, printed, and published the great work of Copernicus, *De revolutionibus*, in 1543, or that Brahe and Kepler were Lutherans. Nor should we overlook the enormous influence of Melanchthon in the history of science. Lutheranism, in short, was very far from opposing the investigation of nature.[50]

In the sixteenth century such investigation had no common method or procedure; indeed after 1550 the best minds of Europe debated the philosophical problem of method with great intensity.

Meanwhile the new dignity granted to practical affairs, along with the growing masses of printed literature dealing with the entire range of human experience, caused the problem of making sense out of the variety of nature to become ever more acute. For people still very much under the influence of medieval conceptions of order, "the result was a heightened awareness of the antithesis between the *observation* of appearance and the *intuition* of an underlying reality."[51] The Lutheran eschatological outlook sought to resolve this antithesis by conceiving the underlying reality as a divine plan for the world. The perception of burgeoning worldly corruption inspired efforts to construe every event in a cosmic sense. The conviction that the end was approaching was probably the simplest form of belief in universal order; at the very least it required that God was preparing to settle all accounts. But it usually implied more than this, for the eyes of faith saw the hand of the Lord everywhere. The divine plan could be glimpsed through biblical prophecy, but the truths of prophecy were verified in the observation of both man and nature. Lutheran teaching always safeguarded God's complete freedom, but it also emphasized that his Word included promises that would be kept.

The Lutheran expectation emphasized the present conflicts and contradictions in the world, and dwelt on them at times with a nearly perverse pleasure, since they pointed to the utter necessity of imminent resolution. Among Lutherans, therefore, the desire for resolution, for an escape from the tension of waiting, was particularly strong. A way out was precisely what magic and the occult offered. Hidden wisdom and hidden answers would set things right for the believer. Indeed among believers who were profoundly conscious of a desperate struggle between good and evil, the search for this hidden wisdom assumed a special intensity and an eschatological character of its own. On the other hand, the magical seeker knew that he could never simply take flight from the repugnant world of appearances His role was primarily to alter sensibilities through the communication of superior understanding. He was, indeed, a kind of preacher of prophetic truth.[52]

The common denominator of the apocalyptic and magical worldviews was the assumption of underlying universal purpose. For the magical outlook as well as for apocalyptic faith, this purpose was God's. As in the study of history and astrology, the ultimate justification for inquiry into nature was that it helped to show this purpose, and therefore to glorify the works of God. For this reason the magician was generally at great pains to show that he was concerned with spiritual, not demonic magic. The distinction was extremely important, because it confirmed that the magician was on the side of faith.

Insofar as the magician was attempting to understand and control the forces of the natural world, he clearly sought a kind of power. This feature of his enterprise is easily misunderstood by the modern observer. The larger magical striving was essentially contemplative and speculative; the power it envisioned came from deep faith and the gift of insight, and carried with it a profound spiritual responsibility. In Lutheran Germany, where eschatological hope emphasized faith, intuitive insight, and careful observation, magic tended to have particularly strong spiritual overtones. It also took on the tension and the future-directed hope characteristic of Lutheranism. The power to which it looked was above all the power for an inner transformation that would be reflected in the phenomenal world. The intuitive approach to knowledge that supported the Lutheran interpretation of prophecy was thus twisted to encourage more radical strivings after prophetic truth.

Once again Philipp Melanchthon exemplifies the confluence of intellectual currents among Lutherans of the late Reformation. It might seem that Melanchthon's intellectualizing tendencies should have been at war with the intuitive and even antirational emphasis of the magical striving. Such a conflict did arise between the strictest Aristotelians of the universities and the popular purveyors of occult wisdom, but in the later sixteenth century there were no clearly formed camps around these positions. In several ways, in fact, Melanchthonian and magical assumptions tended to complement one another.[53] Melanchthon encouraged the effort to find philosophical support for attitudes that were fundamentally intuitive. His teaching on secondary causes, for example, was used in the service of theological convictions about the inevitable course of the future. Similarly, his whole approach toward natural investigation helped to spur speculations about the underlying spiritual dimension of visible reality. As already noted, the great challenge of the age was to understand the increasingly bewildering variety of appearances in terms of prevailing assumptions. Melanchthon's influence on answers to this challenge was not primarily in the direction of a dry, scholastic debate about words; rather his philosophical approach opened the way to all kinds of theorizing about the natural world. What remained the driving force behind such theorizing was the search for prophetic truth, and the sense that the present was a critical time in the history of the world and of spiritual revelation. Job Fincel, as we noted earlier, saw signs of God's wrath everywhere in nature. He thought it possible to distinguish between such divine portents and the deceptive effects of the devil. In other words, there was every reason for a careful study of nature in these Last Times. Andreas Musculus supported his search for signs of the end with the phrase *Deus et natura nihil faciunt frustra*: "God and nature do nothing in vain."[54] If every natural event was directed to an end, would not insight into nature advance an appreciation of the divine plan? Such a belief could easily lead toward a pansophic striving. Doctrinally, Lutheranism maintained a sharp division between creator and created world. Nonetheless, in the late sixteenth century, it was a fairly short and easy step from Melanchthon's philosophical position that God is in nature as creator and maintainer, to the neo-Platonic conception of nature as the embodiment of a spiritual principle.

Not all magic rested on explicit neo-Platonic foundations, but virtually all was associated with some form of mysticism. In other words, magic assumed that knowledge could be gained by direct insight into divine reality. Hence the focus of freedom and transforming power tended to shift away from God to the human mind. This shift of focus above all made magical practitioners like Paracelsus, as well as contemplatives like Valentin Weigel (d. 1588) and Jacob Boehme, heretical in the eyes of orthodoxy.[55] But we should neither overestimate how far sixteenth-century magic rejected Christian doctrines, nor underestimate how far genuine Lutheran piety could bend in the direction of mystical speculation.

Indeed, a revival of mysticism among Lutherans paralleled and complemented the flood of magical speculation in late Reformation Germany. In abstract, theological terms, mysticism and eschatological faith seek very different sorts of fulfillment: mysticism, insofar as it gains its goal in the here and now, has no need of future-directed longing.[56] But Christian mysticism has generally retained, along with the belief in a timeless fulfillment, the hope of a future consummation. The Protestant mysticism of the sixteenth century certainly retained that vision. Luther himself was deeply influenced by medieval German mysticism, but he combined its truths with a powerful eschatological hope. The same was true for the Lutheran thinkers who participated in the revival of medieval mysticism toward the end of the century. The best representative of this group is Johann Arndt (d. 1621), though many more could easily be cited.[57] Filled with a deep and sincere mystical piety, Arndt was at the same time convinced of the decisive eschatological role of his own age. In his sermons and exegetical works he painted a deeply gloomy picture of conditions in his day. Like virtually all of his contemporaries, he sought to understand God's plan. "The Revelation of John," he wrote, "is much concerned with time and number; and therein are the greatest secrets."[58]

Lutheran mysticism had many points of contact with the magical world-view. The fourth book of Arndt's *True Christianity*, for example, entitled *Liber naturae*, read like a textbook of magical principles for the investigation of nature. It was divided into sections on the macrocosm and the microcosm, and the influence of Paracelsus was evident throughout. "Creatures are the hands and messengers of God, which should lead us to him," ran an epigram.[59] The early works of Johann Valentin Andreae similarly show a very close connection between religious speculation and investigation of nature. Andreae recommended mathematics above all else as necessary for a proper understanding of the world; he thought theologians in particular should be versed in this discipline. God himself had revealed that the world had been created according to measure, number, and weight; thus mathematics could help lead to a new and fuller understanding of the Word. It is worth noting that Andreae studied under Matthias Hafenreffer at Tübingen, and had a hand in the composition of the latter's *Templum Ezechielis*.[60] Whether or not it is legitimate to refer to Andreae as a "pansophist," he was certainly caught up in the effort to contribute to prophetic understanding through magical inquiry.

Similarly, elements of nature mysticism appear in the works of the Lutheran divine Philipp Nicolai, who explained in eschatological terms the teaching that Christ was substantially present everywhere. In his *Theoria Vitae Aeternae*, written about 1606, Nicolai dealt at length with the Last Things, and showed how the natural world would necessarily pass away. Christ, the "heavenly phoenix," had three bodies. His personal body was the human nature that he took from Mary. His spiritual body was the Christian church, to which he was spiritually bound. His "world-body," finally, was "the great edifice of the heavens and the earth, which he fills everywhere with his ruling presence." Christ could be depicted as a phoenix because he caused all his bodies to be destroyed and fully renewed. The death and resurrection of his personal body had occurred once in history. The resurrection of his spiritual body occurred in the church. The transformation of his third body would come at the Last Day, when heaven and earth would be consumed in fire and totally renewed.[61] Natural signs everywhere indicated that the world was nearing its final destruction and renewal. Besides the signs announced by Christ, there was such evidence as the astronomers' report that the firmament was contracting.[62] Although Nicolai's attention was focused on the world to come, his assumptions and conclusions fully supported the effort to find prophetic truth through the investigation of nature.

Thinkers like Nicolai, Arndt, and Andreae were usually at pains to make clear the precise theological justification and the limited scope of their magical inquiries. They were careful to avoid compromising basic theological principles, though Arndt's mystical writings brought him under strong suspicion in some quarters. But many Lutherans with just slightly less interest in guarding particular theological formulae did not keep magical speculations at all separate from religious truth. As early as 1575, Aegidius Gutman wrote a treatise of a thousand pages that promised virtually complete understanding of the natural and spiritual worlds to the possessor of godly wisdom. This "theosophical compendium of all things," as Peuckert has described it, was an extended commentary on the first five verses of the first chapter of Genesis, which this author believed encapsulated all prophetic truth, from the "morning" of the world to its "midday" and its "evening" or end, and thence to a new morning. All knowledge was for Gutman ultimately biblical knowledge; nature and the Bible held the same truths.[63] A similar combination of Lutheran and magical ideals can be found in such works as the *Cyclopaedia paracelsica christiana* (1585) of Samuel Eisenmenger.[64] All the liberal arts and sciences, Eisenmenger wrote, were gifts of God; he who sought godly wisdom through faith would be a master of them. For the numerous and often confused seekers who were heirs of both Luther and Paracelsus, the study of occult truths became all but fully equated with the striving for salvation. Yet whether magical research was regarded as only one godly discipline or as an all-important search for universal wisdom, it was pursued with the conviction that it could offer some sort of prophetic insight.

The spread of prophetic speculation tended to feed on itself, generating in the process a common belief that real wisdom was not attained easily or by the unworthy. This trait is clearly visible in major magical enterprises of our period, such as alchemy. This art was concerned with far more than the transmutation of metals; it was posited on the possibility of universal regeneration, and it sought the "moral and spiritual rebirth of mankind."[65] Such high ideals meant that alchemical secrets were not to be broadcast wholesale. The gift of understanding came from God, and only those who understood would be able to grasp the real meaning of arcane alchemical theories. Lutherans respected alchemy for both its allegorical and its scientific value; Luther's son Paul, a physician, employed the art.[66] Beyond both allegory and science lay the occult prophetic wisdom that this and other magical arts promised. The link between alchemy and magical world-reform is evident in late Reformation alchemists, for example Heinrich Kunrath and Michael Maier; the latter became one of the leading defenders of the supposed secret fraternity of the Rosicrucians. The involved imagery in the writings of such figures went hand in hand with a sense of deep mystery, and awe at the sense of responsibility that came with profound revelations concerning the secrets of nature. Only a proper contemplation of these mysteries, and their proper communication, would allow the longed-for transformation of the cosmos.

The notion that God was granting spiritual gifts and responsibility in the Last Times helps to shed light on the popularity of Hermeticism in Germany during our period. The body of writing attributed by many Renaissance scholars to the magician and seer Hermes Trismegistus, often supposed to be a contemporary of Moses, actually dated from late antiquity. These works were "steeped in the gnostic atmosphere of their period, which implied a religious use of magic and an astrological setting for religious experiences."[67] Hermes, Moses, and other eminent ancients were supposed to have possessed profound and godly insight, anticipating Christian as well as classical wisdom. Luther's vision of history as a decline into corruption, and the Lutheran conception of the reign of Antichrist, could make the temporary eclipse of divine wisdom seem inevitable. Now the Reformation had uncovered the light of the Gospel, which was spreading through the world before the Last Day. The enemies of light were still powerful, however, and corruption still reigned; the small band to whom ancient truth was now revealed had a great responsibility. Such ideas made the Hermetic writings most attractive to the seeker after a lost prophetic wisdom. The attraction of Hermeticism helps make sense of such a work as Johann von Jessen's *Zoroaster*, issued in Latin at Wittenberg in 1593.[68] Von Jessen's writing reflected the excitement of one who hoped to share this rediscovered truth.

Apocalyptic concerns may also have played a part in late Reformation interest in the original Cabala, the mystical art of the Jews. Jewish intellectual life underwent a pronounced revival in the later sixteenth century, and much of this activity, rife with messianic excitement, was based on this ancient complex of revelatory methods. In Germany, full of seekers eager for any hint of secret wisdom, the art naturally received a great deal of attention. R. J. W. Evans has pointed out that the followers of Melanchthon inherited an interest in Jewish mysticism from Reuchlin.[69] From the 1540s, when Andreas Osiander used ostensibly cabalistic reckoning in his *Conjectures on the Last Days*, interest in such mysterious methods continued to grow. Not infrequently, as we have seen, Lutherans referred to any prophetic reckoning with letters and numbers as "cabalistic," but by the later decades of the century seekers began to understand that there was far more to the tradition. The attraction of the Cabala for Lutherans lay not simply in the sense of mystery surrounding it, but more particularly in the hope of a revival of ancient wisdom and of a revelation of prophetic truth. Jews and Lutherans shared a feeling of excitement, apprehension, and expectancy during this age, and despite deep-seated Lutheran fear and hatred a good deal of evidence indicates that sharing of insights occasionally took place.[70]

Thus the Lutheran search for certainty in the Last Times is a key element for understanding the burst of magical and occult speculation during the late Reformation. No conflict seemed necessary between evangelical faith and magical theory. As Helisaeus Roeslin declared, "What is opposed to the Holy Scripture and to faith is neither *Astrology* nor *Magic*, nor *true Cabala*, but rather *sheer fictions*, against which arts, as against vain and empty philosophy and loose sophistical prattle, Saint Paul has warned us."[71] Nevertheless, what had begun as an intense quest for prophetic certainty became gradually for some seekers a search for gnosis, for universal saving knowledge. The perils of any such enterprise were certainly not lost on observers in that age; it is no accident that the first Faust book appeared in Lutheran Germany in 1587.[72] Faust epitomized the soul that craved understanding of universal mysteries. But the kind of knowledge and power he sought was forbidden, and hence Faust's obsession led him to the unutterable horror of a pact with Satan. Though the work's scorn for the pope, monks, and nuns was incidental to its central theme, in these details it reflected important features of an apocalyptically tensed Lutheranism. To be sure, there was no direct concern with the end of the world or the universal Judgment; Faust's dilemma is that of the individual soul in its relation to God and the devil. But the origins of the legend are only poorly understood if we ignore the context of Lutheran expectancy and the striving for prophetic understanding that this expectancy encouraged.

THE HEAVENLY SCHOOL

The quest for magical insight was accompanied by a growing habit of conceiving of the earnestly sought prophetic truths as hidden to the everyday sensibilities of most people, as deep and obscure mysteries that could not be understood by everyone. The sense of the hiddenness of prophetic understanding was at least partly an inheritance from the Renaissance tradition, already well established among the Florentine Neoplatonists, of an esoteric learning that would only be sullied and abused through public disclosure. The growth of this sense in late Reformation Germany probably owed something also to the sheer number of prophetic calculations and speculations now in circulation, which exacerbated the already serious confusion of the era and engendered a feeling that real wisdom was somehow hidden from the unworthy.

Other influences may also help explain the spread of popular occultism in Germany. Luther, after all, had rejected the overblown discursive reason of the medieval schools, and put in its place an intuitive approach to knowledge that was inseparable from his prophetic faith. The apocalyptic tension that remained central to Lutheran attitudes made for extreme ambivalence toward learning in general, and such ambivalence is particularly notable in prophetic writings. On the one hand, these writings were increasingly filled with the language of learning, with Latin and Greek phrases, with the technicalities of chronological, astrological, or arithmetical calculation. This language was evidence of a respect for the learned intellect, which offered guidance in an ever more confusing world.[73] On the other hand, the more the prophetic message was surrounded by the language of learning, the more the desire grew to penetrate beyond all this elaborate clothing to the essential and simple insight.

Here the question of the true nature of prophetic insight was manifest once again. We saw earlier that Melanchthon and his contemporaries were somewhat uncertain in their treatment of this matter. In a sense simple faith brought all the saving knowledge that was needed, yet at the same time learned or inspired mediators of prophetic wisdom possessed a special godly gift, and their teachings demanded the attention of the believer. These two thoughts continually appeared together and even tended to merge as the popular quest for wisdom became more explicitly magical. Increasingly, "godly wisdom" was distinguished from mere worldly learning. This wisdom was in one sense the possession of every true believer. Yet at the same time it was often discussed as a deeply buried treasure that required a special gift and great effort to uncover.

The growing sense of a hidden wisdom can be examined in connection with the mystical trend in Lutheranism. A Paracelsian style of nature mysticism blended with the medieval German tradition of more purely spiritual mysticism; the resulting pansophism opened the way to strivings for a very high form of knowledge indeed. It is worth repeating that a striving for such wisdom was not necessarily contrary to confessional loyalty. Indeed for many believers true understanding and true repentance required a true confession of faith. Mystically inspired Lutherans like Arndt were generally also strident opponents of Calvinism, which they saw as a superficial, rationalizing creed. It appealed only to the natural man, not to the depths of the spirit. But the most explicit references to a high and godly wisdom hidden from the unworthy came from popular prophetic writers who, though inspired by Lutheran apocalypticism, were not bound by a sense of confessional orthodoxy.

Aegidius Gutman's massive *Revelation of Divine Majesty*, written in the 1570s but not printed until 1619, was an early example of the conscious search for a wisdom that lay far beyond the realm of confessional boundaries. But this theme did not become really common until the early seventeenth century. Johannes Dobricius, in his *Time-Reminder* of 1612, stressed that to a man "gifted with elevated understanding and wisdom," nothing was hidden, all things could be known. It was necessary to distinguish between mere earthly keenness and godly wisdom. The first came merely from nature; it was represented by the heathen philosophers and all who followed them. Godly wisdom, however, came from above; it was learned in the heavenly school of Christ. Whoever learned in the first school learned many valuable natural things, and was knowledgeable in the eyes of many men. But whoever possessed the second form of wisdom had a glimpse of the eternal light itself. This was a hard and high wisdom, but the closer this old and corrupt world came to its end, the more hidden and secret things would be revealed to those who watched carefully and paid the necessary attention to such events as the great conjunction and the new star of 1604.[74]

In a sense this godly wisdom could be learned from others. Dobricius acknowledged debts to the work of Krentzheim and Poyssel, among others, who had done much to open the secrets of the Last Times. But he also engaged in page after page of his own original and obscure reckonings from biblical and astrological evidence to show that the message of Scripture was identical to that of the heavens. Other inspired writers, such as Paul Nagel, were less willing to acknowledge debts to others. Nagel referred to Eustachius Poyssel as one of the many "learned men of understanding" who had reckoned the times correctly,[75] but he presented his insights as fundamentally his own. The Last Time that would reveal the prophecies of Revelation had now arrived, and Nagel, as one who had learned to understand them, could not remain silent. Stifel and others who had tried to determine when the end would come had erred simply because the time for such revelations had not yet arrived. The mysteries of Scripture and nature had not been rightly understood. Now, however, Nagel promised to write a *prognosticon* that would overshadow the writings of Luther himself.

Yet if Nagel sometimes stressed his own godly gifts, he also emphasized that the insight he enjoyed was potentially open to all. The wise men of old, including Moses, Solomon, Hermes, and many Egyptians and Babylonians, had read the same truths in the heavens, even before the Scriptures were written and gathered together. Yet the understanding of the ancients had been only partial; more-

over Revelation foretold that prophecy from the heavenly book
would cease for many ages. Now the book had been reopened, and
whoever looked with understanding ought to be able to calculate
for himself what would occur in coming years. Whoever compre-
hended the words of Esdras and Revelation would find in them "an
excellent magic, wisdom, and understanding." Nagel had therefore
decided to leave some prophecies unexplained, so that others would
have something to investigate. Every man, after all, carried within
himself the ultimate instrument of discovery, a "golden measure"
that could show him all heavenly things.[76]

As we saw earlier, Nagel used the Paracelsian notion of an "Astronomy of Grace," distinguishing it from astronomy founded on
heathen superstition. In order to understand the Astronomy of
Grace, one needed to learn "in the school of Daniel and the magi,
and in our own school of the Holy Spirit."[77] The school of the Spirit
taught from the great book of the heavens, as well as from Scripture; the properly inspired observation of nature held the same lessons that were learned from the Bible, especially the book of Revelation. The comet of 1618 announced that all who were not found
in this holy school, all who had not put off the old man and entered
into a new birth, would soon fall to the ground and be destroyed.
For those who remained, the coming third age would bring a full
revelation of all the secrets of Scripture and nature; all the learning
of this world would be as nothing.

Nagel rebuked the present leaders of thought and opinion. They
had at best a half understanding of the Scriptures, and now that the
heavenly books were being opened these leaders stood liable to
judgment. Those who thought Nagel had misused numbers or astrology were merely showing folly and blindness. People always
criticized what they could not understand, and only those who understood would mark well and take note. The secrets of the heavenly wonder-book were hidden from the unworthy. Therefore,
Nagel urged, "pray that your eyes will be opened to see. Throw
away your art, your logic and metaphysics, become fools with us
before the world, and children of the new birth before God the
Lord; thus will you be helped; otherwise you remain blind and de-
luded."[78] As his writings encountered mounting criticism, Nagel
increasingly saw himself as in revolt against the narrowing of definitions in both the science and the theology of his time. He defended himself vigorously; he was not inventing a new heresy, but

restoring the truth as preached by Luther and by Christ himself. His work had but one purpose: to help people see what awaited them so that they might be saved. For Nagel, seeing in this sense was believing. What he saw outwardly was a period of profound suffering and purgation, to be followed by a spiritual Advent of Christ in 1624. Then would begin the third age, the final time of peace, which would end in 1666 with the Last Judgment.

Johann Hörner took a tack somewhat different from Nagel's in attempting to divide theology into two sorts, the theology of faith and his own "symbolic theology" or Cabala. The theology of faith, he wrote, was "a godly doctrine of the true saving faith in God and his written and essential Word, touching all men alike, learned and unlearned." The theology of faith informed and illuminated the lives of men. If taught properly, this theology was far from blind. Yet Hörner strongly hinted at the superiority of his symbolic theology or Cabala, which was a fundamental theology of understanding. Its secrets were found above all in Revelation, and to understand its prophetic truths was to be saved. Although it brought a highly necessary wisdom, it was not as common as the theology preached from the chancel and taught in the schools. But by symbolic theology even the common man could grasp many of the deepest mysteries. Human understanding by itself was very weak; one had to open oneself to divine understanding.[79]

Likewise, Paul Felgenhauer emphasized that every person had the ability to discover divine truths. Felgenhauer, who had studied theology at Wittenberg and began his career as a Lutheran preacher, turned against established ecclesiastical authority while still a young man, sometime around 1620. He seems to have combined strong expectations of the Last Day with hope for the possibility of universal reform. Spiritual freedom, he insisted, included the freedom to discover the exact outlines of God's historical plan. In an investigation into biblical chronology published in 1620, he courted "those who understand" with a careful reckoning of the closeness of the end. Those who found fault with his purpose were ignoring Scripture itself, for did not Daniel say that "the wise shall understand"? "Are there not others," he asked, "who interpret him [Daniel], and indeed calculate the last world age, as is to be seen openly in print? Am I then alone among them a sophist, fool, ass, and heretic? But let it be; each will have to give his own accounting of how he has handled himself in this life."[80] Luther himself had hoped for a "Noah" who would be able to reckon the time exactly, but failing the appearance of such a one he had made each believer free to investigate the mysteries. Yet Luther's supposed followers now failed to acknowledge this; they no longer believed that every man possessed his own gifts. Felgenhauer recognized that the truths he sought, of which the theologians were so contemptuous, were not articles of faith. But the prophetic secrets would inevitably be announced and fulfilled. For Felgenhauer the discovery of prophetic wisdom was closely tied to the hope of spiritual transformation.

Thus the apocalyptic notion of revelation in the Last Times led to a more explicitly gnostic emphasis on saving knowledge as insight into universal and divine mysteries. The quest for a high and hidden magical insight could easily grow out of a Lutheran desire for prophetic certainty. As Daniel 12: 9 stated, the secrets were closed up and sealed till the time of the end. Now was that time. The angel of Daniel continued: "Many shall be purified, and made white, and tried; but the wicked shall do wickedly: and none of the wicked shall understand; but the wise shall understand." The strongly Lutheran emphasis remained evident even in extreme expressions of gnostic striving. For the purpose was not simply the salvation of the individual seeker; it was the salvation of all who could and would understand. The secrecy and mystique of these writings was not ultimately an attempt at obfuscation, but rather a recognition that the profoundest prophetic truths were above reason, and reserved for the chosen of God. The mysterious language, the complicated imagery, the insistence on general obscurity—all were ways of emphasizing the ultimate importance of the message. The goal was to evoke in the worthy a conception and assurance of a truth that lay far beyond mundane experience. As Edgar Wind pointed out in his study of pagan mysteries, "disguise is one of the great forces of revelation."[81]

These prophetic writers were preaching what is to us a strange combination of objective and subjective wisdom. It was a combination that characterized the entire culture and age. The truths of the soul and the truths of nature were one. The emphasis was on seeing these truths, on a kind of vision. In this emphasis, certainly, the efforts at prophetic insight inspired by Lutheran expectation came to differ from Luther's own emphasis, which had been on the ear, not the eye, on hearing rather than seeing. But as in the study of natural wonders and astrology, the necessity was to see with more than human vision, to see with the eyes of the inner man. This emphasis on an intuitive, prophetic vision was characteristically Lutheran in its rejection of both scholastic pedantry and false humanist eloquence. Again, the magical seeker was also a preacher of prophetic truth. Indeed it is striking how fully Nagel, Felgenhauer, and others of their ilk fit into the tradition of Lutheran apocalyptic preaching. The writings of these "new prophets" and countless others who expressed similar ideas were filled with the call to repentance. To repent was to be among the worthy, and to be among the worthy was to understand. Having faith meant living a life of repentance, and only such a life could be illuminated by saving knowledge.

THE NEW REFORMATION

The search for occult prophetic wisdom was very closely related to yet another feature of German thought that emerged especially after 1600. This was the hope for a "new reformation." Prophecies of a great spiritual change and breakthrough became increasingly common in the last decades of the sixteenth century, and even more so in the first twenty years of the seventeenth. These hopes have generally been studied in connection with the rise of pansophical or theosophical mysticism in Germany, and as background to the Rosicrucian writings, which will be discussed shortly. Here we will make a brief attempt to cast the whole phenomenon in a somewhat different light by looking at its roots in the tradition of Lutheran apocalypticism.

The usual view of the pansophical or theosophical hopes for a new reformation is based on an analogy with the early years of Luther's Reformation. Those who follow this approach maintain that early Protestantism, like the theosophy of the later period, was in several key respects the child of mysticism. It was in revolt against dry academic disputation and established learning, and sought instead experiential truth and revelation. But, this argument continues, as Protestantism became a state church, identified with the ruling powers, as it established its own strict dogma and again divorced learning from true spirituality, it was inevitably rejected in its turn by those who sought truth, certainty, and revelation. For the new seekers, the orthodoxies of Wittenberg and Geneva became as hateful as that of Rome, and secular authorities as well became generally identified with the Antichrist.[82]

This interpretation would be difficult to refute altogether, but at least one major factor opens it to strong qualification. The argument fails to take into account the powerful continuity of eschatological tension within the Lutheran world of thought, a tension that prompted a continual search for prophetic certainty. Thus, too, it overlooks how much the magical and pansophist strivings of the later period were at least implicitly encouraged by an authentically Lutheran sensibility. The search for certainty, for the true understanding of the Word, never left Lutheranism during these decades, and hopes remained high for reform and renewal. Speculations about the downfall of the Antichrist, the collapse of the Turkish Empire, the conversion of the Jews, and a final spiritual flowering before the end continued to play a role in Lutheran expectation.[83] In explaining the intense hopes for a new reformation it is not enough to cite, as some have done, the relative spiritual freedom within Protestantism in general. For the great majority of these hopes came from a Lutheran background.

That general spiritual freedom did allow speculations about the threats and promises of the future to become gradually bolder in the late sixteenth century. Of this we have had ample evidence. We have seen that Lutherans were open to a broad spectrum of prophetic traditions and scenarios, including for instance Joachimism. Indeed, numerous popular prophetic works from the early seventeeth century demonstrate that even devoted partisans of the Augsburg Confession could invoke Joachim while at the same time launching strong attacks against Calvinists and Catholics.[84] One did not have to know very much about the actual teachings of Joachim to present him as an antipapal prophet of apocalyptic changes and the triumph of true Christianity. His ideas were typically conflated with any number of other prophetic notions, but the Joachimist element is nonetheless clearly evident in the developing hopes for a new reformation. The notion of an Age of the Spirit complemented the belief in a magical or spiritual transformation to be effected by proper contemplation and communication of divine mysteries. Joachim had also foreseen a new order of enlightened believers who would help to usher in the Last Age; with such an assumption the idea that some secret bond linked the truly worthy could flourish. In fact the idea of a secret brotherhood of wise reformers may have been directly encouraged by Joachimism.[85]

Closely associated with these Joachimist conceptions were the prophetic hopes inspired by Paracelsus. The close link between magical discovery and the hope for a new reformation owed much to the followers of the famous physician, who had reinterpreted the old prophecy of a last Elijah, applying it to a man of great wisdom through whom all arts and sciences would be reformed and restored before the end of the world. This *Elias artista* would uncover and reveal all the secrets of nature, for as Christ foretold in Matthew 10: 26, "there is nothing covered, that shall not be revealed, and hid, that shall not be known." Here, then, was a clear expression of the idea that great mysteries would be revealed in the Last Times. Such thorough revelation implied a time of fulfillment, a golden time of peace and understanding. The Paracelsians reckoned carefully on the basis of their master's writings, and word spread that the new reformer would probably appear to initiate this wonderful age in 1603.[86] The breathtaking new star of 1604 excited further forecasts of the last Elijah. But the prophecies of Paracelsus lent themselves equally well to more general expectations of radical spiritual transformation and the end itself, as we saw earlier in connection with astrology.

Still another source for the idea of a new reformation was the Fourth Book of Esdras (2 Esdras in modern editions), which continued to grow in popularity throughout the late sixteenth century. The book foretold terrifying conditions on earth, and revealed the signs by which the degeneration of creation would become evident. The world would be shaken to its foundations. Then, as the Lord told Ezra,

whoever remains after all that I have foretold to you shall himself be saved and shall see my salvation and the end of my world. And they shall see the men who were taken up, who from their birth have not tasted death; and the heart of the earth's inhabitants shall be changed and converted to a different spirit. For evil shall be blotted out, and deceit shall be quenched; faithfulness shall flourish, and corruption shall be overcome, and the truth, which has been so long without fruit, shall be revealed. (2 Esdras 6: 25–28; RSV)

Elsewhere the book announced that the final, Messianic age on earth would last four hundred years, after which would come seven days of judgment and the end of the world (7: 28−43). In other passages there was no mention of a golden time, but such inconsistencies were simply a result of the book's rich diversity of imagery. A sense of mystery was central, and emphasis fell on the role of "the wise among your people" (2 Esdras 14: 46).

Joachimism, Paracelsianism, and expectations based on sources like the Fourth book of Esdras were only a few strands in a fabric of prophetic hopes and apprehensions that had become increasingly dense in the Lutheran world of thought. The various traditions seem to have come together as never before around the time of the new star of 1604. According to many interpretations, such as that of Wilhelm Eo Neuheuser, the star announced a new age.[87] Neuheuser and similar writers typically drew on a wide range of prophetic sources. After 1609 another potent element was added to the brew as the works of the mystic Valentin Weigel found their way into print. This long-dead Lutheran pastor quickly became a saint for many adherents of magical reformism. His writings served to intensify the spiritual element in Paracelsian nature mysticism, deepening the seekers' desire to discover the divine in both nature and the human soul. The appearance of Weigel's books could not have been better timed to reinforce the eclectic striving for prophetic wisdom.

Thus, given the atmosphere of occult and mystical apocalypticism that developed among searchers after prophetic truth in Lutheran Germany, we should not be surprised to find that the most famous of all magical reform movements had its origin in the Lutheran world of thought. In 1614 and 1615 the original Rosicrucian manifestoes appeared at Kassel. These works, whose author has remained unknown, pretended to describe the formation and beliefs of a secret Protestant society that would work quietly but ardently for universal reform in the last age of the world. The tracts had a generally churchly tone, but they also showed strong leanings in the direction of Paracelsian nature mysticism. Though it is all but certain that no secret brotherhood actually existed, these writings made an immediate and enormous splash in Germany. Men of almost every station sought membership in the fraternity, drawn by the high ideals of these first works and by the combination of apocalyptic excitement and magical reformism. Other Rosicrucian writings by other authors soon appeared, some pretending to disclose deep spiritual mysteries, others hoping to lure the secret fraternity out of hiding, still others with a clearly satirical intent. An entire tradition of secret societies, of which Freemasonry is a part, goes back to these Rosicrucian writings. There is no need for us to add to the literature on the authorship of these treatises, or to make a thorough examination of the works themselves. What is important for us is how the burst of Rosicrucian excitement grew organically out of attitudes that were common in Lutheran Germany.

The *Fama Fraternitatis* of 1614 told the story of a noble German youth who made a pilgrimage to the East, where he became profoundly learned in the true ancient wisdom, both natural and spiritual, and in all the ways of peace.[88] His secret fraternity, discovered upon the opening of his grave in the portentous year 1604, sought to live a life of purity, simplicity, and understanding. This society looked to a final, universal reformation. The *Fama* referred to the present as the Last Time, when despite rampant godlessness the knowledge of both Christ and nature was spreading quickly among those whom God blessed with understanding. The Lutheran tone of the work is obvious, as in the confession of "the knowledge of Jesus Christ, as it has clearly and brightly spread in these Last Times, especially in Germany." This knowledge was still resisted by "fanatics, heretics, and false prophets."[89] The elements of apocalypticism, prophetic striving, and occult reformism in this work epitomize the sensibility that had been developing for decades in Germany under the influence of Lutheran eschatological convictions.

This connection is even more evident, however, in the *Confessio fraternitatis* (1615), the central statement of Rosicrucian belief.[90] This work was marked by "anti-papal, cabalistic, astrological chiliasm."[91] The pope was explicitly referred to as the Antichrist, and the imminence of his downfall was asserted. The Order declared that truths at present only whispered or veiled in enigmatic utterances would soon be broadcast openly in the world. A similar event had already happened once in Luther's Reformation, when "after many pious people secretly and very desperately struck out against the pope's tyranny, he was cast out of his seat in Germany with great violence and singular zeal, and abundantly trodden under foot." The final destruction of the Antichrist had been reserved until the present era, when "he will be mangled with nails, and his ass's braying will be silenced by a new voice."[92] The rumblings were already heard among the learned in Germany, in their writings and secret exchanges.

The *Confessio* emphasized in other ways that the present age was decisive. It announced that "God has certainly and actually resolved to show the world, before its destruction [*Untergang*], which will soon ensue, such truth, light, life, and glory as the first man, namely Adam, lost and forfeited, so that his descendants were cast and driven with him into misery."[93] The notion that before the end the creation had to move full circle to its original pristine state was one indication of strong Platonic influence in the prophetic imagination of the period; we have seen hints of it in not a few other writings. The combination of the idea of a return to cosmic unity with the intense Lutheran dwelling on the final earthly struggle and imminent deliverance was at the root of the mystical and chiliastic hopes for a new reformation. In the *Confessio* these hopes did not exclude the old warnings of divine wrath, for "seeing how the world has now almost reached its end, and after the completed period or cycle again hastens to its beginning," God was now directing the course of nature so that the godly experienced steadier joy, while the godless suffered all the more evil and punishment.[94]

Finally, the *Confessio* indicated definite signs that showed that the present world order was rapidly drawing to a close. For example, new stars had appeared in recent years, along with other signs in the book of nature. These signs held the same secrets as the Scriptures. In fact there were certain characters or letters that the *Confessio* described in familiar terms:

As God has here and there incorporated them in the Holy Bible, so he has also imprinted them most clearly on the wonderful work of creation, on the heavens, the earth, and on all beasts, so that just as the mathematician can predict eclipses, we can recognize the obscurations and darkenings of the church, and how long they shall last. From these letters we have borrowed our magic writing, and have made for ourselves a new language, in which the nature of all things is expressed and explained.[95]

It will be remembered that Luther had written of a "new language" that would allow believers to regard the signs rightly, according to the Word.[96] Luther's meaning was obviously perverted by the author of the *Confessio*, but what appeared in these Rosicrucian tracts was nevertheless a primarily Lutheran sensibility with an accretion of magical and occult notions. Those notions had accumulated over several decades, largely as a result of the continuing search for prophetic wisdom.

Many Lutheran clergymen appear to have leaped to explain and defend the Rosicrucian writings; typical of their response was David Meder's *Iudicium Theologicvm* of 1616, which heartily lauded the ideals of the supposed secret society.[97] The generally positive initial reaction of Lutherans is further evidence that theosophical leanings were now commonly combined with expectations of radical transformation. Not surprisingly, the most avid prophetic investigators were often particularly enthusiastic about the manifestoes. Johann Faulhaber has the honor of being one of the first to dedicate a work to the Rosicrucian Order; his *Mysterium arithmeticum* of 1615 was inscribed "with humility and sincerity" to the "most enlightened and famous Brothers R.C."[98] The ideals of the *Fama* and the *Confessio* appealed perfectly to this apocalyptically minded master of reckoning. Numerous works, including Johann Hörner's cabalistic fantasia, presented "discourses" in which members of the supposed Rosicrucian brotherhood took part, thus revealing some of their insights into the Last Times.[99]

The Rosicrucian hopes for a new reformation helped to inspire Paul Nagel, who went on to develop his own complex apocalyptic visions. Although he never claimed to be a member of any secret society, Nagel was clearly in sympathy with the ideals expressed in the mysterious new writings. By around 1620, he seems to have felt that he could confirm their hopes and predictions, since he had himself attained the highest prophetic wisdom. Nagel's prophetic insights went far beyond anything in the Rosicrucian treatises; he probably took no more than general inspiration from the famous anonymous tracts. Indeed the dream of a new reformation should not be associated exclusively with the Rosicrucian phenomenon; it was a common ideal nourished by continuing eschatological excitement. Nagel, Hartprecht, and other preachers of a third age gained their own schools of followers who supported their teachings with further proofs. An apocalyptic writer from Hamburg cited not only these two as inspirers of his thought, but also Johann Arndt, "my much beloved father in Christ."[100] This work spoke of two judgments; in the first the godless would be done away with and Christ would come to rule; the second would bring the end of the world. Between the two would fall the thousand-year reign of Christ.

Although such blatant and literal chiliasm occasionally appeared in popular prophetic works, it was not typical of the prophets of Rosicrucianism and the new reformation. Most of them agreed

with Nagel that the thousand years of Revelation 20 was not to be
understood literally, but rather as a brief rule of Christ in human
hearts before the end. In fact, it may be misleading to group all
the new prophets as sharers of some form of chiliastic vision. In the
writings of several magical reformists the precise character of the
coming new age is left vague. Thus Paul Felgenhauer, for instance,
refused to be called a chiliast; he spoke simply of the coming renewal of the world, leaving some ambiguity about whether the new
world would lie within or beyond history. Felgenhauer was an intensely earnest prophetic preacher for whom the Rosicrucian writings were noble but in no sense normative. His vision of spiritual
transformation included the discovery that the Jews would be converted to Christ before the end. He seems to have combined longing
for spiritual renewal with the expectation of Christ's reign over a
wholly new earth.[101]

The Rosicrucian excitement had a political as well as a magical
dimension, though the political aspect is often overemphasized, as
in the well-known study by Frances Yates.[102] Many German Protestants fastened their hopes to the young elector Frederick of the Palatinate, who in 1617 was elected King of Bohemia as Frederick V.
But Frederick was a Calvinist; how could he become a hero within
apocalyptically inspired Lutheranism? The answer seems to lie in a
growing desire, among those who looked to a universal, magical
transformation, to find concrete evidence for their hopes in the political realm. We noted in an earlier chapter that the tradition of
emperor-prophecies revived among Lutherans in the later sixteenth
century. Already by the 1570s and 1580s, prophetic hopes associated with the House of Saxony were beginning to intensify the political component of the Lutheran prophetic quest.

Eustachius Poyssel, whose reckonings were the origin of expectations for 1623, was not the only prophetic writer who saw in
Saxony the cradle of the reborn Gospel and a final bastion of truth
before the final advent of the New Jerusalem.[103] But Poyssel's later
works, and especially a 1609 tract that was almost certainly from
his pen, show a Lutheran prophetic seeker becoming disenchanted
with institutional Lutheranism, and expanding his hopes to include
the vision of a German Protestant prince who would lead in a universal reformation.[104] Here we have a possible key to the Rosicrucian focus on Frederick V. Poyssel had looked for a time to Frederick IV of the Palatinate as a potential Lutheran hero; many other

writings expressed the hope that a "German Lutheran prince" would play a central role in preparing Christendom for the Second Advent.[105] But as the political scene became more and more confused and threatening, and as the promise of a Lutheran prince remained unfulfilled, those who hoped for some political fulfillment cast their nets a bit farther in the quest for potential heroes.

We also need to recognize, however, that the ideal of political solidarity among German and Swiss-German Protestants, the old ideal of Philipp of Hesse, had never died completely. Among early seventeenth-century Lutherans a spectrum of political outlooks had emerged that corresponded generally with theological differences. Strict, conservative Lutheranism, which dominated the states of the North, tended to shun the idea of political alliances in the defense of Protestantism. A more liberal sort of Lutheran theology, more common in Württemberg and some of the relatively cosmopolitan southern cities, tended to be more open to such alliances and to political activism. In 1609 the latter cities and states formed a Protestant Union that included Calvinists, while the conservative Lutheran states, epitomized by Electoral Saxony, remained aloof. The political aspect of Rosicrucian reformism was strongest among Lutheran prophetic writers who were less than violently anti-Calvinist. Especially by 1618, when political tensions within the empire were reaching a peak, it was natural that some closing of ranks against the common enemy would occur between these Lutherans and other Protestants.[106]

These trends are evident in Simon Studion's "Naometria," completed in 1604, the year of the new star and the supposed date of the Rosicrucian revelation. Studion's reckonings were heavily biblical and strongly Protestant, but in addition to the prophecies of Luther and of Scripture they employed Joachimism and many other sources. Astrological evidence appeared throughout; the new star of 1572 played a key role in several calculations of the time of Christ's return. The work presented impossibly long figurings about the Roman Antichrist, the *filius perditionis* Mohammed, the approaching destruction of Rome and Islam, the political revolutions that would pave the way for the Second Coming, and the return of Christ to establish the Kingdom. Not all of Studion's conclusions seem to have been consistent with one another, but certain main points emerged fairly clearly. The 1260 year-days of Revelation 11 were divided into 42 prophetic months of 30 years each. The last of these prophetic months had fallen between 1560 and 1590; this time had been a preparation for the final earthly drama before the Second Advent. Revolutionary political and religious changes would begin soon afterward, and in these Duke Frederick of Württemberg, to whom the work was dedicated, would play a critical role in alliance with King Henry of Navarre and other prominent Protestant princes. For years the entire world would be embroiled in turmoil. In 1612 the last pope would fall as the world was made ready for its Savior. Then in 1623 Christ would establish his Kingdom on earth, which would last a thousand years.[107]

The "Naometria" has been cited by several scholars as important in the background of Rosicrucianism.[108] Studion identified himself as a member of a "Militia Crucifera Evangelica," a secret society dedicated to the defense, expansion, and enrichment of Protestantism. The group is supposed to have met in Lüneburg in 1586, and to have supplied a model and inspiration to those who held similar ideals. Whether or not the Protestantism of this society included forms other than Lutheranism is unclear. But since Studion's prophetic scenario included some sort of union among Lutherans, Calvinists, and even Anglicans, he appears to have been advancing the belief that the final transformations would include worldly victories for Protestantism generally, preparing the way for the King himself.

Thus prophetic attention could eventually settle on a new Frederick, regarded as a Solomon, who by 1618 ruled over what one prophetic writer had called "the heart of the German nation."[109] Any such shift required, of course, that traditional Lutheran fears about the spread of Calvinism should somehow be mollified. Some apocalyptic writers responded by offering an expanded definition of the true faith. One such writer was Wilhelm Eo Neuheuser, who in 1618 issued a work that looked explicitly to a universal political and religious transformation before the establishment of the New Jerusalem. For Neuheuser, "true Christian belief" meant German Protestantism in the traditions of Luther and Zwingli. The differences between the followers of these two reformers he considered minor; they could and would be overcome as prophetic events led to the final downfall of the Antichrist and the conversion of all people to the true faith. Neuheuser almost always mentioned Luther and Zwingli together; often he invoked Melanchthon as well. His German patriotism probably explains why he never mentioned Calvin. He offered a list of prophetic authorities, including Lichtenberger, Grünpeck, and many others, to show that the papacy would fall, and a universal reformation would take place, before the Last Day.[110] By this time, then, disappointment or desperation led some prophetic seekers to consider that a united German Protestant front against the Antichrist was in the cards.

Another highly patriotic German observer, writing about 1621, expected the downfall of the Antichrist by 1625 and a short reign of peace and truth before the end. He was at pains to explain why the prophecies of Paracelsus and others for a "lion" who would effect great changes in the world had to apply to Frederick of the Palatinate rather than to a Saxon prince. This author, who has not been certainly identified, repeatedly cited Luther while lauding the "holy evangelical belief" and the "evangelical land" of Germany; clearly he was trying to balance inherited Lutheran loyalties with the need to see Germany united under a strong Protestant ruler.[111]

A different solution to the problem was presented in an extremely interesting prophetic tract of 1620 by Johann Wagner, writing under the pseudonym Plaustrarius. His work combined magical apocalypticism with political hopes focused on Frederick V.[112] The magical elements involved an extensive analogy between the beginning of the world and its end. The Creation was the morning and the end was the evening of the world. The six days of Creation would somehow be repeated and fulfilled in the six years from 1618 to 1624. As the world had a good beginning, so it would have a good end. A Fall had followed the Creation; another fall (of all anti-Christian powers) would precede the end. The analogy went on and on, accompanied by much detailed reckoning and magical speculation. The time of peace before the end was announced by Frederick's accession to the Bohemian throne. As a Lutheran writer, Wagner escaped the awkwardness of Frederick's Calvinism by dropping strong hints that very soon Lutheran teachings would triumph as adherents of other creeds recognized their errors and converted to the true faith.[113] Then the final, brief, earthly paradise would be achieved. Wagner preached heavily in traditional Lutheran fashion about the need for prophetic understanding and repentance in these Last Times. In 1621, after the defeat of Frederick V by Catholic forces, Wagner issued another tract that was much more purely spiritual in tone. A punishment was coming over Germany such as no people had ever known. The final time of peace was still awaited, but this time the King who would rule in spirit was Christ himself.[114]

So far as Rosicrucianism and associated hopes for world reformation had direct implications for the worldly regiment, then, some Lutherans allowed their anti-Roman and pro-German sentiments more weight than purely confessional considerations. The new reformation, however, was never primarily a political ideal among those who shared the Lutheran prophetic sensibility. At the heart of their excitement was the possibility of magical, spiritual reform. Since internal transformation would necessarily affect the macrocosm, these hopes had definite political implications. But the notion that world reform could be effectively furthered through a conscious political program was mostly foreign to the prophetic excitement of the period. The events of the Last Times would all follow God's eternal plan. The goal of the Rosicrucian tracts, and the central goal of most other literature on the new reformation, was to spread understanding of that plan among the worthy and faithful. This was a contemplative apocalypticism in the Lutheran tradition, not an activist political creed.[115]

There was, then, a close connection between the search for hidden, prophetic wisdom and the hope for final, spiritual transformation before the Last Day. In the decade 1610–20, the atmosphere of mystery and tension in Lutheran Germany finally produced an eruption of unquestionably unorthodox schemes and dreams. Particularly with the outbreak of what appeared to many to be the final eschatological struggle, visionaries began to declare that all the mysteries of the Last Times were now revealed to those who possessed the gift of wisdom. "He that hath an ear, let him hear," they preached with words of Revelation.[116] These new prophets were bitterly opposed by the defenders of orthodoxy, who were only now coming to a clearer definition of legitimate prophetic insights. But it is no accident that the majority of mystical chiliasts shared a Lutheran background. They had been nurtured in a society where the quest for prophetic understanding had become a universal enterprise, where mystical and magical assumptions had melded with prophetic hopes and fears.

6
❧ Orthodoxy and the End

BABEL

On the eve of the Thirty Years' War, the prophetic mood of Lutheranism was still at its height. The quest for a satisfying comprehension of contemporary conditions and future prospects was of paramount importance, and it now involved a large reading public. In the foregoing chapters we have tried to understand how the search for prophetic truth spread and intensified in the century after Luther's break with Rome. We have seen how this ongoing quest generated an atmosphere of mystery and occultism. Although the pretensions to magical understanding that became so common by the early seventeenth century twisted some original Reformation teachings almost beyond recognition, the quest was encouraged by the continuing Lutheran desire for insight into the culminating divine plan.

By any standard, the early seventeenth century was a time of extreme apprehension and confusion in Germany. The number of prophetic visions, revelations, reckonings, and interpretations in circulation continually expanded, and people of all stations were caught up in the sense of wonder and excitement. Again, the very confusion seemed to many to be a sign of the approaching Judgment. The learned were as absorbed as were common pastors and literate burghers in the discovery of prophetic truth, in reckoning the time, in observing the heavens, and the rest. Even the young Johann Gerhard, later to become one of the most important orthodox theologians of the century, could refer in 1612 to the prophecies of Philipp Nicolai, and announce that "since all the prophecies of Scripture leave no more than about 50 years, the sixth millenary of the world is hastening to its end . . . [and] we will soon see Christ coming."[1] As we have seen, prophetic inquiry became increasingly eclectic, open to any source of insight that was even vaguely anti-Roman, pro-Protestant, and suggestive of changes that stretched the imagination beyond its everyday limits.

Up to the 1620s, this eclecticism becomes more and more evident. We noted it in writers like Gottlieb Heylandt, who cited Luther, Paracelsus, Nagel, Nachenmoser, Nicolai, and Gerhard in support of his own exegesis of Revelation.[2] By the opening of the Thirty Years' War numerous collections of prophetic writings, containing highly diverse visions and scenarios, were being published. Often there was little or no effort to discriminate among the various possibilities. Old prophecies of every sort were revived and reapplied more zealously than ever. The wild visions of the Nuremberg painter Paul Lautensack, for example, who had written in the 1530s, were rediscovered and first published in 1619 under the name of Valentin Weigel.[3] Johann Lichtenberger's predictions and many other old astrological prophecies, the forecasts of the monk John of Capistrano, new editions of the Sibylline Oracles, the supposed vaticinations of a Moslem priest: these and countless other prophetic sources were applied to current conditions and the near future as the sense of crisis reached a climax. Predictably, the well-known verses about 1588 were updated; 1628 fitted the rhyme just as well.[4] All of this was accompanied by a proliferation of efforts to unravel the magical mysteries of space as well as time.

Not surprisingly under such circumstances, some Lutherans began to air serious doubts and fears about what was happening to the evangelical heritage. Johann Valentin Andreae, to take one notable example, expressed a feeling that was growing fast among his contemporaries. Although Andreae's youthful attitudes toward prophetic investigation and magical reform had been highly positive and eager, by 1617 he was rapidly coming to an unhappy estimate of these contemporary preoccupations. A character in his *Menippus* of that year complained that "so many conjectures and speculations, so many confident predictions, so many announcements praised as expressions of the divine Spirit, so many painstaking reckonings of numbers, have done absolutely nothing to enlighten us about events."[5] In fact the world seemed to grow more confused and confusing every day. Andreae complained elsewhere of those

who, calling themselves theosophists, chased after visions, revelations, dreams, auguries, oracles, and countless false prophetic arts.
It had all become a kind of demonic madness. Bad enough were
those who took advantage of popular credulity by hawking insidi-
ous fables; yet many were so caught up in their own conjectures
that they believed them as though they were direct revelations from
God. Men otherwise good and honest were now consumed with
reckonings, harmonies, anagrams, letter and number symbolism,
trigonal progressions, and the like, in vain efforts to predict future
troubles, political changes, the destruction of the pope, the defeat
of the Turk, the renewal of the world, and so on. People were making a virtual religion out of alchemy and related arts. Despite their
good intentions, those who engaged in such activities were now
working against the Gospel and against Luther's achievements.
Their efforts added up to a *Turris Babel*, as Andreae indicated by
so entitling a book in 1619.[6] As many Lutherans now began to see
the situation, overzealous prophetic speculation had led to outright
fanaticism.

In fact, by this time the ferment of prophetic views was beginning
to appear positively dangerous, not only to the right teaching of the
Gospel, but also to the increasingly tenuous social order. For the
new prophets included not only magical seekers like Nagel; they
found a voice in the streets as well. Noah Kalb, for instance, a baker
of Ulm, received a revelation in 1606 that he was the Noah whom
Luther had called for in his exegesis of Daniel 12, one whom God
would raise before the Last Day to reveal the prophetic mysteries.
He proceeded to announce his visions publicly, exciting considerable uproar. For a time Kalb's revelations were regarded as genuine
by some of the local clergy, and the well-known mathematician
Johann Faulhaber became so enthusiastic about them that he ended
up in prison as a result. Kalb himself met his end on the scaffold as
a threat to the peace of the city.[7] A few years later one Philipp
Ziegler of Nuremberg was inspired in part by the Rosicrucian writings to declare himself a spiritual monarch, and to roam the land
issuing various prophecies of both worldly and spiritual change. He
rejected both the teachings of Paul Nagel and those of Nagel's orthodox opponents, promising a spiritual return of Christ as well as
the advent of a new David who would establish a final, godly Kingdom on earth.[8] Kalb and Ziegler were not social revolutionaries in

the tradition of Thomas Müntzer; they were simply very excited prophetic preachers.

More radical, and apparently more popular in their region, were the notions of the Thuringian spiritualist Esaias Stiefel (d. 1627) and his nephew Ezechiel Meth (d. 1640). Between 1604 and 1625, Stiefel had repeated brushes with the authorities in various Saxon cities because of his teaching that to confess Christ was to confess only the living Word; he rejected the written Word of Scripture along with all the sacraments. True Christians of the new birth were already dead to the world and enjoyed eternal life here and now; the resurrection and the otherworldly eternal life were myths. Stiefel recanted his views at least six times, and apparently became at least outwardly reconciled to the Lutheran faith before his death. Meth took up similar teachings, but likewise died at peace with the church.[9] The radical spiritualism these men propounded was not in itself apocalyptic, but it is best understood in light of the striving for spiritual insight that the prophetic excitement of Lutheranism encouraged. The intellectual confusion and excitement of the era led earnest seekers in many different directions.

THE POLARIZATION OF VIEWS

In the second decade of the seventeenth century, the desire for meaningful prophetic insight began to inspire a broad stream of consciously unorthodox speculations. Not until then did orthodox Lutherans begin a serious and concerted campaign against heterodox prophetic tendencies.[10] But one should not assume that the spread of new prophetic trends, having reached a certain threshold, simply provoked a reaction from an already established and well-defined orthodoxy. What occurred in these years was a fairly rapid polarization of ideas on prophetic matters, a polarization that reflected the new intellectual and social conditions of the seventeenth century. The poles do not correlate precisely with elite and popular culture, though that division seems to have been increasingly important. As it first developed, the conflict was essentially a religious quarrel over the character of prophetic faith.

Throughout the later sixteenth century there had been occasional blasts against prophetic calculation and specific prediction. We noted earlier that the central inspiration of Lutheran eschatological excitement throughout the Reformation continued to be a sense of both the imminence and the hiddenness of the end. By 1600 an image commonly used by preachers to convey this sense was that of a snare or trap (Luke 21: 35): people would be caught entirely unawares.[11] Numerous Lutheran preachers and writers continued to warn against dangerous curiosity about the time of the end and the mysteries of the Last Days. Yet the very style of the warnings shows how common was the curiosity they denounced. In a series of sermons published in 1589, Alexandrus Utzinger recognized how appealing the prospect of prophetic insight was. It hardly seemed blameworthy for a Christian to inquire into such high, important, and godly matters. It seemed wonderful to reflect uninterruptedly on the mysteries of time, to open oneself to the workings of the Holy Spirit through which great secrets were revealed. But Utzinger called on believers to recognize that it was actually foolishness to attempt to discover such divine mysteries. Such temptations had plagued Christians since the time of St. Paul and had recently been revived by Michael Stifel, "otherwise a pious man."[12] It was certain that the end was very near, but one had to guard oneself against being drawn away from what was most important.

Utzinger's warnings may have been part of the effort to counteract disappointment or the danger of relaxation after the failure of the prophecies for 1588. But this concern had never disappeared among Lutherans. Already in the 1570s Andreas Schoppe had expressed dismay at the proliferation of attempts to reckon the time of the end. By the last years of the century he felt that the situation was getting out of hand, and he issued a sharp warning against the "false prophets and curious people" who pretended to have uncovered such mysteries.[13] A good Lutheran, Schoppe did not hold that all research into the time of the end was vain or impious. The Holy Scriptures contained many indications that might grant insight into the matter, and the signs announced in the Gospels had almost all been seen already. Luther had said that those who would witness the end were already born in his own day, so in all probability there was not long to wait.

Nevertheless, Schoppe saw great danger in making unguarded pronouncements that might fail to be fulfilled. "For then the simple folk say that the learned are all mixed up [*die Gelerten die Verkehrten*]; they say much but nothing follows from it, so who wants to believe them any more?" What was most important was to watch and to pray in constant readiness; this was what should be taught and preached. The "young prophets" who thought they had the answers were all too full of pride. Their calculations were certainly open to dispute. Even the most learned students of chronology disagreed among themselves about several important dates and periods. The 70 weeks of Daniel 9, for example, allowed for widely different interpretations. A number of different dates were possible for the 430 years the Israelites spent in Egypt. Since these interpretations necessarily affected the reckoning of world ages, the quarrels about them could not be brushed aside.

Schoppe's discussion led him to give what was in effect a history of errors about the Last Day and its time. He recognized that several early Christian writers had held chiliastic beliefs. But the notion that the elect would rule for a thousand years with Christ, which was based almost entirely on a single passage from Revelation 20, he rejected categorically with the help of Augustine. The church had always had to deal with fanatics who thought they had received divine revelations of the Last Things, and those who had made definite predictions had always been wrong. Arnald of Villanova had thought the world would end in 1345; similar errors had arisen in the fifteenth century. In 1527 Melchior Hoffmann, on the basis of passages from Daniel 7 and Revelation 11, had preached openly that the world would last no more than seven years longer. When Nikolaus von Amsdorf warned believers against this new prophet, Hoffmann had insisted furiously that his insights were correct. Many believed him, and confusion had reigned until time had proved him wrong. The confusion was made still worse by the "excellent mathematician [*Arithmeticus*] Michael Stifel," who had set St. Luke's day in 1533 as the time of Christ's return. Schoppe gave a long account of Stifel's tracts and the uproar they had caused. No one who reckoned in this way with words and numbers could be trusted.

More recently, a group of old prophecies had been revived and applied to the year 1560. Although around that time there arose great unrest and persecution, those who had foreseen the Second Advent in that year had been mistaken. Shortly afterwards, a pastor named Johann Beydenrodius had become convinced by pervasive corruption and a terrible outbreak of plague that the end had definitely arrived. When on the feast of St. Michael in 1571, the sun and the moon took on unusual colors, he had quickly concluded that this was the darkening of the sun and the moon mentioned in

Matthew 24: 29, and that the stars would fall at any moment. People of all stations had been badly misled by the many predictions for 1588, which had begun with Regiomontanus. Such errors could have appalling results. Schoppe told the story of a burgher who in 1528 had become so crazed by radical preaching about the coming end that he stopped working altogether, began eating and drinking with abandon, and then stole two horses and went on a rampage. He soon met his end on the gallows, where the birds pecked at his rotting flesh. Several other similarly chilling tales helped warn against an incautious attitude in prophetic matters.

How could any definite reckoning from the prophecies and the numbers of Scripture be certain, asked Schoppe, since God would shorten the days? To be sure, the Lord had commanded his followers to study the Scriptures zealously. But such research had to have proper limits; otherwise there was no defense against utterly fantastic notions. Some argued that Scripture left open the chance that the time of the Last Day might be revealed beforehand; Schoppe rejected their arguments, citing Romans 10 to show that the judgment of God would remain hidden until the very end. Others pointed to the success of important predictions in the past. Hus, for instance, had clearly announced Luther's Reformation. But to generalize from such instances was perilous in the extreme. To do so would be to approve the perverse forecasts of men like Wilhelm Friess, who had predicted the advent of a great savior emperor and a golden age about 1563. Insisting that in no case could the future be known in detail, Schoppe cited a long list of late sixteenth-century predictions that had clearly failed. He also made a general attack on astrological prophecy as unworthy of a Christian. So often had the astrologers been in error that their current apocalyptic predictions were hardly to be believed. In brief, virtually all the precise vaticinations of recent years were bankrupt.[14]

But if this was so, how could the believer know that the Last Day was truly at hand? Schoppe left no uncertainty about his own convictions. He listed reasons to erase doubt. The Apostles had called the time of the New Testament the end of the world and the last hour (1 Corinthians 10). The abandonment of the Gospel by many peoples had long since occurred, and the Roman Antichrist had been clearly revealed (2 Thessalonians 2). The feet of the Roman kingdom were now divided into toes of iron and clay (Daniel 2). The forces of Mesech, Tubal, Gomer, and Bethtogarmah, namely

Spaniards, Muscovites, Italians, and German Papists, raged against the true church (Ezekiel 38). Gog and Magog, to wit Turks and Tartars, laid siege to the true Mount Zion, or Germany. God might indeed allow the Turk to overrun Germany for her sin, in which case he would shortly afterward deliver his chosen. But again Schoppe stressed the central point: the time was known to no mortal.[15]

Though Schoppe's arguments were hardly novel, this sort of detailed criticism of prophetic research was not heard with any great frequency in the sixteenth century. By the second decade of the next century, however, many Lutheran theologians felt that key doctrines were seriously threatened by mystical and chiliastic thinking, and more general reaction to the spread of prophetic inquiry and revelation arose. Leading spokesmen of the Church were increasingly concerned to refute those who claimed to uncover divine secrets or who offered new visions of the end.

Not the least of their reasons was the increasingly precarious position of Lutheranism in the empire. In 1613 the elector of Brandenburg, Joachim II, converted to Calvinism, sending a nervous shock through an already defensive Lutheranism. Equally disturbing was the mounting Catholic aggressiveness and success in many areas. Under these tense circumstances the trend toward increasingly bold apocalyptic speculation reached its fullest expressions. But prophetic excess could easily lay Lutherans open to condemnation by rival confessions, as standard-bearers of the faith now began to see very clearly. In particular, Jesuits were quick to point out that the most extreme and aberrant prophetic schemes came from the Protestant and especially from the Lutheran fold. The reaction among many Lutheran leaders was not only to condemn new and clearly unorthodox positions, but also eventually to reject many prophetic assumptions and methods that had enjoyed general acceptance during the first century of the Reformation.

Before 1630, even the strictest Lutherans still shared the common sense of expectation and generally couched their polemic in apocalyptic terms. Increasingly, however, they tended to deny all but a few basic Reformation insights into the Last Time and to insist that only these were compatible with true prophetic faith. Such was the goal, for example, of Caspar Finck, a professor and preacher at Giessen, in a short work of 1612.[16] Finck reacted to conditions among the "German Israelites" with the usual strong laments, complaining that no one paid attention to the approaching storm of fire. Proper knowledge of the Last Judgment was absolutely crucial for believers. Such knowledge not only corrected such basic errors as the Aristotelian dream that the world was eternal, but also reassured believers of their own eternal life, and warned against human pride and cupidity.

But Finck opposed any and all attempts to determine when the end would come. Under the New Testament dispensation the Second Advent was always imminent in the eyes of God, for whom a thousand years were as a day. One might recall that Michael Stifel had argued precisely the opposite—that biblical references to the approach of the Judgment had to be understood from an earthly, historical perspective; his point had become a common assumption in Lutheran Germany. Finck attacked Stifel and all others who tried to reckon the time; in doing so he rejected not only the pronouncements of the "enthusiasts" and "Anabaptists," but also the prophecy of Elias, heretofore a mainstay of Lutheran prophetic interpretation. This was a false and unscriptural prophecy, Finck said, and he refuted it with his own time-reckoning. The age before the giving of the Law had lasted 2,513 years; the age of the Law itself had been far shorter than the 2,000 years the prophecy claimed. Predictions based on this perversion were contrary to the words of Christ in Acts 1: 7, "It is not for you to know the times or the seasons, which the Father hath put in his own power." Finck's rejection of the prophecy of Elias was still untypical in 1612, but it suggests that the demise of the scheme was slowly beginning. By the 1620s Johann Kepler had joined a number of churchmen in openly attacking the idea, along with all efforts to predict the time of the end.[17] Only a few years later, the notion of the three ages had lost its place in the canon of apocalyptic evidence, and the whole practice of historical time-reckoning had slipped out of the mainstream.

Nor, wrote Finck, did the time of the end depend in any way on the laws or the course of nature. He saw no value in astrological calculations, and he reminded his readers that the famous prediction for 1588 had proved completely untrue. He thus denied several important means by which Lutherans had assured themselves the end was imminent. Only one way did Finck leave open for watching, a way approved by the Bible and St. Jerome. The fate of the Roman Empire provided insight into the nearness of the Judgment; when it was reduced to weak feet of iron and clay, then the entire world would surely be ready to collapse. Like many of his contemporaries, Finck thought it likely that the world would end during Lent, in the springtime, since most of God's greatest miracles had taken place in that season. But the precise year was impossible to know. Having settled these issues, Finck went on to deal at length with the details of the Judgment itself, with eternal life, and with Hell.

Church leaders began to see new errors appearing on all sides in this utterly confused time. Not only was the dangerous mysticism of Paracelsus and Weigel to be combated; Germany was also threatened by new heresies, such as that of the Photinians, who opposed the doctrine of the Trinity.[18] This heresy had spread dangerously in Poland (among the followers of Socinius), and was now rearing its head farther west. Lutheran clergymen responded with lengthy attacks on Photinianism, seeking to show how these ideas contradicted all the authority of Scripture and the fathers. Most latter-day Photinians had first been Calvinists; it was no wonder they had gone further astray.[19] In one sense, the spread of such beliefs only reinforced the Lutheran conviction that the Judgment was close; here were more of the false prophets who would inevitably appear before the end. On the other hand, it was necessary to curb the freedom of speculation that had allowed such errors to arise.

The need to counter free speculation and the occultism that had arisen in its wake led some Lutheran writers to put unprecedented emphasis on clarifying Scripture. Daniel Cramer, for instance, in an exposition of Revelation published in 1619, hoped to make everything in that book crystal clear, a goal Luther himself had thought far from attainable. Cramer's purpose was not to discover new prophetic truths, but rather to quell the notion that hidden in the book were deep secrets that required special gifts or insight to understand. Revelation was a prophetic mirror, in which the whole history of the church was clearly laid out. Cramer found it useful to compare the book to a comic drama, with clearly marked acts and a happy ending. Though he did all he could to give his explanations popular appeal, he explicitly rejected the ideas of the chiliasts and the "cabalistic fantasts."[20] Cramer had in view the same, essentially defensive goal of clarification when he included all the books of Esdras in his 1620 edition of the Luther Bible. The Fourth Book of Esdras was so often cited by seekers of prophetic mysteries that the common man was led to think a key part of the Bible was withheld from him, its secrets reserved for those who could read Greek or Latin. Erroneous teachings could be more easily refuted if such books were made fully public.[21]

More commonly, critics directly attacked the assumption that precise forecasts were possible. Johann Wolther admitted in 1623 that from the Bible one could make reckonings that pointed to the coming of the Last Day around 1670; "but these are conjectures, not demonstrations; surmises, and not proofs."[22] He appears to have been offering an apology for his own earlier efforts to reckon the time. The Bible taught in countless ways, without offering further exactitude or insight, the simple truth that the end was very close. As for the notion that a golden time on earth would follow the tribulations that were now beginning, this idea had no biblical support at all, declared Wolther. "And the reckoning as Nagel produces and presents it is so childish and foolish that it is astonishing that there are people who think there is something to it. For who could not reinforce an already established belief with numbers if he wanted to? But what am I saying, childish and foolish? In his *Prodromus astronomiae apocalypticae* there are such dreadful blasphemies against Christ the eternal Son of God, it is sinful and shameful that they should be tolerated among Christians and put in print."[23] Wolther carefully worded the title of his work to attract readers who were seduced by Nagelian writing. The title was *Golden Arch, Wherein the True Understanding and Contents of the Important Mysteries, Words, and Numbers of the Revelation of John and the Prophet Daniel Are Amply and Superabundantly Discovered....*

Such criticism helped to drive the most ardent seekers for prophetic wisdom into open and vigorous opposition to the leaders of established Lutheranism. Already by the first decade of the seventeenth century, some of these seekers were showing their disappointment with what had become of Luther's heritage, and began to separate themselves from the institutional church. In his 1609 *Magic Proof* of prophetic truth, Eustachius Poyssel cited with seeming approval the opinion of "Schwenckfeld, Osiander, Franck, and others" that "LUTHER AND MELANCHTHON ESTABLISHED AN ARISTOTELIAN THEOLOGY THAT SMACKS MORE OF THE FLESH THAN OF THE SPIRIT." Poyssel's last works, including the *Magic Proof*, were issued anonymously, probably because of growing pressure from orthodox leaders against the kind of speculation for which he was known.[24] But the real divergence seems to have begun slightly later.

Significantly, Paul Nagel thought that a gradual revelation of prophetic truth had taken place between 1610 and 1620, the very decade during which orthodoxy and the new prophets were facing off. Indeed by the early 1620s the gulf was unbridgeable, as attitudes hardened quickly with the onset of the war. Among the most energetic opponents of orthodoxy to emerge about this time was Paul Felgenhauer, who answered the critiques of Georg Rost and others with stinging indictments of these supposed followers of Luther. He denied that he was an enthusiast, an Anabaptist, or a chiliast, as Rost claimed; he was preaching a Christian truth that this "court preacher" was too blind to see. By 1630 Felgenhauer was writing about Lutherans, Calvinists, and Catholics as three equally misled "sects"; he was in open revolt against these and all others.[25]

Symptomatic of the deepening division between an increasingly cautious theological establishment and the seekers of prophetic wisdom was the broad attack on the writings of Johann Arndt that began around 1620. Arndt's mystical piety made him a hero to many magical reformists of the time, and his works thus appeared dangerous and heretical in themselves to those who opposed both mystical and apocalyptic tendencies. He was denounced as a Weigelian and a *Schwärmer* who encouraged the spread of doctrinal confusion and error. Arndt tried to show the clear differences between himself and Weigel,[26] but the harshest opposition to his thought came after his death in 1621. Lucas Osiander of Tübingen issued a particularly strong denunciation, which was answered with passionate defenses by such proponents of Arndtian piety as Paul Egard.[27] The outcome of the dispute was that one part of Arndtian mysticism, namely its more purely spiritual side, was accepted as a legitimate element of Lutheran piety, while the element of Paracelsian nature mysticism was gradually discredited and abandoned. An early and perhaps the best example of this discrimination between forms of mystical thought is found in Johann Valentin Andreae, who as we saw was beginning to divorce himself from Rosicrucian schemes of magical renewal by around 1617, while retaining the warm personal piety inspired by the older tradition of German mysticism.[28]

Adherents of an apocalyptic faith were thus faced with an increasingly clear choice: to maintain a pansophic quest for prophetic wisdom that was now subject to mounting suspicion and discouragement from church leaders, or to abandon the search for gnosis beyond what appeared to many as the lifeless teachings of the church. Although the new prophets who came under attack in the early seventeenth century were usually chiliasts, the dream of an earthly Kingdom was by no means the only thing that separated them from orthodoxy. Their excitement over the new hopes of Rosicrucianism can be understood only in the context of a long and desperate search for prophetic knowledge, and this larger issue of prophetic knowledge and authority was what ultimately divided orthodoxy from its opponents.[29] In certain respects this was, to be sure, a perennial question; many defenders of orthodoxy assumed it was when they equated the errors of the new prophets with those of earlier "fanatics," and styled themselves the defenders of established Lutheran tradition. But in another sense, the early seventeenth-century controversies were of a new and different kind. For some of the assumptions that now came under orthodox attack were extremely common among Lutherans themselves, and many of the new prophets saw themselves as the true heirs of Luther's prophetic faith. In fact, neither the new prophets nor their orthodox opponents were simply defending positions that had been held during the early Reformation. Rather, both groups were developing in new directions attitudes that had strong roots in Lutheran thought.

Thus the years after 1610 saw deep and widespread polarization in Lutheran Germany between an increasingly conservative theological orthodoxy and its malcontents. As orthodoxy sharpened and narrowed its definitions, its leaders hardened their opposition to the bold prophetic and mystical speculations of the age. From the perspective of its critics, orthodoxy had ceased to understand the deep spiritual content of its own preaching, even of the Word. To be sure, aside from Jacob Boehme and a handful of other inspired spirits, those who broke with orthodox teachings in the name of mysticism or magical reform were a deeply confused lot, hardly memorable for their intellectual or religious profundity. Yet it needs to be emphasized that just when many Germans were seeking for prophetic certainty more desperately than ever before, orthodoxy began to find fault with the whole business of prophetic investigation, leaving a kind of vacuum to be filled with the imaginings of self-appointed prophets. At the very time when the desire for prophetic understanding was reaching its peak among many believers who were still nominally followers of Luther, orthodox

Lutheranism began to move toward the doctrinal narrowness that has given it its bad name.

SETTING LIMITS

In earlier chapters we saw time and again that sixteenth-century Lutheranism offered no clear definition of legitimate prophetic insight or methods. Not until the period of the Thirty Years' War did theologians make anything like a consistent effort to establish outlines for acceptable interpretation. When it did develop, the effort was not merely a rejection of particular heretical ideas; it was ultimately a skeptical turning away from the whole enterprise of supporting expectation with evidence from history and nature. Orthodox writers saw themselves as returning to an earlier and purer form of expectancy, but in fact they were beginning to knock down the pillars of the apocalyptic outlook.

The continuing popular success of the new prophets did help to bolster, at least temporarily, the eschatological convictions of many orthodox leaders, who saw the spread of false teachings among Lutherans as yet another proof of the imminence of Judgment. Georg Rost's apocalyptic convictions, for example, were no less intense than those of the prophetic writers he attacked. Rost, a well-known preacher in Mecklenburg, wrote several works aimed at refuting what he saw as rapidly spreading misapprehensions about the Last Times. In 1620 he issued a *Prognosticon Theologicon* to clarify and defend orthodox teachings on the Last Day.[30] That the end would come and that God would effect a universal reformation for eternity were beyond all doubt. Those who did not live by this belief were lost souls. Formal proof was hardly needed that Judgment was at hand; all prophecy and experience forced the conclusion. But although many had tried to calculate the time, their efforts had led to nothing but shame. In book 18 of the *City of God* Augustine had refuted those who had made this mistake during the early days of the church, yet the error had continued to spring up regularly in Christendom. Irenaeus and Lactantius had tried to calculate the end. More recently, Arnald of Villanova, Regiomontanus, Pico della Mirandola, Stifel, Funck, and many others had tried to reckon the time.

Now others not only tried to predict the date of the end, but also held fantastic hopes about a final age of perfection. The Rosicru-

cians and Paul Nagel predicted that Christ would return in 1623 or
1624, but they were trying to discover secrets known only to God.
It was absolutely certain that the end was close, but Christ's coming
would be sudden and unforeseen. Rost's own beliefs were fully literal and were based on historical interpretation of prophecy; he
compared his own age to the one that had preceded the Flood.
Moreover, astrological evidence could supply useful warnings in
these Last Times, and was not to be ignored. The book of nature
complemented the Scriptures, and judicious interpretation of heavenly movements and signs could help believers to understand the
tribulations that were coming. But Rost warned sternly that exces-
sive curiosity brought only danger in these matters; it was best to
regard each day as the last. Hence all attempts to achieve certainty
by calculating with prophetic numbers were wrongheaded.

When Nagel wrote that the wrath of God was soon to come, that
the pouring out of the vials and great suffering were imminent, he
was to be believed, since here his prophecies agreed with the Bible.
In a sense Rost acknowledged in this passage the traditional Lutheran elements of Nagel's apocalypticism. Further than this, he
wrote, Nagel could not be followed, since there was no basis either
for his specific calculations or for his forecast of a "third age."

Broadening his argument to deal with many common prophecies
of his time, Rost rejected as simply unbelievable the idea that the
papacy would be destroyed before the end; Scripture foretold that
the Antichrist would be revealed, but that his persecution of believers would continue until the end of the world. Similarly, despite the
speculations of David Herlicius and others, the book of Daniel
showed that the Turk would not fall until the Last Day. The hope
for a last Elijah was unfounded, for Luther himself had been that
prophet, whose appearance announced the recovery of the Gospel
and the nearness of Judgment. Many of the greatest church fathers
had taught that the Jews would be converted before the Last Day,
but such a conversion was "more to be wished for than hoped
for."[31] A more sober hope was simply that there was still time for
some Jews to see the light. The frequently discussed dream that the
Word might see one final worldly triumph was also vain; Rost
boldly and misleadingly cited Philipp Nicolai's *History of the Kingdom of Christ*, which had hoped for just such a victory, in support
of his own conclusion. The last spread of the Gospel had already

taken place; Luther's prophecies showed that the short time before the end would be a time of trial.

Rost also took care to oppose a larger danger he saw lurking behind all prophetic speculation, that of fatalism. History was not, he insisted, completely determined and unchangeable. Just as an astronomer's prediction of an eclipse did not bring the eclipse about, so God's announcement of evils and suffering before the end did not preordain anything. The cause of suffering and punishment was human sin, and if Germans would now sincerely repent, as the Ninevites had done, God would turn away his wrath and put blessings in its place. Fully the last half of Rost's *Prognosticon* was taken up with discussion of the Judgment itself, the Resurrection, the necessity of preparation, and the like; the author's concern here shifted almost entirely away from prophetic issues toward a more purely individual eschatology of the soul.

Shortly after the publication of his *Prognosticon*, Rost must have seen the necessity of yet stronger medicine to fight the infection of new prophetic schemes. We have observed that the earliest phase of the Thirty Years' War saw an explosion of adventurous apocalyptic writing, and defensive theologians could hardly react fast enough to the ideas now flowing into circulation. In 1622 Rost published a work with the strange title *Heldenbuch vom Rosengarten*, a detailed polemic against the new mystical and chiliastic prophets.[32] The Rosicrucians and their like pretended that they had discovered deep, hidden secrets in the Bible through special prophetic methods and spiritual revelations, and one of these supposed secrets was that a new reformation was coming to usher in an age of earthly perfection. But the true church had always endured horrible persecution, and there was no reason to suppose that conditions would be any different before the Last Day. Christ said that his Kingdom was not of this world. "We are nothing but stinking earthworms," Rost quoted from St. Bernard, "and are at last subjected to death."[33]

When Rost attacked the idea of an earthly Kingdom of God, he usually attributed to the new prophets the idea that this Kingdom would literally last a thousand years. But most of those who looked to a new reformation actually held that the thousand-year period was not to be understood literally, and many conceived of a much shorter spiritual Kingdom to precede the end. Among orthodox theologians this position came to be known as "chiliasmus subtilis"; it was a less blatant but ultimately no less pernicious error.[34] Rost made no such distinctions. It appears that he needed to identify his opponents in some respects with positions that were notoriously heretical, so that he might more easily distinguish orthodox from unorthodox prophecy. Many Lutheran pastors and laymen were powerfully attracted by the hope of new prophetic discoveries; Rost was at the leading edge of an effort to set limits in this realm. Although he took pains to refute the new prophets, Rost's real concern was with prophetic knowledge and its limits. Efforts to calculate the age of the world and the time of Christ's return had always been common; in recent times it was widely assumed that the world would stand six thousand years. The modern chiliasts argued that God had made the world in six days, and a thousand years was as a day to him. But in Rost's view this was idle conjecture, as were all efforts to calculate the age of the world and the time remaining to it. Rost recognized that such reckoning had become common even among respectable theologians, but his rejection was nonetheless categorical. Too many conjectures had led to confusion and doubt, now made far worse by the fantastic and contradictory predictions of Nagel, Felgenhauer, Hartprecht, and the other new prophets.

Many of these would-be prophets drew inspiration from the Fourth Book of Esdras, counting it among the canonical books of the Bible. Nagel, Felgenhauer, and others had misled many in this way. Rost took an approach directly opposed to that of Cramer: he argued forcefully that the book was not canonical, and he had powerful authorities to support him. As for the charge that most preachers and theologians ignored Revelation, Rost protested that nothing was farther from the truth; the entire church held the Apocalypse in the highest regard. Another error about Scripture was perpetrated by Felgenhauer in particular, who held that all the predictions of the prophets, all that they had foreseen and that had happened once already, would be fulfilled again in the Last Days. If so, then a great many things still had to come to pass before the end; how then could the Kingdom of God on earth be expected very soon? Most of these Old Testament prophecies applied only to the Jewish people, as careful study proved. Hurling back a phrase used by his opponents, Rost concluded that these new preachers knew as much about the secrets of the prophets as a dog knows about spelling.

According to Rost, the Rosicrucians were mostly adherents of Paracelsus who hoped to participate in a magical process that would transform the world. They opposed all the learning of the schools, and tried to win converts to their new brand of mystification, a school of the Holy Spirit that had no grades, faculty, or organization. Rost devoted two entire chapters to a defense of schools and the standard academic curriculum, arguing that only by this system could human learning proceed coherently. The chiliastic theology of the Rosicrucians was based on the false assumption that all divine mysteries could be understood through inspiration, but human understanding was in sober truth far too weak to comprehend the ways of God. Paracelsus himself, whom the enthusiasts took as their preceptor, had said that any who tried to learn too much about God's mysteries would inevitably be punished. The new chiliasts were in fact false prophets who, like Calvinists and Papists, perverted the meaning of Scripture.[35]

While the years after 1618 saw a general reaction to the mystical hopes associated with Rosicrucianism, to combat a movement of such broad popular appeal was difficult when its perpetrators remained mostly anonymous. The Lutheran reaction tended to focus on people like Nagel, who wrote in open defiance of the academic and religious establishment. Rost was only one of several Lutherans who responded heatedly to Nagel to discredit the style of thinking this new prophet epitomized. In 1620 a certain Justus Groscurdt pseudonymously issued a severe condemnation of the "new fanatic" Nagel.[36] "Beloved, believe not every spirit," this writer quoted from 1 John 4, "but try the spirits whether they are of God: because many false prophets are gone out into the world." Groscurdt rejected as unscriptural the notion that biblical secrets were also revealed in the heavens. He dismissed as well the hope that Christ would return to establish an earthly Kingdom; when the Lord came again, it would be to judge the living and the dead. Moreover, human knowledge was incomplete and there were many divine mysteries of which nothing could be known in the present life.

Nagel had perverted the meaning of Revelation, according to Groscurdt, and was guilty of the worst sort of presumption. While belittling Luther's achievements, this enthusiast followed the virtually satanic teachings of Paracelsus. In fact, Nagel stood directly in the line of earlier false prophets; Nicholas Storch (a notorious *Schwärmer* of the early Reformation) was his spiritual grandfather.

Recently cabalists such as Johann Hörner and other followers of Paracelsus had revived old errors, including the belief that the future could be predicted with certainty. The astrologer Antonius Torquatus had predicted that the downfall of the Turk would come in 1596; this and a great many similar forecasts had failed completely. What reason was there now for believing Nagel's prophecies for coming years? Michael Stifel's attempts to discover the time of the end were notorious, and such foolishness was still common. Nagel and the Paracelsians tried to give a magical interpretation to the book of Revelation, and dreamed of a golden age. But the prophecies that they so hopefully applied to the near future had already been largely fulfilled in the Reformation; now there was nothing to hope for except the Last Day itself, but when this would come it was impossible to know.

Another bitter orthodox opponent of Nagel was Philipp Arnoldi of Tilsit, whose *Antinagelius* appeared at Königsberg in 1622.[37] Arnoldi's main purpose was to refute the expectation of a third age of earthly perfection. The visions of the Rosicrucians and of Nagel were not supported by Scripture, but were vain dreams and illusions. If people regarded them only as dreams, Arnoldi wrote, there would be no danger. But these recent writings had received much attention and applause. All sorts of schemes and calculations were now widely printed and read; the common man should be warned against such errors. Many of Nagel's predictions relied on confused and empty methods like the Cabala, and on a perversion of astrology. One could not doubt that comets and other miraculous signs in the heavens indicated God's wrath. But Nagel's prediction of a new star in 1623, which would announce the fulfillment of all that those of 1572 and 1604 had indicated, found no support in Scripture or the fathers.

Arnoldi produced pages of biblical evidence against the idea of an earthly Kingdom. That the Last Day was fast approaching was sure, but Nagel's reckonings twisted the entire Christian message. Still, Arnoldi was not above responding to Nagel's calculations with one or two of his own. The number of the beast, for instance, 666, stood for the period when the tyranny of the Antichrist was most complete. This period had begun in 864 under Pope Nicholas, and ended in 1530 with the Augsburg Confession. This modest sort of reckoning was still fully acceptable, as long as it supported the orthodox Lutheran view that the Reformation was the last flash of the Gospel before the end.

The Lutheran opposition to the prophetic quest we have examined had become organized into a well-defined doctrinal front by the time Nicolaus Hunnius issued his *Comprehensive Account of the New Prophets* in 1634.[38] Hunnius's work was essentially an attack on chiliasm as a thoroughly satanic notion, invented, he said, by Jews and heretics, that had seduced many souls away from the true church. For Hunnius chiliasm epitomized virtually the whole range of theological error. The chiliast had forgotten the essential Christian value, humility, and from this one failing derived every intellectual perversion of the Weigelians, the Boehmists, and all other fanatics. By thus lumping together almost all forms of unorthodoxy and discussing them as a single enemy, Hunnius was helping to establish a position that would characterize orthodoxy for many decades to come. He was joined in this view by Johann Gerhard, who also worked to formulate a general concept of illegitimate future expectations. Among orthodox theologians, the term "chiliasm" gradually came to mean any form of eschatological heterodoxy.[39] The notion that virtually all doctrinal error grew from the same diseased root would become standard among orthodox theologians later in the century; Daniel Colberg epitomized the trend in his *Platonisch-Hermetisches Christenthum*, where "Paracelsists, Weigelians, Rosicrucians, Quakers, Boehmists, Anabaptists" and many others, including chiliasts, were found to be closely related in their errors.[40]

The defensive movement of orthodoxy reflected in part a larger seventeenth-century reaction against magic and the occult. In Lutheranism, that reaction went hand in hand with the triumph of strict scholastic methods in the universities. Free speculation was heavily discouraged, and in such an atmosphere prophetic methods like astrology were bound to come under attack. While astrology certainly continued to thrive in many quarters until much later, after 1620 it was gradually abandoned as a direct support of biblical prophecy. Relatively few astrological writings from this later era show the sort of religious emphasis and apocalyptic implications that had been evident in earlier decades. The movements of celestial bodies were less often interpreted as harbingers of divine punishment, and even comets began to lose their threatening aspect.

Some people had always been skeptical of the common claims about new stars and comets, but by 1620 the many new and radical interpretations had begun to provoke a more general reaction to the practice of attributing prophetic import to such phenomena. A tract of 1619 by Friedrich Grick dismissed the uproar over the comet of the previous year, and hurled ridicule at the crowd of ignorant writers in Germany who had rushed their confused interpretations into print. All the prophecies of doom, disaster, political changes, and a new age to come were so much nonsense. If one tried to publish such things in France he would pay a quick price. As much good as evil followed the appearance of comets, and those who tried to make any kind of prediction from them were engaging in fantasy. This truth applied to respectable theologians and astrologers as well as to raving fanatics working with the Cabala.[41] Grick was soon moved to answer criticisms of his work with another and even more strident attack on the dozens of "fantasts," like Faulhaber, who thought they could uncover the supernatural meaning of cometary appearances. Grick now ridiculed the whole tradition of apocalyptic astrology and the interpretation of heavenly wonders. It was foolish to suppose that the comet had anything to do with the recent news of Bohemia and Spain, "for the dispute in Bohemia had begun before the comet appeared," and it had long been clear that the Spaniards were preparing for a conflict.[42]

A decade later, critics were questioning the assumptions of apocalyptic astrology even more openly and more comprehensively. In 1631, for example, Johann Stilsov of Erfurt published a popular work bluntly challenging the idea that the heavens were contracting.[43] A great many learned astronomers and preachers, wrote this author, had been announcing that the heavens had sunk some 2,266 miles, and were now preparing to collapse altogether. Long and careful investigation had led Stilsov to the conclusion that it was not so. Surely God could make the heavens contract or collapse at any time, but what was possible was not necessary. The argument was long and often technical, but simple experience also helped to make the point: the sun's rays had grown no hotter, and the days had become no shorter. Stilsov energetically denied that nature was growing old and weak, that the entire system was about to break up. God was a good creator, and he did not abandon his creation. To be sure, a large number of works appearing around this time still vigorously harped on the apocalyptic significance of heavenly signs and configurations. But the beginnings of a major change in outlook were manifest in the spread of doubt about assumptions long held. It seems more than coincidental that the change occurred during the same decades in which Copernicanism began to receive wide acceptance among astronomers.[44]

The various reactions to the speculative mania of the age were not in themselves opposed to apocalyptic belief. But the cumulative effect of such challenges to gnostic striving was ultimately to discredit traditional assumptions that were required for the inherited apocalyptic world-picture. All groups and individuals who speculated in any way that contradicted the new orthodoxy were lumped together in one class of heretics, fanatics, chiliasts. Even key ideas that Luther himself had accepted, such as the prophecy of Elias, were increasingly excluded from the realm of legitimate evidence. Orthodoxy successfully clamped down on the quest for prophetic insight; orthodox prophetic teachings represented only one very small fraction of the old realm of prophetic knowledge. Thus early Lutheran orthodoxy shared in the larger skeptical movement against the prophetic and magical world-view in the early seventeenth century.

PROPHECY AND THE WAR

The first decade of the Thirty Years' War saw the last great explosion of eschatological excitement in Germany. This is hardly surprising given the devastating effects of the war, not only in actual destruction and loss of life, but also in its psychological impact after decades of tense expectation. The disruption of life in many parts of Germany at this time would be difficult to overestimate. Few Lutheran areas remained completely unaffected. The belief that the great struggle of the Last Days was coming to a climax was commonly shared; it was as widespread among representatives of the emerging orthodox establishment as among the new prophets and their confused audience. At the same time, however, the polarization of prophetic attitudes and orthodoxy's attempt to rein in apocalyptic speculation were greatly intensified by the rapid changes and upheavals of the war. The long military conflict was ultimately the most important reason why the apocalyptic world-view dissolved so rapidly in the decades after 1630.

The first years of the war witnessed a feverish excitement in the Lutheran world. Many believers fastened with renewed seriousness on the bleak prophecies of Luther about the future of Germany, while at the same time the hope of a final evangelical victory exercised an ever stronger appeal. During the 1620s and early 1630s, there appeared prophetic visions and revelations of every sort, in which the conviction of an approaching Armageddon, to be followed either by the eternal Kingdom or a final age of peace, was central.[45] Far more commonly than in earlier apocalyptic writings, direct connections between political or military events and apocalyptic imagery are evident in popular works of this period. The events of the time made inevitable a closer linking between spiritual forms of apocalypticism and more concrete political hopes and fears. As we hope to show, however, the effect of this rapid politicization of expectations was finally to hasten the decline of the traditional apocalyptic outlook.

The political prophecy of the Thirty Years' War period cannot be considered here in any detail, but we need to note some important trends. Throughout the first century of the reform movement, prophetic inquiry in the Lutheran realm tended to avoid becoming too directly tied to concrete political concerns. We have, to be sure, seen a continuation of the messianic emperor tradition in the latter half of the sixteenth century, and ideas about the prophetic role of the House of Saxony or other Protestant dynasties had some currency around 1600. In such highly developed prophetic schemes as those of Adam Nachenmoser and Philipp Nicolai, there was also a clear political element, as there was in the Rosicrucian hopes. But even these elaborate schemes were relatively short on political detail. The spiritual aspect remained heavily predominant in the early Lutheran prophetic tradition.

The war, however, evoked a large number of prophecies that were more political than spiritual, reflecting a more immediate concern with the basic earthly goals of peace and security. After 1618, a growing number of popular prophecies appeared, in which spiritual rhetoric was often little more than an adornment for hopes of military victory or stable, peaceful government. The prophecies of the Silesian leatherworker Christopher Kotter, who in 1620 predicted the return of Frederick to the Bohemian throne, the fall of the Hapsburgs, and the destruction of the papacy, were typical of those that gained wide popularity. Kotter's political forecasts were combined with hopes for the conversion of the whole world to the true faith, but they marked a visible shift toward the mundane in popular prophecy. They had many echoes, especially during the early phases of the war.[46]

Political prophecies attributed to Lichtenberger, Grünpeck, Carion, Paracelsus, and other famed astrologers gained widespread popular attention. In one typical collection of such prophetic writings, the anonymous editor explained that the forecasts of Lichtenberger and Paracelsus for great troubles to be followed by world reformation had been essentially accurate; these seers had simply misinterpreted the dates of the earthshaking changes to come.[47] Countless similar popular forecasts focused especially on the events in Bohemia as a prelude to the final earthly struggles. The prediction of future victory for the godly was almost always accompanied by a clear message of repentance, and the call gained urgency by the common adoption of 1623 or 1624 as the critical year to be awaited. In the popular mind political prophecy probably went hand in hand with the more spiritual insights of the pansophic and theosophic seekers. But the pressure of events increasingly pushed political and military developments into the foreground of prophetic attention.

Not surprisingly, whatever old political vaticinations appeared useful and appropriate were revived and recast to fit the new circumstances in Germany. Thus for instance the political prophecies of Paul Graebner, a preacher active at Magdeburg in the late sixteenth century, became commonly known only after the beginning of the war. Around 1619 a collection of Graebner's conjectures appeared, predicting that 1619 and 1620 would see the outbreak of a terrible conflict, and that a split between the Catholic and Spanish party and the defenders of the Augsburg Confession would lead to the election of two emperors in Germany. The pope would continue to perpetrate evils, and God would pour out his wrath in countless ways, until in 1624 all enemies of the Word were utterly destroyed. Like Nagel, Graebner foresaw that the final age of the world would last until 1666, though the time might well be shortened. Do penance now, he warned.[48]

Closely associated with the spread of this sort of political prophecy was a final culmination of hopes for a messianic German emperor. The defeat of Frederick V in 1620 was a setback for one strain of such hopes, but it does not appear to have seriously affected the tradition as a whole, which had been gaining ground in Lutheranism for several decades. This strain of hopeful expectancy continued to gain strength at least until the advent of Gustavus Adolphus.

The emperor prophecy of the era took typical form in a work published in 1631 under Graebner's name, on the effects of the 1618 comet.[49] The author of this tract claimed to have communicated directly with God in visions and dreams. God had revealed that a last great German emperor would appear in 1634, who would change the entire face of Europe. He would bring peace and stability, and through a powerful council would establish the one true religion. After a truce with the Turk expired, the German emperor would conquer the peoples of Asia and Africa, and peace would be established, which would continue until the Last Day. The significance of the "comet-star" itself was both religious and political. It portended a bloodbath for sinners, but great rejoicing among true Christians. True believers were easily identified, for

> Martin Luther is the last prophet of Holy Scripture, and no one else shall appear with such great gifts, and endure such great danger with all peoples, as Luther. Luther is indeed dead, yet all kings, princes, and human powers, as well as all bands and sects, must fear this man; indeed it will happen that many of you when you hear this name Luther spoken will tremble, and both learned and unlearned will be amazed and frightened.[50]

So the victory of the great German emperor would also be the victory of Lutherans. The star announced all good things for them and for Luther's doctrine, especially since "no man of learning can subdue Luther with the pen, and no king with all the power of kings can oppress Luther with pikes, gold, or silver."[51] Papists and Calvinists were to take somber warning. God was to be thanked for revealing such high things in his creation and in the order of nature. Although this tract may well have been based on a prophecy written by Graebner as much as a half century earlier, it nevertheless reflected hopes that were very much alive around 1630. It is significant that Graebner's political prophecies gained far wider circulation in this later period than they had in earlier decades.

The tradition of prophecies about a great German emperor was seriously undermined by the entry of the Swedish king Gustavus Adolphus on the stage of the war. In fact such hopes appear to have died out very quickly around this time. Gustavus himself became the object of a more intense, if far briefer, eruption of political prophecy in Germany. The apocalyptic imagery applied to him was based on a prophecy of Paracelsus about a "Lion of the North" (*Löwen aus Mitternacht*), who would come to defeat the powers of evil in the Last Days.[52] Clearly, one did not need to be a narrow partisan of Lutheran doctrine to see in Gustavus a hero of messianic proportions, and the king's swift military success ensured an even closer focusing of popular prophetic hopes on the realm of concrete political developments. But with the king's death at Lützen in 1632, there was no longer anyone on whom prophetic dreams could settle. Another main avenue of prophetic hope had reached a dead end.

The spread of political prophecy was soon accompanied by the proliferation of popular literature consisting of purely political reporting and discussion. An example of the practical attitude that was beginning to appear was a 1631 tract offering *Apocalyptic, yet Political Considerations* of the circumstances facing German Protestant princes; this work was not apocalyptic at all, but rather showed a blunt preoccupation with worldly affairs and "German liberty."[53] Other popular writings from the 1630s show less and less sense of imminent catastrophe or deliverance, and the emergence of simple concern for "the ancient liberty of the German fatherland."[54] The prevailing attitude in popular literature on the war was becoming one of simple complaint about worldly troubles rather than expectation of imminent upheaval and resolution. Increasingly, too, prophetic interpretations of the events of the war were outnumbered by simple news sheets reporting significant developments and the prospects for peace.[55] Peter Burke has pointed to the appearance of newspapers during the Thirty Years' War as evidence of the rise of popular political consciousness in Europe; this trend needs to be understood as the other side of a simultaneously waning apocalyptic consciousness. For the first time, too, something like a common Protestant awareness was emerging, not only in Germany but in Northern Europe generally, as more practical political alliances became necessary.[56] News began to replace prophecy as the effort to fit current events into a transcendent scheme of meaning was gradually abandoned.

The pronouncements of Johann Warner, who became a sort of prophetic adviser to the Swedish military command, reflected the growing political emphasis in the prophecy of the period. Warner was an ardent Lutheran who foresaw a wonderful reign of peace to precede the Last Day, but not before Christians had passed through terrible trials. As time passed his predictions took on a much more practical tone, as though plans for political action were being suggested. He was careful to divorce his prophecies from all association with the mystical chiliasm and sectarianism that had grown up among the new prophets. "I have nothing to do with such fanatical spirits, except that I too struggle against them," he wrote.[57] Warner's was a straightforward, visionary prediction in the service of Lutheranism. Although this sort of political prophecy could be couched in thoroughly eschatological terms, and was often applauded even by orthodox theologians, it nonetheless represented a falling away from the sort of spiritual questing we have examined. It was more and more a reflection of hopes and fears for the earthly future. The function of prophecy was beginning to contract, as on balance it would continue to do throughout the seventeenth century.

Among some orthodox writers and preachers the war continued to evoke apocalyptic warnings and exhortations to repentance. Georg Rost's reactions to the conflict and the confusion of his time are illustrated in a work of 1625 in which he compared the Germans to the Ninevites of Jonah.[58] Rost directly related the words of Matthew 24 on wars, pestilence, false prophets, and iniquity to the contemporary scene. All these miseries had fallen on Germany because of her sins. The warnings of war had not been heeded, so God had now sent hunger, plague, and other afflictions as well. A further punishment was the rash of enthusiasts who misled many Christians by predicting that Christ would return in 1625 to establish a thousand-year Kingdom. The nearer the end, the worse such tribulations would become, but the lesson of Jonah was paramount. If Germans would repent, they might be delivered.

Yet Rost's zealous and heartfelt apocalyptic warnings were hardly typical of Lutheran orthodoxy. In the works of most theologians the war was rarely mentioned,[59] and the Last Things were often treated as a wholly abstract theological category with no connection to everyday experience. The sermons and edificatory writings of the period show a rapid waning of efforts to breathe new life into old eschatological teachings. The desire for some form of future-directed religious hope did not, of course, disappear in war-torn Germany. But the writings of the preachers and theologians were losing touch with the lives of the people; orthodox prophecy was quickly becoming mere theology. How many Lutherans, we may wonder, were likely to read the huge tome on the Last Things by Paul Jenisch, which took well over a thousand pages to plough through the standard teachings, and avoided all but the tamest prophetic speculation?[60] This work, which included a preface by Johann Valentin Andreae, had been written in 1628, but remained unpublished until 1645 because of the disruptions of war. Jenisch seems to have intended to reassert pure evangelical eschatology, but for many Lutherans this aim now implied a general weakening of the old apocalyptic excitement.

Far better known Lutheran theologians also show the same tendency to restrict the realm of eschatology. Johann Matthaeus Meyfart, who combined strict orthodoxy with a true reforming zeal, was deeply affected by the chaos of his age. Meyfart's influential sermons on the Last Things, published in 1626 as the *Tuba Novissima*, show a real and powerful eschatological sensibility, but they are not truly apocalyptic in character. They make very little if any effort to show that signs of any sort prove the historical closeness of the end. Meyfart preached as though God's Judgment hung over all men at every moment. His message was a powerful and persuasive call to repentance, but there were no references to the natural world, no use of celestial signs, no mention even of Antichrist as playing a role in the Last Days of the world. This was, in fact, no longer Reformation-style eschatology. Meyfart's sermons reflect rather a movement toward the purely orthodox eschatology that stood apart from all efforts to dig into divine mysteries.[61]

The same is true of Meyfart's other works, notably his eschatological trilogy of 1627–32. In the first work of the trilogy, *The Heavenly Jerusalem*, he clearly put himself within the tradition of Arndtian personal piety, minus the aspect of nature mysticism. What he had to say about the Last Day and its coming was extremely reserved, compared to the sort of speculation that orthodox thinkers had been commonly engaging in a few years earlier.[62] In the other works of the trilogy, the lack of an effort to buttress prophetic preaching with evidence from history and the natural world is notable. The final volume, *The Last Judgment*, includes some very general references to the historical significance of the Reformation: the Last Day could not come, for example, until the Antichrist was revealed. Now the fourth monarchy wobbled on its last legs and was about to fall; the forces of the Antichrist raged in desperate fury. But Meyfart was highly reserved about other signs. Almost all the celestial signs were still in the future; they would occur directly before the end. Meyfart did cite evidence that the position of the stars was beginning to shift, suggesting that the breakup of the firmament could not be far off.[63] But such evidence was rare in his writings; he was not engaged in the search for prophetic proof that had so engaged earlier generations.

Among dissenters from the Lutheran establishment, the war encouraged the rise of an ardent antimilitarism and pacifism that would have broad European influence through the seventeenth century. Paul Felgenhauer was among the leading preachers of the idea that any and all war, even war in defense of German freedom, was against the commandment of God; the children of God were called to a different kind of freedom. For the first time, the earlier pacifist teachings of Sebastian Franck and groups such as the Mennonites began to gain a truly widespread popular following in the Lutheran regions of Germany.[64] Such teachings could gain common acceptance only after war ceased to be regarded as one of God's punishments sent upon a sinful mankind.

Thus the Thirty Years' War brought a rapid divergence of political and spiritual hopes. Thus too it played a major role in the collapse of the quest for universal prophetic insight. It is important to remember that apocalyptic beliefs can be disconfirmed without being discredited; individual cases of failed prophecy do not necessarily destroy the apocalyptic mentality.[65] The fundamental reason for the waning of the apocalyptic sensibility was not simply gradual disillusionment, but the overexpansion of the apocalyptic outlook into a pansophic cloud; the deflation of this confused atmosphere was sooner or later inevitable. But the war clearly played a part in the timing of this process in Germany. As the conflict dragged on and spread, daily events began to appear too sordid to be part of a divine scheme for history. The events of the war proved too unpredictable, too drawn out, and too human to support the continuation of earlier intense beliefs in imminent resolution.

THE WANING

Much of the evidence examined in this chapter has suggested that by the 1630s the old prophetic excitement had begun to wane quickly among Germans influenced by the Lutheran tradition. To illustrate with any degree of thoroughness how this process continued in later decades would take us far beyond the scope of this study. But we can hardly avoid a glance at the larger outlines of this striking change in outlook and some of its implications.

Luther's heirs did not consciously turn away from apocalyptic belief. But as the more cautious proponents and followers of theological orthodoxy felt it necessary to repudiate the unruly prophets in their midst, they also gradually abandoned the tense eschatological hope that had characterized the first century of the Reformation in Germany. This abandonment was perhaps first manifest in the retreat to more purely biblical forms of prophecy, evident in writers like Meyfart and Paul Jenisch.[66] It becomes much clearer in later orthodox theology. Werner Elert has pointed to a "cooling off" of the Lutheran passion for history in the seventeenth century; the whole concern with the place of the present in a universal scheme of time was on the wane.[67] In place of the earlier concern with time and history, orthodoxy tended to put a wholly personal concern with the eternal benefits of justification. This emphasis spiritualized and individualized eschatology, and the coming Kingdom as a collectivity grew less important. The way was thus opened, as one scholar has put it, "for Protestant eschatology to sink into a rationalistic individualism."[68] Mystical, individualizing tendencies had grown in Lutheran eschatology in the last decades of the sixteenth century and the first years of the seventeenth, but during that era these tendencies had remained within the frame of the apocalyptic world-picture; indeed they had intensified that outlook by underlining the profound duality between the spiritual life of the chosen and the decadent world, soon to be destroyed. It was now increasingly common for disillusioned believers to break free from the assumptions of the apocalyptic outlook, to return to an inner spirituality that resembled more closely the piety of the *Devotio moderna* than the Reformation hope of the coming Kingdom. Here lay the roots of Pietism.

The more purely mystical piety of the seventeenth century could only emerge when eschatological thought had been divorced from historical reckoning and the observation of nature. In other words, faith and cosmology had to separate. The waning of apocalypticism was at the same time the waning of the theory of man as microcosm, and of the entire magical world-picture. The microcosm theory, to be sure, came under general attack in Europe during the seventeenth century,[69] but among few groups was the turning away so marked or so consistent as it was in Lutheran orthodoxy. The apocalyptic world-view had been essential to the union of faith and cosmology, prophecy and gnosis, throughout the Reformation. But as orthodoxy put serious expectancy at arm's length, the links between prophecy and gnosis were broken. Prophetic faith without gnosis turned in the direction of a personal mystical belief that often verged on quietism. Gnosis without prophecy would eventually take shape in the realms of rational, empirical science.

This process, we have suggested, was greatly accelerated by the outbreak of war, "by the political blows of 1618–20 and the necessity for a militant simplification of ideas," as R. J. W. Evans has put it with reference to Central Europe as a whole.[70] In Lutheran Germany this simplification implied restriction of the traditional freedom of apocalyptic faith. The goal of Lutheran churchmen in the first century of their movement had been largely the reform of the individual conscience in the face of the impending Judgment. Apocalyptic belief tended to preclude any long-term program of social discipline; one sought to save souls, not to impose a program of reform on Christian society. But now, with the very conditions of daily life often tenuous, spiritual leaders felt a new challenge. As Johann Valentin Andreae saw it, "purity of religion had been established with the Reformation, but the task of his century was to establish purity of life."[71] Andreae's reaction against the prophetic mania in which he himself had been caught up as a youth eventually led him to dedicate his life to the more worldly concerns of education and Christian discipline; in this he typified broad trends in German Lutheran society. The new programs of church discipline that were introduced in Württemberg and elsewhere by the middle decades of the century were one reflection of a changed social scene, in which traditional expectancy had at best a radically reduced role. The proper ordering of Christian society, conceived in newly practical terms, hardly allowed for the continued open pursuit of apocalyptic insight by individual believers.[72]

By 1630, apocalyptic expectation was already becoming a characteristic of separatist groups, a mode of dissent; it no longer reflected deep and universally shared assumptions. Even among radical separatists, prophetic and magical speculation appears to have become less prominent than the themes of tolerance, pacifism, and personal, practical piety. All but forgotten figures like Hans Engel-brecht (d. 1642) and Ludwig Gifftheil (d. 1661), both mystical en-thusiasts opposed by the established church, seem to have been far more interested in the teaching and practice of a personal, everyday piety than in magical or prophetic speculation per se. The same was true of Nikolaus Teting, who wandered through Germany in the 1620s preaching on the inner Kingdom of God.[73] The pacifist spiri-tualism of Christian Hoburg (d. 1675) similarly typified the anti-clerical piety of the seventeenth century. The dreams of magical reform that had been so common before 1620 withered in later decades, leaving in their place a mysticism of a different sort.[74]

Even with the most ardent, unchurchly seekers, the sort of pro-phetic hope that inspired definite predictions of future events did not fare well as the seventeenth century progressed. Late in his life Paul Felgenhauer, who for decades had predicted imminent upheav-als, divine punishment, and the advent of a new age, began to sound a new note: "I am no prophet or fortune-teller, but a liar, as are all men." It was difficult and dangerous to try to foretell par-ticular events; all was in the hands of God and of time. Felgenhauer had not given up the hope of an imminent godly Kingdom, but his attitude toward prophecy had grown more reserved.[75] Again, it is worth noting that Felgenhauer was a strong proponent of religious tolerance, and had a practical reform program for the church. He was in revolt against all "sects," against any person or group who claimed unequivocal authority for particular confessional beliefs or definite prophetic visions.

Naturally the disappearance of apocalyptic attitudes was an un-even process. There were occasional upswellings of the old hopes and fears, as for example in 1666 and the immediately preceding years. Not only had 1666 long been a focus of speculation because the date included the number of the beast; there was also a major comet in 1664–65 which was widely proclaimed as a divine warn-ing.[76] But even the popular literature of this period shows a far less consistent and powerful sense of expectancy than had obtained just a few decades earlier. Wonder-books of various sorts, for example, were still appearing in Germany in the 1660s, but the wonders were no longer generally regarded as signs of God's wrath or of the com-ing Judgment. For some writers reports of natural wonders became a proof of God's benevolence; for Johannes Prätorius (d. 1680) they were even an occasion for amusing wordplay. And prodigy writing itself died out fairly quickly in the second half of the seventeenth century.[77]

In other German literature of the seventeenth century, the theme of the Last Day receded far into the background. When the Last Things were mentioned in popular literature late in the century, they generally had individual rather than historical or cosmic significance. Eschatology gradually became a point of abstract dogma, or a merely aesthetic form. By midcentury the doctrine of the Last Judgment could even be used for comic satire.[78] One good index of broad movements in piety is offered by hymns of the period, and here too there was a clear dwindling of apocalyptic emphasis after about 1620.[79]

Not only in Lutheran orthodoxy, then, but in the wider world of Lutheran piety and its various offspring, the apocalyptic tensions of the Reformation era were waning markedly by the middle decades of the seventeenth century. The war in Germany had greatly hastened the process by which eschatological expectancy lost its universality. To a certain extent, nonconformists kept alive a tradition of chiliastic hope, which saw a final and not insignificant flowering in German Pietism. But on balance the apocalyptic world-view had lost its central role; prophecy and gnosis had gone their separate ways.

✑ Conclusion

Martin Luther would have been disappointed to know that his five hundredth birthday would be celebrated on earth.[1] He believed in the imminence of the end of the world and the Last Judgment; this belief was widely shared among his colleagues and followers. Much more than Catholics or Calvinists, Lutherans kept alive the tense hopes and fears for the future that had characterized the late Middle Ages. Luther did seek to shift the emphasis of expectation from the terrible prospect of divine wrath and punishment to the joyful promise of redemption and resurrection, a new heaven and a new earth. But the anxious experience of looking forward and waiting remained a central feature of piety in the Lutheran realm; in fact this kind of expectancy now had explicit support from the leaders of an established church. The nearness of the Second Advent was confirmed by the discovery of the Antichrist, by the interpretation of biblical prophecy, by other signs and prophetic traditions, and by the simple witness of faith. Moreover, far from waning as the sixteenth century progressed, the sense of expectation in Lutheran Germany tended to become more explicit, more reasoned, and more comprehensive. Inasmuch as this attitude of expectancy was more commonly expressed and explored, we can also say that it became more intense.

This study has concentrated mostly on the latter broadening and intensification of the apocalyptic sensibility. The process can be clearly discerned in the troubled times after Luther's death, and it becomes especially noticeable in the confused era around 1600. We have seen some of its manifestations in the effort to reckon the ages of world history, and to speculate about the nearness of the end on the basis of chronological evidence. Many of the same tendencies were evident in astrological prediction, which in Lutheran Germany was heavily influenced by apocalyptic assumptions. And the search for prophetic knowledge, as it developed from Lutheran attitudes about the Last Times, had much to do with the spread of interest in magic and the occult.

Despite the formal Lutheran acknowledgment of the Augustinian conception of God's absolute freedom, all these types of prophetic inquiry took for granted some sort of divine plan or structure. In chronological reckoning this plan applied essentially to the outlines of history. Astrology shared an interest in an orderly historical scheme, but it also assumed a stable and discoverable network of influences in the structure of creation. Magical inquiry, finally, depended fully on the assumption of universal correspondences that extended to the human mind and to nature. These types of inquiry into God's plan were all encouraged by the feeling that the Last Days of the world had arrived. One common corollary of this conviction was that God intended profound secrets to be revealed so that people might be saved. The overriding concern was, after all, salvation; and since the Judgment was approaching, this concern turned into an earnest, often confused, and at times desperate striving for saving knowledge. The apocalyptic believer sought reassurance through insight into a reality far greater than self, greater than human society, greater than the world that could be grasped through human reason or discourse.

In Lutheran teaching, the Reformation itself had brought the final recovery of divine truth. The true Gospel was preached once again, the light of truth was flashing over the world to prepare the way for the Judge. At the same time, however, Luther's followers developed a profound sense of collective guilt at Germany's failure to accept God's blessings. Increasingly, attention turned to the terrible punishments that were coming, so much so that the joyous message of the Gospel was often obscured. This world no longer held out any hope, only the threat of God's wrath. The late sixteenth-century and early seventeenth-century yearning for the Last Day was not at heart a rejoicing, but a longing for deliverance from a thoroughly corrupt world. This longing helps to explain why Germans sought so desperately for a way out of their spiritual malaise through prophetic insight, through occult schemes, and through new hopes for a universal spiritual transformation.

The waxing pessimism of the age, the wailing over the present vale of tears and the longing for salvation from it, moved toward gnostic revulsion from the world. The gnostic tendency is a revulsion from time itself, a seeking for deliverance in the purely spiritual, the timeless, the perfect; it therefore looks to the destruction of this world. The saved is one who sees, who knows; the ignorant are damned to eternal suffering. Time itself is for the gnostic a product of ignorance; this is why in some magical schemes of late Reformation apocalypticism, knowledge of the universal scheme could actually help to bring about the final, much desired transformation. Naturally, the Christian presuppositions of Lutheranism put a limit to this revulsion against the world, this radical dualism. The world was a divine creation, and one's place in it was ordained by God. But the desire to understand one's place in the plan, to see how and when the time of trial and suffering would end, was given powerful justification by the apocalyptic outlook that prevailed in Lutheranism.

For Lutherans, of course, all prophetic truth was biblical. Whatever one learned about the deepest truths of nature and history could be expected to complement, if not to confirm, biblical truth. It was but one short step from here to the assumption that the prophetic truths of Scripture could in fact be confirmed in both the macrocosm and the microcosm, and only one more to the supposition that it was positively necessary to complete one's understanding of the Word by reading in the book of nature and in one's own soul. To be sure, the most radical steps along this line of thought were often taken by magical seekers, like Paul Nagel, who were at least as deeply influenced by Paracelsian and other forms of magical thought as they were by Lutheran teachings. But such attitudes gained their broadest acceptance where apocalyptic tension awoke a strong desire to understand prophetic secrets, and Luther's teachings had helped produce such a tension among many of his cultural heirs. Much of European society in the sixteenth century, of course, was affected to some degree by an apocalyptic sensibility, and questers after magical insight could be found almost anywhere. But one suggestion of this study has been that German culture was distinctive partly because the apocalyptic currents remained strongest there after Luther's Reformation. I strongly suspect that nowhere else did these various trends merge in quite the same way; nowhere else did the combination of prophetic preaching, disappointed hopes, confusion, pessimism, and popular curiosity create so intense an atmosphere of watchfulness.

Repeatedly, the ideas of Philipp Melanchthon have proved important for understanding these trends in late Reformation thought. In him were combined genuine evangelical piety and the broad-minded interests of late humanism. Countless anxious souls who shared both his piety and his interests, but who were either unable or unwilling to maintain a certain reserve and a larger perspective on the search for prophetic understanding, produced biblical, mathematical, and magical reckonings in hopes of illuminating their uneasy present and their uncertain future. Insofar as Reformation culture was burgher culture, these speculations reflected the hopes and fears of the German townsmen. Indeed the variety of literature we have reviewed suggests that the apocalyptic world-view may actually have been a unifying force in German town life, forming a bridge between popular culture and the world of the learned. Judging from the pervasiveness of apocalyptic hopes, fears, and expectations, learned and popular culture may not have been as separate as we are sometimes led to believe. Only in the seventeenth century did learned and popular attitudes toward prophecy begin to diverge noticeably, and even then, as we have suggested, there was not so much a divergence as a waning that affected the assumptions of a whole society.

The atmosphere at the turn of the century was one of mystery, esotericism, rumor, and excited expectation. The unceasing waves of literature—astrological, alchemical, medical, visionary, and prophetic—had created conditions in which the grossest sort of intellectual pretension could flourish. But to dismiss the age on this account as one of rank, unproductive superstition is to overlook the creative aspects of this great ferment. Moreover, this sort of dismissal is simply bad history. As Frances Yates tells us, "Too often, the mistake is made of judging people of the sixteenth century as if they knew, what we know, that no great, general, religious change was about to come."[2] The sense of imminent universal change was above all a response to the need for a sense of order in the world; in the absence of any other real certainty, it was comforting to know that the inevitable cosmic resolution was soon to occur. This attitude also had its creative sides, one of which was to spur on the crucial debate over method in philosophy and science. The question grew more and more pressing: how could proper insight into the fundamental truths of the universal scheme be gained? At the same time this sense of imminent change, though it could take several different forms, was almost always accompanied by the call for thorough personal transformation, for repentance. All the prophetic schemes and dreams of the late Reformation period were variations on the combined themes of repentance, Judgment, and the coming Kingdom.

The prophetic dreams and reckonings of the time were already beginning to discredit themselves in the early seventeenth century. But the process was greatly hastened by the Thirty Years' War; that holocaust did much to end the last great age of apocalyptic hope in Germany. The trend toward increasingly radical prophetic speculations was intensified by the conflict, but at the same time, many uneasy Lutherans began to react by seeking more mundane forms of order, and thus tended to turn their backs on all but the most traditional and general prophetic interpretation. Moreover the war itself, which many Germans had seen at first as the final earthly struggle, ultimately contributed to disillusionment when the expected cosmic changes did not occur. Under these pressures the realms of subjective and objective experience, which had been held in tenuous union by the apocalyptic imagination, broke apart remarkably quickly. Among the many transitions that we might choose to call the end of the medieval world, this one has a better claim than most.[3]

Although this study does not extend to the later seventeenth century, I have adduced some general evidence to suggest that prophetic excitement continued to wane in Lutheran Germany after 1630. The number of popular tracts devoted to apocalyptic themes appears to have dwindled rapidly after the early decades of the seventeenth century. While I have made no attempt to marshal evidence for the point, it is probably not too risky to assert that German piety became more mystical and personal in this later period. It is true that there was a strong chiliastic strain in German Pietism, best illustrated in the works of Johann Albrecht Bengel (d. 1752). But Pietist millenarianism tended toward a melioristic rather than truly apocalyptic outlook; it looked to gradual fulfillment, not sudden spiritual transformation. Pietism reflected a confidence that the final divine transformation was in some respects already underway within history, an idea that had emerged earlier among Calvinist prophetic thinkers. Moreover, the eschatological hopes of Pietism were far less reflective of an entire *Zeitgeist* than were those of the Reformation era. They were more than balanced by the individualistic and subjective religiosity that prevailed in the late seventeenth and early eighteenth centuries.

Other sorts of prophetic hope and fear have continued to play an important role in Western attitudes throughout the modern age. But never again would religious prophecy be as fully integrated with the quest for gnosis as it was in the late Reformation. This study has looked at the apocalyptic sensibility in its time of greatest intensity and pervasiveness; what followed was a gradual, if uneven, disappearance, and the rise of very different assumptions about nature, history, and the future.

Our study of the apocalyptic sensibility in the era of the Reformation provokes a final speculation about Luther's influence upon the German mind. The Reformation in Germany had directed hopes to an imminent, objective end of history, and thus a resolution of all earthly problems, with the Second Advent. Lutheran apocalypticism did not, of course, encourage an abandonment of history or of Christian responsibility. But it did tend to subordinate earthly hopes so thoroughly to the promise of the coming Kingdom that historical existence could be felt as a heavy and unwanted burden. Unlike Calvinism, which left the door open to meliorism and the vision of progress that eventually marked the Anglo-American experience and the rise of Western liberalism, Lutheranism looked to immediate transformation and liberation from history. Then, too, the swing of the pendulum to a radically subjective piety among seventeenth-century Germans effectively distanced the believer from the uncertainties of historical change; faith looked entirely beyond history. If the German idea of freedom has differed from that of other Western peoples, perhaps it may be traced to a deep and ultimately gnostic revulsion against the reality of history itself, an impatient longing, often inspired but often misdirected, for the Kingdom of God.

᪥ Reference Matter

✥ Notes

The following abbreviations are used in the notes:

WA   D. Martin Luthers Werke: Kritische Gesamtausgabe. Weimar, 1883–.
CR   Corpus reformatorum. Vols. 1–28: Philipp Melanchthon: Opera ... omnia. Ed. C. G. Bretschneider. Halle, 1834–52; Braunschweig, 1853–60. Vols. 88ff: Huldreich Zwinglis sämtliche Werke. Ed. Emil Egli et al., Berlin, Leipzig, Zürich, 1905–.
ADB   Allgemeine deutsche Biographie. 56 vols. Leipzig, 1875–1912.

Introduction

1. The quotation is found in Leonard Krentzheim's Coniecturae. Christliche vermuttungen, von künfftiger Zeit, Zustand, in Kirchen vnd Regimenten (Görlitz, 1583), "Vorrede" of Marcus Rullus, fols. b vii, b vii/v. These particular words may be inexact or even apocryphal; I have been able to verify them in neither the CR nor the Supplementa Melanchthoniana (Leipzig, 1910–). But they are certainly not uncharacteristic of Melanchthon. Rullus reported that Melanchthon was speaking before "etliche hunderte studenten."

2. Ibid., fol. b viii/v.

3. See Frank Kermode, The Sense of an Ending: Studies in the Theory of Fiction (London, 1966).

4. John Headley, Luther's View of Church History (New Haven, 1963), pp. 245ff.

5. See Gunnar Hillerdal, "Prophetische Züge in Luthers Geschichtsdeutung," Studia Theologica 7 (1953), 107.

6. Nothing could be further from the truth than the often repeated assertion that with the Peace of Augsburg the Lutherans "came to enjoy a recognized status and thereafter relaxed." See Roland H. Bainton, The Reformation of the Sixteenth Century (Boston, 1952), p. 111.

7. Bryan W. Ball, *A Great Expectation: Eschatological Thought in English Protestantism to 1660* (Leiden, 1975), p. 16. Other recent works on the English scene that share this mistaken outlook to one degree or another include: Richard Bauckham, ed., *Tudor Apocalypse* (Oxford, 1978); Paul Christianson, *Reformers and Babylon: English Apocalyptic Visions from the Reformation to the Eve of the Civil War* (Toronto, 1978); Katharine R. Firth, *The Apocalyptic Tradition in Reformation Britain 1530–1645* (Oxford, 1979); and C. A. Patrides and Joseph Wittreich, Jr., eds., *The Apocalypse in English Renaissance Thought and Literature* (Ithaca, 1985).

8. On the whole *renovatio mundi* theme in the later Middle Ages and the sixteenth century, see the magisterial work by Marjorie Reeves, *The Influence of Prophecy in the Later Middle Ages: A Study in Joachimism* (Oxford, 1969), as well as her more recent work, *Joachim of Fiore and the Prophetic Future* (London, 1976). It is significant that in both of these works Reeves's treatment of Joachimist prophecy after the early sixteenth century is focused mostly on Northern Europe.

9. Denis Crouzet, "La Représentation du temps à l'époque de la Ligue," *Revue historique* 270, no. 2 (1983), 297–388. Crouzet does not acknowledge to what extent the apocalyptic works he cites from the late 1580s drew upon German Protestant sources. In a study ostensibly devoted to expectancy in France, many if not most of the writings cited are German. Crouzet argues that in the rituals associated with the League an eschatological myth "devient acte collectif" (p. 322).

10. Gerhard Ebeling, *Luther: An Introduction to His Thought* (Philadelphia, 1970), p. 92.

11. Friedrich Wilhelm Kantzenbach, *Orthodoxie und Pietismus* (Gütersloh, 1966), pp. 32, 33.

12. Unless otherwise noted, biblical quotations are from the Authorized (King James) Version.

13. Gerald Strauss, *Luther's House of Learning: Indoctrination of the Young in the German Reformation* (Baltimore and London, 1978), p. 307.

14. Bernard McGinn, "Introduction" to *Apocalyptic Spirituality: Treatises and Letters of Lactantius, Adso of Montier-en-Der, Joachim of Fiore, the Franciscan Spirituals, Savonarola* (New York, 1979), p. 15.

15. For a discussion of examining social worlds from the "inside" and the "outside," see J. G. A. Pocock, *Politics, Language, and Time* (London, 1972), title essay.

16. Among the most important studies is R. J. W. Evans, *Rudolph II and His World* (Oxford, 1973). Of the many excellent works of Frances Yates dealing with this period, the indispensable one is *Giordano Bruno and the Hermetic Tradition* (Chicago, 1964).

17. Wilhelm Koepp, *Johann Arndt: Eine Untersuchung über die Mystik im Luthertum* (Berlin, 1912), p. 9.

Chapter 1

1. Bernard McGinn, *Visions of the End: Apocalyptic Traditions in the Middle Ages* (New York, 1979), pp. 2–6.

2. This tack has been taken by more than a few students of Luther's thought. See for example Hans Preuss, *Martin Luther: Der Prophet* (Gütersloh, 1933).

3. I hope to avoid the sticky problems of historical definition surrounding the terms "gnosis" and "gnosticism," around which a small corpus of works has grown up. "Gnosis," "gnostic," and "gnosticism" are here used interchangeably to refer to a general eschatological orientation, rather than to the beliefs of any particular ancient sect. For a recent discussion of the problems surrounding the historical use of these terms, see Kurt Rudolph, "'Gnosis' and 'Gnosticism'—the Problems of Their Definition and Their Relation to the Writings of the New Testament," in A. H. B. Logan and A. J. M. Wedderburn, eds., *The New Testament and Gnosis: Essays in Honor of Robert McL. Wilson* (Edinburgh, 1983), pp. 21–37.

4. Walter Schmithals, *The Apocalyptic Movement: Introduction and Interpretation* (Nashville and New York, 1975), p. 102.

5. Ibid., p. 104.

6. Ibid., p. 107.

7. Rudolph Otto, *The Kingdom of God and the Son of Man* (London, 1943), p. 15; quoted in Schmithals, *The Apocalyptic Movement*, p. 93. On the similarities between apocalypticism and gnosticism see also Carl-A. Keller, "Das Problem des Bösen in Apokalyptik und Gnostik," in Martin Krause, ed., *Gnosis and Gnosticism: Papers Read at the Seventh International Conference on Patristic Studies* (Leiden, 1977), pp. 70–90. See also C. Kingsley Barrett, "Gnosis and the Apocalypse of John," in Logan and Wedderburn, *The New Testament and Gnosis*, pp. 125–37. Barrett concludes (p. 133) that "in Judaism there is a kinship and propinquity between Apocalyptic and the sort of mystical speculation that is one, and indeed a major, component among the phenomena of Gnosticism." See also Kurt Rudolph, *Gnosis: The Nature and History of Gnosticism* (New York, 1983), esp. p. 278: "Apocalyptic and Gnosis . . . have a whole series of mythological themes in common." George MacRae has written that "both apocalyptic and Gnosticism center on the acquisition (by revelation) and the communication of a knowledge that exercises saving power in the present by its future-oriented content. It is true that the vast bulk of Gnostic revelations are much more obviously centered on the origins of humanity and world, but the perspective is future nevertheless: it is in the return to the precosmic that human destiny lies. And the presence of explicit passages of apocalyptic eschatology in Gnostic revelations is further evidence that the categories of apocalyptic and Gnosticism should not be too sharply divided. The latter is one manifestation of the former, albeit in extreme form." "Apocalyptic Eschatology in Gnosticism," in David Hellholm, ed., *Apocalypticism in the Mediterranean World and the Near East: Proceedings of the International Colloquium on Apocalypticism, Uppsala, August 12–17, 1979* (Tübingen, 1983), p. 324.

8. Schmithals, *The Apocalyptic Movement*, pp. 94–95.

9. Christopher Rowland, *The Open Heaven* (London, 1982), p. 21; cited by C. K. Barrett in Logan and Wedderburn, p. 127.

10. Reeves, *The Influence of Prophecy*, p. 295.

11. Marjorie Reeves, Preface to *Apocalyptic Spirituality*, ed. McGinn, p. xiv.

12. Bernard McGinn, Introduction to *Apocalyptic Spirituality*, p. 14.

13. Norman Cohn, *The Pursuit of the Millennium: Revolutionary Millenarians and Mystical Anarchists in the Middle Ages* (New York, 1961). Cohn's view of apocalypticism in general shares much with the understanding of Gnosis propounded by Hans Jonas (*The Gnostic Religion: The Message of the Alien God and the Beginnings of Christianity*; Boston, 1978) and by the political philosopher Eric Voegelin (in many works, including *The New Science of Politics*; Chicago, 1952). In this view any form of mystical dualism is essentially revolutionary, since it places all value on some supposed higher reality, or a reality to come.

14. See for example Michael Barkun, *Disaster and the Millennium* (New Haven, 1974).

15. Robert E. Lerner, "The Black Death and Western European Eschatological Mentalities," *American Historical Review* 86, no. 3 (June 1981), 537.

16. Ibid., pp. 537–38.

17. Robert E. Lerner, *The Powers of Prophecy: The Cedar of Lebanon Vision from the Mongol Onslaught to the Dawn of the Enlightenment* (Berkeley, 1983), p. 193 et passim.

18. McGinn, *Visions of the End*, p. 10.

19. Ibid., p. 33.

20. Keller, "Das Problem des Bösen," in Krause, ed., *Gnosis and Gnosticism*, p. 75.

21. Schmithals, *The Apocalyptic Movement*, p. 148, quoted in McGinn, Introduction to *Apocalyptic Spirituality*, p. 8.

22. McGinn, Introduction to *Apocalyptic Spirituality*, p. 8.

23. Karl Löwith, *Meaning in History* (Chicago, 1949), p. 155.

24. Ernest Lee Tuveson, *Millennium and Utopia: A Study in the Background of the Idea of Progress* (Berkeley, 1949), pp. 15ff. See also Theodor E. Mommsen, "St. Augustine and the Christian Idea of Progress: The Background of the City of God," *Journal of the History of Ideas* 12 (1951), 346–74.

25. On Byzantine apocalypticism see especially Paul J. Alexander, *The Byzantine Apocalyptic Tradition* (Berkeley, 1985).

26. McGinn, *Visions of the End*, pp. 62–65.

27. Richard Kenneth Emmerson, *Antichrist in the Middle Ages: A Study of Medieval Apocalypticism, Art, and Literature* (Seattle, 1981), pp. 53–54. The notion that there were pronounced and widespread expectations in the West for the return of Christ in 1000 A.D. was long ago shown to be mistaken. See George L. Burr, "The Year 1000 and the Antecedents of the Crusades," *American Historical Review* 6 (Apr. 1901), 429–39. The myth was also debunked by A. Vasiliev, "Medieval Ideas of the End of the World: East and West," *Byzantion* 16 (1942–43), 462–502; but Vasiliev wrongly reported that Burr shared the myth. A far more thorough and subtle analysis of the whole question is found in Henri Focillon, *The Year 1000* (New York, 1969).

28. McGinn, *Visions of the End*, p. 108.

29. On Rupert, Anselm, and Richard, particularly with regard to changes in commentaries on Revelation, see Barbara Nolan, *The Gothic Visionary Perspective* (Princeton, 1977), pp. 15–34.

30. Marjorie Reeves, Preface to *Apocalyptic Spirituality*, ed. McGinn, p. xvii. For a general guide to Joachim and Joachimism, I have depended on Reeves's indispensable *The Influence of Prophecy*.

31. Robert E. Lerner, "Refreshment of the Saints: The Time after Antichrist as a Station for Earthly Progress in Medieval Thought," *Traditio* 32 (1976), 97–144. See also Emmerson, *Antichrist in the Middle Ages*, pp. 104–6.

32. McGinn, *Visions of the End*, p. 147.

33. Ibid., pp. 224–25.

34. Emmerson, *Antichrist in the Middle Ages*, p. 54.

35. See William Heist, *The Fifteen Signs Before Doomsday* (East Lansing, Mich., 1952); also Emmerson, *Antichrist in the Middle Ages*, p. 83.

36. McGinn, *Visions of the End*, pp. 230–33.

37. Preuss, *Martin Luther: Der Prophet*, pp. 11–12; Emmerson, *Antichrist in the Middle Ages*, pp. 95–101. The key biblical passage on Enoch and Elijah is Revelation 11: 3–7.

38. Emmerson, *Antichrist in the Middle Ages*, p. 59.

39. On prophecies about emperor and pope, see the very brief survey in Preuss, *Martin Luther: Der Prophet*, pp. 4–11. A fuller treatment is found in Reeves, *The Influence of Prophecy*. On emperor prophecies see also the still useful work of Franz Kampers, *Die deutsche Kaiseridee in Prophetie und Sage* (Munich, 1896).

40. Paul Russell, "'Your Sons and Your Daughters Shall Prophesy . . .' (Joel 2: 28): Common People and the Future of the Reformation in the Pamphlet Literature of Southwestern Germany to 1525," *Archive for Reformation History* 74 (1983), 122–39; here p. 138.

41. Gerald Strauss, *Manifestations of Discontent in Germany on the Eve of the Reformation* (Bloomington, 1971), "Introduction," pp. ix–xxiii.

42. Emmerson, *Antichrist in the Middle Ages*, pp. 72–73.

43. See Howard Kaminsky, "Chiliasm and the Hussite Revolution," *Church History* 26 (1957), 43–71.

44. Stewart C. Easton, *Roger Bacon and His Search for a Universal Science: A Reconsideration of the Life and Work of Roger Bacon in the Light of His Own Stated Purposes* (New York, 1952), p. 169.

45. According to Marjorie Reeves (*The Influence of Prophecy*, p. 48n), Easton "argues too easily that Bacon was a Joachite."

46. On Lichtenberger the fullest study is Dietrich Kurtze, *Johannes Lichtenberger: Eine Studie zur Geschichte der Prophetie und Astrologie* (Lübeck, 1960). See also his shorter study, "Prophecy and History: Lichtenberger's Forecasts of Events to Come . . . Their Reception and Diffusion," *Journal of the Warburg and Courtauld Institutes* 21 (1958), 63–85.

47. On the influence of fatalism in the early Reformation era, see Aby Warburg, *Heidnisch-antike Weissagung in Wort und Bild zu Luthers Zei-*

ten (Heidelberg, 1920); also in Aby Warburg, *Gesammelte Schriften* (Nendeln, 1969), vol. 2, pp. 487–558. Fatalism in popular propaganda of the era is explored by Robert Scribner, *For the Sake of Simple Folk: Popular Propaganda for the German Reformation* (Cambridge, 1981); see esp. pp. 117ff.

48. Marjorie Reeves, "The Development of Apocalyptic Thought: Medieval Attitudes," in Patrides and Wittreich, eds., *The Apocalypse in English Renaissance Thought and Literature*, pp. 40–72; here p. 62. On the *renovatio mundi* theme in the Renaissance generally, see also Reeves's *The Influence of Prophecy*, pp. 429–62.

49. Pauline Moffitt Watts, "Prophecy and Discovery: On the Spiritual Origins of Christopher Columbus's 'Enterprise of the Indies,'" *American Historical Review* 90, no. 1 (Feb. 1985), 73–102; here p. 92.

50. An excellent introduction to the topic is John Leddy Phelan, *The Millennial Kingdom of the Franciscans in the New World: A Study of the Writings of Geronimo de Mendieta (1525–1604)* (Berkeley and Los Angeles, 1970; first ed. 1956).

51. Preuss, *Martin Luther: Der Prophet*, pp. 20–21.

52. Hans Preuss, *Die Vorstellungen vom Antichrist im späteren Mittelalter, bei Luther und in der konfessionellen Polemik* (Leipzig, 1906), p. 6.

53. Robert Lerner, "Medieval Prophecy and Religious Dissent," *Past and Present* 72 (Aug. 1976), 19–20.

54. George H. Williams, *The Radical Reformation* (Philadelphia, 1962), p. 857.

55. See Günther List, *Chiliastische Utopie und radikale Reformation: Die Erneuerung der Idee vom tausendjährigen Reich im 16. Jahrhundert* (Munich, 1973). Also valuable on Luther and Müntzer is Hans-Ulrich Hofmann, *Luther und die Johannes-Apokalypse* (Tübingen, 1982), pp. 647–55.

56. This point is made in reference to Protestantism in England by Keith Vivian Thomas, *Religion and the Decline of Magic* (London, 1971); see esp. ch. 5. Thomas also points out that in England, while the Reformation had put an end to miracles, orthodox believers were not so sure about the status of religious prophecy. Many took the position that further messages from God could not be ruled out. These statements are equally applicable to Lutheran Germany.

57. R. J. W. Evans, *The Making of the Habsburg Monarchy 1550–1700: An Interpretation* (Oxford, 1979), p. 394.

58. Natalie Zemon Davis, "From Popular Religion to Religious Cultures," in Steven E. Ozment, ed., *Reformation Europe: A Guide to Research* (St. Louis, Mo., 1982), p. 325.

59. Headley, *Luther's View*, esp. pp. 106–61.

60. Heinrich Quistorp, *Calvin's Doctrine of the Last Things* (Richmond, Va., 1955), p. 113.

61. John Calvin, *Institutes of the Christian Religion*, ed. J. T. McNeil (Philadelphia, 1960), vol. 2, pp. 905–6.

62. The best work on Brightman and his English colleagues is Bryan W. Ball, *A Great Expectation* (see above, Introduction, note 7). There is no

good modern study of Alsted's eschatological thought; a brief treatment may be found in R. G. Clouse, "The Rebirth of Millenarianism," in Peter Toon, ed., *Puritans, the Millennium and the Future of Israel: Puritan Eschatology 1600 to 1660* (Cambridge, 1970), pp. 42–54.

63. The aggressive, international character of Calvinism is well analyzed in Claus-Peter Clasen, *The Palatinate in European History 1555–1618* (Oxford, 1963).

64. Gottfried W. Locher, "Huldrych Zwingli's Concept of History," in Locher, *Zwingli's Thought: New Perspectives* (Leiden, 1981), p. 103.

65. Zwingli, *Commentarius de vera et falsa religione* (1525), CR 90, 633ff. I have used the translation of S. M. Jackson (Philadelphia, 1929), p. 49.

66. On Zwingli's positive outlook on the earthly future, see Locher, "Huldrych Zwingli's Concept of History," in *Zwingli's Thought*, p. 111. For Zwingli's words to posterity see CR 92, 751ff. Although later Zwinglianism reflected some strong apocalyptic tendencies, the materials for the present study were so rich that I have not extended my treatment to cover apocalypticism in the Zwinglian tradition. Heinrich Bullinger was only one of many Zwinglians who by the middle and late decades of the sixteenth century began to dwell with considerable intensity on the Last Things and the closeness of the end. By far the best known of Bullinger's works of prophetic interpretation is his *One Hundred Sermons on the Apocalypse of Jesus Christ*, which was first published in Latin in 1557. But he also preached sermons on the Last Judgment that appeared in German in 1555; two years later he issued the Latin work *On the End of the Ages and the Coming Judgment of Our Lord Jesus Christ*. In these writings Bullinger showed himself to be far less hesitant than Zwingli to interpret the often obscure imagery of Daniel and Revelation. Zwinglian scholars such as Theodor Bibliander were equally interested in the historical interpretation of prophecy; Bibliander issued for example a *Precise Reckoning and Division of the Ages from the Creation of the World to Its Last Epoch* (*Genauere Ausrechnung und Einteilung der Zeiten von der Schöpfung der Welt bis zu ihrem letzten Zeitalter*). Other Zwinglian apocalyptic writers included Sebastian Meyer, Rudolf Gwalther, Ludwig Lavater, and Johannes Stumpf.

Despite their confessional agreements with a confident and aggressive Calvinism, the Zurichers shared with the Lutherans a growing mood of defensive nervousness as the sanguine assurance of the early Reformation faded. An enormous mass of prophetic and apocalyptic literature, printed in German in Lutheran centers, probably contributed to this spread of characteristically Lutheran apocalyptic attitudes, and the Swiss-German Reformation continued to be affected by this sort of expectancy. In this important respect, sixteenth-century Zwinglians had more in common with Luther's heirs than with Calvin's.

67. Bernd Moeller, *Imperial Cities and the Reformation: Three Essays*, trans. H. C. Erik Midelfort and Mark U. Edwards (Philadelphia, 1972); see the title essay.

68. Ibid., pp. 49, 85.

69. While according to Moeller the early Zwinglian movement was characterized by a "surge of communal thinking," by 1540, he states, this surge was beginning to decrease (Moeller, pp. 103–5). During the crisis years from 1547 to 1555, forces entirely alien to the mentality of the city triumphed, and "the old urban mentality was systematically broken to pieces" (p. 110). Lutheranism took control of the church in the Protestant cities of Upper Germany. It would appear that the same tendency toward the breakup of the old communal mentality must have affected Zurich and the other Swiss-German cities. In the light of these changes, it is hardly surprising that the "second generation" of the Zwinglian reform was apocalyptically minded in a way that Zwingli himself had not been. As the Swiss and Upper German Protestants lost the sense of a connection between community and salvation, the apocalyptic sense of an impending universal transformation gained ground.

70. See Lionel Rothkrug, *Religious Practices and Collective Perceptions: Hidden Homologies in the Renaissance and Reformation* (*Historical Reflections*, 7, no. 1, Spring 1980). These ideas form only a small part of Rothkrug's much broader canvas.

71. Will-Erich Peuckert, *Die grosse Wende: Das apokalyptische Saeculum und Luther* (Darmstadt, 1966), vol. 2, p. 546.

72. Paul Althaus, "Luthers Gedanken über die letzten Dinge," in *Luther-Jahrbuch* 22 (1941), 13–14. On Luther's notion of the sleep of the soul, see also the longer work of Althaus, *Die letzten Dinge* (Gütersloh, 1933), p. 144. Luther's conception was not the same as the teaching known as "psychopannychism," which was simply that souls slept in total unconsciousness between death and the Last Judgment; here all was seen from the perspective of time, while for Luther death takes the soul beyond the world of time.

73. T. F. Torrance, *Kingdom and Church: A Study in the Theology of the Reformation* (Fair Lawn, N.J., 1956), p. 17.

74. Althaus, *Die letzten Dinge*, p. 350. The doctrine of the Resurrection poses no contradiction to this position, since Luther taught that the original corrupt body would be totally renewed; no material connection would remain. See *Evangelisches Kirchen-Lexicon*, "Auferstehung der Tödten," vol. 1, pp. 243–45.

75. Ulrich Asendorf, *Eschatologie bei Luther* (Göttingen, 1967), pp. 207ff, 228–32.

76. Preuss among others seeks to make this distinction, calling Luther's eschatology "prophetic" but not "apocalyptic." See *Martin Luther: Der Prophet*, pp. 210–13.

77. Karl Holl, "Martin Luther on Luther," trans. H. C. Erik Midelfort, in Jaroslav Pelikan, ed., *Interpreters of Luther: Essays in Honor of Wilhelm Pauck* (Philadelphia, 1968), p. 13.

78. Luther, "Vorrede vber den Propheten Daniel," *WA Deutsche Bibel* 11, II, 13.

79. Headley, *Luther's View*, pp. 123–24.

80. Cf. Werner Elert, *Morphologie des Luthertums* (Munich, 1965), vol. 1, p. 448.

81. Preuss, *Die Vorstellungen vom Antichrist*, p. 173.
82. See Headley, *Luther's View*, p. 228. This did not, of course, make of Luther a "chiliastic" thinker; the spread of the Gospel did not imply any kind of worldly progress.
83. *WA Deutsche Bibel* 11, II, 125. I have used the translation of Gerald Strauss, "The Mental World of a Saxon Pastor," in Peter Newman Brooks, ed., *Reformation Principle and Practice: Essays in Honor of Arthur Geoffrey Dickens* (London, 1980), p. 169.
84. *WA Deutsche Bibel* 7, 404: "meyn geyst kan sich ynn das buch nicht schicken." On the illustrations to Revelation see Peter Martin, *Martin Luther und die Bilder zur Apokalypse* (Hamburg, 1983); for the points made here, esp. pp. 100–108.
85. Hans-Ulrich Hofmann, *Luther und die Johannes-Apokalypse* (Tübingen, 1982), pp. 395ff. Luther's attitude toward the book of Revelation thus came to differ greatly from the positions of both Zwingli and Calvin. Zwingli, drawing on the arguments of Erasmus, seriously doubted the canonicity of the book. The Apocalypse was the one biblical book on which Calvin wrote no commentary.
86. See Warren A. Quanbeck, "Luther and Apocalyptic," in Vilmos Vajta, ed., *Luther and Melanchthon in the History and Theology of the Reformation* (Philadelphia, n.d.).
87. This point is made by Firth, *The Apocalyptic Tradition*, p. 12.
88. See Firth, *The Apocalyptic Tradition*, esp. pp. 1–23. Firth generally downplays Luther's importance for Protestant apocalypticism; she is also one of the many English scholars who imply that the greatest flowering of Reformation apocalypticism occurred in Britain. Typical of her mistaken views on these matters is the suggestion that Luther "seems to have borrowed his view of Antichrist from the Wyclifite tradition" (p. 12).
89. Luther, "Vorrede auf die offenbarung S. Johannis," *WA Deutsche Bibel* 7, 407–21. First published in 1530; a revised, final edition was issued in 1545.
90. Ibid., 409. The translation is from the American Edition (St. Louis, 1955–), vol. 35, p. 400.
91. In a letter to Wenzeslaus Link: *WA Briefwechsel* 1, no. 121. The most important scriptural reference was 2 Thessalonians 2: 3–4: "for that day [of Christ] shall not come, except there come a falling away first, and that man of sin be revealed, the son of perdition; who opposeth and exalteth himself above all that is called God, or that is worshipped; so that he as God sitteth in the temple of God, shewing himself that he is God."
92. Preuss, *Die Vorstellungen vom Antichrist*; see esp. pp. 102–20.
93. Hillerdal, "Prophetische Züge," pp. 111. See *WA Tischreden* 3, no. 3055a.
94. Hillerdal, "Prophetische Züge," pp. 111–12; Preuss, *Die Vorstellungen vom Antichrist*, pp. 170–75.
95. Emmerson, *Antichrist in the Middle Ages*, pp. 213–14.
96. See Scribner, *For the Sake of Simple Folk*, pp. 148–63.
97. For Luther the Antichrist represented an entire age in world history, that of the third and final persecution of the true church. The idea that the

church would undergo three trials had strong roots in the fathers and in medieval schemes of periodization, and was closely associated with the temptations of Christ as pictured in Matthew 4: 1–11. On this idea see Headley, *Luther's View*, pp. 148–50.

98. Preuss, *Die Vorstellungen vom Antichrist*, pp. 2, 96, et passim.

99. "Ein tröstliche predigt von der zukunfft Christi vnd den vorgehenden zeichen des Jüngsten tags" (1532), *WA* 34, II, 459–82.

100. "Vorrhede Martini Luthers. Auff die Weissagung des Johannis Lichtenbergers" (1527). I have used the edition found in Aby Warburg, *Heidnisch-antike Weissagung*, reprinted in *Gesammelte Schriften* (Nendeln, 1969), vol. 2, pp. 545–50. See esp. pp. 548ff.

101. *WA* 34, II, 481.

102. See Marjorie O'Rourke Boyle, *Rhetoric and Reform: Erasmus' Civil Dispute with Luther* (Cambridge, Mass., and London, 1983), esp. pp. 132–52. Another student of Luther's thought maintains that the Reformer's central christological conceptions were influenced in the direction of Gnostic dualism by the teachings of Hermetic literature: Theobald Beer, *Der fröhliche Wechsel und Streit. Grundzüge der Theologie Martin Luthers* (Einsiedeln, 1980).

103. Heiko A. Oberman, *Luther: Mensch zwischen Gott und Teufel* (Berlin, 1982), pp. 79, 109, 112, 307, et passim.

104. Headley, *Luther's View*, p. 227. See *WA* 30, III, 387. See also Robert W. Scribner, "Incombustible Luther: The Image of the Reformer in Early Modern Germany," *Past and Present* no. 10 (Feb. 1986), 36–68; on the goose and swan prophecy, pp. 41–42.

105. Headley, *Luther's View*, p. 232.

106. Preuss, *Martin Luther: Der Prophet*, pp. 4ff.

107. On Hilten see the literature listed in Headley, *Luther's View*, p. 246n, and Hofmann, *Luther und die Johannes-Apokalypse*, pp. 662–72. Scholars disagree on the extent to which Luther saw himself as a prophetic figure. Headley rejects the view of Preuss (*Martin Luther: Der Prophet*), arguing that "it is . . . misleading to consider Luther's awareness of himself under the concept of a prophet" (p. 232), for as Karl Holl points out, Luther sought to conceal his person behind his work. But as Mark Edwards shows, there were clearly points at which "Luther explicitly saw himself, and his fellow pastors, performing the same role as the prophets in the Old Testament." *Luther's Last Battles: Politics and Polemics, 1531–46* (Ithaca, 1983), p. 103.

108. See Headley, *Luther's View*, p. 234.

109. Luther's opposition to astrology was at any rate certainly not part of a "struggle for the inner intellectual and religious liberation of modern man," as Aby Warburg suggests (*Heidnisch-antike Weissagung*, in *Gesammelte Schriften*, p. 531). Warburg clearly exaggerates how far Luther's world picture diverged from that of his astrologically minded colleagues.

110. Oberman, *Luther*, p. 55.

111. Headley, *Luther's View*, pp. 240–43; Hillerdal, "Prophetische Züge," pp. 117–18.

112. *WA* 10, II, 57ff. Cited in Asendorf, *Eschatologie bei Luther*, p. 223; see also Hillerdal, "Prophetische Züge," p. 119.

113. In his most important work on the Turkish threat, "Eine Heerpredigt wider den Türken" (1529), *WA* 30, II, 149–97, Luther thought it unlikely that Germany would fall to the Turk before the Last Day, since Revelation 20 predicted that Gog and Magog would be cast down. But elsewhere Luther spoke of the real threat that Christendom would be overrun, and on balance he must be regarded as a perpetuator of late-medieval fears of the eastern infidel. An excellent treatment of Luther's sermon against the Turk and the apocalyptic expectations reflected therein is offered by Mark. U. Edwards, *Luther's Last Battles: Politics and Polemics, 1531–46*, pp. 97–114. See also Rudolf Mau, "Luthers Stellung zu den Türken," in Helmar Junghans, ed., *Leben und Werk Martin Luthers von 1526 bis 1546; Festgabe zu seinem 500. Geburtstag* (Berlin, 1983), vol. 1, pp. 647–62.

114. Hillerdal, "Prophetische Züge," pp. 119–22.

115. The *Table Talk* offers many examples of this sort of grim prediction. Hans Preuss presents a list of references: *Martin Luther: Der Deutsche* (Gütersloh, 1934), pp. 96–100. The parallel between Germany and the sufferings of the ancient Jews is clearly presented in "Ein Sermon von des Judischen reichs vnd der welt ende. Matth. 24" (1524), *WA* 15, 738–58.

116. For the quotation from the 1533 preface, see *WA* 38, 72. The *Table Talk* quotation: *WA Tischreden* 5, no. 5506. I have been directed to many of Luther's prophetic pronouncements by the helpful work of Heinrich Fausel, *D. Martin Luther: Leben und Werk 1522 bis 1546* (Munich and Hamburg, 1966). For predictions regarding the future of Germany and the Last Day, see esp. vol. 2, pp. 294–303.

117. Edwards, *Luther's Last Battles*, pp. 113, 208.

118. For example: *WA Tischreden* 6, no. 6677; 5, no. 5504.

119. *WA Tischreden* 5, no. 5686. I was directed to this passage by Peuckert, *Die grosse Wende*, vol. 2, p. 546.

120. Luther, *Supputatio annorum mundi* (1541; 1545). *WA* 53, 1ff. A German translation by Johann Aurifaber appeared in 1550 at Wittenberg: *Chronica des ehrnwirdigen Herrn D. M. Luther deudsch*.

121. Headley, *Luther's View*, p. 52.

122. Torrance, *Kingdom and Church*, p. 21.

123. Headley, *Luther's View*, pp. 108–10. "Elias" is the grecized form of "Elijah" used by Luther and his contemporaries; it was also used in the New Testament of the AV. Perhaps because this scheme or prophecy does not appear in the Bible, scholars have generally retained the name "Prophecy of Elias" to avoid confusion with biblical prophecies.

124. *WA* 53, 12.

125. *WA* 15, 13.

126. Ibid.

127. Marjorie O'Rourke Boyle, "Stoic Luther: Paradoxical Sin and Necessity," *Archive for Reformation History* 73 (1982), 69–93. The argu-

ment is ingenious and provocative, but in the last analysis ridiculous. Luther's apocalypticism (to take only the example nearest at hand) is impossible to reconcile with a genuinely Stoic outlook.

128. Robert Lerner, *The Powers of Prophecy*, p. 159.

129. Arthur Rich, *Die Anfänge der Theologie Huldrych Zwingli* (Zurich, 1949), p. 76; Hans Volz, *Die Lutherpredigten des Johannes Mathesius* (Leipzig, 1930), p. 64; Preuss, *Martin Luther: Der Prophet*, p. 49.

130. Stifel, *Bruder Michael Styfel Augustiner von Esslingen, Von der Christförmigen rechtgegrundten leer Doctoris Martini Luthers, ain überauss schönkünstlich Lied, sampt seyner nebenausslegung. In Bruder Veyten Thon* (Augsburg, 1522).

131. Robert Scribner has acknowledged this in his recent work on popular propaganda, *For the Sake of Simple Folk*; see pp. 117, 187. Preuss's claim that Luther's prophetic preachings dissolved the eschatological tension of the later Middle Ages is not sustainable.

132. Scribner, *For the Sake of Simple Folk*, pp. 169–75, 185–89.

133. Martin, *Martin Luther und die Bilder zur Apokalypse*, pp. 88–90, 115ff, 197, et passim.

134. Osiander, *Eyn wunderliche Weyssagung von dem Bapstum, wie es ihm bis an das Ende der Welt gehen sol . . .* (Nuremberg, 1527). I have been helped by the analysis in Scribner, *For the Sake of Simple Folk*, pp. 142–47.

135. Osiander, *Sant Hildegardten weissagung vber die Papisten, vnd genanten geistlichen, wilcher erfüllung zu unsern zeiten hat angefangen, vnd volzogen sol werden* (Nuremberg, 1527).

136. Scribner, *For the Sake of Simple Folk*, p. 185.

137. Lerner, *The Powers of Prophecy*, pp. 164–66.

138. An example is the short tract by Martin Schrot, *Apocalypsis. Ain frewden geschray über das gefallen Bapstumb so yetz diser zeit durch Gottes wort vnd schwerdt überwunden ist* (Augsburg, c. 1546), which drew on the Sibyls, biblical prophecy, and other sources to argue that the fall of the papacy was inevitable.

139. Scribner, *For the Sake of Simple Folk*, pp. 137–40. Luther's work was titled *Ein gesichte Bruder Clausen ynn Schweytz* (Wittenberg, 1528); I have not seen this work.

140. A little-known figure, Grünpeck was a humanist, a physician, and sometime imperial historiographer to Maximilian I. In the early sixteenth century he issued a series of popular works, including a commentary on monstrous births and a number of astrological prophecies. Among his most influential works was a *Spiegel der naturlichen himlichen vnd prophetischen sehungen aller trubsalen, angst, vnd not, die vber alle stende, geschlechte, vnd gemayn . . . in kurtzen tagen geen werdenn* (Leipzig, 1522). See the biographical sketch by Albin Czerny, "Der Humanist und Historiograph Kaiser Maximilians I. Joseph Grünpeck," *Archiv für österreichische Geschichte* 73 (1888), 315–64.

141. Scribner, *For the Sake of Simple Folk*, p. 133.

142. On Lautensack, see *ADB*, vol. 18, p. 72, and Hofmann, *Luther und die Johannes-Apokalypse*, pp. 551–63.

143. Scribner, *For the Sake of Simple Folk*, pp. 147, 184.

Chapter 2

1. Preuss, *Martin Luther: Der Prophet*, pp. 49–57. On Luther as the third Elijah (the second being John the Baptist), see also Hans Volz, *Die Lutherpredigten des Johannes Mathesius*, pp. 63ff. Volz also notes comparisons of Luther with David, Samson, and Moses (pp. 68ff), and other interpretations of the Reformer as a prophet sent before the Last Day (pp. 72ff, 92). Hans-Ulrich Hofmann has examined anew the whole issue of Luther and the Enoch-Elijah tradition: *Luther und die Johannes-Apokalypse*, "Excurs I," pp. 656–61.

2. Ibid., pp. 71–73.

3. Antonius Otho Hertzberger, *Etliche Propheceysprüche D. Martini Lutheri, Des dritten Elias* (Magdeburg?, 1552).

4. Peter Glaser, *Hundert vnd zwanzig Propheceyunge, oder Weissagung, des Ehrwirdigen Vaters Herrn Doctoris Martini Luthers, von allerley straffen, so nach seinem tod vber Deutschland von wegen desselbigen grossen, vnd vielfaltigen Sünden kommen solten* (Eisleben, 1557); *Zwey Hundert Propheceyunge oder weissagunge, des tewren Mans D. Martini Lutheri, von allerley Straffen* . . . (Bautzen, 1574).

5. Georg Walther, *Prophezeiungen D. Martini Lutheri. Zur erinnerung vnd anreitzung zur Christlichen Busse, ordentlich vnd mit vleis getragen* (Wittenberg, 1559), fol. a/v. The major collections of Luther's prophecies are noted in Volz, *Die Lutherpredigten des Johannes Mathesius*, pp. 74n, 75n; see also Preuss, *Martin Luther: Der Prophet*, p. 161n. To understand the full scope of the effort to popularize Luther's expectations, we need to consider other works as well, such as *Ein Christliche vermanung vnd erinnerung, D. Martini Luthers . . . Von den letzten schweren zeiten, des Jüngsten tages* . . . (Schleusingen, 1555). This short tract was a reprinted version of a 1533 preface that expressed warnings of darkest doom for this world; for the original see *WA* 38, 70–74.

6. Melchior Specker, *Von der Herrlichen Zükunfft Jesu Christi, zum Jüngsten Gericht. Vnd was im selben vnnd darnach geschehen werde. Alles was hievon im H. Neuwen Testament geoffenbart* . . . (Strassburg, 1555).

7. Wolfgang Waldner, *Bericht Etlicher furnemsten Stücke, den Jüngsten tage, vnd was darauff folgen wirdt, betreffend. Zu diesen letzten Zeyten allen Menschen, nützlich vnd nötig zu betrachten* . . . (Nuremberg, 1567), fol. Bi.

8. Hieronymus Menzel, *Einfeltige, vnd Christliche Ausslegung, des Herrlichen vnd trostlichen Evangelii, von der Verkelerung des Herrn Jhesu Christi, in drey Predigten gefast. Samt kurtzem Bericht, von der letzten Zukunfft des Herren Christi, und dem Process des Jüngsten Gerichts, aus Göttlicher Schrifft zusammen gezogen* (Eisleben, 1570).

9. Johann Garcaeus, *Eine Christliche kurtze Widerholung der warhafftigen Lere und bekentnis unsers Glaubens von der Zukunfft des Herrn Christi zum Gericht* (Wittenberg, 1569).

10. Other didactic treatises of this sort include Basilius Faber, *Allerley Christliche, nötige . . . vnterrichtung, von den letzten Hendeln der Welt* (Eisleben, 1565, and many other eds.); Erasmus Alberus, *Vom jüngsten Tag vnd Auferstehung* (1566); Alexandrus Utzinger, *Process Des Jüngsten*

Gerichts (Schmalkalden, 1589); K. Althaus, *Predig von kommenden Gerichten* (1563).

11. Robert Kolb, *Nikolaus von Amsdorf (1483–1565): Popular Polemics in the Preservation of Luther's Legacy* (Nieuwkoop, 1978), p. 185.

12. For general background on this debate, see Robert Kolb, "Dynamics of Party Conflict in the Saxon Late Reformation: Gnesio-Lutherans vs. Philippists," *The Journal of Modern History* 49, no. 3 (Sept. 1977), pp. 1289–1305.

13. Ibid.; see esp. pp. 1293–94.

14. See Martin Stupperich, "Das Augsburger Interim als apokalyptisches Geschehnis nach den Königsberger Schriften Andreas Osianders," *Archive for Reformation History* 64 (1973), pp. 225–45.

15. Andreas Musculus, *Christliche Trewe Warnung, vnd Vermanüg, wider die grewliche vñ verdamliche Sicherheit der gantzen Welt* (Lemgo, 1562), fols. Fviii/v, G.

16. Jacob Andreae, *Ein Christliche Predigt Vber das Euangelium auff den XXV. Sontag nach Trinitatis, Matthei am 24. Von vielen vnd mancherley verfürungen in der Kirchen Gottes, vor dem Jüngsten tage* (Leipzig, 1578), Vorrede.

17. In this paragraph and elsewhere in this chapter, I have drawn from the massive two-volume work of the nineteenth-century Catholic historian J. Döllinger, *Die Reformation, ihre innere Entwicklung und ihre Wirkungen im Umfänge des Lutherischen Bekenntnisses* (Regensburg, 1846, 1848; unaltered reprint: Frankfurt a.M., 1962). On Eber see vol. 2, p. 396. Döllinger's aim was to show that the Reformation wreaked a nearly complete moral and social degeneration in Germany. His method was mainly to cite the wailings, laments, denunciations, and quarrels of Lutheran preachers and theologians themselves; the Reformation was thus condemned through the words of its own perpetrators. Not surprisingly, then, the study cites countless Lutherans who expressed the conviction that since this world went so rapidly from bad to worse, the Last Day had to be close at hand. Indeed, the work is a mine of illustrations for the pessimistic side of the Lutheran expectation. But these judgments of Lutherans on the condition of their own society fall into clearer perspective if we understand their growing impatience; compared to the coming Kingdom of God, earthly society was bound to appear hopelessly corrupt. On the mind of the typical Lutheran pastor, see the excellent study by Gerald Strauss, "The Mental World of a Saxon Pastor" (see above, Ch. 1, note 83).

18. Döllinger, *Die Reformation*, vol. 2; on Spalatin, p. 113; Cruciger, 151–52; Kaufman, 284; Bartholomaus Gernhard, 300–301; Josua Loner, 311–12; Andreae, 375ff; Chytraeus, 507ff.

19. Barthol[omaus] Wolfhart, *Vom jüngsten Tage* (n.p., 1563). Cited in Döllinger, *Die Reformation*, vol. 2, pp. 303–5.

20. Andreas Musculus, *Vom jüngsten Tage* (Erfurt, 1559). Cited in Christian Wilhelm Spieker, *Lebensgeschichte des Andreas Musculus* (Frankfurt a.O., 1858), p. 212.

21. Waldner, *Bericht Etlicher furnemsten Stücke, des Jüngsten tage*, fol. B.

22. For this view see Werner Elert, *Morphologie des Luthertums*, vol. 1, pp. 409–10.

23. Glaser, *Zwey Hundert Propheceyungen oder weissagunge*. . . , fols. [)(vi/v]ff.

24. Nikolaus von Amsdorf, *Eine Predigt aus Luthers Schrifften vber die Propheten gezogen, dass Deutschland wie Israel, Judaea vnd Jerusalem wird zerstöret vnd verwüstet werden* (Jena, 1562).

25. Spieker, *Lebensgeschichte des Andreas Musculus*, pp. 399–402.

26. Quoted in Spieker, *Lebensgeschichte des Andreas Musculus*, pp. 224–25.

27. Richard Gawthrop and Gerald Strauss, "Protestantism and Literacy in Early Modern Germany," *Past and Present* 104 (1984), pp. 31–55.

28. This point has been made about Luther himself by John Headley: "The imminence of his eschatology has well been designated as the limiting principle to all his pronouncements and actions in the worldly Regiment." *Luther's View*, p. 263.

29. Gerald Strauss, *Luther's House of Learning*, p. 31.

30. Ibid., p. 33. According to Rudolf Otto, "genuine" eschatological teaching is essentially inconsistent. On the one hand is the sense that the Kingdom is at hand and the end is coming immediately. On the other hand is a message that assumes future duration, the call for a certain disposition toward the world and its affairs. The former would seem to call for nothing but "a swift and complete surrender to the mercy of the judge," while the latter assumes "lasting relationships and attitudes." This inconsistency, this irrationality appears wherever there is genuine eschatological teaching, and can be seen not only in Jesus but in Zoroaster, in Mohammed, in St. Francis, and in Luther. See Otto's *Kingdom of God and the Son of Man*, ch. 5, "Concerning the Eschatological Type and Its Essential Irrationality," esp. pp. 61–63.

31. Paul Engricens, *Trewhertzige Ermanung Der Zeichen, so für dem Jüngsten Tage hergehen* . . . (Eisleben, 1560?), fol. Avi/v.

32. For a convincing argument that Melanchthon's interest in prodigies, portents, divination, and so forth represented a "popular" train of thought, see Stefano Caroti, "Comete, portenti, causalità naturale e escatologia in Filippo Melantone," in *Scienze, credenze occulte, livelli di cultura*, Convegno Internazionale di Studi, Florence, June 26–30, 1980 (Florence, 1982), pp. 393–426, esp. pp. 425–26.

33. Jaroslav Pelikan has made this point clearly, though in connection with formal theology rather than popular literature, in his *From Luther to Kierkegaard* (St. Louis, 1950), pp. 46–48.

34. See Elert, *Morphologie des Luthertums*, vol. 1, p. 389.

35. Lucien Febvre and Henri-Jean Martin, *L'Apparition du livre* (Paris, 1958), p. 443. On the rise of a "print culture" in Europe see also E. L. Eisenstein, *The Printing Press As an Agent of Change: Communications and Cultural Transformations in Early-Modern Europe* (Cambridge, 1979).

36. See Miriam U. Chrisman, *Lay Culture, Learned Culture: Books and Social Change in Strasbourg, 1480–1599* (New Haven and London,

284 Notes to Pages 75–80

1982), p. 260. My characterization of popular religious belief follows that of Chrisman. A valuable discussion of the curiosity of laymen is found in Steven Ozment, *The Reformation in the Cities*, pp. 38–40.

37. My thinking here has been influenced by E. Eisenstein, "The Advent of Printing and the Problem of the Renaissance," *Past and Present* 45 (1969), pp. 19–89, here esp. p. 73. Eisenstein refers here to the influence of the press on approaches to the Scriptures in general. John Bossy has recently made the suggestion that "it was as much as anything by putting a face to the Vision of St. John that the press contributed to launching the experience of the gospel in another mode." *Christianity in the West 1400–1700* (Oxford and New York, 1985), p. 104.

38. Eisenstein, *The Printing Press as an Agent of Change*, vol. 1, pp. 74–76.

39. Matthias Flacius Illyricus, *Catalogus testium veritatis, qui ante nostram aetatem reclamarunt papae . . .* (Basel, 1556; German ed. Frankfurt a.M., 1573).

40. Marjorie Reeves, *Joachim of Fiore*, pp. 137–38.

41. Melchior Ambach, *Vom Ende der Welt, Vnd zukunfft des Endtchrists. Wie es vorm Jüngsten tag in der Welt, ergehn werde . . .* (Frankfurt a.M., c. 1550).

42. Ibid., fol. Aiiii.

43. *CR* 14, 984; *CR* 8, 663.

44. Garcaeus, *Ein Christliche kurtze Widerholung*, fol. Ciiii/v.

45. McGinn, *Visions of the End*, p. 24.

46. Caspar Füger, *Ein Erschröckliche propheceyung, vnd Weyssagung Lactantij Furmiani . . . von dieser vnser jetzigen bösen zeit vnd jüngsten Tage . . .* (Hoff, 1581; another ed. 1585; revised and reissued by Michael Meltzer in 1615). Füger also edited a collection of prophecies by Hilten, Lactantius, Luther, and various astrologers: *Prognosticon Oder Weissagung . . . biss auffs 84. vnd 88. Jar, ja biss ans ende der Welt . . . aus Johan Hilten, vnd Lactantio Firmiano . . . auch D. Martini Lutheri . . .* (Eisleben, 1584).

47. Andreas Musculus, *Vom Mesech vnd Kedar, vom Gog vnd Magog, von dem grossen trübsal für der Welt Ende. Wie viel vorgehender Zeichen erfullet, welche noch sollen erfullet werden. Wie nahe solches alles für der Thür.* (Frankfurt a.O., 1577), Vorrede.

48. Henricus Neotechnus [pseudonym], *VI. Prognostica Von Verenderung vnd zufalligem Glück vnd Vnglück der höchsten Potentaten im Römischen Reich, Auch des Türcken vnd Pabst . . .* (Hall in Sachsen, 1613).

49. For Luther's positive comment see *WA Tischreden*, I, no. 268. His desire to throw the "dreamer" into the Elbe is cited in Schmithals, *The Apocalyptic Movement*, pp. 197–98.

50. Caspar Goldwurm, ed., *Prognosticon. Weissagungen vñ Vrtheyl, von betrübungen vnnd grossen anfechtungen Europe, Durch den Hochberhümbten Astronomum . . . D. Anthonium Torquatum gestelt* (Frankfurt a.M., 1558). The work was reprinted at Leipzig in 1594.

51. Johann Capistranus [pseudonym], *Woldenckwürdige Weissagungen vnd Propheceyung von den jetzigen Läufften . . . Vnd nachfolgenden . . . Jahren* (Breslau, 1619), fol. A/v.

52. Newe Zeyttung. Ein wunderbarlichen Historien von Zweyen Meidlein, so in jrer Kranckheyt seltzam ding reden (n.p., n.d.).

53. Johann Schütz, *Newe Zeitung vnd Wunderpredig. Dadurch eine Arme einfeltige verachte Jungfraw ohne gefehr xvij. jar alt, alle stende zur busse vnd besserung jres sündlichen lebens vermanet hat* ... (Erfurt, 1560). This is only one example of a great many works of this sort; a helpful though very incomplete index can be found in Emil Weller, *Die ersten deutschen Zeitungen 1505–99* (Tübingen, 1872; reprinted Hildesheim, 1962).

54. *Newe Zeitung: Eine Warhafftige Historia, so sich am heiligen Ostertage dieses L.xxxj. Jahrs* ... *begeben vnd zugetragen* (Schweinfurt, 1581).

55. Jacob Coler, Doct. *Iacobi Coleri Probst zu Berlin Eigentlicher bericht, Vō den seltzamen vnd zu vnserer Zeit vnerhörten, Wunderwercken vnd Geschichten, so sich newlicher zeit in der Marck Brandenburg zugetragen* ... (Erfurt, 1595).

56. Wilhelm Friess, *Prognosticatio. Etliche seltzame Propheceyung, geweyssaget von dem Allten M. Wilhelmo Friesen, von Mastricht* ... (Nuremberg, 1558?).

57. Friess, *Ein Grausame vnnd Erschröckliche Propheceyhung, oder Weissagung vber Pollerland vnd Teutschland, Brabant vnd Franckreich* (Basel, 1577; another ed. 1586). This prophecy, which concerns the appearance in a dream of a handsome young man who predicts the future of the nations of Christendom, has a vague resemblance to the so-called "Prophecy of Gamaleon," which circulated widely in the Middle Ages. On the Gamaleon prophecy see McGinn, *Visions of the End*, pp. 251–52.

58. *Zwo warhafftige Propheceyungen von zukünfftigen dingen. Die erste, von einem newen Propheten, Welcher zu Stettin in Pommern* ... *erschienen. Die andere Von einem Fewrigē Sternen, welcher in Calabria gesehen worde* ... (n.p., 1586).

59. See Melanchthon's commentary on Matthew 24: CR 14, 985.

60. Niclas von Amsdorff (sic), *Fünff fürnemlich vnd gewisse Zeichen aus heiliger göttlicher Schrifft, so kurtz vor dem Jüngsten tag geschehen sollen* (Jena, 1554).

61. The work in which this list of signs appeared was titled *Propheceien vnd Weissagungen. Vergangne, Gegenwertige, vnd Künfftige ding, Geschichten vnnd Zufall, aller Stende* ... (Augsburg, 1549). The 1560 adaptation was that of Paul Engricens, *Trewhertzige Ermanung*. Another edition appeared in 1592, and early in the next century the list was included in an altered version of the 1549 collection cited above: *Propheceyen Vnd Weissagungen jetzt gegenwertig vnd kunfftige sachen, Geschicht vnd Zufäll, biss zum Ende der Welt ankündend* (n.p., 1620).

62. Paul Engricens, *Trewhertzige Ermanung*, fol. Bvii.

63. Richard Emmerson agrees: the legend was "apparently of little interest to Protestants." *Antichrist in the Middle Ages*, p. 210.

64. Nicolaus Winckler, *Bedencken Von Künfftiger verenderung Weltlicher Policey, vnd Ende der Welt* ... (see below, Ch. 3, note 53), fol. Fii.

65. Wolfgang Waldner, *Bericht Etlicher furnemsten Stücke, den Jüngsten tage*, fol. Dv/v.

66. The view of Preuss (*Die Vorstellungen vom Antichrist*) that Luther's vision of the Antichrist represented some sort of spiritual peak from which later conceptions declined is hardly convincing.

67. Jacob Andreae, *Dreizehen Predigten vom Türcken* (Tübingen, 1568).

68. See John W. Bohnstedt, "The Infidel Scourge of God: The Turkish Menace As Seen by German Pamphleteers of the Reformation Era," *Transactions of the American Philosophical Society*, n.s., 58, pt. 9 (December, 1968), esp. p. 23; also Edwards, *Luther's Last Battles*, p. 112.

69. Caspar Füger, *Weissagung, von der künfftigen zerstörung Deutsches Landes, durch den Turckischen Keyser Soldan* . . . (n.p., 1568).

70. Johann Lapaeus, ed., *Practica vnd Prognostica, Oder Schreckliche Propheceiung D. Martin Luthers, des ausserwehlten Rustzeugs vnd Propheten des Deutschen Landes* . . . (Ursel, 1578), fol. (:)/v.

71. Musculus, *Vom jüngsten Tage*, cited in Spieker, p. 212.

72. Philipp Nicolai, *Theoria Vitae Aeternae. Historische Beschreibung desz gantzen Geheimnisses vom Ewigen Leben* (Hamburg, 1620), p. 629.

73. Ibid., pp. 630–31.

74. On Grünpeck as a wonder-writer see Rudolf Schenda, "Die deutschen Prodigiensammlungen des 16. und 17. Jahrhunderts," *Archiv für Geschichte des Buchwesens* 4 (Frankfurt a.M., 1963), 642–43.

75. Ibid., pp. 644f.

76. Melanchthon's general understanding of the signs to precede the end is summarized in a sermon on Luke 21: CR 24, 17–32. On prodigies, monsters, etc., see *Narratio de prodigio*, CR 7, 611; *De monstris* (fragment), CR 10, 111.

77. Job Fincel, *Wunderzeichen. Warhafftige beschreybung vnd gründlich verzeichnuss schröcklicher Wunderzeichen vnd Geschichten* . . . (Nuremburg, 1556). A much enlarged edition appeared at Frankfurt am Main in 1566; the work was further expanded in 1567.

78. For this paragraph and what follows on Fincel I am heavily indebted to Heinz Schilling, "Job Fincel und die Zeichen der Endzeit," in Wolfgang Brückner, ed., *Volkserzählung und Reformation: Ein Handbuch zur Tradierung und Funktion von Erzählstoffen und Erzählliteratur im Protestantismus* (Berlin, 1974), pp. 326–92.

79. Joel 2: 28–32. Cited in Fincel's 1556 edition, fol. A/v. Luther's reference: WA Deutsche Bibel 7, 409.

80. Schilling, "Job Fincel und die Zeichen der Endzeit," pp. 348–57.

81. Quoted in Schilling, p. 344.

82. Schilling, pp. 359–63.

83. Ibid., p. 361.

84. Ibid., p. 365. On Luther's questions about the necessity of reading the signs see WA 15, 620.

85. Conrad Lycosthenes, *Prodigiorum ac ostentorum chronicon, quae praeter naturae ordinem* . . . *ab exordio mundi* . . . *ad haec* . . . *tempora, acciderunt* . . . (Basel, 1557); *Wunderwerck Oder Gottes vnergründtliches vorbilden, das er in seinem geschöpffen allen* . . . *erscheynen, hören, brieuen lassen* (Basel, 1557).

86. Marcus Fritsch, *Meteorum, hoc est, impressionum aerearum et mirabilium naturae operum . . . item: catalogus prodigiorum atque ostentorum . . .* (Nuremberg, 1563), republished at Wittenberg in 1581 and 1598.

87. Caspar Goldwurm, *Wunderzeichen: Das ist . . .* (Frankfurt, 1567). This was apparently the same work as Goldwurm's *Warhaftige Beschreibung vieler Wunderwerke,* issued in 1557, 1567, and 1579. See J. Janssen, *A History of the German People at the Close of the Middle Ages* (London, 1900–1912), vol. 12, p. 244n.

88. Christoph Irenaeus, *De Monstris. Von seltzamen Wundergeburten* (n.p., 1584), and *Prognosticon Aus Gottes Wort nötige Erinnerung, Vnd Christliche Busspredigt zu dieser letzten bösen Zeit . . .* (n.p., 1578). On the literature of wonders and horrors in general see J. Janssen, *A History of the German People,* vol. 12, ch. 5, pp. 228ff. Like Döllinger (see note 17 above), Janssen can be a valuable source despite his anti-Protestant bias.

89. Iohann Letzner, *Wunder Spiegel, Das Erste [Ander] Buch. In welchem die fürnemsten Cometen vnd Wunderstern, von anfang der Welt her . . . beschrieben werden . . .* (Erfurt, 1604). Fuller treatment of the literature on such celestial signs as new stars and comets is reserved for Chapter 4.

90. For Fincel's discussion of the division of wonders into classes ("prodigium," "ostentum," "portentum," etc.), see his 1566 edition, part 2, "Der ander theil Wunderzeichen," fol. Bv/v. For the more involved treatment of Lycosthenes, see his *Wunderwerck,* fols. av/v–aviii/v. Herlicius denied the importance of these distinctions and discussed the various sorts of strange precipitation in his *De Pluviis Prodigiosis Speculatio Physica et Historica. Von Blutregen vnd andern Wunderbaren Vnnatürlichen Vngewöhnlichen Regen . . .* (Greifswald, 1597).

91. There was, to be sure, a considerable wonder-literature produced elsewhere. See for example Katharine Park and Lorraine J. Daston, "Unnatural Conceptions: The Study of Monsters in Sixteenth- and Seventeenth-century France and England," *Past and Present* 92 (Aug. 1981), 20–54. But Park and Daston point out that in the latter half of the sixteenth century monsters and prodigies "began to cast off their religious associations" in France and England (p. 41), a finding that cannot be duplicated for Lutheran Germany.

92. Johann Engerdus (?), *Preseruatiu, Cur vnnd Seelen-Artzney, wider die gifftige jetzoschwebende Seuch der New Evangelischen Secten, bevorab dess hochschädlichen Lutherthumbs . . .* (Ingolstadt, 1581). A printed comment in the margin (fol. Bii) summarized the major point of this work clearly: "Die Christenheit begert keines Wunderzeichen bey der zukunfft eines Apostaten vnd abtrinnigen Münchs."

93. Probably the best available collection of sixteenth-century German broadsheets is that made by Johann Jacob Wick (1522–88), Archdeacon of the Great Minster in Zurich. The Wickiana in the Zentralbibliothek of Zurich have been closely studied by Bruno Weber, *Erschröckliche und warhafftige Wunderzeichen, 1543–1586* (2 vols., Zurich, 1971–72). It is worth noting that most of the pamphlets and broadsides in Wick's collection were published in Lutheran cities.

94. Quoted in Spieker, *Lebensgeschichte des Andreas Musculus*, pp. 224–25.

95. Musculus, *Von Mesech vnd Kedar* (see note 47 above).

96. For example: Helisaeus Roeslin, *Gründliche, Warhafftige vnnd rechtmessige Erklerung, der Charactern vñ Buchstaben, so vff dem in Norwegen gefangnen Hering gestanden, Durch einen gelehrten, an einen fürnemen geschrieben* (n.p., 1588). This work probably inspired a similar effort ten years later by the Zwinglian churchman Raphael Eglin, *Newe Meerwunderische Prophecey, Auff Danielis vnnd der Offenbarung Johannis Zeytrechnung gezogen, die aller erst durch Gottes gnad an das liecht gebracht* (Zurich, 1598).

97. The Wettin preacher was Ambrosius Taurer, *Der Geistliche, Uberflüssig gnugsam ausschlagende Feigenbaum. Das ist . . . warnung, das der Jüngste tag nahe ist . . .* (n.p., 1594). Taurer wrote at least two other apocalyptic works, *Von der Grundsuppe der Welt* (Eisleben, 1588), and *Bericht von mancherley schrecklichen Wunderzeichen die vns vom nahen Ende der Welt predigen* (Halle, 1592). Daniel Schaller points to the decreasing longevity of men in his *Herolt. Aussgesandt In allen Landen offendtlich zuuerkündigen vnnd auszuruffen. Das diese Weldt mit Irem wesen bald vergehen werde . . .* (Magdeburg, 1595), fol. O.

98. Daniel Schaller, *Vom Ende der Welt. Aus Prophetischer vnnd Apostolischer Schrifft bericht . . .* (Magdeburg, 1599), and *Theologischer Heroldt. In Alle Lande vnd vier winckel der Weldt, Aussgesandt . . .* (Magdeburg, 1604).

99. Melanchthon, *Confessio augustana* XVII. See CR 26, 569–70. This article did denounce the "Jewish" error of belief in an earthly Kingdom of God.

100. Karl Holl, "Die Kulturbedeutung der Reformation," in *Gesammelte Aufsätze zur Kirchengeschichte* (Tübingen, 1948), vol. 1, p. 526. For a more detailed examination of the issue see Friedrich Beisser, *Claritas scripturae bei Martin Luther* (*Forschungen zur Kirchen- und Dogmengeschichte*, no. 18; Göttingen, 1966).

101. Quoted in Elert, *Morphologie des Luthertums*, vol. 1, p. 167.

102. On these different attitudes of Lutherans and Calvinists see Thomas Klein, *Die Kampf um die zweite Reformation in Kursachsen 1586–91* (Cologne, 1962). The push for a "second Reformation" was, according to Klein, a major theme of German Protestantism in the late sixteenth century. A move in the direction of an activist, disciplined form of Protestantism was the answer to the manifold challenges that faced the Lutheran states, above all the challenges of post-Tridentine Catholicism and a secularized humanism. An alliance of humanists, Philippists, and Calvinists developed, held together by the assumption that Luther's Reformation was not an end in itself, but a giant step on the road to Christian reform and revival, a road that now had to be followed further if German Protestantism was not to succumb to the counterreformation. But it must not be forgotten that this sentiment was limited to a fairly small group of government councillors and academics; the notion of a "second Reformation" never penetrated the populace at large or the Lutheran clergy in any of these Lutheran states.

103. Melanchthon on prophetic dreams: "Erinnerung Philippi Melanchthonis von mancherley Geschlächten der Träume samt ihrer bedeutung," *CR* 20, 677–85; see also 686–92.

104. Johannes Funck, *Apocalypsis. Der Offenbarung Künfftiger Geschicht Johannis, . . . bis an der welt ende, Auslegung . . . Mit einer Vorrede Philip. Melanth.* (n.p., first published 1559; this ed., 1561). The editor was Zacharias Engelhaubt, a preacher at Regensburg. The work was signed "J. F."—almost certainly Funck. According to H.-U. Hofmann (*Luther und die Johannes-Apokalypse*, p. 511, note 21), this work was composed around 1546–47, and apparently circulated in manuscript.

105. Melanchthon used the term "vorwitz." I believe that "curiosity," with the connotation of arrogance or presumption, best conveys the meaning here.

106. Funck, *Apocalypsis*, "Vorrede Philippi Melanthon," fols. Aij ff.

107. Caspar Peucer, *Commentarius de praecipuis generibus divinationum . . .* (Wittenberg, 1580, first published, 1553).

Chapter 3

1. The best general introduction to the "prophetic history" discussed in this chapter is R. W. Southern, "Aspects of the European Tradition of Historical Writing: 3. History as Prophecy," *Transactions of the Royal Historical Society*, Ser. 5, 22 (1972), 159–80. See also Peter Burke, *The Renaissance Sense of the Past* (New York, 1969).

2. Eric Auerbach, *Mimesis: The Representation of Reality in Western Literature* (Princeton, 1953), pp. 73–76 et passim.

3. See Reinhart Koselleck, "Vergangene Zukunft der frühen Neuzeit," in Hans Barion et al., eds., *Epirrhosis: Festgabe für Carl Schmitt* (Berlin, 1968), pp. 549–66.

4. Sarah Hutton, "Aspects of the Concept of Time in Elizabethan and Jacobean England" (diss., Warburg Institute, University of London, 1977), p. 35.

5. Torrance, *Kingdom and Church*, p. 3.

6. Headley, *Luther's View*, p. 269.

7. Elert, *Morphologie des Luthertums*, vol. 1, pp. 423–36. See also *Encyclopedia of the Lutheran Church*, s.v. "History, Lutheran Understanding of," vol. 2, pp. 1025–31.

8. Valentine Engelhart, *De Mvndo et Tempore. Das ist Von der Welt vñd der Zeit, ein nützlich Büchlein . . .* (n.p., 1562), "Das Ander Theil . . . von der zeit," fol. a.

9. Johann Garcaeus, *Primus tractatus brevis et utilis de tempore* (Wittenberg, 1563).

10. Klaus Maurice and Otto Mayr, eds., *The Clockwork Universe: German Clocks and Automata 1550–1650* (Washington, D.C., 1980), pp. vii, viii.

11. Hartmann Schedel, *Liber chronicarum* (Nuremberg, 1493). On this and other universal chronicles of the period around 1500 see Paul Joachimsen, *Geschichtsauffassung und Geschichtschreibung in Deutschland unter dem Einfluss des Humanismus* (Leipzig, 1910), chapter 4, pp. 80–104.

12. Adalbert Klempt, *Die Säkularisierung der universalhistorischen Auffassung: Zum Wandel des Geschichtsdenkens im 16. und 17. Jahrhundert* (Göttingen, 1960), p. 23; Hans-Jürgen Schönstadt, *Antichrist, Weltheilsgeschehen und Gottes Werkzeug* (Wiesbaden, 1978), pp. 102–3. Schönstadt notes (citing Christopher Dawson) that the prophecy of Elias came to enjoy biblical authority, and brought Protestants into closer contact with the Jewish and apocalyptic elements in the Christian tradition.

13. Schönstadt, *Antichrist, Weltheilsgeschehen und Gottes Werkzeug*, p. 105.

14. The question whether the use of such world-historical patterns in the German world chronicles of the sixteenth century was fundamentally a continuation of medieval attitudes, or involved key steps in the direction of a more modern approach, has occasioned decades of scholarly quarrels. Much of the older literature is reviewed in Klempt, *Die Säkularisierung der universalhistorischen Auffassung*, pp. 7–20. Klempt argues that these essentially medieval and eschatological schemes were first used as truly systematic tools of ordering by Melanchthon and his students, but that in the very process of applying them more systematically than ever, late sixteenth-century students of chronology like Caspar Peucer began to recognize the shortcomings of these schemes, and thus began the process in which the eschatological approach to history would eventually dissolve. Klempt would admit, however, that to recognize certain particular problems in one's understanding of history is not necessarily to reject the assumptions on which that understanding is based. My argument is that the eschatological outlook continued to dominate the sense of history in Lutheran Germany until well into the seventeenth century.

15. Friedrich von Bezold, "Astrologische Geschichtskonstruction im Mittelalter," in *Aus Mittelalter und Renaissance: Kulturgeschichtliche Studien* (Munich and Berlin, 1918).

16. Matthias Flacius, *Ecclesiastica historia integram ecclesiae Christi ideam . . . complectens . . . congesta per aliquot studiosos et pios viros in urbe Magdeburgica* (Basel, 1559–74).

17. S. L. Verheus in *Zeugnis und Gericht: Kirchengeschichtliche Betrachtungen bei Sebastian Franck und Matthias Flacius* (Nieuwkoop, 1971) recognizes that there are passages of clear eschatological import in the *Centuries*, but argues that eschatology is so subordinated that it stands as an "opus alienum" in the work. This position cannot be maintained when the aims of Flacius and his associates are rightly considered.

18. Schönstadt, *Antichrist, Weltheilsgeschehen und Gottes Werkzeug*, pp. 100, 101.

19. Robert Stupperich, *Der unbekannte Melanchthon: Wirken und Denken des Praeceptor Germaniae in neuer Sicht* (Stuttgart, 1961), pp. 72–84.

20. Melanchthon, *Chronica durch Magistrum Johann Carion fleissig zusammengezogen, menigklich nützlich zu lesen* (Wittenberg, 1532), CR 12, 708. I have also used a later version edited by Caspar Peucer, *Chronica Carionis* (Wittenberg, 1573). On the popularity of the *Chronica* I have followed Lerner, *The Powers of Prophecy*, p. 170.

21. Firth, *The Apocalyptic Tradition*, p. 6.

22. Melanchthon, *Chronica durch Magistrum Johann Carion fleissig zusammengezogen* (1532), "Einleitung."

23. Peucer, ed., *Chronica Carionis* (Wittenberg, 1573), pp. 1145–46.

24. Firth, *The Apocalyptic Tradition*, pp. 15–16.

25. Caspar Peucer, "Vorrede" to *Chronica Carionis*, fols. b–ciii/v.

26. Ibid., p. 124.

27. Sebastian Franck, *Chronica. Zeyt-buch und geschychtbibel von anbegyn biss inn diss gegenwertig MDXXXJ jar* (Strassburg, 1531).

28. Johann Funck, *Chronologie von Erschaffung der Welt bis auf das Jahr 1560* (Wittenberg, 1570, 1578, 1602).

29. Abraham Bucholzer, *Isagoge chronologia. Id est: Opusculum, ad annorum seriem in sacris bibliis contexendam, compendio viam monstrans ac fundamenta indicans* (Görlitz, 1580), *Index chronologicus* (Görlitz, 1580), and *Isagoge chronologica ab initio mundi ad exsilium Israelitarum in Babylone* (Görlitz, 1584). This last work has been unavailable to me.

30. Laurentius Faustus, *Anatomia Statvae Danielis. Kurtze vnd eigentliche erklerung der grossen Bildnis des Propheten Danielis . . .* (Leipzig, 1586); Heinrich Bünting, *Chronologia hoc est, omnium temporum et annorum series . . .* (Zerbst, 1590), and *Chronologia catholica . . . ab initio mundi* (Magdeburg, 1608); Elias Reusner, *Isagoges historicae libri duo* (Jena, 1600). Klempt argues (*Die Säkularisierung der universalhistorischen Auffassung*, pp. 41–42) that although Reusner clearly separates political and sacred (church) history, he "does not want to dissolve altogether the universal historical structure." Indeed he does not, since Reusner used evidence from both realms to show that the world would probably end in 1670!

I make no claims to thorough coverage of the major chronological writings. Other such works include for example Sethus Calvisius, *Chronologia, ex autoritate potissimum sacrae scripturae et historicum fide dignissimorum . . .* (Leipzig, 1605); *Opus chronologicum, ex autoritate potissimum sacrae scripturae et historicum fide dignissimorum . . .* (Frankfurt, a.O., 1620).

31. Ioannes Sleidanus [Johannes Sleidan], *De quatuor summis imperiis lib. III* (Strassburg, 1556).

32. David Chytraeus, *Chronologia . . . ab initio mundi* (Rostock, 1573), and Michael Neander, *Compendium chronicorum, sive historiarum omnium aetatum, gentium, imperiorum, ac regnorum* (Leipzig, 1586), fols. 32/v–38/v.

33. Conrad Baur in Normberg, *Compendiolvm Chronologicvm: Das ist: Kurtze Chronica oder Zeitregister . . .* (n.p., 1607).

34. Georg Nigrinus, *Ein wolgegründe Rechnung vnd Zeitregister* (Ursel, 1570), fol. Aiiij.

35. Ibid., fol. biii/v.

36. Georg Nigrinus, *Apocalypsis. Die Offenbarunge Sanct Johannis . . . In diesen letzten trübseligen Zeiten . . . in Sechszig Predigen verfasset, Vnd . . . auffs trewlichst vnd fleissigst erkleret vnd ausgelegt* (Ursel, 1573), and *Funffzig Prediglen über den Daniel* (Ursel, 1574).

37. Leonard Krentzheim, *Chronologia. Das ist, Gründtliche vnd fleissige Jahrrechnung . . . Von anfang der Welt, biss auff unsere [Zeit] . . .* (Görlitz, 1577), fol.)(iii.

38. Michael Aitzinger [Michael von Eytzing], *Nova Qvaestionis Solvtio. Nämlich Wie lang die Welt Revera gestanden sey, von Anfang biss auff das gegenwürtig Jar . . .* (Augsburg, 1566).

39. An old but still useful account is F. Kaltenbrunner, "Die Polemik über die gregorianische Kalender Reform," in *Sitzungsberichte der . . . Kais. Akad. Wiss.,* 87 (Vienna, 1877). See also Ernst Zinner, *Geschichte und Bibliographie der astronomischen Literatur in Deutschland zur Zeit der Renaissance* (Stuttgart, 1964), pp. 25ff.

40. Lambertus Floridus Plieninger [Helisaeus Roeslin?], *Kurtz Bedencken Von der Emendation dess Jars, durch Babst Gregorium den XIII fürgenomen, vñ von seinem Kalender, nach ihm Kalendarium Gregorianum perpetuum intituliert, Ob solcher den Protestierenden Ständen anzünemen seie oder nicht. Mit angehencktem Prognostico inn was zeiten wir seien, auss den Propheten Daniele, Zacharia, vnd Apocalypsi Johannis hergefürt, vnd was wir zügewarten haben* (Strassburg, 1583). The popular edition of Luther's critique of the Nicene Council was titled *Herrlich Bedencken, Des tewren Mannes Gottes Lutheri seligen, von den jtzundt newen Bepstlichen Calender . . .* (n.p., 1584).

41. Maestlin edited a collection of writings on the calendar reform, which included a reprint of Plieninger's tract: *Notwendige vnd gründtliche Bedenncken Von dem allgemeinen, uhralten, und nu mehr bey sechtzehen hundert Jaren gebrauchten Römischen Kalender . . .* (Heidelberg, 1584). His own contribution was titled "Ausführlicher Bericht, Von dem allgemeynen Kalender oder Jahrrechnung . . . vnd was darvon zu halten sey."

42. Kepler's work on the date of Christ's birth is available in *Johannes Kepler gesammelte Werke,* vol. 5, *Chronologische Schriften* (Munich, 1953), *Widerholter Aussführlicher Teutscher Bericht, Das vnser Herr vnd Hailand Jesus Christus nit nuhr ein Jahr vor dem anfang vnserer heutiges tags gebreuchigen Jahrzahl geboren sey: Wie . . . Roslinus . . . neben Henrico Buntingo . . . fürgibt: auch nicht nuhr zwey Jahr, wie Scaliger vnd Calvisius mit vilen alten Kirchen Scribenten darfür halten, sonder fünff gantzer Jahr . . .* (Strassburg, 1613). Kepler had first entered the debate with an appendix to his tract on the new star of 1604, entitled "De vero anno natalitio Christi." Calvisius issued an *Admonitio . . . ad chronologiae studiosos . . . annum nativitatis, & tempus ministerii Christi concernentium . . .* (Erfurt, 1610), which was an answer to calculations made by Reusner in his *Isagoges historicae libri duo.*

43. Francis C. Haber, *The Age of the World: Moses to Darwin* (Baltimore, 1959), p. 33. The definitive work on Scaliger is that of Anthony Grafton, *Joseph Scaliger: A Study in the History of Classical Scholarship,* but only the first volume (Oxford, 1983) has appeared. The second, on Scaliger's chronological studies, is still to come. On Bodin see Klempt, *Die Säkularisierung der universalhistorischen Auffassung,* pp. 50ff; and especially the fine work of George Huppert, *The Idea of Perfect History* (Urbana, 1970), pp. 93ff.

44. See Klempt, *Die Säkularisierung der universalhistorischen Auffassung*, pp. 55ff: not until the 1640s did Germans begin seriously to question the idea of the four monarchies.

45. Martin Mirus, *Postilla: Das ist: Ausslegung der Evangelien* (Jena, 1605), pp. 13ff.

46. Andreas Osiander, *Coniecturae de ultimis temporibus, ac de fine mundi, ex sacris literis . . .* (Nuremberg, 1544), and *Vermütung von den letzten Zeiten, vnd dem Ende der Welt, aus der Heiligen Schrifft gezogen* (Nuremberg, 1545). An English translation appeared as early as 1548: *The Coniectures of the last dayes, & end of the worlde, gathered out of scriptures by Andrewe Oseander, and translated by George Joye* (Antwerp?, 1548).

47. Musculus, *Vom Mesech vnd Kedar*, fols. Dij ff.

48. Henricus Efferhen, *XIII Christenliche Predigten auss dem XXXVIII. vnd XXXIX. Capitel Ezechielis. Von Gog vnnd Magog, oder den Türcken* (Strassburg, 1571).

49. Paulus Severus, *Prophezeyung vnnd Weissagung, von dem M.D.LX. Jar, Biss auff das M.D.LXX. Jar werendt . . .* (n.p., 1560?)

50. Johann Rasch, *Weissag der Zeit. Allgemaine Himels vnd Weldpractic . . . immer fort auff alle kunfftigfolgende Jahr . . .* (Munich?, 1596), fol. Cij/v.

51. Theodorus Ursinus, *Sonderliche Propheceyungen Vom heiligen Römischen vnd Teutschen, vnd vom Türckischen Reiche, wie es mit solchen Reichen zugehen werde?* (Nuremberg?, 1605), fol. Aiiij/v.

52. Heinz Duchhardt, *Protestantisches Kaisertum und altes Reich* (Wiesbaden, 1977), esp. ch. 2, pp. 54ff.

53. Nicolaus Winckler, *Bedencken Von Künfftiger verenderung Weltlicher Policey, vnd Ende der Welt, auss heyliger Göttlicher Schrifft vnnd Patribus, auch auss dem Lauff der Natur des 83. biss auff das 88. vnd 89. Jar . . .* (Augsburg, 1582?), fol. Aiij/v.

54. Ibid.

55. Habakkuk 3:2: "O Lord, revive thy work in the midst of the years, in the midst of the years make known."

56. Winckler, *Bedencken Von Künfftiger verenderung Weltlicher Policey, vnd Ende der Welt*, fol. Jij.

57. Adam Nachenmoser, *Prognosticon Theologicvm. Das ist: Gaistliche Grosse Practica auss Hailiger Biblischer Schrifft vnd Historien. Von der Welt Nahe vnd Garaus . . .* (Leyden [Strassburg?], 1595). According to E. Weller (*Lexicon pseudonymorum*, Regensburg, 1886; rpt. Hildesheim, 1963), Adam Nachenmoser was a pseudonym for Johann Fischart, the well-known German satirist. I find no other evidence suggesting or corroborating that Fischart was the author, and given the nature of the work itself it seems highly unlikely that he was. Weller elsewhere (*Die falschen und fingierten Druckorte*, Leipzig, 1864; rpt. Hildesheim, 1960–61; vol. 1, p. 8) states that Leyden was not the real place of publication; the *Prognosticon* was printed at Frankfurt in 1588 and 1591, at Strassburg in 1595. The date of the general introduction, however, and several of the prophecies themselves, suggest that the work was first written by 1584.

58. Nachenmoser, *Prognosticon Theologicvm,* "An Christlichen Guthertzigen Leser, von dem 1588. Jar," fol.):(vj.

59. Philipp Nicolai, *Historia des Reichs Christi, Das ist: Gründliche Beschreibung der wundersamen Erweiterung, seltzamen Glücks, vnd gewisser bestimmte Zeit der Kirchen Christi . . .* (first published 1598; this ed. Frankfurt, a.M., 1659).

60. See above, Chapter 1, note 97.

61. Nicolai, *Historia des Reichs Christi,* esp. ch. 6, pp. 640–64.

62. Erich Trunz, "Meyfarts Leben und Werke," in *Johann Matthaus Meyfart: Tuba Novissima . . .* (reprinted with commentary, Tübingen, 1980), pp. 55–56.

63. I have used a German translation of Hoe's commentary on Revelation: *Extremum et Totale Romae Papalis Excidium. Das ist: Dasz das Päbstiche Rom vnd AntiChristische Reich vorm Jüngsten Tage noch solle vnd müsse zerstöret vnd vmbgekehret werden: Auss dess Herrn Doctoris Mattiae Hoen von Hoenegg . . . Commentario vber die Offenbarung . . . vnd von Wort zu Wort verteutscht* (n.p., 1631).

64. Nicolaus Hartprecht, *Tuba Temporis, Oder Warhafftige, Vnfeilbare Zeit Rechnung, Dergleichen die Welt noch nie gesehen hat, Darinnen augen scheinlich demonstriret vnd erwiesen wird, wie die Welt von anfang biss in diss lauffende 1620 Jahr ein gantz vollkommenes Seculum . . . erfüllet . . .* (Erfurt, 1620).

65. Gottlieb Heylandt [Henr. Wesener?], *Examen Chronologicum: Oder Gründtliche, hochnützliche Erzehlung der Jahr dieser Welt, von dero Anfang, biss auff das nechstkunfftige 1623. Jahr . . .* (n.p., 1622). The seventeenth-century bibliographer Martin Lipen identified Gottlieb Heylandt as Heinrich Wesener, but *Jöcher's allgemeine Gelehrten-Lexicon* has a full bibliographical entry for Heylandt, listing him as a Master of Philosophy and preacher at Greifswald.

66. Gottlieb Heylandt [Henr. Wesener?], *Enarratio Chronologo-Historica Apocal ypseus S. Iohannis: Das ist . . .* (n.p., 1623), p. 152.

67. *Coniectura domini Nicholai de Cusa, de novissimis diebus,* cited in Leroy Edwin Froom, *The Prophetic Faith of Our Fathers* (Washington, D.C., 1946–54), pp. 130–37. Froom's work, though often eccentric in interpretation, offers generally reliable summaries.

68. I have used the edition of Cusa's work appended to Leonard Krentzheim's *Coniecturae* under the title "Coniecturae Oder Christliche Vermutungen des Herren Nicolai Cusani, Cardinaln, Von dem Zustandt der Kirchen Christi, in den letzten Zeiten . . ." See fol. Mv/v.

69. Ibid., fols. O ff.

70. The jubilee derived from a Hebrew tradition that celebrated every 50th year (i.e. the year after the lapse of seven seven-year periods) as a time of perfect rest. See Leviticus 25: 8–55. The idea was carried over into the Christian church, for which the jubilee year became a time for special solemnity and prayer. In the late Middle Ages the interval was reduced; by the end of the fifteenth century the jubilee was officially celebrated every 25 years.

71. Pauline Moffitt Watts, *Nicholas Cusanus: A Fifteenth-Century Vision of Man* (Leiden, 1982), p. 101.

72. Nikolaus von Amsdorf, *Das Melchior Hoffman ein falscher Prophet vnd sein leer vom Jüngsten tag vnrecht, falsch vnnd widder Gott ist* (n.p., 1528).
73. David Meder, *Zehen Christliche Busspredigten, Vber die Weissagung Christi dess grossen Propheten, vom Ende der Welt vnd Jüngsten Tage* . . . (Frankfurt a.M., 1581), fols. Miiij/v–Nij.
74. Froom, *Prophetic Faith*, vol. 2, p. 298.
75. See Emanuel Hirsch, *Die Theologie des Andreas Osiander* (Göttingen, 1919), pp. 131–35, 166–70; also Kolb, *Nikolaus von Amsdorf*, p. 109.
76. *CR* 13, 823–980. Melanchthon's exegesis of Daniel was in its main outlines similar to Luther's.
77. Osiander, *Vermütung von den letzten Zeiten*, fol. cij/v. The translation is from the English edition of George Joye.
78. Ibid., fol. Oiij.
79. Johann Funck, *Apocalypsis: Der Offenbarung Kunfftiger Geschicht Johannis* . . . (see above, Ch. 2, note 104). See esp. ch. 23.
80. *Chunmanni Flinspachii Tabernomontani conjecturae extremorum temporum* (1559). I have not had access to an original edition of this work, but have used the redaction in Johann Wolf, *Lectiones memorabiles et reconditarum* . . . (Frankfurt a.M., 1671), vol. 2, pp. 761–68. Flinsbach also wrote a *Confirmatio chronologiae* (1552), and a *Chronologiam und genealogiam Christi & omnium populorum* (Basel, 1567), neither of which I have seen.
81. Leonard Krentzheim, *Coniecturae*. The work was ostensibly delivered as an address to an assembly of the preachers of Liegnitz in 1577. In 1593 Krentzheim's teachings on the person of Christ caused him to be accused of crypto-Calvinism and to lose his position as superintendent at Liegnitz. He later served as pastor in a small town in Bohemia, while his earlier works continued to be highly regarded. See Zedler's *Universal-Lexicon*.
Rullus, a pastor at Liegnitz, introduced the work with a preface that left no doubts about the main point: the Last Judgment was due very soon; the signs were unambiguous. Those who laughed at the idea would soon pay the full penalty. Rullus quoted Melanchthon at length to quash the doubts of educated sceptics, and cited the well-known prophecies of the monk Johann Hilten. The translator had high praise for Krentzheim's *Chronologia*, which had shown conclusively that as the world had a beginning so it must have an end, and that the time had now nearly arrived. A second preface by Lorentz Ludewig lauded not only the historical reckonings of Krentzheim, but also those of Abraham Bucholzer and the teachings of Philipp Melanchthon on the signs of the coming end. Ludewig also showed the harmony between the periods of the Old and New Testaments. From the flight out of Egypt to the birth of Christ, 1517 years had elapsed, and the period from Christ to the Reformation was exactly the same. And since from the flight out of Egypt to the final destruction of Jerusalem was 1588 years, the prediction made a hundred years earlier by "our distinguished and renowned mathematician," that is, Regiomontanus, was con-

firmed: in that year of the Christian era there would be great changes, if not the end of the world itself.

82. Krentzheim, *Coniecturae*, fol. Hiiij/v.

83. He reckoned that the 1290 days (or years) of Daniel 12 began in 302 A.D. with the persecution of the church under Diocletian. Simple addition rendered 1592—only a few short years after the great changes expected in 1588. It was not to be concluded, though, that the world would necessarily end in 1592. That time was after all hidden to men. A further calculation suggested that the end would probably come later anyway. Using the other figure from Daniel 12, 1335, Krentzheim added as before and arrived at 1637.

84. See note 68 above.

85. At the same time, however, Krentzheim took strong exception to Cusa's division of world history into four ages marked off by the Creation, the Flood, Moses, Christ, and the end. He urged that in this case the Cardinal's thoughts should be left to the Cardinal himself.

86. *Eustachii Poyssels VII. Tractetlein. Darine die ersten drey melden, Von verenderung der Newen vñ Alten Ostern* (n.p., 1594). Several of these apocalyptic treatises, including some devoted to the implications of the calendar change, were published earlier, in 1589, 1590, and 1591. The tracts on the calendar were titled *Von Christi vnd Antichristi Ostern*. See fols. Aij–Ciiij. A number of these works went through later reprintings, for example: *Etliche tractetlein, jetziger zeit nützlich und nötig zu lesen. Darinnen gehandelt wird, Von verenderung etlicher verlauffner Zeit, etc. Item, Wie lang die Welt noch zustehen habe . . . Neben einem wunderlichen Gesicht, so bey der Nacht am Himmel gesehen worden* ("Jetzo nachgedruckt ann der Oder," 1595).

87. David Herlicius, *Tractatus Theologastronomistoricus. Von des Türckischen Reichs vntergange vnd endlicher zerstörung etliche conjecturen vnd vermutungen, auss der H. Schrifft, Sternkunst, vnd den Historien genommen: Neben gründlicher Erklerung vnd Beweiss, dass . . . viel trawrige betrübte zeiten, verfolgungen vnd zerrüttungen gewiss vor der thür stehen . . .* (n.p., 1596).

88. On Herlicius and astrology see below, Chapter 4.

89. Nicolai, *Historia des Reichs Christi*, p. 332.

90. Ibid., p. 333.

91. Reymers spent most of his life in Lutheran lands, and was always in close contact with leading Lutheran clergymen. He was certainly influenced by Lutheran eschatological views, and was in all probability a Lutheran himself.

92. Nicolai Raimari ursi Ditmarsi [Nicolas Reymers], *Chronologische, Gewisse vnd vnwiderlegliche Beweisung, auss heiliger Gottlicher Schrifft vnd heiligen Vättern, dass die Welt vergehen, vnd der Jüngste tag kommen werd, innerhalb 77. Jaren: Anzurechnen von disem jetzlauffenden Jar Christi 1596 . . .* (Nuremberg, 1606), fol. Aij.

93. Jacob Tilner, *Chronologische Zeit Rechnung, vnd gewisse Beweisung aus heiliger gottlicher Schrifft das die Welt in der kürtze vergehen, vnd der liebe Jüngste Tag jnnerhalb 44. Jahren . . . kommen werde. Sampt*

etlichen angehenckten Propheceyungen, des theuren Mannes Gottes D. Martin Luthers, vnd anderer seligen (Halle?, 1613), fols. A/v–Aij.
94. Albert Hitfeld, *Jegenbeweiss. Das die Welt nicht noch 42 Jahr stehen könne, wie Jacobus Tilnerus . . . beweisen will* (n.p., 1613). Hitfeld also wrote a *Betglocke, wegen dess Römischen, Mahometischen vnnd Bäpstlichen Reichs Endschafft vnd darauff fürstehenden jüngsten Tags* (1614). See also below, Chapter 4, note 95.
95. Johann Wolther, *Chronologia Oder Zeit vnd Jahrrechnung, in welcher etliche schwere Örter der Bibel, was Zeit vnd Jahr anlanget, erkleret werden, vnd demnach . . . dargethan wird, Dass die Welt ein Hundert vnd acht Jahr lenger gestanden habe, denn die Chronologi führen . . .* (Königsberg, 1611).
96. Hartprecht, *Tuba Temporis*, fols. A2, A2/v.

Chapter 4

1. I have made an effort in this chapter to avoid the technical details of astrology where possible. At some points, however, an understanding of the basic principles of the art as practiced in the early modern era will be helpful. A good historical introduction is Franz Boll, Carl Bezold, and Wilhelm Gundel, *Sternglaube und Sterndeutung: Die Geschichte und das Wesen der Astrologie* (Darmstadt, 1966). The efforts of the French clergy to control astrological discourse are noted by Denis Crouzet, "La Représentation du Temps" (see above, Introduction, note 9), p. 307. A particularly good discussion of astrology in early modern England is found in Keith Thomas, *Religion and the Decline of Magic*. The present book was already in press when I gained access to the valuable collection of studies edited by Paola Zambelli: *'Astrologi hallucinati': Stars and the End of the World in Luther's Time* (Berlin and New York, 1986). I find nothing in these writings that would lead me to any substantial qualification of my own arguments.
2. See Johann Friedrich, *Astrologie und Reformation. Oder die Astrologen als Prediger der Reformation und Urheber des Bauernkrieges. Ein Beitrag zur Reformationsgeschichte* (Munich, 1864).
3. See above, Chapter 1, note 46.
4. Kurtze, "Prophecy and History" (see above, Chapter 1, note 46). According to George Sarton, Albumazar, whose work was published as *De magnis coniunctionibus* at Augsburg in 1489, had himself plagiarized from the earlier (ninth-century) Arab astrologer Alkindi. *An Introduction to the History of Science* (Baltimore, 1927), vol. 1, p. 568.
5. On Grünpeck see above, Chapter 1, note 140.
6. The anonymous tract was *Ein Ausszug etlicher Practica vnd Propheceyen auff vergangne vñ zükünfftige jar, Sibille, Brigite, Cirilli, Joachim des Apts, Methodii, vnd brüder Reinharts, Von dem letzten Türckischen kaiser . . .* (n.p., n.d.; c. 1518?)
7. On the planetary conjunction of 1524 and the expectations for a flood, see Lynn Thorndike, *A History of Magic and Experimental Science*, vol. 5 (New York, 1941), pp. 178–233.

8. Thorndike, vol. 5, p. 181. Stoeffler's work was the *Almanach nova plurimis annis venturis inserviens* (Ulm, 1499).

9. Leonhard Reinmann, *Practica vber die grossen vnd manigfeltigen Coniunction der Planeten, die im jar M.D.XXiiij. erscheinen, vñ vngezweiffelt vil wunderparlicher ding geperen werden* (Nuremberg, 1523). I have been helped in this paragraph by Zinner, *Geschichte und Bibliographie der astronomischen Literatur*, p. 19.

10. On the elector's supposed ascent of the mountain, see Thorndike, *A History of Magic and Experimental Science*, vol. 5, p. 202. On Dürer's dream, see Crouzet, "La Représentation du temps," pp. 376–77. The argument that alarmist forecasts served as propaganda for the early Reformation is advanced by Paola Zambelli, "Fine del mondo o inizio della propaganda?" in Zambelli, ed., *Scienze, credenze occulte, livelli di cultura* (Florence, 1982), pp. 291–368.

11. In 1522 Carion published a *Prognosticatio vnd Erklerung der grossen Wesserung: Auch anderer erschrockenlichen würchungen, so sich begebe nach Christi vnsers lieben hern gepurt . . .* [1524] (Leipzig, 1522). Here he made his forecast for the flood to result from the conjunctions of 1524. He also foresaw a golden age of peace to begin in 1532 (he made reference to Joachim of Fiore), and predicted that the Antichrist would be born in 1693. Some time shortly afterward, Christ would return in glory for the Judgment. Carion's expectations at this point had clearly not yet been directly influenced by those of early Protestantism.

12. Thorndike, *A History of Magic and Experimental Science*, vol. 5, p. 382.

13. Paracelsus, *Prognostication auff xxiiij jar zukünfftig, durch den hochgelerten Doctorem Paracelsum* (Augsburg, 1536). I have used the edition in A. Ritter, ed., *Collectio vaticiniorum* (Berlin, 1923).

14. *Propheceien vnd Weissagungen.* See above, Chapter 2, note 61.

15. Melanchthon's lectures were the *Initia doctrinae physicae dictata in academia Witebergensi*, first published in Wittenberg in 1549 and very often thereafter.

16. R. J. W. Evans, *The Making of the Habsburg Monarchy*, p. 348.

17. See above, Chapter 1, note 100.

18. Elert, *Morphologie des Luthertums*, vol. 1, p. 381.

19. On the issue of Luther's birthdate, in which Melanchthon was much influenced by the Italian astrologer Lucas Gauricus, see Aby Warburg, *Heidnisch-antike Weissagung*, in *Gesammelte Schriften*, vol. 2, pp. 500ff. Reinhart Staats has recently criticized Warburg and others for placing too much weight on Melanchthon's astrological motivations in this matter. Staats argues that most evidence in fact points to 1484 as the date of Luther's birth, that Melanchthon knew this, and that the astrological evidence was for Melanchthon merely confirmation of this fact, in "Luthers Geburtsjahr 1484 und das Geburtsjahr der evangelischen Kirche 1519," *Bibliothek und Wissenschaft*, 18 (1984), 61–84. Still, Melanchthon was pleased and reassured that the celestial evidence fit so nicely with his understanding of events. Oberman, *Luther* (p. 88), appears to be slightly mixed up on this point; most of the astrologers argued for 1484, not 1483 as he suggests.

20. This is suggested by Warburg, *Heidnisch-antike Weissagung*, esp. pp. 497ff.

21. See Elert, *Morphologie des Luthertums*, vol. 1, p. 389. John Warwick Montgomery has gone farther, maintaining that "Melanchthon's theocentric belief that God providentially guides the world through 'secondary causes' is one with Luther's conviction that the risen Christ is dynamically present in even the apparently trivial natural occurrences of the world." This statement confuses Luther's view with a metaphysical doctrine, and it seems doubtful that Luther himself could have agreed with it. Montgomery is right, however, in holding that Melanchthon's position "gives astrological and astronomical research a theological dynamic which it heretofore lacked." *Cross and Crucible: Johann Valentin Andreae (1586–1654), Phoenix of the Theologians* (The Hague, 1973), p. 10.

22. Thorndike, *A History of Magic and Experimental Science*, vol. 5, pp. 381–82.

23. Caspar Peucer, *Commentarius de praecipuis generibus divinationum*, esp. pp. 376ff.

24. Thorndike, *A History of Magic and Experimental Science*, vol. 6, p. 99.

25. Cyprian Leowitz, *Grundliche, Klärliche beschreibung, vnd Historischer bericht, der fürnemsten grossen zusamenkunfft der obern Planeten, der Soñen Finsternussen, der Cometen, vnd derselben wirckung, so sich in der vierten Monarchien erzaigt vnnd begeben, sampt einem Prognostico von dem 1564. Jar, biss auff nachvolgend zweintzig Jar werende* (Lauingen, 1564), fol. V/v.

26. Georg Caesius, *Prognosticon Astrologicvm, Oder Practica Teutsch* . . . (Nuremberg, 1574). Caesius appears to have issued a similar practica almost every year between 1570 and 1604.

27. Georg Caesius, *Prognosticon Astrologicvm* (Nuremberg, 1580).

28. Georg Friederich Caesius, *Prognosticon Astrologicvm* (Nuremberg, 1602), fol. Aij.

29. Adam Ursinus, *Prognosticatio. Auff das M.D.LXXI. Jhar* (Erfurt, 1570?), fol. Aij.

30. Arndt's original *Vier Bücher* appeared at Magdeburg in 1610; the first book had been printed separately at Frankfurt as early as 1605. I have used a later, expanded edition of Arndt's work: *Fünff Bücher Vom Wahren Christenthum* (Lüneburg, 1684). See esp. book 2, chapter 58, pp. 677ff.

31. Ibid., p. 678.

32. Ibid., p. 680.

33. Lorentz Eichstadt, *Prognosticon de Conjunctione Magna Saturni & Iovis . . . Oder Discurs Von der Grossen Zusammenkunfft Saturni vnd Jovis vnter dem Himlischen Trigono dess Fewrigen Löwen im Jahr Christi 1623* (Alten Stettin, 1622).

34. Melchior Schaerer, *Verantwortung vnd Rettung der Argumenten vnd Vrsachen, welche M. Melchior Scherer, in den Vorreden seiner zweyen Prognosticorum verschienen 1608. vnd 1609. Jahren . . . eingeführet . . .* (n.p., 1611). See p. 170.

35. Johann Kepler, *Tertivs Interveniens. Das ist, Warnung an etliche*

Theologos, Medicos vnd Philosophos, sonderlich D. Philippum Feselium, dass sie ... nicht das Kindt mit dem Badt aussschütten ... (Frankfurt a.M., 1610).

36. Christopher Cnoll, *Prognosticon Generale Perpetuum. Ein allgemeine Practica, auff alle vnd jede Jahr, biss ans ende der Welt ...* (Görlitz, 1616), p. 68.

37. The idea was derived from Arabic sources, particularly from Albumazar's *De magnis coniunctionibus* (see above, note 4).

38. Krentzheim's use of this astrological method of reckoning is found in his *Coniecturae*, fols. Liiij–Lv.

39. See above, note 26. Leowitz also issued an important Latin work predicting all the major eclipses to occur between 1564 and 1607. This work was used in turn by many popular writers who offered their own predictions on the basis of major celestial events of this sort. For example: *Prognosticon Vnd Weyssagung der fürnemsten dingen so vom [1564–1607] sich zutragen werden, auss den Finsternussen vnd grossen Ephemeri des Hochgelerten Cypriani Leouicij, vnd auss dem Prognostico Samuelis Syderocratis, gezogen vnd zusamen gestelt* (n.p., 1564?). The author of this tract emphasized that the increasing frequency of such signs indicated the nearness of the end. Denis Crouzet ("La Représentation du temps," p. 311) deals with a French edition that is almost certainly a translation of this work.

40. In the Latin edition, according to Thorndike, the *Prognosticon* has a separate title page, but in the German edition I have used the two parts form an integral work. Thorndike hardly notes the strongly apocalyptic tone of the work (see *A History of Magic and Experimental Science*, vol. 6, p. 117).

41. Leowitz, *Grundliche, Klärliche beschreibung...*, fol. Rij.

42. Ibid.; see preface and dedication to Maximilian II, dated September, 1563.

43. Ibid., fol. V.

44. Johann Hebenstreit, *Prognosticon Historicvm vnd Physicvm. Auffs M.D.LXVI Jhar ...* (Erfurt?, c. 1565).

45. Nicolaus Orphanus, *Ivdicivm Astrologicvm. Von dem Tausend, Fünffhundert, Vier vnd siebenzigsten Jare, bis in das 1578. Jar, darinnen gantz gründlichen vnd warhafftig, warnungsweise wird angezeiget, was sich für Trübsal, vnd Vnglück, in Deutschlanden vnd andern Königreichen, zutragen vnd begeben werde* (Nuremberg?, 1573?).

46. Nicolaus Orphanus, *Ivdicivm Astrologicvm. Auff die Jahr vnsers Heylandes Jhesu Christi Geburt 1577. vnd 1578.* (Nuremberg, 1576?), fol. [Bvij].

47. Thorndike, *A History of Magic and Experimental Science*, vol. 5, p. 417.

48. Typical of Henisch's many annual prognostications was a *Practica: Auff das Jar nach der Gnadenreichen Geburt vnsers Herren vnd Heylands Jhesu Christi M.D.LXXXVII* (n.p., c. 1586). He also wrote several works on the new stars and comets, and worked as a theoretical adviser to two clockmakers in constructing the great clock of the Augsburg Cathedral

(Maurice and Mayr, *The Clockwork Universe*, p. 78). See also Thorndike, *A History of Magic and Experimental Science*, vol. 6, pp. 142–43.

49. Tobias Mvller [Moller], *Prognosticon Astrologicvm . . . 1592* (Frankfurt a.O., 1591). From about 1570 until well into the early seventeenth century, Nicolaus Winckler issued annual practica and prognostica full of such warnings. Most of these were published at Nuremberg or at Augsburg. One Nicholas Eberhard Winckler (his son?) also published numerous works of this sort in the early seventeenth century, as well as a *Beschreibung von künstlicher Veranderung Theatri Naturae, Ende der Welt vnd ordentlicher Process Judicii finalis, wie es endlich am Jüngsten Tag werde zugehen* (Lauingen, 1611).

50. For examples of works by Caesius see above, notes 26 and 27. It is not always possible to tell whether an astrological author was also a pastor, but a remarkable number did identify themselves as such.

51. Some of the early satires are briefly discussed in Zinner, *Geschichte und Bibliographie der astronomischen Literatur*, p. 23. Fischart's *Aller Practick Grossmutter* (Strassburg, 1572–74) shared its inspiration with another satire from the same period, the *Aller Practicken vnnd Prognosticken Grossvater* (n.p., 1575), probably by Hans Christoph Becker. Oswald Anderman issued a *Sehr gewisse Prognostica . . . biss zum ende der Welt* (Magdeburg, 1582) that made fun of the common prophecies and almanacs. Another satirical work was titled *Prognostica. Das sind etzliche vor vnd anzeigungen aller Jaren . . .* (n.p., 1586). This latter tract poked fun especially at the writings of one Wilhelm Misocacus, who had forecast horrible things for 1588. Misocacus was also ridiculed by the Catholic astrologer Johann Rasch; see note 54 below. Such satirical writings were still common in the early seventeenth century; a 1611 work entitled *Newe vnd trewe Baurhaffte vnnd jmmer Daurhaffte Practica, auch Bosserliche doch nicht verführliche Prognostica vnd Wetterbuch* mocked not only the dark yearly warnings of the astrologers but also the expectation that some great prophetic figure was soon to appear.

52. Goldwurm's edition of Torquatus was titled *Prognosticon. Weissagungen vñ Vrtheyl, von betrübungen vnnd grossen anfechtungen Europe, Durch den Hochberhümbten Astronomum . . . D. Anthonium Torquatum gestelt . . .*

53. Georg Friederich Caesius, *Prognosticon Astrologicvm*, Vorrede. Leonhardt Thurneisser's published prophecies were apparently numerous and highly popular. His annual practica were fairly standard, but he also issued more obscure works such as an *Impletio, oder Erfüllung der verheissung* (Nuremberg, 1581). In his *Alter vnd newer corrigirter Allmanach vnd Schreib Kalender, sampt verenderung des Wetters, mit eingeführter Practick, auff dz Schaltjahr . . . M.D.LXXXIIII.* (Berlin, 1583), he offered calculations on the basis of both the old Julian calendar and the revised Gregorian system; his willingness to acknowledge the value of the calendar change may have been another reason he was attacked by Protestant astrologers.

54. Johann Rasch, *Gegenpractic, Wider etliche aussgangen Weissag, Prognostic vnd Schrifften, sonderlich des Misocaci, vber das 84. vnd 88.*

Jare, von vntergang hohes Geschlächts, änderung der Reich vnd Religion, Newen Calender, Letzten Zeit, Antichrist, vnd End der Welt (Munich, 1584).

55. Johann Rasch, *Weissag der Zeit.* Rasch attacked what he saw as unacceptable prophecies in the Catholic camp as well. Thus for example he criticized those of Wolfgang Lazius of Vienna, who issued several emperor-prophecies to show that the House of Hapsburg would soon reform the church and unite the whole world.

56. Jonas Philognysius [Johann Nas], *Die vnfelig gewisest Practica practicarum, auff das yetzig vnd nachfolgende jar auss grund der grossen Coniunction, langer erfarnuss, vnd steter übung mit vergleichung der siben irrdischen Planeten, vnd zwölff Himlischen zaichen beschriben* . . . (Ingolstadt, 1566), fols. D, D/v.

57. Simon Pauli, "Perikopenpredigt auf den zweiten Advent, über Luc 21, 25–36," from *Postilla* (Magdeburg, 1574). In Wilhelm Beste, *Die bedeutendsten Kanzelredner der lutherschen Kirche des Reformationszeitalters* (Leipzig, 1856), vol. 2, pp. 275ff.

58. Lucas Pollio, *Vom Jüngsten Gericht, Sechss Fasten Predigten. Anno MDLXXX.* (Nuremberg, ca. 1601); Martin Mirus, *Postilla.* A useful listing of published sermons of the sixteenth and early seventeenth centuries is found in Martin Lipen, *Biblioteca realis universalis* (Frankfurt a.M., 1685), vol. 2; see esp. under "Postille" and "Sermones."

59. Jacob Andreae, *Christliche, notwendige vnd ernstliche Erinnerung, Nach dem Lauff der irdischen Planeten gestelt, Darauss ein jeder einfeltiger Christ zusehen, was für glück oder vnglück, Teutschland diser zeit zugewarten. Auss . . . Luc. 21 . . .* (Tübingen, 1567).

60. Michael Eichler, *Biblisch Calender, Darinnen vff alle vnnd jede Jar, Tag vnnd Stund . . .* (Frankfurt a.M., 1579).

61. For example: Balthasar Wilhelm, *Practica oder Prenostication auff tzuokunfftig tzythe, auss der heyligen schrifft getzogenn* (n.p., 1524?).

62. Heinrich Winand, *Concilivm Olympicvm. Reichstag der Sieben Firmamentischen Fürsten . . . zu Rahtschlagen vber die Straffen, mit welchen die Gottlose Welt sol vberfallen werden, auff das Jar M.D.LXXXX.* (Magdeburg, 1589?).

63. Caspar Stiller, *Geistliche Practica Astrologica. Oder Kirchen-Calender, Darinne von Geistlichen Sonnen vnd Mond-Finsternissen, wie auch von bösen Aspecten gehandelt . . .* (Leipzig, 1620).

64. The quatrain is found so frequently in literature of the period that it would be pointless to offer a list. It was adapted to support expectations for earlier years, as for example in the work of Johann Garcaeus (see Chapter 2, note 9): "Wenn man wird zelen, 1582 Jhar / Geschicht nichts newes so zergehet die Welt gar." Once 1588 was past, the rhyme was not forgotten, but used to show that big changes were overdue. And, inevitably, it was updated for later years; one version applied it to 1628.

65. David Meder, *Zehen Christliche Busspredigten.*

66. Nicolaus Weiss, *Prognosticon Astrologicvm. Von dem 1572. bisz auff das 1588. Jar werende . . .* (Vienna, 1571?; other editions Dresden, 1572, and Frankfurt a.M., 1573); and *Practica auff Zehen Jar . . . biss auff*

das 1588. Jar werende . . . (n.p., 1578). Weiss was almost certainly a Lutheran.

67. Among Weiss's other prophecies was a *Prognosticon: Von dem 1575. Jahr an, werende bis in das 1580. Jar, Darinnen gantz gründlich vnd warhafftig warnungs weise angezeigt wirdt, was sich für Trübsal, Jammer vnd Vnglück in Deutschland vnd andern Königreichen begeben vnd zutragen werde* . . . (n.p., 1575).

68. Johann Rasch, *Practica Auff das grosswunder Schaltjar. 1588.* (Munich, 1587; another edition 1588).

69. Sociological investigations have shown that the unequivocal disconfirmation of an expectation may, under certain circumstances, actually lead to an intensification of the underlying belief. Such findings may shed light on the continuance of apocalyptic expectations throughout the sixteenth century. See Leon Festinger, Henry Riecken, and Stanley Schachter, *When Prophecy Fails* (Minneapolis, 1956).

70. Daniel Schaller, *Ein New Theologisch Prognosticon auff das 89. vnd folgende Jar. Wider die grosse Hochschedliche Sicherheit der Welt, die da meinet sie sey mit dem 88. Jahr vber den Angstberg hinüber, vnd es habe nunmehr kein noth* . . . (Magdeburg, 1589).

71. Georg Rollenhagen, *Der Hinckende Both, schlahe jhn die Gicht, Ist komen bringt viel andern bericht, Dann wir zuuorn, vff diese Reim, Mit Warheit nicht berichtet sein* (n.p., 1589). On Rollenhagen see *ADB*, vol. 29, pp. 87–95.

72. Thomas Hartman, *Cometen Spiegel: Oder: Bericht von Cometen* . . . (Hall in Sachsen, 1605), pp. 5ff.

73. Michael Babst, *Der Sieben Planeten lauff vnnd Wirckung, auff das Menschliche Leben, in diesem letzten Zeiten gerichtet* . . . (Leipzig, 1594).

74. Isaac Habrecht, *Kurtze vnd Gründliche Beschreibung, Eines Newen vngewöhnlichen Sterns, oder Cometen* . . . (Strassburg, 1618).

75. Lorentz Eichstadt, *Prognosticon De conjunctione magna.*

76. Valesius Minymus, *Hoch nötiges vnd zu dieser betrübten zeit allen bedrängten Christen tröstliches bedencken, Vber der beschaffenheit itziger Zeit, sonderlich aber dess instehenden Jahres 1623.* (n.p., 1622). Minymus's work differed in several key respects from that of Eichstadt (see note 75). Minymus openly rejected the notion that the downfall of the Antichrist had occurred with Luther, and suggested that this key prophetic event was still to come (fols. K, K/v); Eichstadt equally clearly asserted that the downfall of the pope had to be understood in spiritual terms and that it had been effected by Luther; he rejected the projection of an earthly downfall of the pope as too literal an interpretation of Daniel and Revelation (fol. Iij/v).

77. This position is also argued by Ernst Zinner, *Geschichte und Bibliographie der astronomischen Literatur*, pp. 20–21.

78. Chrisman, *Lay Culture, Learned Culture*, pp. 257–58.

79. Johann Pfeffinger, *Christliche gewisse deutung der zeichen, die für vnd in diesem 1562. Jar geschehen* (Leipzig, 1562), fol. Aiij.

80. Quoted in Thorndike, *A History of Magic and Experimental Science*, vol. 6, p. 69. Brahe, however, not only viewed the new star as a sign of the end but also thought it might herald a new age of peace.

81. John Warwick Montgomery, *Cross and Crucible*, p. 8. Chytraeus's work was titled *De stella inusitata et nova quae mense Novembri anno 1572. conspicit coepit. Et ... de comato sidere, quod hoc mense Novembri anno 1577 videmus* (Rostock, 1577).

82. Thorndike, vol. 6, p. 78.

83. Sigismundus Sueuus [Schwabe], *Cometen, Was sie für grosse Wunder vnd schreckliche ding zu bedeuten, vnd ankündigen pflegen ...* (Görlitz, 1578).

84. Christoph Irenaeus, *Prognosticon Aus Gottes Wort.*

85. Jacob Heerbrand, *Ein trewe Warnung vnd gutthertzige Vermanung zur Büss ... vber das schröckliche Wunderzeichen, den Cometen ... oder Pflawenschwantz ... 1577* (Tübingen, 1578).

86. Some examples of other such works: Johann Praetorius, *Narratio oder Historische erzelung dern Cometen, so vor diser zeit sind gesehen worden ...* (Nuremberg, 1578); Georg Busch, *Von den Cometen ... 1572* (Erfurt, 1573), and *Von dem erschrecklichen grausamen grossen Cometstern ...* (Prague, 1578); Andreas Celicius, *Christliche, notwendige, nützliche vnd theologische Erinnerung, von dem newen Cometen* (Leipzig, 1578). On the comet of 1577 in general see Clarisse Doris Hellman, *The Comet of 1577: Its Place in the History of Astronomy* (New York, 1944). Hellman's work does not, however, do justice to the apocalyptic interpretations of the comet.

87. Typical of the excited works inspired by the new star was a tract by Wilhelm Eo Neuheuser, *Tractatvs: De Nova Stella; Oder Von dem newen Abent Stern ...* (Strassburg?, 1604). For an interesting though rather myopic treatment of expectations in connection with 1604 see Will-Erich Peuckert, *Die Rosenkreutzer: Geschichte einer Reformation* (Jena, 1928), "Die Wunderzeit 1604," pp. 51–58.

88. David Herlicius, *Astronomische vnd Historische Erklerung Des Newen Sterns oder ... Cometen ... 1604* (Alten Stettin, 1605).

89. I have used a 1605 edition of Kepler's work that appeared along with another tract on the new star by Helisaeus Roeslin: *Gründlicher Bericht vnd Bedencken, Von einem vngewöhnlichen Newen Stern ... dess 1604. Jahrs ...* (Amberg, 1605), fols. B, B/v.

90. It would take us too far afield to examine the arguments of Kepler and his responses to Roeslin in any detail. Kepler's disagreement with Roeslin's mode of interpretation was already clear from his tract on the new star of 1604. He responded to Roeslin's highly popular work on the comet of 1607 (see note 91) with an *Antwort Joannis Keppleri ... Auff D. Helisaei Röslini Medici & Philosophi Discurs Von heutiger zeit beschaffenheit ...* (Prague, 1609), in which he called into question the whole assumption that comets portended disaster. Kepler also argued here in favor of Copernicus, whose cosmology Roeslin rejected. Many avid astrologers, however, were early defenders of Copernicus.

91. Helisaeus Roeslin, *Historischer, Politischer vnd Astronomischer naturlicher Discurs Von heutiger zeit Beschaffenheit, Wesen vnd Stand der Christenheit, vnd wie es künfftig in derselben ergehn werde ...* (Strassburg, 1609), fol. Jiij/v.

92. Ibid.

93. Ibid., fol. Fij.

94. David Herlicius, *Kurtzer Discvrs Vom Cometen, vnnd dreyen Sonnen, so am ende des 1618. Jahrs erschienen sind* . . . (Alten Stettin, 1619).

95. Albert Hitfeld, *Ivdiciolvm. Kleiner Vorstand* . . . *Der bedeutung des Cometen* . . . *1618.* (n.p., 1619).

96. Erasmus Schmidt, *Prodromus conjunctionis magnae, anno 1623. futurae* . . . (Wittenberg, 1619).

97. Philipp Melanchthon, *Postilla. Dominica II adventus. Evangelium Lucae 21, CR 24,* 18.

98. Johann Garcaeus, *Eine Christliche kurtze Widerholung* . . . , fol. J/ v; Daniel Schaller, *Herolt,* fol. Niiij/v; Valerius Herberger, *Predigt am zweiten Advent-Sonntage. Luc. 21, 25–36.* (1613), in R. Nesselman, *Buch der Predigten oder 100 Predigten und Reden* . . . (Elbing, 1858), p. 10.

99. Isaac Habrecht, *Kurtze vnd Grundliche Beschreibung, Der dreyen Sonnen* . . . *im Jahr 1622. zu Strassburg* . . . (Strassburg, 1622?). A deacon at Strassburg contributed another commentary on this appearance: Oseas Schadaeus, *Eine dreyfache, kurtze, vnd einfältige Betrachtung, Desz herrlichen Wundergesichts der dreyen Sonnen* . . . (Strassburg, 1622). This latter tract is a long, heavily Lutheran, heavily apocalyptic work that cites Fincel, Lycosthenes, Sleidan, Goldwurm, Peucer, Garcaeus, Krentzheim, Nigrinus, Arndt, and Luther to argue that such signs held a profound message.

100. Lorentz Eichstadt, *Novum & Rarissimum Ostentum Quinque Pareliorum. Oder Einfeltiges Bedencken vber die fünff Sonnen* . . . (Alten Stettin, 1625).

101. Thomas, *Religion and the Decline of Magic,* pp. 634–36.

102. Montgomery, *Cross and Crucible,* pp. 12, 13.

103. Ibid., pp. 196, 197.

104. These themes are admirably explored in Kurt Goldammer, "Paracelsische Eschatologie: Zum Verständnis der Anthropologie und Kosmologie Hohenheims," *Nova acta paracelsica* 5 (1948), 45–85; 6 (1952), 68–102.

105. Will-Erich Peuckert has described these trends in Germany around 1600, and has given astrology its deserved notice. What is missing in his discussion is a sense of the Lutheran background to the expectancy in general, and to the astrological apocalypticism in particular, of the age. See his *Die Rosenkreutzer* (Jena, 1928).

106. The most readily available edition of Weigel's work is *"Astrology Theologized." The Spiritual Hermeneutics of Astrology and Holy Writ* . . . , ed. Anna Bonus Kingsford (London, 1886).

107. Montgomery, *Cross and Crucible,* p. 12.

108. There is no good scholarly treatment of Nagel. He is discussed as a representative of the chiliasm of the Thirty Years' War period in Roland Haase, *Das Problem des Chiliasmus und der dreissigjährige Krieg* (Leipzig, 1933), pp. 93, 94. Haase is, however, to be read with discretion. Nagel's place in the history of mathematics is considered in A. G. Kästner, *Geschichte der Mathematik* (Göttingen, 1796–1800), vol. 4, pp. 399–403.

109. Paul Nagel, *Himmels Zeichen. Grosse Conjunctiones Planetarum superiorum, vnd newer Wunderstern, so Anno 1604 . . . erschienen* (Hall in Sachsen, 1605).
110. Paul Nagel, *Catoptromantia Physica. Diviniatio ex speculo Astrologico. Das ist: Grundlicher Bericht vnd naturliche Weissagung aus der . . . gestirneten Firmaments . . .* (Leipzig, 1610). Nagel's astrological analyses of biblical prophecy were not without foundation in the sources themselves, since the visions of Revelation did probably owe a debt to astrological mysticism. See Boll, et al., *Sternglaube und Sterndeutung*, p. 30.
111. Paul Nagel, *Prognosticon Astrologo-Cabalisticum, Auff das Jahr MDCXX. beschrieben, In welchem der grundt vnserer warhafftigen Astronomiae entdecket vnd eröffnet wird . . .* (n.p., 1619).

Chapter 5

1. Frances Yates, *Giordano Bruno*, pp. 306–7.
2. Bruno, "Die Abschiedsrede, welche Giordano Bruno vor den Professoren und Hörern auf der Akademie zu Wittenberg im Jahre 1588 am 8. März gehalten hat," *Gesammelte Werke* (Leipzig, 1904–9), vol. 6, p. 81.
3. Yates, *Giordano Bruno*, p. 312, points out that while in England Bruno had made similar remarks about the possibility that truth might be discovered there, amongst the nymphs of the Thames. While this is so, I have been unable to find in Bruno's writings the same enthusiasm for England as in this speech about Germany. Yates herself acknowledges that Bruno "evidently liked the Lutherans very much better than the Calvinist heretics of France or the Puritan Anglicans" (pp. 306–7).
4. See Thomas Klein, *Die Kampf um die zweite Reformation*, p. 138. Klein believes that once the government of Christian I began a concerted effort to establish a reformed (Calvinist) church polity in Saxony, Bruno had no choice but to leave Wittenberg. His view is plausible, but it does not follow that the magician's stay at the university had been possible only because of unusually confused circumstances.
5. Arthur D. Imerti, "Editor's Introduction: 'The Making of a Heretic,'" in Giordano Bruno, *The Expulsion of the Triumphant Beast* (New Brunswick, 1964), p. 15. Imerti suggests that Bruno left Wittenberg because as a champion of Copernicus he no longer felt safe among Calvinists (or Philippists) who had declared Copernicus's views heretical.
6. Ibid.
7. The shakeup of the faculty in 1588 saw Mylius, Leyser, and other upholders of conservative Lutheranism dismissed and replaced with theologians who leaned toward Calvinism. It is possible that the magician might have felt some marginal sense of solidarity with the prophetic faith of the old-style Lutherans against the strict Aristotelianism and the rationalizing tendencies of the new theologians.
8. See Elizabeth Eisenstein, "The Advent of Printing and the Problem of the Renaissance," p. 79.
9. Christopher Cnoll, *Prognosticon Generale Perpetuum*, Vorrede, fol. Ciiij/v.

10. See R. J. W. Evans, *Rudolph II and His World* and *The Making of the Habsburg Monarchy.*

11. Augustine, *On Christian Doctrine,* trans. D. W. Robertson (Indianapolis, 1958), p. 52. Augustine also commented on the value of numbertheory in *The City of God,* book 11, ch. 30.

12. On the general topic of the role of numbers in medieval thought, see Albert Zimmermann, ed., *Mensura. Mass, Zahl, Zahlensymbolik im Mittelalter (Miscellanea Mediaevalia,* vol. 16; Berlin and New York, 1983–84).

13. Stifel reported these matters in a preface to a later work, *Ein sehr Wunderbarliche wortrechnung* (n.p., 1553). See esp. fol. Aiij. The order of the letters in LEO X DECIMVS was irrelevant; thus while the letters could have added up to 664 or 666, Stifel was free to choose the latter, and far more significant, figure.

14. Stifel's *Rechenbüchlein* was published in Wittenberg, 1532. A valuable treatment of this work can be found in H.-U. Hofmann, *Luther und die Johannes-Apokalypse,* pp. 533–36; see also Hofmann's general treatment of Stifel, pp. 530–49.

15. Stifel, *Ein sehr Wunderbarliche wortrechnung,* "Vorrede"; see also the article on Stifel in *ADB,* vol. 36, pp. 208–16. There are also numerous descriptions of this incident in later sixteenth-century literature. The various accounts of the affair differ on some details; I have followed none of them to the letter, but have tried simply to give a generally acceptable account of what is important.

16. "Er Michael hat ein kleines Anfechtlein bekommen, aber es soll ihm nicht schaden, gottlob, sondern nütze sein." See *ADB,* vol. 36, p. 212.

17. See the literature listed in *ADB,* especially A. G. Kästner, *Geschichte der Mathematik,* vol. 1, pp. 112–28.

18. Michael Stifel, *Arithmetica integra . . . cum praefatione Philippi Melanchthonis* (Nuremberg, 1544); *Deutsche Arithmetica* (Nuremberg, 1545).

19. Stifel, *Ein sehr Wunderbarliche wortrechnung,* fol. Cij/v.

20. Ibid., fol. Niij. Stifel was still involved in apocalyptic reckoning as late as 1560 at Jena. See H.-U. Hofmann, *Luther und die Johannes-Apokalypse,* p. 547.

21. Christoff Rudolph, *Behend vnnd Hubsch Rechnung durch die kunstreichen regeln Algebre—so gemeincklich die Coss genent werden* (Vienna?, 1524?).

22. On Rudolph's use of addition and subtraction symbols, see Chrisman, *Lay Culture, Learned Culture,* p. 184. Rudolph published other works that show even more clearly his interest in playing with numbers, including for example a *Künstliche rechnung mit der Ziffer vñ mit den zal pfennige, sampt der Wellischen practica, vnd allerley vorteil auff die Regel de Tri* (first published 1526; I have seen only the edition of Nuremberg, 1532).

23. See *ADB,* vol. 36, p. 214.

24. Stifel, *Arithmetica integra,* preface of Melanchthon.

25. Georg Walther, *Prophezeiungen D. Martini Lutheri,* fol. a vj/v.

Walther was probably not the first to use this chronogram; see Volz, *Die Lutherpredigten des Johannes Mathesius*, p. 78.

26. Nicolas Selnecker, *Der Prophet Daniel, vnd die Offenbarung Johannis* (n.p., 1567). In "The Apocalypse: A Bibliography," Joseph Wittreich reports that this work had been published at Geneva in 1547; I have not located this edition (see Patrides and Wittreich, eds., *The Apocalypse in English Renaissance Thought and Literature*, p. 377).

27. Ibid., fols. liij, liij/v.

28. Sigismundus Sueuus [Schwabe], *Arithmetica Historica. Die Löbliche Rechenkunst. Durch alle Species vnd fürnembste Regeln . . . zu gutte erkleret . . .* (Breslau, 1593), "Vorrede."

29. This chronogram had been used earlier (see Volz, *Die Lutherpredigten des Johannes Mathesius*, pp. 77–78). It was only one among very many Schwabe presented.

30. Christopher Cnoll, *Prognosticon Generale Perpetuum*, pp. 65–66.

31. I have not seen this work. Herlicius refers to it in his *Tractatus Theologastronomistoricus* (see above, Chapter 3, note 87), fol. [Eiiij].

32. Eustachius Poyssel, *Die Schlüssel David, Esaie: 22. Apocalip: 3.* (n.p., 1594). Regarding the reign of Frederick IV in the Palatinate I have depended on *ADB*, vol. 7, pp. 613–21.

33. Eustachius Poyssel, *Die Braut dess Lambs, Das Himlische Newe Jerusalem, wie dasselb der Heilige Johannes im 21. vnd 22. Capitel seiner Himlischen Offenbarung beschreybet . . .* (n.p., 1591).

34. Studion, "Naometria, seu nuda, et prima libri intus, et foris scripti per claven Davidis, et calamum virgae similem apertio: in quo non tantum ad cognoscendatum S. Scripturae totius: quam naturae quoque universae mysteria brevis sit introductio: verum etiam prognosticus. (Stellae illius natutinae anno domini 1572 conspectae ductu.) Demonstratur adventus ille Christi ante diem novissimum secundus per quem, homine peccati, papa, cum filio suo perditionis Mahometo, divinitus devastato, ipse ecclesiam suam, et principatus mundi restaurabit, ut in iis posthac sit cum ovili uno pastor unus . . . In cruciferae militiae evangelicae gratiam. Authore Simone Studione, inter Scorpiones . . . anno 1604." The manuscript is at the Württembergische Landesbibliothek in Stuttgart; a copy is on microfilm at the Warburg Institute, University of London.

35. Matthias Hafenreffer, *Templum Ezechielis, sive in IX postrema prophetae capita commentarius . . .* (Tübingen, 1613). This work is an outstanding example of the magical mentality shared by Lutherans in this age; the concern with numbers and measurement is evident throughout the work, but is especially manifest in the "Appendix geometrica," pp. 340–44. Luther had interpreted the temple described at the end of Ezekiel as the heavenly Jerusalem described in Revelation 21–22 (*WA Deutsche Bibel* 11, I, 392), and had written, "Wer müssig und lüstig ist, der kan wol viel drinnen sehen und forschen . . . Vnd die Offenbarung Johannis kan auch dazu helffen" (Ibid., 408). An Apocalypse illustration in the full German Bible of 1534 prominently displayed an angel holding a golden staff to measure the city (Revelation 22: 15ff). See Peter Martin, *Martin Luther und die Bilder zur Apokalypse*, pp. 136, 196.

36. Paul Nagel, *Raptusastronomicus. Das ist Astronomische gewisse warhafftige Prophecey vnd Weissagung, aus dem Ersten, Andern vnd Dritten Himmel* . . . (n.p., 1627).

37. Johannes Dobricius, *Chronomenytor das ist, Zeiterinner, in welchem* . . . *erkleret vnd angezeiget wird, In was vor einer zeit wir Jetzo sein, vnd was nun mehr vnfehlbar der Welt vnd vns schierkünfftig zugewarten* (Liegnitz, 1612), p. 49.

38. Even Descartes came to Ulm in 1620 seeking instruction from Faulhaber. See *ADB*, "Faulhaber, Johann," vol. 6, pp. 581–83.

39. Urim and Thummim: objects mentioned in several passages of the Old Testament as mediums for the revelation of the will of God to his people. See Deuteronomy 33: 8; Exodus 28: 30; Leviticus 8: 8, etc.

40. Johann Faulhaber, *Himlische gehaime Magia Oder Newe Cabalistische Kunst, vnd Wunderrechnung, Vom Gog vnd Magog. Darauss die Weisen, Verstandigen vnd Gelerten* . . . *heimlich observiren vnd fleissig aussrechnen mögen, die Beschaffenheit dess grossen Christenfeindts Gog vnd Magogs* . . . (Nuremberg, 1613), fol. [Aiiij/v].

41. Johann Faulhaber, *Andeutung, Einer vnerhörten newen Wunderkunst. Welche der Geist Gottes* . . . *biss auff die letzte Zeit hat* . . . *verborgen* (Nuremberg, 1618), fol. B. Faulhaber is here quoting directly from the work of Dobricius (see note 37 above), p. 50.

42. I have not attempted to solve the puzzle. It was based on the same sort of correlation of numbers and letters that Stifel and Poyssel had used; the idea may have come directly from Stifel.

43. Johann Faulhaber, *Fama Syderea Nova. Gemein offentliches Ausschreiben, Dess Ehrnvestern, Weitberühmbten vnd Sinnreichen Herrn Johanni Faulhabers* . . . (Nuremberg, 1618).

44. In 1632 Faulhaber's mathematical mind was still seeking out deep prophetic mysteries. In a work dedicated to Gustavus Adolphus he analyzed several natural wonders by means of the prophetic numbers of Daniel and Revelation: *Vernunfftiger Creaturen Weissagungen, Das ist: Beschreibung eines Wunder Hirschs, auch etlicher Heringen vnd Fisch, vngewohnlicher Signaturen vnd Characteren, so vnderschidlicher Orten gefangen, vnd den hochsten Potentaten zugeschickt worden* . . . (Augsburg, 1632). The work was partly inspired by the minor tradition of fish-prophecies that included writings by Helisaeus Roeslin and Raphael Eglin. The fish was an ancient symbol of Christ. At the end of this tract Faulhaber quoted from Philipp Nicolai's *Historia des Reichs Christi*: "zweiffelt mir nicht, es werden einmahl dise dunckele Weissagungen hell vnd klar werden, sonderlich weil es sich zum Ende nahet, da man alle Geheimnuss je länger je besser wirdt verstehen vnd erraichen können. . . ."

45. There were many other works of this sort besides those we have discussed. A great many prophetic investigations appear to have been inspired by Faulhaber and his work; indeed he seems to have spawned a whole new generation of number-reckoners, judging by the multitude of obscure works that were dedicated to him.

46. Johann Hörner, *Problema Summum, Mathematicum & Cabalisticum. Das ist. Ein hohe, versiglete, Mathematische vnd Cabalistische Auff-*

gab vnd Figur, an alle Gelehrten vnnd Kunstliebende Europae (Nuremberg, 1619).

47. *WA* 23, 134ff. Cited in Montgomery, *Cross and Crucible*, p. 6.

48. Montgomery in *Cross and Crucible* equates this notion of the ubiquity of Christ with a principle of Melanchthonian metaphysics. See above, Chapter 4, note 21.

49. *WA TR* 1, 1160.

50. On the Lutheran openness to natural science in general see Elert, *Morphologie des Luthertums*, vol. 1, pp. 355–406.

51. R. J. W. Evans, *Rudolf II and His World*, p. 248.

52. Here and in the following paragraphs, I have benefited from the insights of Evans, *Rudolf II and His World*, especially pp. 196ff, 274ff.

53. Melanchthon, like the greater number of his philosophically minded contemporaries, was no slavish upholder of the authority of Aristotle. He held, for example, that Plato's views were equally venerable, and necessary as a complement to Aristotelianism. "Let us love both," he concluded. See Neal W. Gilbert, *Renaissance Concepts of Method* (New York, 1960), pp. 36–37.

54. Andreas Musculus, *Vom Mesech vnd Kedar.*

55. I make no effort to deal directly here with the thought of relatively well-known figures like Paracelsus, Weigel, and Boehme. My concern is with the atmosphere that encouraged the kinds of speculation they engaged in.

56. See Paul Althaus, *Die letzten Dinge*, p. 11.

57. See Koepp, *Johann Arndt*. Koepp sees the revival of mystical trends even in Andreas Musculus, and offers a substantial survey of Lutheran mysticism in the late sixteenth century. Koepp sees a deep antagonism between genuine Lutheran mysticism and the "theosophical-gnostic" mysticism of Paracelsus and many strains of Renaissance magic. My suggestion is precisely the opposite: the two were actually closely related. On Lutheran and Renaissance mysticism see also Heinrich Bornkamm, "Renaissancemystik, Luther, und Böhme," *Luther-Jahrbuch* 9 (1927), 156–97. Bornkamm distinguishes the Neoplatonic vision of a harmonious cosmos from the vision, shared by Luther and Boehme, of a nature full of necessary contradictions and pain. But there was an important common ground between these perspectives in the sixteenth century. For the Neoplatonic conception admitted *present* duality and contradiction; the harmony was hidden or somehow to be realized in a coming transformation of nature.

58. Johann Arndt, *Fünff Bücher Vom Waren Christenthum*, book 2, p. 678.

59. Ibid., book 4.

60. Harald Scholtz, *Evangelischer Utopismus bei Johann Valentin Andreae: ein geistiges Vorspiel zum Pietismus*, esp. p. 41. (*Darstellungen aus der württembergischen Geschichte*, vol. 42, Stuttgart, 1957.)

61. Philipp Nicolai, *Theoria Vitae Aeternae*, pp. 710–12. Nicolai died in 1608; the preface is dated 1606.

62. Ibid., pp. 633, 634.

63. Aegidius Gutman, *Offenbarung Göttlicher Mayestat, Darinnen an-*

gezeygt wird, Wie Gott der Herr Anfänglich, sich allen seinen Geschöpffen, mit Worten vnd Wercken geoffenbaret . . . (Hanau, 1619). The work apparently circulated widely in manuscript for several decades. See Peuckert, *Die Rosenkreutzer,* pp. 31–32 (where the work is described as a "theosophical compendium of all things"); also Peuckert's *Pansophie* (Berlin, 1956), pp. 366–67.

    64. Samuel Siderocrates [Eisenmenger], *Cyclopaedia Paracelsica Christiana. Drey Bücher von dem warē vrsprung vnd herkommen der freyen Künsten . . .* (n.p., 1585). A discussion of this work can be found in Peuckert, *Pansophie,* pp. 363–66.

    65. Evans, *Rudolf II and His World,* p. 201.

    66. Montgomery, *Cross and Crucible,* pp. 13–20. Montgomery must be accused of ignoring, or at least playing down, the occultism inherent in alchemy.

    67. Frances Yates, "A Great Magus," review of Peter J. French, *John Dee: The World of an Elizabethan Magus,* in Yates, *Ideas and Ideals in the North European Renaissance* (London and Boston, 1984), p. 58.

    68. Johann von Jessen, *Zoroaster. Nova, brevis, veraque de universo philosophia* (Wittenberg, 1593), "Praefatio," fol. A4/v.

    69. Evans, *Rudolf II and His World,* p. 237.

    70. Numerous works on the Cabala were published in Lutheran Germany, but it is beyond my purpose here to discuss specific writings. Examples from the late sixteenth century include: Elchanan Paul, *Mysterium novum. ein neu herrlich Beweiss aus den prophetischen Schriften nach der Hebräer Cabala, dass der Name Jesus Christus Gottes Sohn . . . in den fürnehmsten Prophezeiungen von Messia verdeckt bedeutet* (Helmstedt, 1580); Johann Pistorius, *Ars cabalistica* (Basel, 1587). In the 1580s Valentin Schindler, professor of Oriental languages at Wittenberg, travelled often to Bohemia for the purpose of learning eastern languages from the Jews; we may suppose that he picked up some other sorts of learning there as well. In the early seventeenth century, Paul Felgenhauer was only one of many seekers who took a great interest in Jewish wisdom in connection with the hope for a new reformation. On Felgenhauer, see below, pp. 214–15. For a general treatment of the Cabala in this period see J. L. Blau, *The Christian Interpretation of the Cabala in the Renaissance* (New York, 1944).

    71. Roeslin, *Historischer, Politischer vnd Astronomischer naturlicher Discvrs . . . ,* fol. bij/v. For Paul's warning see Colossians 2: 8.

    72. This was the anonymous *Historia von D. Johann Fausten, dem weitbeschreyten Zauberer und Schwartzkunstler . . .* (Frankfurt a.M., 1587). The work was published by Johann Spiess, and is therefore commonly referred to as the "Spiess Faustbook." On the Faust legend generally, the best treatment is still E. M. Butler, *The Fortunes of Faust* (Cambridge, 1952).

    73. On this idea of "the mediation of the learned intellect," see Evans, *Rudolf II and His World,* p. 254.

    74. Dobricius, *Zeiterinner,* esp. fols.):(2,):(2/v,):(3.

    75. Paul Nagel, *Cursus Quinquenalis Mundi. Wundergeheime Offenbarung, dess trawriger vnnd betrübten zustands, welcher in Nechstkunff-*

tigen Jahren, vermutlich sich begeben vnd zutragen soll... (Hall in Sachsen, 1620), fol. Eij/v.

76. Paul Nagel, *Raptusastronomicus*, fols. Aij ff.

77. Paul Nagel, *Stellae prodigiosae* (n.p., 1619), fol. Ciij.

78. Paul Nagel, *Prognosticon Astrologo-Cabalisticum*, p. 29.

79. Johann Hörner, *Problema Summum, Mathematicum & Cabalisticum* (see note 46 above). Hörner tried earnestly to head off criticism of his work. He made a solemn protest that "I write in a philosophical manner, and not as a theologian about God and godly things." Thus, he wrote, no theologian should accuse him of writing anything against God or his Word. Hörner did not see himself as opposing established theologians; see fol.)( )( )(.

80. Paul Felgenhauer, *Rechte, Warhafftige vnd gantz Richtige Chronologia, Oder Rechnung der Jare der Welt*... (n.p., 1620), fol. Ciij. I am unable to ascertain just when Felgenhauer thought the end would come, but he did say explicitly that the world would not last another 45 years.

81. Edgar Wind, *Pagan Mysteries in the Renaissance* (New Haven, 1958), p. 23.

82. This is generally the approach taken by Will-Erich Peuckert, *Die Rosenkreutzer*. A student of Peuckert, Roland Haase, also adopted this view in his work *Das Problem des Chiliasmus und der dreissigjährige Krieg*; see pp. 90, 91.

83. On ideas about the downfall of the Antichrist and the collapse of the Turk, see Chapter 3, esp. pp. 115–34. The conversion of the Jews before the end continued to be a Lutheran hope despite Luther's growing pessimism and bitterness in his later years. In the early seventeenth century, the Lutheran Christopher Besold, a friend of Johann Valentin Andreae, wrote a work entitled *De conversione Hebraeorum*, which I have not seen. On seventeenth-century attitudes toward the Jews see especially Hans Joachim Schoeps, *Philosemitismus im Barock* (Tübingen, 1952).

84. This was done, for example, by a writer calling himself Henricus Neotechnus, who edited a work titled *VI. Prognostica Von Verenderung vnd zufälligem Glück vnd Vnglück der höchsten Potentaten im Römischen Reich*.... See esp. "Beschluss," fols. [Siiij/v]–T3.

85. See Marjorie Reeves, *Joachim of Fiore*, esp. chapter 6, "Joachim and Protestantism," pp. 136–65.

86. Peuckert, *Die Rosenkreutzer*, pp. 49–51.

87. Wilhelm Eo Neuheuser, *Tractatvs: De Nova Stella; Oder Von dem newen Abent Stern Scheinende*....

88. *Fama Fraternitatis Oder Bruderschafft des Hochloblichen Ordens des R. C. An die Häupter, Stände und Gelehrten Europae* (Kassel, 1614), in Richard van Dülmen, ed., *Joh. Valentin Andreae: Fama Fraternitatis; Confessio Fraternitatis; Chymische Hochzeit: Christiani Rosencreutz. Anno 1459 (1616)* (Stuttgart, 1973). The attribution of the first Rosicrucian works, namely the *Fama* and the *Confessio*, to the Lutheran theologian and pastor J. V. Andreae is highly questionable and has long been a matter of debate. The most thorough recent treatment of the problem, in Montgomery, *Cross and Crucible*, may well have dealt the final blow to the

theory of Andreae's authorship. The last work in van Dülmen's collection, the *Chymische Hochzeit*, did unquestionably come from Andreae's pen, but lies outside our present interests. W. E. Peuckert has recognized the Lutheran context of the Rosicrucian writings, and I owe much to his insights (see the Bibliography for a listing of his works). But he did not take into account the role of Lutheran apocalypticism.

89. *Fama Fraternitatis*, in van Dülmen, p. 28. It is worth noting that Christian Rosenkreutz's grave was supposed to have been opened 120 years after it was sealed. Rosenkreutz thus died in 1484, the year of the great conjunction and the supposed year of Martin Luther's birth. Surely there was some hint here that one prophet had followed another.

90. *Confessio Fraternitatis Oder Bekanntnuss der löblichen Bruderschafft dess hochgeehrten Rosen Creutzes an die Gelehrten Europae geschrieben* (Kassel, 1615), in van Dülmen, pp. 31–42.

91. Montgomery, *Cross and Crucible*, p. 169.

92. *Confessio Fraternitatis*, p. 37. The language here recalls the imagery of Melanchthon's papal ass.

93. *Confessio Fraternitatis*, p. 38.

94. Ibid., p. 33.

95. Ibid., p. 39.

96. See Chapter 1, p. 46.

97. A. E. Waite, *The Brotherhood of the Rosy Cross* (New Hyde Park, N.Y., 1961), p. 224. Waite discusses much other general evidence linking Rosicrucianism to Lutheranism, including for example the rose and cross in Luther's coat of arms.

98. Johann Faulhaber, *Mysterium arithmeticum, sive, cabalistica et philosophica inventio, nova admiranda et ardua, qua numeri ratione et methodo computentur . . . illuminatissimis laudatissimisque fratribus R. C. fama viris humiliter et sincere dicata* (Ulm, 1615).

99. Johann Hörner, *Problema Summum, Mathematicum & Cabalisticum*, esp. book 2, pp. 1–53.

100. J. C. C. H. (anonymous), *Clangor buccinae propheticae de novissimis temporibus* (n.p., 1620?), fol. [Cij].

101. Paul Felgenhauer, *Rechte, Warhafftige vnd gantz Richtige Chronologia*. See fol. Biij: "es ist gewiss, dass die Juden künfftig sollen vnd werden zu Christo bekehret werden, wie Paulus deutlich [macht] Rom. 11, v. 25." In general on Felgenhauer and the Jews see Schoeps, *Philosemitismus im Barock*, pp. 18–45. In many of his works Felgenhauer appears to approach chiliasm, but equally often he writes simply of the Last Day and its nearness. Dietrich Korn has called this an "attempt at obfuscation," maintaining that the distinction between chiliastic and more orthodox expectations was clearly recognized by all in this period, in his *Das Thema des jüngsten Tages in der deutschen Literatur des 17. Jahrhunderts* (Tübingen, 1957), p. 5. But the idea that Felgenhauer was trying to keep his real expectations under cover seems questionable. He was preaching repentance, and in his early writings in particular he had probably not developed a very clear prophetic scheme. He could therefore emphasize either the approaching Judgment, or the wonderful transformation to come.

102. Frances Yates, *The Rosicrucian Enlightenment* (London, 1972).
103. Eustachius Poyssel, *Die Schlüssel David* (see above, note 32). More explicit than Poyssel in expounding the prophetic role of Saxony was Georg Molysdorf, *Der Edle Rautenkrantz, Mit seinem schönen Geheimnis, welchs bedeut, Den herrlichen Einzug des Ehrenkönigs Jhesu Christi, ins hochlöbliche Chur vnd Fürstliche Haus zu Sachsen . . .* (Erfurt, 1585). Another significant expression of such hope was Laurentius Faustus, *Anatomia Statvae Danielis.* In the 1570s Paul Gräbner of Magdeburg also lionized the Saxon elector and prophesied that he would become emperor (see Haase, *Das Problem des Chiliasmus*, p. 79n).
104. Eustachius Poyssel (probable author), *Magischer Beweiss Alles dess jenigen, was der Autor dieses Tractats, seydhero des verschinen 1583. Jahrs vnnd dess Newen Calenders anfang, in dem offen druck hat aussgehen lassen* (n.p., 1609). In his *Zeiterinner* of 1612 Johann Dobricius wrote that Poyssel was the author of this tract, and internal evidence supports the same conclusion. Poyssel began to issue his writings anonymously after about 1600 or slightly later; he may have sensed that the tide was starting to turn against prophetic quest and preaching. Another anonymous tract probably from Poyssel's pen was *Der von Gott bestimpten Zahlen dess Antichrists, 1260. endlicher Aussgang vnd Ende, Apocal. 11. 12. 13.* (n.p., 1608).
105. For example "Henricus Neotechnus" in his *VI. Prognostica,* "Beschluss," fol. Tij/v.
106. On these political differences among German Lutherans see Schönstadt, *Antichrist, Weltheilsgeschehen und Gottes Werkzeug*, pp. 4, 5; also Klein, *Der Kampf um die zweite Reformation*, p. 189.
107. See above, note 33. Studion offered an immense variety of highly complex reckonings, and it is difficult to sort them out, not to mention to read them. In some places it appeared that Christ would return in 1620, not 1623. Marjorie Reeves has discussed the "Naometria" in her *Joachim of Fiore*, p. 150.
108. See for example Peuckert, *Die Rosenkreutzer*, pp. 38–40; Frances Yates, *The Rosicrucian Enlightenment*, p. 33; Karl R. H. Frick, *Licht und Finsternis* (Graz, 1975), vol. 1, pp. 287–88.
109. Cyprian Leowitz, *Grundliche, Klärliche beschreibung*, fol. Siiij/v.
110. Wilhelm Eo Neuheuser, *Victoria Christianorum verissimorum universalis: Das ist: Ein Gründliche Beschreibung, welcher gestallt alle waare Evangelische Christen von heutiger zeit an . . . zu reinem Christlichen Glauben/Sieg vnd Vberwindung erhalten werden* (Friedwegen, 1618).
111. Jano Henuriades du Verduns (?), *Apocalyptische Satzstück vnd Vrsachen von jetzo instehender grossen Veränderung vieler mächtigster Regimentern . . . vnd . . . bald am hernach inbrechenden Jüngsten Gericht . . .* (n.p., 1623).
112. Johann Wagner (Plaustrarius), *Wunder- vnd Figürlich Offenbahrung: Das ist: I. Vergleichung der Welt Anfang vnd Ende, darinnen der jetzigen Zeit trübsäliger Zustandt begriffen . . .* (n.p., 1620).
113. The treatment of this work in Roland Haase, *Das Problem des Chiliasmus*, pp. 54–59, is marred by errors of both fact and interpretation.

Haase suggests that "Plaustrarius" was probably a Calvinist; how he concludes this I do not know. It is true that the writer expresses disillusionment
with Saxony and with "those who first helped plant the Gospel, and now
help out of blind zeal to drive it into the ground again" (p. 59). But the
overall tone of the work suggests that its author was a disappointed Lutheran who maintained a strongly apocalyptic outlook. Among the more
interesting hints is his reference to "die drey Haupt Religion (P.V.C.). . . ."
I make of this "Papistische, Vnsere, Calvinistische." "Our" religion,
namely Lutheranism undefiled by the "blind zeal" of its new orthodox proponents, would triumph, as the three "Hauptreligion" would "einander
nicht aussrotten, aber doch wird eine vber die ander zu herrschen haben,
vnd wirt nach solcher Trangsal ein jedweder seine Fehle selbst erkenen, vnd
sich zu Gott bekehren . . ." (pp. 48–49).

114. Johann Wagner (Plaustrarius), *Prognosticon, Oder Weissagung
auff diese jetzige Zeit, darinn vermeldet, wie Gott der Allmächtige die
gantze Welt, ihrer Sünde wegen daheim suchen wolle mit allerley Plagen
vnnd Straffen* (n.p., 1621). Another work from Wagner's hand was a
*Schrifftmesige Offenbahrung vnd erklärung etlicher geheimer Figuren, so
in dem 1621. jahr zu Prag . . . gefunden worden* (n.p., 1621). This writing
predicted a great punishment to come in 1624 on account of what had
happened in Bohemia, with the destruction of the earthly enemies of the
Gospel following before the universal reformation of the world.

115. The suggestion that many Lutherans took refuge in "the arcane
revelations of the Rosicrucian movement" is made by R. J. W. Evans, *The
Making of the Habsburg Monarchy*, p. 110. The connections between Rosicrucianism and the "ancient tradition of gnosis" are mentioned in Keith
Thomas, *Religion and the Decline of Magic*, p. 269.

116. Revelation 2: 7, 3: 6, etc.

Chapter 6

1. Johann Gerhard, *Postilla* (Jena, 1613), vol. 1, p. 27, cited in Korn,
Das Thema des jüngsten Tages, p. 10.

2. See above, Chapter 3, notes 65 and 66.

3. [Paul Lautensack], *Offenbahrung Jesu Christi, das ist: Ein Beweisz . . . welcher Gestalt der einige Gott . . . in der person Jesu Christi sich
geoffenbahret habe . . .* (Frankfurt a.M., 1619), cited in Hofmann, *Luther
und die Johannes-Apokalypse*, p. 687.

4. Lichtenberger's prophecies appeared in several collections in the early
1620s, including one titled *Propheceyen Vnd Weissagungen jetzt gegenwertig vnd künfftige sachen, Geschicht vnd Zufall, biss zum Ende der Welt
ankündend. Als nemblich: M. Johann Lichtenbergers, Johann Carionis,
M. Josephi Grunpeck, Der Sibyllen, vnd vil anderer* (n.p., 1620). Capistrano's prophecies were published again as *Woldenckwürdige Weissagung
oder Propheceyung*. The 1588 rhyme was updated in a *Prognostica Von
gefährlichen verenderungen in dieser Welt, welche in diesem 1628. Jar angehen . . .* (n.p., 1628).

5. Johann Valentin Andreae, *Menippus, s[ive] dialogorum satyricorum centuria, inanitatem nostratium speculum, cum quibusdam aliis liberioribus* (1617), 28th dialogue, quoted in Wilhelm Hossbach, *Johann Valentin Andreae und sein Zeitalter* (Berlin, 1819), p. 26.

6. Andreae on the seekers who despite good intentions were now working against the revived Gospel: *De curiositatis pernicie syntagma* (1621), quoted in Hossbach, *Johann Valentin Andreae*, pp. 60–62; *Turris Babel, sive judiciorum de fraternitate rosaceae crucis chaos* (n.p., 1619).

7. See "Faulhaber, Johann," *ADB*, vol. 6, p. 582; also J. Jansen, *Geschichte des deutschen Volkes*, vol. 6, p. 449.

8. Roland Haase, *Das Problem des Chiliasmus*, pp. 102–3. Ziegler styled himself "Origines Philippus von Gottes Gnaden, erwählter und gekrönter König zu Jerusalem, Siloh, Joseph und David, der Brüder des Rosenkreutzes Oberster und unüberwindlichster Zepter des Königs in Sion."

9. On Stiefel and Meth, see "Stiefel, Esaias," *ADB*, vol. 36, pp. 173–74. See also *Herzog's Realencyclopädie fur Theologie und Kirche*, vol. 9, pp. 679ff.

10. Although it should be used with caution, the eighteenth-century work of J. G. Walch still offers useful and interesting reading on these controversies of the early seventeenth century: *Historische und theologische Einleitung in die Religions-Streitigkeiten, Welche sonderlich ausser der Evangelisch-Lutherischen Kirche entstanden*, parts 4 and 5 (Jena, 1736). In the same category stands Gottfried Arnold's famous *Unpartheyische Kirchen und Ketzerhistorie* (Frankfurt a.M., 1699).

11. This biblical image was not infrequently used by Luther himself, but it seems to have been invoked more often in this later period—partly, perhaps, in reaction to the proliferating efforts to reckon the time of the end. Gregor Strigenitz, for example, preached a whole series of sermons on this theme around 1600: *Laqveus Aucupis, Das ist, Sechs Adventspredigten Vom Fallstricke, Aus den worten des Herrn Christi, Lucae am 21. Capit.* (Leipzig, 1614).

12. Alexandrus Utzinger, *Process Des Jüngsten Gerichts*, fol. Cij/v.

13. Andreas Schoppe, *Christliche vnnd Nötige Warnung für dem erdichten Lügen Geist der falschen Propheten vnd fürwitzigen Leute, so die gewisse zeit des jüngsten Tages auszurechnen . . . sich bemühen . . .* (Wittenberg, 1596). The tract appeared a year later under a different title: *Weissagung Etlicher falscher Calender schreiber, welche sich unterstehen vnd propheceyen dürffen die geheimnuss Gottes auszugründen vnnd ausrechnen, auff welche zeit der Jüngste tag gewis kommen sol . . .* (n.p., 1597). According to Schoppe's preface, he had published a similar work 24 years earlier (c. 1572) in response to numerous speculations of that time.

14. Ibid., fols. G2–J3/v (chronicle of errors on reckoning the time of the end); fols. L3–L4 (attack on astrological prophecy).

15. Ibid., fols. M, M/v.

16. Caspar Finck, *Kurtzer, Notiger, vnd in Gottes Wort wolbegründter Bericht, Von dem Jüngsten Gericht, Ewigen Leben, Vnd Hellen . . .* (Giessen, 1612).

17. Kleopas Herennius [Johann Kepler], *Kanones Pveriles: Id est, Chro-*

nologia Von Adam biss auff diss jetz lauffende Jahr Christi 1620., in Kepler's *Gesammelte Werke*, vol. 5, *Chronologische Schriften* (Munich, 1953). This work includes attacks on the chronological writings of Felgenhauer, Tilner, and others.

18. Renaissance Photinianism took its name from Photinus, a fourth-century bishop of Sirmium in Pannonia, who denied the separate personality of the Logos and held that Christ was the adopted Son of God. It was thus a form of unitarianism.

19. For example: Georg Rost, *Gründtlicher Bericht von den Newen Photinianern . . .* (Magdeburg, 1613). The Wittenberg faculty responded to the Photinians in an *Auszführliche vnnd Gründliche Wiederlegung Des Deutzschen Arianischen Catechismi Welcher zu Rackaw in Polen anno 1608 gedruckt . . .* (Wittenberg, 1620).

20. Daniel Cramer, *Apocalypsis, Oder Offenbarung S. Johannis, Sampt einer richtigen Erklerung, so wol wegen Historischer erfüllung aller vnd jeden hierin erhaltenen Geheimnussen, wie auch Lehrn, Besserungen, Trost vnd Warnungen . . .* (Alten Stettin, 1619).

21. Johannes Wallmann, "Zwischen Reformation und Pietismus: Reich Gottes und Chiliasmus in der lutherischen Orthodoxie" in Eberhard Jüngel et al., *Verifikationen: Festschrift für Gerhard Ebeling zum 70. Geburtstag* (Tübingen, 1982), pp. 187–205; here p. 193.

22. Johann Wolther, *Aureum Johannis Woltheri Peinensis Saxonis: Das ist: Gulden Arch, Darinn der wahre Verstand vnd Einhalt der wichtigen Geheimnussen, Wörter vnd Zahlen, in der Offenbahrung Johannis, vnd im Propheten Daniel . . . gefunden wird . . .* (Rostock, 1623), p. 101.

23. Ibid., fol. B. Much of Wolther's book was devoted to harsh denunciations of Calvinism and of the reckonings of the Calvinist chiliast John Napier. The Calvinist churches, wrote Wolther, were empty not only of crucifixes, but of Christ himself.

24. [Eustachius Poyssel], *Magischer Beweis* (see Chapter 5, note 104), p. 39.

25. Felgenhauer's works against Rost include his *Apologeticus contra invectivas aeruginosas Rostij. Kurtze Verantwortung, Auff das Heldenbuch vom Rosengarten . . .* (n.p., 1622) and his *Disexamen vel Examen Examinis . . . Gegen Examen Oder Bescheidene antwort, auff das Rostische Examen-vexamen . . .* (Wahrenburg[?], 1623). Felgenhauer attacked Lutherans, Calvinists, Catholics, and other "sects" in his tract *Der Vorhof am Tempel des Herrn* (n.p., 1630); similar views were expressed in many other of his writings, including for example a *Sendtbrief an die Hirten vnd an die Schafe, vnter allerley Secten* (n.p., 1632).

26. Arndt tried, for instance, to show where he clearly disagreed with Weigel in a *Kurtzes Bedencken Uber Valentin Weigels Dialogum, de Christianismo, zu Halle gedrucket Anno 1615* (n.p., n.d.)

27. Koepp, *Johann Arndt*, p. 116. I have not seen Osiander's work against Arndt.

28. On the development of Andreae's attitudes and mystical piety see Scholtz, *Evangelischer Utopismus*, esp. pp. 17–18, 46–47.

29. This key point has been missed in the learned and otherwise accurate

work of Johannes Wallmann (see note 21 above). Wallmann views the main issue between orthodoxy and its prophetic opponents as that of chiliasm, but these debates went deeper than disagreement over particular expectations.

30. Georg Rost, *Prognosticon Theologicon Oder Theologische Weissagung, Vom Jüngsten Tage, Darinnen mancherley schöne, liebliche vnd anmütige fragen, von den letzten handeln dieser Welt werden erörtert . . .* (Rostock, 1620).

31. Ibid., fols. K, K/v.

32. Rost's title is worth quoting at length: *Heldenbuch vom Rosengarten. Oder Gründlicher vnd Apologetischer Bericht von den Newen Himlischen Propheten, Rosenkreutzern, Chiliasten vnd Enthusiasten, Welche ein new Irrdisch Paradiss vnd Rosengarten auff dieser Welt ertrewmen, vnd allerley Schrifftlose vnd Vntheologische paradoxa vnd Irrthumb in der werthen Christenheit, öffentlich ausssprengen, Benamentlich M. Valentinus Weigelius . . . M. Paulus Nagelius . . . Paulus Felgenhawer . . . Wie alle dinge in vns verborgen sind, vnd das man geschwinde vnd behende ohne mühe vnd arbeit allerley gute Künste vnd Sprachen, auch ohne Bücher allein durch die Salbung kan studieren, allerley geheimnissen verstehen, auch die zeit vom Jüngsten Tage aussforschen, wie Christus Anno 1623. widerkommen, vnd ein Irrdisch Paradiss auff Erden anrichten, vnd 1000. Jahr mit seinen Reichsgenossen in allerley wollust herrschen soll, wie alle Jüden bekehret, dass Evangelium aussgebreitet, vnd der Turcke, Bapst vnd die 4. Monarchy sollen vntergehen, etc.* (Rostock, 1622).

33. Ibid., fols. Aiiij, Aiiij/v.

34. Wallmann, "Zwischen Reformation und Pietismus," p. 191. Daniel Cramer apparently introduced the term "chiliasmus subtilis."

35. Other works in which Rost sought to discredit the new prophets included *Reformation. Das ist: Bericht, auff eine dieser zeit schwebende hochwichtige Frage: was von der allgemeinen Reformation der Kirchen . . . zu halten seye?* (Rostock, 1624), and *Theologische Weissagung von der Zweifachen Kirchen Reformation* (Rostock, 1625).

36. Justus Groscurdt, *Bacchationum Nagelianarum Prima: Das ist, Ein sonderlicher vnd zwar Erster FastnachtsAuffzug des newen Schwermers, der sich nennet Paulum Nagelium . . .* (n.p., 1620). The title page bears the name "Anania Solingio in Valle Gratiarum"; a note in the copy at the Herzog August Bibliothek in Wolfenbüttel identifies this author as Justus Groscurdt, about whom I have been unable to find any reliable biographical information.

37. Philipp Arnoldi, *Antinagelius. Das ist: Gründlicher Beweisz, Dass nach dieser Welt Zustande nicht ein tertium Seculum oder dritte irrdische Zeit . . . zu hoffen sey . . .* (Königsberg, 1622).

38. I have read the 1708 edition of Hunnius by the severely orthodox J. H. Feustking, who added a long preface of his own: *Mataeologia Fanatica, Oder Ausführlicher Bericht Von der Neuen Propheten, Die sich Erleuchtete und Gottsgelehrte nennen, Religion, Lehr und Glauben* (Leipzig, 1708). Hunnius had reacted earlier to what he saw as a powerful and dangerous movement in his *Christliche Betrachtung der Newen Paracelsisten*

vnd Weigelianischen Theology (Leipzig, 1622). Here he attacked both the gnostic mysticism and the chiliasm of the new prophets.

39. List, *Chiliastische Utopie und radikale Reformation*, p. 75.

40. Daniel Colberg, *Das Platonisch-Hermetisches Christenthum, Begreiffend Die Historische Erzehlung vom Ursprung und vielerley Secten der heutigen Fanatischen Theologie* . . . (Frankfurt and Leipzig, 1690).

41. Friedrich Grick, *Cometenbutzer, Das ist: Eine glaubwürdige Copey Articulierter vnd rechtmassiger Klag, dess guten, vnschuldigen Cometen* . . . (n.p., 1619). On Grick see Zinner, *Geschichte und Bibliographie der astronomischen Literatur in Deutschland*, p. 24.

42. Friedrich Grick, *Cometenbutzers Schutzer, Das ist, Eine glaubwürdige Copey articulierter, rechtmessiger Exceptionum* . . . *dess guten, Vnschuldigen Cometen* . . . (n.p., 1619), fol. Diij.

43. Johann Stilsov, OYPANOΠΙΠΙTIA. *Das ist: Kurtze Erörterung dess Zweiffels, ob der Himmel von Ptolomaei Zeit an biss hieher sich* . . . *gesencket haben könne* . . . (Erfurt, 1631).

44. See John Dillenberger, *Protestant Thought and Natural Science* (New York, 1960), p. 78.

45. Typical of such visions was a *Göttliches Wunder-Buch, Darinnen auffgezeichnet vnd geschrieben stehen, I. Himlische Offenbahrungen vnd Gesichte, einer gottfürchtigen Jungfrawen auss Böhmen* . . . *II. Propheceyungen* . . . *eines frommen Christlichen Mägdleins zu Cottbus in Nieder-Lausitz. III. Christliche Sprüche* . . . *einer gottsehligen Jungfrewen* . . . *zu Stettin in Pommern* . . . (n.p., 1630).

46. Haase, *Das Problem des Chiliasmus*, pp. 65–66.

47. *Propheceyen Vnd Weissagungen jetzt gegenwertig vnd künfftige sachen* (see note 4 above), p. 2. Another similar collection of popular astrological prophecies was a *Vaticinium Trin-Uni-Sonum. Das ist Dreyerley Propheceyung oder Weissagung gleiches Lauts vnnd Inhaldts, beschrieben Von Sebald Brand* . . . *D. Johann Carion* . . . *Jacob Hartmann* (Mittelburg?, 1620).

48. Paul Graebner, *Conjecturen oder Muhtmassungen, Welche Herr Paulus Gräbner publicirt, vnd an Tag gegeben* . . . (Warmünster?, 1619).

49. Paul Graebner, *Prognosticon oder Erklärung: Vber den Anno 1618. erschienen Comet Stern, vnd dessen Operation. Von Veränderung der höchsten Potentaten dieser Welt, vnd von dem Vntergang dess Türckischen Kaysers, u. Beschrieben: Durch Paulum Gräbnern, Weyland Pfarrherrn im Stifft Magdeburg* (n.p., 1631).

50. Ibid., p. 23.

51. Ibid. Haase (*Das Problem des Chiliasmus*) completely ignores this part of the work.

52. This prophecy of Paracelsus became very widely known only at this time. It was publicized in a host of popular writings, such as a *Propheceyung, Doct. Philippi Theophrasti Paracelsi, Anno 1546. Vom Löwen ausz Mitternacht* (n.p., 1631), and a *Postilion: Oder Englische Posaun der Heimsuchung, Welche mit grosser Stim* . . . *die Drey schröckliche Wehe* . . . *verkündiget: Vom Löwen von Mitternacht* . . . (n.p., 1630). On the "Lion of the North" prophecy in general, see Haase, *Das Problem des Chilias-*

mus, p. 69, and Felix Berner, *Gustav Adolph: Der Löwe aus Mitternacht* (Stuttgart, 1982).

53. Irenaeus Heilandt, *Apocalyptisches, Doch Politisches Bedencken, Was die Evangelischen vnd Protestirenden Churfürsten vnd Stände . . . zu gewarten . . .* (n.p., 1631). Similar political warnings appeared in an anonymous *Prognosticon, Wegen Des künfftigen Auszgang vnd Effect. Dess Leipzigischen Schluss. Sampt angehaffter Vermahnung an die Evangelischer Stände* (n.p., 1631).

54. *Wohlgegründeter Politischer Discurs, Vom jetzigen Zustande vnd Kriegeswesen im gantzen Römischen Reich . . . Verfertiget Von einem alten redlichen Deutschen, deme die vhralte Freyheit dess Deutschen Vaterlandes nichts weniger als die Religion selbsten hoch angelegen ist* (n.p., 1631).

55. Typical of the newssheets that began appearing frequently in the 1630s was a *Teutscher Nation Newer Post-Reuter, Welcher Berichtet Von dem Zustand . . . des Menschlichen Leibes vnd Lebens Zufallen . . .* (n.p., 1639).

56. On the rise of popular political consciousness, see Peter Burke, *Popular Culture in Early Modern Europe* (New York, 1978), pp. 262–63. For the point about a common Protestant awareness I am indebted to Prof. Thomas Brady.

57. Quoted in Haase, *Das Problem des Chiliasmus*, p. 72n.

58. Georg Rost, *Ninivitisch Deutschland, Welchem der Prophet Jonas Schwerdt, Hunger, Pestilentz, vnd den endlichen Vntergang ankündiget . . .* (Lübeck, 1625).

59. Jaroslav Pelikan, *From Luther to Kierkegaard*, p. 79.

60. Paul Jenisch, *Christlicher vnd Nothwendiger Bericht auss Gottes Wort vnd der fürnemsten Kirchen Lehrer reinen heilsamen Schrifften, Von den letzten Händeln der Welt, vom Jüngsten Tage vnd Ewigen Leben . . .* (Ulm, 1645).

61. Johann Matthaeus Meyfart, *Tuba Novissima, Das ist, Von den vier letzten dingen des Menschen . . .* (Coburg, 1626; reprinted Tübingen, 1980).

62. Erich Trunz, "Meyfarts Leben und Werke," in Johann Matthaeus Meyfart, *Tuba Novissima* (reprinted Tübingen, 1980), p. 74. The eschatological trilogy consisted of *Das Himlische Jerusalem* (1627), *Das höllische Sodoma* (1630), and *Das Jüngste Gericht* (1632).

63. Johann Matthaeus Meyfart, *Das Jüngste Gericht in zweyen Buchern . . .* (Nuremberg, 1652), book 1, pp. 206–7.

64. Schoeps, *Philosemitismus im Barock*, pp. 38ff.

65. See above, Chapter 4, note 69.

66. For comments on the larger trend of a seventeenth-century retreat into biblical prophecy, see Burke, *Popular Culture in Early Modern Europe*, p. 274.

67. Elert, *Morphologie des Luthertums*, vol. 1, pp. 430f.

68. James Perry Martin, *The Last Judgment in Protestant Theology from Orthodoxy to Ritschl* (Grand Rapids, 1963), p. 12 et passim.

69. See Keith Thomas, *Religion and the Decline of Magic*, p. 643.

70. Evans, *Rudolf II and His World*, p. 289.

71. David Warren Sabean, *Power in the Blood: Popular Culture and Village Discourse in Early Modern Germany* (Cambridge, 1984), p. 207. Sabean is here citing J. V. Andreae's *Theophilis*, ed. Richard van Dülmen (Stuttgart, 1973).

72. On these programs of church discipline see Sabean, *Power in the Blood*, pp. 73, 79, 207, 209, et passim.

73. On all these see Walch, *Historische und theologische Einleitung.*

74. W. E. Peuckert has pointed to the victory of "pure mysticism" over pansophy in the early seventeenth century: see *Pansophie*, pp. 382–84.

75. Schoeps, *Philosemitismus im Barock*, p. 42.

76. Typical of the sort of tract that saw a warning from God in the comet of 1664–65 was one by Christopher Neubarth, *Astrologische Gedancken Uber die Zween neulich enstandene erschreckliche Comet-Sterne . . . 1664 . . . 1665* (Breslau, 1665); also Tobias Beuteln, *Dreyfache Zugabe Der Admirabilium in Aere et Aethere Oder Wunderbaren Wercke Gottes In der Lufft und am Gestirnten Himmel, So auff vorher erschienenen grossen Cometen . . .* (Leipzig, 1665). On expectations for 1666 in England see Thomas, *Religion and the Decline of Magic*, p. 141.

77. Schenda, "Die deutschen Prodigiensammlungen," pp. 667–68.

78. Johann Michael Moscherosch, *Visiones De Don Quevedo*, "Letztes Gericht," 1642.

79. The gradual disappearance of the theme of the Last Day in German literature of the seventeenth century is described in Korn, *Das Thema des Jüngsten Tages.*

Conclusion

1. Oberman, *Luther*, p. 21.

2. Yates, *Giordano Bruno and the Hermetic Tradition*, p. 355n.

3. My views on this point about the lingering of the Middle Ages in Germany have been strengthened by W. E. Peuckert, who writes of the world of German magic as a "Mittelalter in der Neuzeit." See, for example, the preface to his *Pansophie*. I will also admit to the lingering impression of Ernst Troeltsch upon my thought.

৺ Bibliography

Primary Sources

Agricola, Philipp. *Ein gar Schöne Christliche vnd liebliche Comedia von dem letzten tage des Jüngsten Gerichts.* Frankfurt a.O., 1573.
——. *Klaren Ausszug der Propheten vnd Weissagung, auch der Erklerenden Zeichen dess Sons Gottes selber, vnd der gantzen heiligen Schrifft Offenbarung, vff den baldt herantrettenden Jüngsten Tag seines Gerichts.* Berlin, 1577.
Alberus, Erasmus. *Vom jüngsten Tag vnd Auferstehung.* N.p., 1566.
Albrecht, Georgius. *Tuba novissima, oder vom Jüngsten Gericht.* Nordlingen, 1645.
Albrecht, Lorenz. *Evangelisch Prognostic. Ein bewärte augenscheinerfahrliche weissag, aus allen alten vnd newen sectereygeschichten abgenuṁen.* . . . Munich, [1589?].
——. *Predicanten Practic. Prognostic oder Iudicium von der Predigkunden stand, glück, vnd früchten.* . . . Munich, 1589.
Alsted, Johann Heinrich. *Diatribe de mille annis apocalypticis.* Frankfurt, 1627.
Althamer, Andreas. *Anzeugung warumb Gott die welt so lange zeyt.* . . . Nuremberg, 1527.
Althaus, K. *Predig von kommenden Gerichten.* N.p., 1563.
Ambach, Melchior. *Vom Ende der Welt, Vnd zukunfft des Endtchrists. Wie es vorm Jüngsten tag in der Welt, ergehn werde.* . . . Frankfurt a.M., [c. 1550].
Ammersbach, Henr. *Geheimniss der letzten Zeit.* N.p., [c. 1666].
Amsdorf, Nikolaus von. *Fünff fürnemliche vnd gewisse Zeichen aus heiliger göttlicher Schrifft, so kurtz vor dem Jüngsten tag geschehen sollen.* Jena, 1554.
——. *Das Melchior Hoffman ein falscher Prophet vnd sein leer vom Jüngsten tag vnrecht, falsch vnnd widder Gott ist.* N.p., 1528.
——. *Eine Predigt aus Luthers Schrifften vher die Propheten gezogen, dass Deutschland wie Israel, Judae vnd Jerusalem wird zerstöret vnd verwüstet werden.* Jena, 1562.

Anderman, Oswaldt. *Sehr gewisse Prognostica... von diesem 1582. jar an, biss zum ende der Welt....* Magdeburg, 1582.

Andreae, Jacob. *Christliche, notwendige vnd ernstliche Erinnerung, Nach dem Lauff der irdischen Planeten gestelt, Darauss ein jeder einfeltiger Christ zusehen, was für glück oder vnglück, Teutschland zugewarten... Auss... Luc. 21.* Tübingen, 1567.

———. *Ein Christliche Predigt Vber das Euangelium auff den XXV. Sontag nach Trinitatis, Matthei am 24. Vom vielen vnd mancherley verfürungen in der Kirchen Gottes, vor dem Jüngsten tage....* Leipzig, 1578.

———. *Dreizehen Predigten vom Türcken.* Tübingen, 1568.

Andreae, Johann Valentin. *Turris Babel, sive judiciorum de fraternitate Rosaceae Crucis chaos.* N.p., 1619.

Angli, Andreae. *Bericht von Johan Hilten, vnd seinen Weissagungen.* Frankfurt a.O., 1597.

[Anleitung]. *Gründliche vnd kurtze Anleitung zum Verstande der Offenbahrung Johannis vnd Propheceyung Danielis.* Oppenheim, 1611; Breslau, 1612.

[Antichrist]. *De Anti-Christo & fine mundi s. scripturae prognostica.* Basel, 1567.

[Antichristus]. *Antichristus Demonstratus, Oder: Wohlgegründter Bericht von dem grossen Antichrist....* N.p., 1624.

Arndt, Johann. *Fünff Bücher Vom Wahren Christenthum....* Lüneburg, 1684.

———. *Johann Arndts sel. Postilla, oder Ausslegung der Sontags vnd aller Festen Evangelien, durchs gantze Jahr....* Lüneburg, 1680.

———. *Kurtzes Bedencken Uber Valentin Weigels Dialogum, de Christianismo, zu Halle gedrucket Anno 1615.* N.p., n.d.

———. *Paradieszgärtlein, voller Christlichen Tugenden....* Amsterdam, 1682.

Arnoldi, Philipp. *Antinagelius. Das ist: Gründlicher Beweisz, Dass nach dieser Welt Zustande nicht ein tertium Seculum... zu hoffen sey.* Königsberg, 1622.

Artopoeus, Petrus [Peter Becker]. *Pro consolatione afflictae nostrae ecclesiae Apocalypseos isagoge et propheticae imaginia nostri temporis explicatio.* Frankfurt a.O., 1549.

[Astrologische]. *Astrologische Bedencken, Von der Erschröcklichen, gantz Europa gefährlichen, Land vnd Leut betrohlichen, ins gemein hochschädlichen Würkung, der Sonnen Finsternuss... 1630.* N.p., 1630.

Augustine. *On Christian Doctrine,* Trans. D. W. Robertson. Indianapolis, 1958.

[Ausszug]. *Ein ausszug etlicher Practica vnd Propheceyen auff vergangne vñ zükünfftige jar, Sibille, Brigitte, Cirilli, Joachim... Methodii, vnd brüder Reinharts....* N.p., [c. 1518].

———. *Ein kurtzer Auszug der Cronica, gedechtnuss wirdiger geschicht, von dem 1175 Jar an biss auff diss vnser 1564. Jar....* Nuremberg, 1564.

Babst, Michael. *Ein kurtzer Tractat, Darinnen neben der Erklerung dess alten Kirchengesangs: Da Pacem Domine, auch angezeigt wird, was von dem jetzigen angehenden Seculo Propheceyet worden.* . . . Freiburg in Sachsen, 1600.

———. *Der Sieben Planeten lauff vnnd Wirckung, auff das Menschliche Leben, in diesem letzten Zeiten gerichtet.* . . . Leipzig, 1594.

———. *Wunderbarliches Leib vnd Wund Artzneybuch.* . . . Eisleben, 1596–97.

Balduinus, Fridericus. *Diatribe theologica de Anti-Christo.* . . . Wittenberg, 1607.

Baur in Normberg, Conrad. *Compendiolvm Chronologicvm: Das ist: Kurtze Chronica oder Zeitregister . . . von anfang der Welt.* . . . N.p., 1607.

[Bawren klag]. *Die New vermehrte, vnd gebesserte Bawren klag, vber den Newen . . . Bäpstische Kalender.* N.p., 1584.

[Bawren Rathschlag]. *Bawren Rathschlag, Vber den Neuwen Kalender, auch ihnen zugemessene vnd aussgegangene Bauwrenklag.* . . . N.p., 1585 (earlier ed. c. 1583?).

[Becker, Hans Christoph?] *Aller Practicken vnnd Prognosticken Grossvater.* N.p., [c. 1570].

Beham, Hans Sebald. *Typi in Apocalypsi Ioannis depicti ut clarius vaticinia Ioannis intelligi possint.* Frankfurt, 1539.

Beineken, David. *Astrologische Wunder-Schrifft . . . In den jetzigen 1632. 33. vnnd 34. Jahren.* N.p., 1633.

[Bericht]. *Kurtzer Bericht, von gemeinen Kalender, Woher er kommen, wie er mit der zeit verrücket, ob vnd wie er widerumb zuersetzen sey.* Neustadt an der Hart, 1583.

Beuteln, Tobias. *Dreyfache Zugabe Der Admirabilium in Aere et Aethere Oder Wunderbaren Wercke Gottes in der Lufft und am Gestirnten Himmel.* . . . Leipzig, 1665.

Bibliander, Theodor. *Ad omnium ordinum republicae Christianae principes, viros populumque Christianum relatio fidelis.* Basel, 1545. The work was reprinted under the title *Diligens et erudita libri Apocalypseos enarratio* in Petrus Artopoeus [Peter Becker], *Pro consolatione afflictae nostrae ecclesiae. . .* , Frankfurt a.O., 1549.

Birgitte, St. *Das buch der himelischen offenbarung sant Birgitten wie es yetz in der welt ergen sol.* Augsburg, 1504; another ed. Dillingen, 1569.

Böhme, Jacob. *Sämtliche Schriften,* ed. W. E. Peuckert. Stuttgart, 1955.

Brand, Sebald. *Prognosticon Sebaldi Brandini. Das ist: Prognosticirung Von Zustandt der Welt von . . . 1614 biss auff . . . 1623.* N.p., 1615.

———. *Propheceyung vnd wunderbahre Weissagungen von allerley, niemaln erhörten Veränderungen . . . 1605. biss auff . . . 1623.* Bern, 1607.

———, et al. *Vaticinium Trin-Uni-Sonum. Das ist Dreyerley Propheceyung oder Weissagung gleiches Lauts vnnd Inhaldts, beschrieben Von Sebald Brand . . . D. Johann Carion . . . Jacob Hartmann.* Mittelburg(?), 1620.

Brenz, Johannes. *Homiliae vel sermones nonulli in prophetam Danielem,* in *Werke,* ed. Martin Brecht and Gerhard Schäfer, *Schriftauslegungen,* Teil I. Tübingen, 1972.

Bruno, Giordano. "Die Abschiedsrede, welche Giordano Bruno vor den Professoren und Hörern auf der Akademie zu Wittenberg im Jahre 1588 am 8. März gehalten hat," in Giordano Bruno, *Gesammelte Werke*, ed. Ludwig Kuhlenbeck, vol. 6, pp. 72–93. Leipzig, 1909.

Bucer, Martin. *De regno Christi*, ed. Wilhelm Pauck, Philadelphia, 1969. Library of Christian Classics, vol. 19.

Buchas, Caspar. *Prognosticon astrologicon . . . 1594*. Magdeburg, 1594.

Bucholzer, Abraham. *Index chronologicus*. Görlitz, 1580.

———. *Isagoge chronologia . . . ad annorum seriem in sacris bibliis. . . .* Görlitz, 1580.

———. *Isagoge chronologica ab initio mundi ad exsilium Jsraelitarum in Babylone*. Görlitz, 1584.

Bullinger, Heinrich. *Daniel sapientissimus Dei propheta. . . .* Zurich, 1565.

———. *De fine seculi et iudicio venturo domini nostri Jesu Christi . . . orationes duo*. Basel, 1557.

———. *In Apocalypsim Jesu Christi . . . conciones centum*. Basel, 1557. Later Latin eds. Basel 1559, 1570; German ed. *Die Offenbarung Jesu Christi. . . .* Mühlhausen, 1558.

———. *Von höchster Freude vnd grösstem Leid des kunftigen Jüngsten Tags. . . .* Zürich, 1572.

Bünting, Heinrich. *Chronica catholica . . . ab initio mundi. . . .* Magdeburg, 1608.

———. *Chronologia hoc est, omnium temporum et annorum series. . . .* Zerbst, 1590.

———. *Itinerarium Sacrae Scripturae. Das ist, Ein Reisebuch, Vber die gantze heilige Schrifft. . . .* Helmstedt, 1582.

Busch, Georg. *Die andere Beschreibung von dem Cometen . . . 1572*. [Erfurt?], 1573.

———. *Von dem Cometen, welche in diesem 1572. Jar . . . erschienen*. Erfurt, 1573.

———. *Von dem erschrecklichen grausamen grossen Cometstern*. Prague, 1578.

Caesareus, Nicolaus. *Bedeutung vnd Offenbarung wahrer himlischer Jnfluxion, nemblich der Finsternissen, so die folgender 7 Jhar nacheinander geschehen. . . .* Nuremberg, 1558.

———. *Prognosticon Astrologicvm . . . 1577*. N.p., [1576?].

Caesius, Georg. *Catalogus numquam antea visus omnium cometarum secundum seriem annorum. . . .* Nuremberg, 1578.

———. *Prognosticon Astrologicvm, Oder Practica Teutsch . . . 1575*. Nuremberg, 1574. Caesius published many similar annual works.

Caesius, Georg Friederich. *Prognosticon Astrologicvm . . . 1603*. Nuremberg, 1602. A similar work appeared in 1603.

Calvin, John. *Institutes of the Christian Religion*, ed. J. T. McNeil. Philadelphia, 1960.

Calvisius, Sethus. *Admonitio Sethi Calvisii ad chronologiae studiosos. . . .* Erfurt, 1610.

———. *Chronologia, ex autoritate potissimum sacrae scripturae. . . .* Leipzig, 1605.

———. *Opus chronologicum, ex autoritate potissimum sacrae scripturae et historicum fide dignissimorum.* . . . Frankfurt a.O., 1620.
Camerarius, Joachim. *Notatio figurarum orationis et mutatae simplicis elocutionis in apostolicis scriptis.* Leipzig, 1556.
Capistranus, Johann [pseudonym]. *Woldenckwürdige Weissagung oder Propheceyung von den jetzigen Läufften . . . 1619. Vnd nachfolgenten 1620 . . . 1623 Jahren.* . . . Breslau, 1619.
Carion, Johann. *Prognosticatio vnd Erklerung der grossen Wesserung: auch anderer erschrockenlichen würchungen.* . . . Leipzig, 1522.
———. *Propheceiung Johan Carionis, Das ist, Auslegung der verborgenen Weissagung Doctor Johannis Carionis, von Verenderung vnd Zufelligem Glück der höchsten Potentaten des Römischen Reichs.* N.p., 1594; another ed. Mittelburg [false; Wittenberg?], 1620.
———. *Chronica Carionis.* See Melanchthon, Philipp.
Celicius, Andreas. *Christliche, notwendige, nützliche vnd theologische Erinnerung, von dem newen Cometen.* Magdeburg (also Leipzig), 1578.
———. *Notwendige Erinnerung. Von des Sathans letzten Zornsturm.* . . . Wittenberg, 1594.
Christian, Hulderich. *Drey Propheceyung, Bedeutung, Warnung vnd Vermahnung.* . . . N.p., 1606.
Chytraeus, David. *Auslegung der Offenbarung Johannis.* Rostock, 1572; Rostock, 1585; Wittenberg, 1585. Latin ed. Wittenberg, 1563.
———. *Chronologia . . . ab initio mundi.* . . . Rostock, 1573.
———. *De stella inusitata et nova quae mense Novembri anno 1572. conspicit coepit. Et . . . de comato sidere, quod hoc mense Novembri anno 1577 videmus.* Rostock, 1577.
Cnespelium, Jacob. *Practica: Auff das 1585. Jar.* . . . N.p., [1584?].
Cnoll, Christopher. *Calendarium Generale Perpetuum. Ein Allgemeiner Calender, auff alle vnd jede Jahr biss ans Ende der Weld.* . . . Liegnitz, 1619.
———. *Prognosticon Generale Perpetuum. Ein allgemeine Practica, auff alle vnd jede Jahr, biss ans ende der Welt.* . . . Görlitz, 1616.
Colberg, Daniel. *Das Platonisch-Hermetisches Christenthum.* . . . Frankfurt and Leipzig, 1690.
Coler, Jacob. *Doct. Iacobi Coleri Probst zu Berlin Eigentlicher bericht, Võ den seltzamen . . . Wunderwercken vnd Geschichten, so sich newlicher zeit in der Marck Brandenburg zugetragen . . . vnd noch teglich geschehen.* . . . Erfurt, 1595.
———. *Notwendige Erinnerung auff daz schreckliche Fewerzeichen, so . . . 1580. Jahrs am Himmel gesehen worden sampt einer . . Rechnung aus Gottes Wort, dass das Ende der Welt . . . nahe für der Thüren.* Berlin, 1581.
Confessio fraternitatis. See Van Dülmen, Richard.
Cramer, Daniel. *Apocalypsis, Oder Offenbarung S. Johannis.* . . . Alten Stettin, 1619.
Cusanus, Nicholas. *Die Kunst der Vermutung: Auswahl aus den Schriften* [von Nikolaus von Cues], ed. Hans Blumenberg. Bremen, 1957.
[Daniel]. *De lapide fortissimo qui imaginem Danielis capite.* . . . N.p., 1623.

[Deutschland]. *Wache auff Deutschland, denn es ist hohe Zeit.* N.p., 1625.

Dieterich, Cunrad. *Vlmische Cometen Predigte, Von dem Cometen . . . 1618.* Ulm, 1619.

[Discurs]. *Wohlgegründeter Politischer Discurs, Vom jetzigen Zustande vnd Kriegeswesen im gantzen Römischen Reich. . . .* N.p., 1631.

Dobricius, Johannes. *Chronomenytor das ist, Zeiterinner, in welchem . . . erkleret vnd angezeiget wird, In was vor einer zeit wir Jetzo sein, vnd was nun mehr vnfehlbar der Welt vnd vns schierkünfftig zugewarten.* Liegnitz, 1612 (earlier ed. c. 1605?).

Dolingius, Johannes. *Nothwendiger Bericht vom bevorstehenden Ende der Welt. . . .* Rostock, 1637.

Draud, Georg. *Bibliotheca librorvm Germanicorvm classica: Das ist: Verzeichnuss aller vnd jeder Bucher, so . . . in Teutscher Spraach . . . in Truck aussgangen. . . .* Frankfurt a.M., 1625.

Efferhen, Henricus. *XIII Christenliche Predigten auss dem XXXVIII. vnd XXXIX. Capitel Ezechielis. Von Gog vnnd Magog, oder den Türcken.* Strassburg, 1571.

Egardus, Paul. *Erklärung des XX. Capitels Apocalypseus.* Lüneburg, 1620.

―――. *Geheimniss dess Reichs Gottes im Menschen, das ist: die tröstliche Lehre von dem Reich Gottes, was es sey, wie es komme, wo es zu finden. . . .* Lüneburg, 1626.

―――. *Schatz der himmlischen Weisheit.* Lüneburg, 1625.

Eglin, Raphael. *Epilysis Apocalypseos S. Joannis.* Zurich, 1601.

―――. *Newe Meerwunderische Prophecey, Auff Danielis vnnd der Offenbarung Johannis Zeytrechnung gezogen. . . .* Zurich, 1598.

―――. *Prophetia haliuetica nova et admiranda, ad Danielis et sacrae Apocalypseos calculum chronographicum.* Zurich, 1598.

Ehinger, Elias. *Ivdicivm Astrologicvm Von dem Newen Cometa . . . 1618.* Augsburg, [1619?].

Eichler, Michael. *Biblisch Calender, Darinnen . . . einem jegklichen Menschen, auss der allergewissesten Astronomia der heiligen Schrifft, sein Glück oder Vnglück . . . angezeigt. . . .* Frankfurt a.M., 1579.

Eichstadt, Lorentz. *Novum & Rarissimum Ostentum Quinque Pareliorum. Oder Einfeltiges Bedencken vber die fünff Sonnen. . . .* Alten Stettin, 1625.

―――. *Prognosticon de conjunctione magna Saturni & Iovis in trigono igneo Leonis . . . 1623.* Alten Stettin, 1622.

Eisenmenger, Samuel [pseudonym: Samuel Siderocrates]. *Cyclopaedia Paracelsica Christiana. Drey Bücher von dem warē vrsprung vnd herkommen der freyen Künsten. . . .* N.p., 1585.

Engelhart, Valentin. *De Mvndo et Tempore. Das ist Von der Welt vn̄d der Zeit, ein nützlich Büchlein. . . .* N.p., 1562.

Engerdus, Johann (?). *Preseruatiu, Cur vnnd Seelen-Artzney, wider die gifftige jetzoschwebende Seuch der New Evangelischen Secten, bevorab dess hochschädlichen Lutherthumbs. . . .* Ingolstadt, 1581.

Engricensis, Paulus. *Trewhertzige Ermanung Der Zeichen, so für dem Jüngsten Tage hergehen. . . .* Eisleben, [c. 1560].

Eytzing [Aitzinger], Michael von. *Nova Qvaestionis Solvtio. Nämlich Wie lang die Welt Revera gestanden sey, von Anfang biss auff das gegenwür-tig Jar....* Augsburg, 1566.

Faber, Basilius. *Allerley Christliche, nötige vnd nützliche vnterrichtung, von den letzten Hendeln der Welt, Als: Vom Jüngsten tage . . . Mit an-gehenckten warnungen vnd Prophezeien D. Mart. Luthers. . . .* Eisleben, 1565; many other eds.

Fabricius, Paulus. *Iudicium de cometa . . . M.D.LXXVII . . . Viennae con-spectu est. . . .* N.p., [1578?].

Fagius, Caspar. *Wunder Stern, vnd Zornzeichen. So an Sonn, vnd Monde, des 1568. Jarss . . . Sampt einer verwarnung, was drauff folgen möge. . . .* Erfurt, 1569.

Fama fraternitatis. See Van Dülmen, Richard.

[Faulhaber, Johann?]. *Analysis, Das ist: Aufflösung der Wortrechnung Jo-hannes Krafften Schulmodisten in Vlm. . . .* Nuremberg, 1614.

Faulhaber, Johann. *Andeutung, Einer vnerhörten newen Wunderkunst. Welche der Geist Gottes, in etlichen Prophetischen, vnd Biblischen Ge-heimnuss Zahlen, biss auff die letzte Zeit hat wöllen versigelt vnd ver-borgen halten. . . .* Nuremberg, 1613.

———. *Arithmetischen, Cubicosischen Lustgarten. . . .* Tübingen, 1604.

———. *Fama Syderea Nova. Gemein offentliches Aussschreiben, Dess Ehrnvestern, Weitberümbten vnd Sinnreichen Herrn Johanni Faulha-bers. . . .* Nuremberg, 1618.

———. *Gemein offen AussSchreiben . . . An alle Philosophos, Mathema-ticos, sonderlich Arithmeticos vnd Künstler . . . in Europa. . . .* Augs-burg, 1615.

———. *Herrn Johann Faulhabers . . . Continuatio, Seiner neuen Wunder-kunsten, oder Arithmetischen wunderwercken. . . .* Nuremberg, 1617.

———. *Himlische gehaime Magia Oder Newe Cabalistische Kunst, vnd Wunderrechnung, Vom Gog vnd Magog. . . .* Nuremberg, 1613.

———. *Mysterium arithmeticum, sive, cabalistica et philosophica inven-tio, nova admiranda et ardua, qua numeri ratione et methodo compu-tentur . . . illuminatissimis laudatissimisque fratribus R.C. fama viris hu-militer et sincere dicata.* Ulm, 1615.

———. *Numerus figuratus, sive arithmetica analytica arte mirabili. . . .* [Nuremberg?], 1614.

———. *Vernunfftiger Creaturen Weissagungen, Das ist: Beschreibung eines Wunder Hirschs, auch etlicher Heringen vnd Fisch . . . Auss den gehaimen Zahlen dess Propheten Danielis, vnd der Offenbarung S. Jo-hannis erklärt. . . .* Augsburg, 1632.

Faustus, Laurentius. *Anatomia Statuae Danielis. Kurtze vnd eigentliche erklerung der grossen Bildnis des Propheten Danielis. . . .* Leipzig, 1586.

Felgenhauer, Paul. *Das Allerheiligste am Tempel dess Herrn. . . .* N.p., 1630.

———. *Apologeticus contra invectivas aeruginosas Rostij. Kurtze Verant-wortung, auff das Heldenbuch vom Rosengarten.* N.p., 1622.

———. *Disexamen vel examen examinis. . . .* Wahrenburg(?), 1623.

———. *Das Heilige am Tempel des Herrn. . . .* N.p., 1631.

———. *Rechte, Warhafftige vnd gantz Richtige Chronologia, Oder Rech-nung der Jare der Welt. . . .* N.p., 1620.

————. *Sendtbrief an die Hirten vnd an die Schafe, vnter allerley Secten.* N.p., 1632.

————. *Speculum Temporis. Zeit Spiegel.* . . . N.p., 1620.

————. *Der Vorhof am Tempel des Herrn.* . . . N.p., 1630.

Fincel, Job. *Wunderzeichen. Warhafftige beschreybung vnd gründlich verzeichnuss schröcklicher Wunderzeichen vnd Geschichten.* . . . Nuremberg, 1556; enlarged ed. Frankfurt a.M., 1566.

Finck, Caspar. *Kurtzer, Notiger, vnd in Gottes Wort wolbegründter Bericht, Von dem Jüngsten Gericht, Ewigen Leben, Vnd Hellen.* . . . Giessen, 1612.

Fischart, Johann. *Aller Practick Grossmutter.* Strassburg, 1572–74.

Flacius Illyricus, Matthias. *Catalogus testium veritatis, qui ante nostram aetatem reclamarunt papae.* . . . Basel, 1556; German ed. Frankfurt a.M., 1573.

————. *Ecclesiastica historia integram ecclesiae Christi ideam . . . complectens . . . gongesta per aliquot studiosos et pios viros in urbe Magdeburgica.* Basel, 1559–74.

Flinsbach, Cunman. *Chunmanni Flinspachii Tabernomontani conjecturae extremorum temporum,* in Johann Wolf, *Lectiones memorabiles et reconditae.* . . , Frankfurt a.M., 1671. First published 1559.

Franciscus, M. *Offenbartes Geheimnuss Der Juden-Plag. Dass ist: Erschrockliche, zum theil Wunderliche Straffen . . . Gottes, über die Juden.* . . . N.p., 1627.

Frank, Sebastian. *Chronica. Zeyt-buch und geschycht-bibel von anbegyn bis inn diss gegenwertig MDXXXJ jar.* Strassburg, 1531.

Fridericus, Daniel. *Expositio 12. priorum capitum Apocalypseos.* Wittenberg, 1614.

Friedrich, Henr. *Gründliche Widerlegung der Aberglaubischen Astrologorum so auss dem Gestirn vnd derselben Influenz prognosticiren vnd Nativitäten stellen.* . . . Erfurt, 1624.

Friess, Wilhelm. *Ein Grausame vnnd Erschröckliche Propheceyhung, oder Weissagung vber Pollerland vnd Teutschland, Brabant vnd Franckreich.* Basel, 1577; reprinted 1586.

————. *Prognosticatio. Etliche seltzame Propheceyung, geweyssaget von dem Allten M. Wilhelmo Friesen, von Mastrich.* . . . Nuremberg, [c. 1558].

Frisius, Matthias. *Tabula synopticae Apocalyptiae Novi Testamenti.* Lüneburg, 1583.

Fritsch, Marcus. *Meteorum, hoc est, impressionum aerearum et mirabilium naturae operum . . . item: catalogus prodigiorum atque ostentorum.* . . . Nuremberg, 1563.

Füger, Caspar [trans.]. *Ein Erschröckliche propheceyung, vnd Weyssagung Lactantij Furmiani . . . von dieser vnser jetzigen bösen zeit vnd jüngsten Tage.* . . . Hoff, 1581. The work appeared under slightly different titles in 1585 and 1615.

————— [ed.]. *Prognosticon Oder Weissagung . . . biss auffs 84. vnd 88. Jar, ja biss ans ende der Welt . . . aus Johan Hilten, vnd Lactantio Firmiano . . . auch D. Martini Lutheri.* . . . Eisleben, 1584.

———. *Weissagung, von der künfftigen zerstörung Deutsches Landes, durch den Turckischen Keyser Soldan.* . . . N.p., 1568.

Funck, Johann. *Apocalypsis: Der Offenbarung Künfftiger Geschicht Johannis* . . . *Mit einer Vorrede Philip. Melanth.* N.p., 1561; another ed. Frankfurt, 1586. The work apparently existed in manuscript as early as 1546 under a different title: "Was widerwertigkeit vnd verfolgung die heilig, christliche kirche . . . von der apostel zeit her in gemain erlitten habe vnd was noch . . . zu warten sein. . . ."

———. *Chronologia: hoc est omnium temporum et annorum ab initio mundi usque ad resurrectionem domini nostri Jesu Christi, computatio.* . . . Nuremberg, 1545. The work, updated to 1560, was reprinted at Wittenberg in 1570, 1578, 1602, and later. German ed. *Chronologie von Erschaffung der Welt bis auf das Jahr 1560.*

Garcaeus, Johann. *Eine Christliche kurtze Widerholung der warhafftigen Lere vnd bekentnis unsers Glaubens von der Zukunfft des Herrn Christi zum Gericht.* Wittenberg, 1569.

———. *Primus tractatus brevis et utilis de tempore.* . . . Wittenberg, 1563.

Gigas, Johannes. *Von der Stuffen zum Himelreich, wieder die Papisten, Wiederteuffer, vnd Schwenckfelder.* Frankfurt a.O., 1564.

Glaser, Peter. *Hundert vnd zwanzig Propheceyunge, oder Weissagung, das Ehrwirdigen Vaters Herrn Doctoris Martini Luthers.* . . . Eisleben, 1557.

———. *Zwey Hundert Propheceyunge oder weissagunge* . . . *D. Martini Lutheri.* . . . Bautzen, 1574; another ed. 1628.

Goldwurm, Caspar. *Biblische Chronica.* . . . Frankfurt a.M., 1576.

———. [trans.]. *Prognosticon. Weissagungen vñ Vrtheyl, von betrübungen vnnd grossen anfechtungen Europe, Durch den Hochberhümbten Astronomum* . . . *D. Anthonium Torquatum gestelt.* . . . Frankfurt a.M., 1558. Reprinted Leipzig, 1594.

———. *Wunderzeichen: Das ist, Warhaftige Beschreibunge aller fürnemen, seltzamen, vngewönlichen, Göttlichen vnd Teuffelischen* . . . *gesichte vnnd missgeburt.* . . . Frankfurt a.M., 1567.

Golitzschen, Johan. *Ein Erschröckliche Geburt, vnd Augenscheinlich Wunderzeichen des Allmechtigen Gottes.* . . . Strassburg, 1564.

Graebner, Paul. *Conjecturen oder Muhtmassungen.* . . . [Warmünster?], 1619.

———. *Pauli Secvndi Gesang, Vom Antichrist.* Hamburg, 1600.

———. *Prognosticon oder Erklärung: Vber den Anno 1618. erschienen Comet Stern, vnd dessen Operation.* N.p., 1631 (Vorrede 1621).

Grick, Friedrich. *Cometenbutzer, Das ist: Eine glaubwürdige Copey Articulierter vnd rechtmassiger Klag.* . . . N.p., 1619.

———. *Cometenbutzers Schutzer, Das ist, Eine glaubwürdige Copey articulierter, rechtmessiger Exceptionum.* . . . N.p., 1619.

Groscurdt, Justus. *Bacchationum Nagelianarum Prima: Das ist, Ein sonderlicher vnd zwar Erster FastnachtsAuffzug des newen Schwermers, der sich nennet Paulum Nagelium.* . . . N.p., 1620.

Gross, Johann. *Christliche Predigt Von dem Wahrsagen der Abergläubigen.* Basel, [1619?].

Grünpeck, Joseph. *Ein newe ausslegung. Der seltzamen, wundertzaichen vnd wunderpürden.* . . . N.p., [c. 1530].

———. *Practica der gegenwertigen grossen Trübsaln, vnnd vilfaltiger Wunder.* . . . Strassburg, [c. 1530].

———. *Prognosticon Doctor Joseph Grünpecks, von zwey vnd dreyssigsten Jar an bis auff das viertzigst Jar.* . . . Nuremberg, [c. 1532].

———. *Spiegel der naturlichen himlischen vnd prophetischen sehungen aller trubsalen, angst, vñ not, die vber alle stende . . . in kurtzen tagen geen werdenn.* Leipzig, 1522.

Gutknecht, Friedrich. *Practica auff das Jar, M.D.LXXI.* Nuremberg, 1570.

Gutman, Aegidius. *Offenbarung Göttlicher Mayestat, Darinnen angezeygt wird, Wie Gott der Herr Anfänglich/sich allen seinen Geschöpffen, mit Worten vnd Wercken geoffenbaret.* . . . Hanau, 1619.

Gwalther, Rudolf. *Aussführliche Trostpredigten von der letzten Zukunfft Christi.* Zurich, n.d.

———, and Heinrich Bullinger. *Archetypi homelarium . . . in Apocalypsin divi Johannis.* Zurich, 1598.

Habrecht, Isaac. *Kurtze vnd Gründliche Beschreibung, Eines Newen vngewöhnlichen Sterns, oder Cometen.* . . . Strassburg, 1618.

———. *Kurtze vnd Grundliche Beschreibung, Der dreyen Sonnen . . . im Jahr 1622. zu Strassburg.* . . . Strassburg, [1622?].

Hafenreffer, Matthias. *Templum Ezechielis, sive in IX. postrema prophetae capita commentarius.* . . . Tübingen, 1613.

Hafftirn, Petrus. *Trostbüchlein vnd Lehr vom Jüngsten Gericht.* Leipzig, 1575.

Hamel, Laurentius. *Einfaltiger theologischer Bericht, von dem erschrecklichen Cometen . . . der in dem nechst vorgangenen 1577. Jar . . . ist erschienen.* Frankfurt a.O., 1578.

Hantschmann, Urban. *De novissimis mundi oratio apodicta.* Wittenberg, 1611.

Hartman, Thomas. *Cometen Spiegel: Oder: Bericht von Cometen.* . . . Hall in Sachsen, 1605.

Hartprecht, Nicholaus. *Tuba Temporis, Oder Warhafftige, Vnfeilbare Zeit Rechnung, Dergleichen die Welt noch nie gesehen hat.* . . . Erfurt, 1620.

Hassler, Johan. *Astrologische Practica, Auff das 1590 Jar.* . . . Basel, [1589?].

Hebenstreit, Johan Baptistam. *Cometen Fragstuck, auss der reinen Philosophia, Bey Anschawung dess . . . 1618 . . . Cometen.* . . . Ulm, 1618.

Hebenstreit, Johann. *Prognosticon von allerley seltzamen zufellen des 1559. Jhars.* Erfurt, 1558.

———. *Prognosticon Historicvm vnd Physicvm. Auffs M.D.LXVI. Jhar.* . . . Erfurt, 1565.

———. *Prognosticon Physicum: Des Jhars . . . 1565.* Erfurt, [1564?].

Heerbrand, Jacob. *Ein trewe Warnung vnd gutthertzige Vermanung zur Büss . . . vber das schröckliche Wunderzeichen, den Cometen . . . 1577.* Tübingen, 1578.

Heidegger, Joh. Frid. *Das Lied Mosis, oder Schrifftmässiger Bericht von denen Zeichen derer Zeiten vnd Vorboten des Jüngsten Gerichts.* Zurich, n.d.

Heiden, Christian. *Practica . . . Auff das M.D.L.XX. Jahr. . . .* Nuremberg, 1570.

Heilandt, Irenaeus. *Apocalyptisches, Doch Politisches Bedencken, Was die Evangelischen vnd Protestirenden Churfürsten vnd Stände . . . zu gewarten. . . .* N.p., 1631.

Heilbrunner, Philipp. *Ezechielis propheta vaticinia.* Lauingen, 1587. Heilbrunner apparently wrote other works on the prophecies of Daniel and the minor prophets.

Helbach, Wendelin von. *Warhafftige newe Zeitung, wie drey Engel von Himmel, in die Stat Cassaw im Vngerlandt auss befelch des Herrn Christi zur Busse vermanet haben. . . .* Tübingen, 1565.

Heller, Joachim. *Practica . . . Auff das M.D.LXI. Jar. . . .* Nuremberg, [1560?].

Helwig, Andr. *Antichristus romanus, in proprio suo nomine, numerum illum apocalypticum (DCLXVI) continente proditus.* Wittenberg, 1612.

Henisch, Georg. *Alter vnd Newer Schreybkalender, Auff das Jar: M.D.LXXXV.* [Augsburg?], 1584.

———. *Iudicium de Pogonia ad finem anni 1577. conspecto.* Augsburg, 1578.

———. *Kurtze Beschreibung, Desz Cometen, oder Strobelsterns . . . dieses 1596. Jars. . . .* Nuremberg and Augsburg, 1596.

———. *Practica: Auff das Jar nach der Gnadenreichen Geburt vnsers Herren vnd Heylands Jhesu Christi M.D.LXXXVIII.* N.p., [c. 1586].

———. *Practica: Oder Iudicivm Astrologicvm . . . Auff das Jahr . . . 1585.* Basel, [1584?]. Henisch wrote similar annual works throughout the 1580s and 1590s.

Henuriades, Jano. *Apocalyptische Satzstück vnd Vrsachen von jetzo instehender grossen Veränderungen vieler mächtigster Regimentern. . . .* N.p., 1623.

Herberger, Valerius. *Predigt am zweiten Advent-Sonntage. Luc. 21, 25–36,* in R. Nesselman, ed., *Buch der Predigten,* Elbing, 1858. First published 1613.

Herlicius, David. *Astronomische vnd Historische Erklerung Des Newen Sterns oder . . . Cometen . . . 1604.* Alten Stettin, 1605.

———. *De Pluviis Prodigiosis Speculatio Physica et Historica. Von Blutregen vnd andern Wunderbaren Vnnatürlichen Vngewöhnlichen Regen. . . .* Greifswald, 1597.

———. *Kurtze aber Trewhertzige Erklerung, des . . . newen Sterns oder Cometen . . . dieses 1607 Jahrs. . . .* Lübeck, 1607.

———. *Kurtzer Discvrs vom Cometen, vnnd dreyen Sonnen . . . 1618.* Alten Stettin, 1619.

———. *Prodromus vnd Erster Theil Gründtlicher Wiederlegung oder Refutation des Newen Babstischen Calenders. . . .* Alten Stettin, 1605.

———. *Prodromus vnd Erster Vortrab . . . Dess Cometen . . . dess M.DC.XVIII. Jahres.* Nuremberg, 1618.

———. *Tractatus Theologastronomistoricus. Von des Türckischen Reichs vntergange. . . .* N.p., 1596.

Herold, Balthasar. *Kurtze gründliche vnd warhafftige Beschreibung von einem vngewohnlichen newen Stern . . . 1604.* N.p., 1605.

Hertzberger, Antonius Otho. See Otho, Anton.
Heshusius, Tilemann. "Predigten 1568–70." Untitled collection, Staats-
und Universitätsbibliothek Hamburg.
Heunisch, Caspar. *Hauptschlüssel der offenbarung Ioannis.* Schleusingen,
1684.
Heuring, Simon. *Practica Teutsch auff das M.D.LXIII. Jar.* . . . Nurem-
berg, [1562?]. Similar annual works by Heuring appeared in the 1560s.
Heylandt, Gottlieb. *Enarratio Chronologo-Historica Apocal ypseus S. Io-
hannis: Das ist: Historische Ausslegung.* . . . N.p., 1623.
———. *Examen Chronologicum: Oder Gründtliche . . . Erzehlung der
Jahr dieser Welt.* . . . N.p., 1622.
Hildebrand, Wolfgang. *Zehen Jährig Prognosticon . . . von dem 1627.
Jahre an, biss man schreiben wird 1638.* N.p., 1628.
Hildegard, St. *Prophetia oder Weissagung Hildegardis, darinnen sie vor
ungefähr 450 Jahren von diesen vnsern letzten Zeiten . . . geschrieben
hat . . . in Druck gegeben . . . vnd offerirt von Georgio Bellamera.* N.p.,
1620.
Hiller, Matth. *Von gefehrlichen verenderung in dieser Welt, die vns durch
des 1588. Jahres wunderliche constellation trewet, anzeiget.* Leipzig,
1586.
Hitfeld, Albert. *Alberti Hitfelds Betglocke, wegen dess Römischen, Mahometischen vnnd Bäpstlichen Reichs Endschafft vnd darauff fürstehenden jüngsten Tags.* Magdeburg, 1614.
———. *Ivdiciolvm. Kleiner Vorstand . . . Der bedeutung des Cometen . . .
1618.* N.p., 1619.
———. *Jegenbeweiss. Das die Welt nicht noch 42 Jahr stehen könne, wie
Jacobus Tilnerus . . . beweisen will.* N.p., 1613.
Hoe von Hoenegg, Matthias. *Commentarius in Apocalypsin.* 2 vols. Leip-
zig, 1610–40.
———. *Extremum et Totale Romae Papalis Excidium. Das ist: Dasz das
Päbstische Rom vnd AntiChristische Reich vorm Jüngsten Tage noch
solle vnd müsse zerstöret vnd vmbgekehret werden.* . . . N.p., 1631.
Höffler, Caspar. *Bericht von der letzten Zukunfft Christi.* Hamburg, 1599.
———. *Evangelischer Rhum vnd Ehrenpreiss, Des Hochlöblichen Chur-
vnd Furstlichen Hauses Sachsen, auss dem CXLVII Psalm.* . . . Alten-
burg, 1618.
Hoffman, Erhard. *Practica Deutsch, auff das Jar . . . M.D.LXXI.* . . . Er-
furt, [1570?].
Hoffmann, Christopher. *De Christiana religione, et de regno Antichristi.*
Frankfurt, 1545.
Holtheuser, Joh. *Vom jüngsten Tag.* Nuremberg, 1584.
Hörner, Johann. *Problema Summum, Mathematicum & Cabalisticum.
Das ist: Ein hohe, versiglete, Mathematische vnd Cabalistische Auffgab
vnd Figur, an alle Gelehrten vnnd Kunstliebende Europae.* Nuremberg,
1619.
Huber, Samuel. *Zwo Predigten . . . Darinnen der Grundt des Calvinischen
Abfals vom heiligen Evangelio, kurtzlich entdeckt wird.* Wittenberg,
1593.

Hunnius, Nicolaus. *Christliche Betrachtung der Newen Paracelsisten vnd Weigelianischen Theology.* Leipzig, 1622.

———. *Mataeologia Fanatica, Oder Ausführlicher Bericht Von der Neuen Propheten, Die sich Erleuchtete und Gottsgelehrte nennen, Religion, Lehr und Glauben,* ed. J. H. Feustking. Leipzig, 1708. First published 1634.

Iordan, Gregor. *Propheceyung vnd Weissagung von erschrecklichen vnnd grewlichen widerwertigkeiten.* . . . Cologne, 1592.

Irenaeus, Christoph. *Abtruck eines schröcklichen Zornzeichens, sampt Christlicher Erinnerung von den Zeichen vor dem Jüngsten Tag.* Eisleben, 1565.

———. *De Monstris. Von seltzamen Wundergeburten.* N.p., 1584.

———. *Prognosticon Aus Gottes Wort nötige Erinnerung, Vnd Christliche Busspredigt zu dieser letzten bösen Zeit . . . Auff den Cometen . . . 1577.* N.p., 1578.

[J.C.C.H.] *Clangor buccinae propheticae de novissimis temporibus.* . . . N.p., 1646. First published c. 1620.

Jenisch, Paul. *Christlicher vnd Nothwendiger Bericht auss Gottes Wort vnd der fürnem̃sten Kirchen Lehrer reinen heilsamen Schrifften, Von den letzten Händeln der Welt, vom Jüngsten Tage vnd Ewigen Leben.* . . . Ulm, 1645.

Jessen, Johann von. *Zoroaster. Nova, brevis, veraque de universo philosophia.* Wittenberg, 1593.

Kepler, Johann. *Antwort Joannis Keppleri . . . Auff D. Helisaei Röslini . . . Discurs Von heutiger zeit beschaffenheit.* . . . Prague, 1609.

———. *Gesammelte Werke,* ed. W. von Dyck and M. Caspar. Vol. 5, *Chronologische Schriften.* Munich, 1953.

———. *Tertius Interveniens. Das ist, Warnung an etliche Theologos, Medicos vnd Philosophos, sonderlich D. Philippum Feselium, das sie . . . nicht das Kindt mit dem Badt aussschütten.* . . . Frankfurt a.M., 1610.

———, and H. Roeslin. *Gründlicher Bericht vnd Bedencken, Von einem vngewöhnlichen Newen Stern . . . 1604.* . . . Amberg, 1605.

Klain, Johann. *Prognosticon. Oder: Practica Teutsch, auff das M.D.LXXI. Jar.* . . . Nuremberg, [1570?]. Klain issued several similar annual works in the 1570s.

Köppen, Joachim. *Wunder vber Wunder, Das ist: Seltzame vnd Ebenthewrliche Geschicht vnd Gesicht, welche sich zu Stargardt in Pommern . . . bey Observation des Cometen, so sich . . . 1618 . . . sehen lassen.* N.p., 1619.

Krauss, Daniel. *Warhafftiger Bericht vnd erschröckliche Newe Zeitung.* Zurich, 1628.

Kreützhelm, Leonard. *Chronologia. Das ist, Gründtliche vnd fleissige Jahrrechnung, Sam̃pt verzeichnung der fürnemsten Geschichten, Verenderungen vnd Zufell . . . Von anfang der Welt.* . . . Görlitz, 1577.

———. *Coniecturae. Christliche vermuttungen, von künfftiger Zeit, Zustand, in Kirchen vnd Regimenten . . . Sampt den Weissagungen . . . Nicolai Cusani.* . . . Görlitz, 1583.

Lachtern, Jacob. *Bericht auss Gottes Wort, vom Jüngsten Gericht Gottes.* Nuremberg, 1566.

Laelius, Laurentius. *Fünff Predigten, Von dem Evangelischen Jubelfest.* . . . Nuremberg, 1618.

Lambert, Franz. *Exegeseos, Francisci Lamberti Auenlonensis, in sanctam diui Ioannis Apocalypsim, libri VII.* Marburg, 1528.

Lapaeus, Johann. *Warhafftige Prophezeiungen des thewren Propheten, vnd heiligen Manns Gottes, D. Martini Lutheri seliger Gedechtnis.* . . . Ursel, 1578; new, enlarged ed. 1592.

————, ed. *Practica vnd Prognostica, Oder Schreckliche Propheceiung D. Martin Luthers, des ausserwehlten Rustzeugs vnd Propheten des Deutschen Landes.* . . . Ursel [Oberursel?], 1578.

Lavater, Ludwig. *Predigt von des gedültigen Jobs Glauben vnd bekandtnuss von Aufferstehung der Todten, vom Jüngsten tag vnd ewigen Leben.* Zurich, 1577.

Leisentritt, Johann. *Fragmenta. Missivae seu relationis cuiusdam de certis Antichristi praecursoribus, extremum Dei iudicium & veram Christi ecclesiam exprimentis.* N.p., 1571.

Leowitz, Cyprian. *De coniunctionibus magnis insigniorum superiorum planetarum, solis defectionibus et cometis.* . . . Lauingen, 1564.

————. *Grundliche, Klärliche beschreibung, vnd Historischer bericht, der fürnemsten grossen zusam̃enkunfft der obern Planeten, der Soñen Finsternussen, der Cometen, vnd derselben wirckung . . . biss auff nachvolgend zweintzig Jar werende.* . . . Lauingen, 1564.

————. *Von dem newen Stern . . . oder Cometen, welcher gesehen ist worden . . . 1572.* Lauingen, 1573. Latin ed. *De nova stella,* Lauingen, 1573.

Letzner, Iohann. *Wunder Spiegel, Das Erste [Ander] Buch. In welchem die fürnem̃sten Cometen vnd Wunderstern, [Finsternis] von anfang der Welt her . . . beschrieben werden.* . . . Erfurt, 1604.

Libavius, Andreas. *D.O.M.A. Wolmeinendes Bedenken von der Fama vnd Confession der Bruderschafft des Rosenkreutzes.* N.p., 1616.

[Lied]. *Das Lied Im thon, Gott hatt das Euangelium, gegeben das wir werden frumb.* . . . Tübingen, n.d.

[Lied]. *Ein Lied von den Alten vnnd Newen Calvinisten, Vnd trewe warnung, sich für jrem Gifft zühuten.* Dresden, 1576.

Lipen, Martin. *Bibliotheca realis universalis omnium materiarum, rerum et titulorum, in theologia, jurisprudentia, medicina et philosophia occurentium.* . . . 6 vols. Frankfurt a.M., 1679–85.

Listenius. Georgius. *Ein Erschreckliches warhafftiges Gesicht vnd Zeichen, so am Himel gesehen ist worden.* . . . Nuremberg, 1565.

Luginsland, Urban [pseudonym?]. *Prognosticon. Die vil berümpte Practica von Himmel vnd erden abgesehen.* . . . N.p., 1576.

————. *Prognosticon. Warsagung aus Würckung des Himmels vnd erden figur vnd gestalt.* . . . N.p., 1570.

Lungwitz, Matthaeus. *Wetterglocke. Notwendiger Bericht Was ein jeder Christ bey grossen Gewitter bedencken.* . . . Leipzig, 1628.

Luther, Martin. *Ein Christliche vermanung vnd erinnerung, D. Martini Luthers (Gottseligers) des Mans Gottes, Von den letzten schweren zeiten, des Jüngsten tages.* . . . Schleusingen, 1555.

———. *D. Martin Luthers Werke: Kritische Gesamtausgabe.* Weimar, 1883–.

———. *Erschröckliche Prophecey: vnd Weissagungen, anzeygendt, dess gantzen Teutschlands Vntergang . . . Gezogen auss den Schrifften: Herrn D. Martini Lutheri. . . .* Nuremberg, 1628.

———. *Herrlich Bedencken, Des tewren Mannes Gottes Lutheri seligen, von dem jtzundt newen Bepstischen Calender. . . .* N.p., 1584.

———. "Vorrhede Martini Luthers. Auff die Weissagung des Johannis Lichtenbergers," in Aby Warburg, *Heidnisch-antike Weissagung in Wort und Bild zu Luthers Zeiten,* in *Gesammelte Schriften,* vol. 2, pp. 545–50. Nendeln, 1969.

———. *Warhafftige Weissagung des letzten Deutschen Propheten D. Martini Luters. . . .* N.p., 1630.

Lutz, Renhardus. *Verzaichnuss vñ kurtzer begriff der Kätzerischen, vñ verdampten lehr Martin Steinbachs. . . .* Strassburg, 1566.

Lycosthenes, Conrad [Conrad Wolffhart]. *Wunderwerck Oder Gottes vnergründtliches vorbilden, das er in seinen geschöpffen allen . . . erscheynen, hören, brieuen lassen.* Basel, 1557; first Latin ed. Basel, 1557.

Maestlin, Michael. *Ephemeris nova anni 1577. sequens ultimam hactenus a Ioanne Stadio ed. ephemeridum, supputata ex tabulis Prutenicis. . . .* Tübingen, 1576.

———. *Notwendige vnd gründtliche Bedenncken . . . von dem . . . Römischen Kalender. . . .* Heidelberg, 1584.

Maier, Simon. *Kurtze vnd eigentliche Beschreibung des Cometen oder Wundersterns . . . 1596.* Nuremberg, 1596.

Major, Georg. *Erinnerung vom Jüngsten Gericht. . . .* Wittenberg, 1569.

Mardochai, Simson. *Prognostische Propheceyhung. Von den Natürlichen Influentzen des 1606. vnd 1607. Jahrs. . . .* Prague, 1606.

Meder, David. *Judicium Theologicvm von Bruderschafft des Rosen Creutz.* N.p., 1616.

———. *Zehen Christliche Busspredigten, Vber Die Weissagung Christi dess grossen Propheten, vom Ende der Welt vnd Jüngsten Tage. . . .* Frankfurt a.M., 1581.

Medler, Nicolaus. *Ein wunderlich Gesicht newlich bey Braunschweig am himmel gesehen. . . .* N.p., 1549.

Melanchthon, Philipp. *Chronica durch Magistrum Johann Carionis fleissig zusammengezogen, menigklich nützlich zu lesen.* Wittenberg, 1532.

———. *Philippi Melanthonis opera quae supersunt omnia,* ed. C. G. Bretschneider, in *Corpus reformatorum,* vols. 1–28. Halle, 1834–52; Braunschweig, 1853–60.

———. *Supplementa Melanchthoniana.* Leipzig, 1910–.

Menzel, Hieronymus. *Einfeltige, vnd Christliche Ausslegung, des . . . Evangelii . . . Sampt kurtzem Bericht, von der letzten Zukunfft des Herren Christi. . . .* Eisleben, 1570.

Merclius Joannem. *Himlische Fewerzeichen . . . 1560.* Nuremberg, [c. 1560].

Meyer, Sebastian. *D. Sebastiani Meyer, ecclesiastae Bernensis, in Apocalypsim divi Iohannis apostoli commentarius. . . .* Zurich, 1534, 1539, and 1584.

Meyfart, Johann Matthaeus. *Himlisches Jerusalem.* Nuremberg, 1633; first published 1627.

——. *Das Jüngste Gericht in zweyen Buchern.* . . . Nuremberg, 1652.

——. *Tuba Novissima, Das ist, Von den vier letzten dingen des Menschen.* . . . Coburg, 1626; reprinted with introduction and commentary by Erich Trunz, Tübingen, 1980.

Minymus, Valesius. *Hoch nötiges vnd zu dieser betrübten zeit allen bedrängten Christen tröstliches bedencken, Vber der beschaffenheit itziger Zeit, sonderlich aber dess instehenden Jahres 1623.* N.p., 1622.

Mirus, Martin. *Postilla: Das ist: Ausslegung der Evangelien.* . . . Jena, 1605.

Misocacus, Wilhelm. *Prognosticvm Oder Practica, auffs Jahr . . . 1585.* Danzig, [1584?]. Misocacus wrote several other annual practica in the 1580s and 1590s.

Moller, Albin. *Practica Astrologica . . . 1595.* Leipzig, 1594.

Moller [Müller], Tobias. *Prognosticon Astrologicvm . . . 1592.* Frankfurt a.O., 1591. One of many such annual works from Moller's hand.

——. *Widerlegung . . . der jenigen Restitution Anni vnnd Kalendarii.* . . . Leipzig, 1583.

Molysdorf, Georg. *Der Edle Rautenkrantz, Mit seinem schönen Geheimnis . . . Den herrlichen Einzug des Ehrenkönigs Jhesu Christi, ins hochlöbliche Chur vnd Fürstliche Haus zu Sachsen.* . . . Erfurt, 1585.

Musaenius, Simon. *Newe Prophetin. Von Schönbethe, in der alten Marck.* . . . Eisleben, 1580.

Musculus, Andreas. *Christliche Trewe Warnung, vnd Vermanūg, wider die grewliche vñ verdamliche Sicherheit der gantzen Welt.* Lemgo, 1562.

——. *Nützliche vnd seligliche Betrachtung des zunahenden Jüngsten Gerichts.* . . . Frankfurt a.O., 1578.

——. *Prophecey vnd Weissagung des Sons des lebendigen Gottes . . . Von dem zunahendem vnd allbereit vorhandenem Zorn, Straff, Jammer vnd Vnglück, vber Deutschlandt.* Erfurt, 1557.

——. *Vom jüngsten Tage.* Erfurt, 1559.

——. *Vom Mesech vnd Kedar, vom Gog vnd Magog, von dem grossen trübsal für der Welt Ende . . . Wie nahe solches alles für der Thür.* . . . Frankfurt a.O., 1577.

——. *Von des Teufels Tyranney, Macht vnd Gewalt, Sonderlich in diesen letzten tagen, vnterrichtung.* Erfurt, 1561.

——. *Warnung vnd vermanung wieder die greuliche vnnd verdamliche sicherheit dieser zeit.* . . . Frankfurt a.O., 1558.

Musculus, W. *Weissagung D. M. Lutheri, der Deutschen Apostel vnd Prophet, von dem grossen zunahenden Vnglück vber Deutschland.* Frankfurt a.O., 1567.

Mylius, Georg. *Augspurgische Calender Zeitung. Kurtze historische erzölung des Calender streits.* . . . Wittenberg, 1584.

——. *Bapstpredigten, In welchen gehandlet . . . Was, vnd Wer der Bapst zu Rom sey, vnd nicht sey.* . . . Frankfurt a.M., 1615.

Nachenmoser, Adam. *Prognosticon Theologicvm. Das ist: Gaistliche Grosse Practica auss Hailiger Biblischer Schrifft vnd Historien.* . . . Leiden [Strassburg?], 1595.

Nagel, Paul. *Catoptomantia Physica. Divinatio ex speculo Astrologico. Das ist: Grundlicher Bericht vnd naturliche Weissagung aus der* . . . *gestirneten Firmaments.* . . . Leipzig, 1610.

———. *Complementum astrologiae.* . . . Hall in Sachsen, 1620.

———. *Cursus Quinquenalis Mundi. Wundergeheime Offenbarung, dess trawriger vnnd betrübten zustands, welcher* . . . *begeben vnd zutragen soll.* . . . Hall in Sachsen, 1620.

———. *Himmels Zeichen. Grosse Conjunctiones Planetarum superiorum, vnd newer Wunderstern, so Anno 1604* . . . *erschienen.* Hall in Sachsen, 1605.

———. *Philosophia nova.* N.p., 1621.

———. *Prodromus astronomia apocalyptica.* . . . Danzig, 1620.

———. *Prognosticon Astrologicum* . . . *M.DC.XX.* Leipzig, [1619?].

———. *Prognosticon Astrologo-Cabalisticum, Auff das Jahr MDCXX. beschrieben.* . . . N.p., 1619.

———. *Prognosticon Astrologo Harmonicum.* . . . Hall in Sachsen, n.d.

———. *Raptusastronomicus. Das ist Astronomische gewisse warhafftige Prophecey vnd Weissagung, aus dem Ersten, Andern vnd Dritten Himmel.* . . . N.p., 1627.

———. *Stellae prodigiosae.* N.p., 1619.

———. *Wächterbuchlein vnd Letztes Stundengeschrey, wie hoch es am Tage sey.* . . . N.p., 1622.

Nas, Johann [pseudonym: Jonas Philognysius]. *Die vnfelig gewisest Practica practicarum, auff das yetzig vnd nachfolgende jar.* . . . Ingolstadt, 1566.

Neander, Michael. *Compendium chronicorum, sive historiarum omnium aetatum, gentium, imperiorum ac regnorum.* . . . Leipzig, 1586.

Neotechnus, Henricus [pseudonym]. *VI. Prognostica Von Verenderung vnd zufalligem Glück vnd Vnglück der höchsten Potentaten im Römischen Reich, Auch des Türcken vnd Pabst.* . . . Hall in Sachsen, 1613; another ed. 1621.

Neubarth, Christopher. *Astrologische Gedancken Uber die Zween neulich enstandene erschreckliche Comet-Sterne* . . . *1664* . . . *1665.* Breslau, [c. 1665].

Neuheuser, Wilhelm Eo. *Consideratio et enarratio Brevis de nova stella seu cometa. Das ist.* . . . Friedwegen [Salzburg?], 1619.

———. *Mystica Tempora Patefacta. Das ist: Gründliche Erklärung vnd Offenbahrung der geheimen vnd verborgenen Zeit vnd Zahl, in heiliger Schrifft mehr Orthen gemelt.* . . . Friedwegen [Salzburg?], 1623.

———. *Tractatvs: De Nova Stella; Oder Von dem newen Abent Stern Scheinende.* . . . Strassburg, 1604.

———. *Victoria Christianorum verissimorum universalis: Das ist.* . . . Friedwegen [Salzburg?], 1618.

Nicolai, Philipp. *Freudenspiegel des ewigen Lebens.* Frankfurt a.M., 1599; reprinted Soest, 1963.

———. *Historia des Reichs Christi, Das ist: Gründliche Beschreibung der wundersamen Erweiterung, seltzamen Glücks, vnd gewisser bestimmte Zeit der Kirchen Christi im Newen Testament.* . . . Frankfurt a.M., 1598.

———. *Theoria Vitae Aeternae. Historische Beschreibung desz gantzen Geheimnisses vom Ewigen Leben.* Hamburg, 1620.

Nigrinus, Georg. *Apocalypsis. Die Offenbarunge Sanct Johannis des Apostels vnd Euangelisten.* . . . Ursel, 1573.

———. *Ein wolgegründe Rechnung vnd Zeitregister, von anfang der Welt, die Jarzal vnd Zeit begreiffend bis auff vns.* . . . Ursel, 1570.

Nosseni, Joh. Mar. *Chronologia vnd Beschreibung des grossen Bildes, welches dem König Nebukadnezar im Traum erschienen.* Dresden, 1611.

[Offenbahrungen]. *Engelische Erscheinungen, Offenbahrungen vnd Gesichte.* . . . N.p., 1630.

Orphanus, Nicolaus. *Ivdicivm Astrologicvm. Von dem Tausend, Fünffhundert, Vier vnd siebenzigsten Jare, bis in das 1578. Jar.* . . . [Nuremberg?, c. 1573].

———. *Ivdicivm Astrologicvm. Auff die Jahr . . . 1577. vnd 1578.* Nuremberg, [c. 1576].

Osiander, Andreas. *Sant Hildegardten weissagung vber die Papisten, vnd genanten geistlichen, wilcher erfüllung zu unsern zeiten hat angefangen, vnd volzogen sol werden.* Nuremberg, 1527.

———. *Vermütung von den letzten Zeiten, vnd dem Ende der Welt, aus der heiligen Schrifft gezogen.* Nuremberg, 1545. Latin ed. *Coniecturae de ultimis temporibus, ac de fine mundi, ex sacris literis* . . . Nuremberg, 1544.

———. *Eyn wunderliche Weyssagung von der Bapstum, wie es ihm bis an das Ende der Welt gehen sol.* . . . Nuremberg, 1527.

Osiander, Lucas. *Bawren-postille, Dass ist.* . . . Tübingen, 1601.

———. *Bedencken, Ob der newe Bäpstliche Kalender ein Nohtturfft bey der Christenheit seye.* . . . Heidelberg, 1584.

Otho, Anton [Antonius Otho Hertzberger]. *Etliche Propheceysprüche D. Martini Lutheri, Des dritten Elias.* N.p., 1552.

Otto, Johann. *Calculator. Ein newes, liebliches, vnd nutzliches ausgerechnetes Rechenbuch.* . . . Leipzig, 1579, 1580.

Paracelsus, Theophrastus. *Prognostication auff xxiiij jar zukünfftig, durch den hochgelerten Doctorem Paracelsum.* Augsburg, 1536. Also ed. by A. Ritter in *Collectio vaticiniorum,* Berlin, 1923.

———. *Propheceyung, Doct. Philippi Theophrasti Paracelsi, Anno 1546. Vom Löwen ausz Mitternacht.* N.p., 1631.

Particlius, Simeon. *Eine newe, jedermannigliche sehr nützliche Himlische Sternwarnung, von sehr grossen schrecklichen Verenderungen.* . . . Amsterdam, 1631.

Pastoris, Heinrich. *Practica Teutsch.* N.p., 1524.

Paul, Elchanan. *Mysterium novum. ein neu herrlich Beweiss aus den prophetischen Schriften nach der Hebräer Cabala, dass der Name Jesus Christus Gottes Sohn . . . in den fürnehmsten Prophezeiungen von Messia verdeckt bedeutet.* Helmstedt, 1580.

Pauli, Simon. *Bildnus vnd Gestalt einer erschrecklichen vnnatürlichen . . . Geburt eines Kindes.* . . . Rostock, 1578.

———. *Postilla.* Magdeburg, 1574.

Peucer, Caspar [ed.]. *Chronica Carionis.* Wittenberg, 1573.
————. *Commentarius de praecipvis generibus divinationum. . . .* Wittenberg, 1580.
Pfeffinger, Johann. *Christliche gewisse deutung der zeichen, die für vnd in diesem 1562. Jar geschehen.* Leipzig, 1562.
Pflaum, Jacob. *Etliche weissagung durch den hochgelarten Astronomum Jacob Pflawmen zu Vlm zusamen getragen, Anno M.CCCCC.* Wittenberg, 1532.
Pfriem, Hans. *Ein gar lustig merklich Geticht wider den unzeyttigen Fürwitz, göttliche Geheymnussen zuerforschen.* N.p., n.d.
Pistorius, Bartholomaeus. *Teutsche Rithmi von Betrachtung dess Jüngsten gerichts. . . .* N.p., 1604.
Pistorius, Johann. *Ars cabalistica.* Basel, 1587.
Plieninger, Lambertus Floridus. *Kurtz Bedencken Von der Emendation dess Jars, durch Babst Gregorium den XIII fürgenomen. . . .* Strassburg, 1583.
Pollio, Lucas. *Vom Jüngsten Gericht, Sechss Fasten Predigten, Anno MDLXXX.* Nuremberg, 1601.
————. *Vom Jüngsten Gericht, 10 Fasten Predigten.* Nuremberg, [c. 1601].
Portantius, I. *Kurtze Erklerung, von den eigenschafften dess grossen . . . Cometen. . . .* Nuremberg, 1577.
[Postilion]. *Postilion: Oder Englische Posaun der Heimsuchung. . . .* N.p., 1630.
Poyssel, Eustachius. *Apocal. 11. Gar lange Zeit, die Heylig Stadt, Der Antechrist vertreten hatt. . . .* N.p., 1590.
————. *Die Braut dess Lambs, Das Himlische Newe Jerusalem. . . .* N.p., 1591.
————. *Das dreyzehende Capitel der Offenbarung Johannis, mit kurtzer Ausslegung.* N.p., 1589.
————. *Das dritte Theyl, Von Christi vnnd Antechristi Ostern. . . .* N.p., 1589.
————. *Eustachii Poyssels VII. Tractetlein.* N.p., 1594. Also published as *Etliche tractetlein, jetziger zeit nützlich vnd nötig zu lesen. . . .* N.p., 1595.
————. *Luc. 21. Wenn ihr aber sehen werdet Jerusalem belegert mit einem Heer. . . .* N.p., 1590.
————. *Die Schlüssel David, Esaie: 22. Apocalip: 3.* N.p., 1594.
————. [probable author]. *Der von Gott bestimpten Zahlen dess Antichrists, 1260. endlicher Aussgang vnd Ende. . . .* N.p., 1608.
————. [probable author]. *Magischer Beweiss Alles dess jenigen, was der Autor dieses Tractats, seydhero des . . . 1583. Jahrs . . . hat aussgehen lassen.* N.p., 1609.
[Practica]. *Newe vnd trewe Baurhaffte vnnd jmmer Daurhaffte Practica . . . Prognostica vnd Wetterbuch. . . .* N.p., 1611.
Praelius, Thomas [pseudonym?]. *Böhmischer Warheitsager. Dass ist, Wahrer vnd Klarer beweiss, das es mit Böhmen also ergehen müssen. . . .* N.p., 1621.
Praetorius, Johann. *Narratio Oder Historische erzelung dern Cometen. . . .* Nuremberg, 1578.

Praetorius, Stefan. *58. Schöne, Ausserlesene, Geist- vnd Trostreiche Tractätlein, Von der gülden Zeit* ... [ed. Johann Arndt]. Lüneburg, 1622.

[Prodromus]. *Prodromus Evangelij Aeterni seu Chilias Sancta. Vortrab des Ewigen Evangelij* ... *durch den Kleinen, gewürdigten Diener* ... *zu Philadelphia.* ... N.p., 1625.

[Prognostica]. *Prognostica Von gefährlichen verenderungen in dieser Welt, welche in diesem 1628. Jar angehen, vnd biss auff 1640. sich erstrecken sollen.* N.p., 1628.

———. *Prognostica. Das sind etzliche vor vnd anzeigungen aller Jaren* ... *bis an das ende der Welt.* ... N.p., 1586.

[Prognosticon]. *Nova Novorvm. Ein new Prognosticon aus Calabria, auff das 87. Jahre* ... *biss ins künfftige 1588.* ... Cologne, c. 1585.

———. *Prognosticon, Das ist, Weissagung Auff das Jahr* ... *M.DC.XX.* Prague, 1620.

———. *Prognosticon, Wegen Des künfftigen Auszgang vnd Effect. Dess Leipzigischen Schluss. Sampt angeheffter Vermahnung an die Evangelischer Stände.* N.p., 1631.

———. *Prognosticon vnd Weyssagung der fürnemsten dingen so vom M.D.LXIIII. Jar biss auff das M.D.C.VII. sich zutragen werden, auss* ... *Cypriani Leouicij, vnd auss dem Prognostico Samuelis Syderocratis, gezogen vnd zusamen gestelt.* N.p., [c. 1564].

Prolaeus, Andreas. *Babylon. Das ist: Theologischer Schrifftmassiger Erklärung des sechsten General-Gesichtes der heiligen geheimen Offenbahrung S. Johannis.* ... Leipzig, 1632.

[Prophecey]. *Propheceien vnd Weissagungen. Vergangne, Gegenwertige, vnd Künfftige ding* ... *Als: Doctoris Paracelsi, Johann Lichtenbergers, M. Josephi Grünpeck, Joan. Carionis Der sibyllen, vnd anderer.* Augsburg, [c. 1549]. Reissued in revised and expanded form in 1620 under the title *Propheceyen Vnd Weissagungen jetzt gegenwertig vnd künfftige sachen, Geschicht vnd Zufäll, biss zum Ende der Welt ankündend. Als nemblich: M. Johann Lichtenbergers, M. Josephi Grunpeck, Der Sibyllen, vnd vil anderer.* N.p., 1620. Also as *Trübsal der gantzen Welt auch Veränderung vieler Herrschafft vnd Regimenten.* N.p., 1620.

———. *Prophecey vnd Weissagungen. Ein Vorwarnung dreier Fromen, fürsichtigen Weysen Männern.* ... Erfurt, 1586.

[Propheceyhung]. *Wunderbarliche Propheceyhung vnd weissagung eines sibenbürgischen Propheten, betreffende was sich im 1630. Jahr, mit den vornembsten Potentaten der Welt* ... *zutragen werde.* Hermanstadt in Siebenburgen(?), 1630.

[Propheceyung]. *Eine Warhafftige vnd Gewisse Propheceyung, Welche in Westphalen in einem Kloster Offenbruck, auff Bergament geschrieben* ... *gefunden ist.* ... Lemgo, 1592.

[Propheceyungen]. *Zwo warhafftige Propheceyungen von zukünfftigen dingen. Die erste, von einem newen Propheten* ... *Die andere Von einem Fewrigē Sternen.* ... N.p., 1586.

[Prophezeyung]. *Warhaffte Prophezeyung Dreyer Im Bapstumb Hochberümbter Fürtrefflicher Männer, Welche lange vor D. Luthers Seel: zeiten, von* ... *Verenderungen im Römischen Reich, Geweissaget.* ... N.p., 1632.

Pscherer, Lorentz. *Trost vnd Schrecken. Das ist: Göttliche Offenbahrügen, Geschichte vnd Propheceyungen, so Lorentz Pscherer ein Gottsfürchtiger Schulmeister . . . gehabt.* N.p., 1630.

Rasch, Johann. *Gegenpractic, Wider etliche aussgangen Weissag, Prognostic vnd Schrifften . . .* Munich, 1584.

——. *New Losstag. Nutzliche bedencken vnd vnterscheidung der pöslischen alten Losstag.* Rorschach am Bodensee, 1590.

——. *Practica Auff das grosswunder Schaltjar. 1588.* Munich, 1587; another ed. 1588.

——. *Weissag der Zeit. Allgemaine Himels vnd Weldpractic. . . .* [Munich?], 1596.

Reinmann, Leonhard. *Practica vber die grossen vnd manigfeltigen Coniunction der Planeten, die im jar M.D.XXiiij. erscheinen, vñ vngezweiffelt vil wunderparlicher ding geperen werden.* Nuremberg, 1523.

Remmelin, Johann Ludwig. *Formatio figurati numeri miraculosa.* Augsburg, 1617.

——. *Mysterium arithmeticum, sive cabalistica & philosophica inventio. . . .* Nuremberg, 1615.

Rensberger, Nicolaus. *Astronomia Teutsch.* Augsburg, 1569.

Reusner, Elias. *Commentariolum de vera annorum mundi ad natum Christum supputatione: chronologiae. . . .* Jena, 1600.

——. *Isagoges historicae libri duo.* Jena, 1600.

Reymaldus, Christianus. *Teutscher Nation Newer Post-Reuter, Welcher Berichtet Von dem Zustand, beyde an Fried vnd Vnfried, Gesundheit vnd Kranckheit. . . .* N.p., 1639.

Reymers [Raimarus Ursus], Nicolas. *Chronologische, Gewisse vnd vnwiderlegliche Beweisung, auss heiliger Gottlicher Schrifft vnd heiligen Vättern, dass die Welt vergehen, vnd der Jüngste tag kommen werd, innerhalb 77. Jaren: Anzurechnen von disem jetzlauffenden Jar Christi 1596. . . .* Nuremberg, 1606.

——. *Chronotheatrum.* Prague, 1597.

Rhelasus, Theodorus [Joh. Hasler?]. *Fröliche Practick Auff das 1588. Jar, wider aller alten Astrologen langher Practicirte meinunge, gerichtet. . . .* [Basel?], 1588.

Richter, Balthassar. *Buch der heimlichen offenbarung Ioannis.* Leipzig, 1602.

Ritter, Albert [ed.]. *Collectio vaticiniorum das ist, Propheceien vnd Weissagungen Vergangene, Gegenwartige vnd Kunfftige Sachen. . . .* Berlin, 1923. Reprinted from a collection from c. 1550.

Rober, Martin. *Im Christlichen Evangelischen Lutherischen Jubel Jahr I. Ein schön Braut Lied II. Das rechte Hochzeit Kleid III. Die Päbstische Grewel vnd Menschen Tand. . . .* Halle, 1618.

Rodtbart, Christoph. *Extremum iudicium. Die gantze Lehr vom Jüngsten Tag. . . .* Hildesheim, 1605.

Roeslin, Helisaeus. *Gründliche, Warhafftige vnnd rechtmessige Erklerung, der Charactern vñ Buchstaben, so vff dem in Norwegen gefangnen Hering gestanden. . . .* N.p., 1588.

——. *Historischer, Politischer vnd Astronomischer naturlicher Discurs*

Von heutiger zeit Beschaffenheit, Wesen vnd Stand der Christenheit, vnd wie es künfftig in derselben ergehn werde. . . . Strassburg, 1609.
———. *Theoria nova coelestium.* . . . Strassburg, 1578.
Rollenhagen, Georg. *Der Hinckende Both, schlahe jhn die Gicht, Ist komen bringt viel andern bericht, Dann wir zuuorn, vff diese Reim, Mit Warheit nicht berichtet sein.* N.p., 1589.
Rose, Andreas. *Practica oder Prognosticon, auff das M.D.LXXXV. Jar.* . . . N.p., c. 1584.
Rost, Georg. *Gründtlicher Bericht von den Newen Photinianern.* . . . Magdeburg, 1613.
———. *Heldenbuch vom Rosengarten. Oder Gründlicher vnd Apologetischer Bericht von den Newen Himlischen Propheten, Rosenkreutzern, Chiliasten vnd Enthusiasten.* . . . Rostock, 1622.
———. *Ninivitisch Deutschland, Welchem der Prophet Jonas Schwerdt, Hunger, Pestilentz, vnd den endlichen Vntergang ankündiget.* . . . Lübeck, 1625.
———. *Prognosticon Theologicon Oder Theologische Weissagung, Vom Jüngsten Tage.* . . . Rostock, 1620.
———. *Reformation. Das ist: Bericht, auff eine dieser zeit schwebende hochwichtige Frage: Was von der allgemeinen Reformation der Kirchen . . . zu halten seye?* Rostock, 1626.
———. *Theologische Weissagung von der Zweifachen Kirchen Reformation.* Rostock, 1625.
Rudolph, Christoff. *Behend vnnd Hubsch Rechnung durch die kunstlichen regeln Algebre—so gemeincklich die Coss geneñt werden.* [Vienna?, c. 1524].
———. *Künstliche Rechnung mit der Ziffer.* . . . Nuremberg, 1526, 1532.
Ruppelich, Georg. *Glaubens Büchlein, Das ist, bestendige Versicherung vnsers . . . Glaubens, auff die zeit dess Jüngsten Tags gerichtet.* . . . Frankfurt a.O., 1582.
Sachse, Michael. *Acht Predigten . . . von der letzten Posaunen Gottes.* Leipzig, 1598.
———. *Newe Keyser Chronica.* Magdeburg, 1615.
Sagan, Johannem Stralen. *Wunderglöcklein Aus dem Propheten Joel . . . angeleutet.* . . . Wittenberg, 1630.
Salmuth, Johann. *Zwo vnterschiedene Predigten: Von dem Evangelischen Jubelfest.* Amberg, 1617.
Saubert, Johann. *Betrachtung der künfftigen Ewigkeit.* . . . Nuremberg, 1639.
———. *Lutherus propheta Germaniae.* Nuremberg, 1632.
Schadaeus, Oseas. *Eine dreyfache, kurtze, vnd einfältige Betrachtung, Desz herrlichen Wundergesichts der dreyen Sonnen.* . . . Strassburg, 1622.
Schaerer, Melchior. *Verantwortung vnd Rettung der Argumenten vnd Vrsachen, welche M. Melchior Scherer . . . eingeführet: Wider den Hochgelehrten Herrn Philippum Feselium.* . . . N.p., 1611.
Schaller, Daniel. *Herolt. Aussgesandt In allen Landen offendtlich zuuerkündigen vnnd auszuruffen. Das diese Weldt mit Irem wesen bald vergehen werde.* . . . Magdeburg, 1595.

————. *Ein New Theologisch Prognosticon auff das 89. vnd folgende Jar.* . . . Magdeburg, 1589.

————. *Theologischer Heroldt. In Alle Lande vnd vier winckel der Weldt, Aussgesandt.* . . . Magdeburg, 1604.

————. *Vier Advents Predigten.* Magdeburg, 1612.

————. *Vom Ende der Welt. Aus Prophetischer vnnd Apostolischer Schrifft bericht* . . . *Wider den Newen Propheten Adolbertum Termopedium.* Magdeburg, 1599.

Schedel, Hartmann. *Liber chronicarum.* Nuremberg, 1493.

Schelhammer, Johann. *Dreitzehen Trostliche Predigten, vber den ein vnd neuntzigsten Psalm.* . . . Hamburg, 1597.

Schickhart, Philipp. *AbendLiecht. Auss dem Propheten Sacharia vierzehenden Capitel. Vmb den Abend würdts Liecht sein.* Tübingen, 1617.

Schmidt, Erasmus. *Prodromus Conjunctionis Magnae, anno 1623. futurae. Das ist.* . . . Wittenberg, 1619.

Schmidt, Philipp. *Geistreiche Prophetische weissagungen, die wir innerhalb Sechzig vnd Siebentzig Jahren ipso Eventu augenscheinlich in der Christenheit erfüllet gesehen, vnd was wir* . . . *noch in Teutschland zugewarten.* . . . Wittenberg, 1619; another, slightly revised ed. Wittenberg, 1629. The work, which contained prophecies of Luther, N. Selneccer, and P. Nicolai, had apparently been edited and issued at Wittenberg in 1615 by one Philipp Fabri.

Schönwald, Abr. *Das Buch der versiegelten Rede des Propheten Daniels am XII. vnd Offenbahrung Johannis am XIII.* Küstrin, [c. 1572].

Schoppe, Andreas. *Christliche vnnd Nötige Warnung für dem erdichten Lügen Geist der falschen Propheten vnd fürwitzigen Leute, so die gewisse zeit des jüngsten Tages auszurechnen, zu nennen vnd zu Weissagen sich bemühen.* . . . Wittenberg, 1596.

Schopper, Jacob. *Christliche Ausslegung Der Schonen Weissagung dess H. Propheten Danielis, auss seinem 9. Capitel, von den 70. Wochen.* . . . Nuremberg, 1615.

Schrot, Martin. *Apocalypsis. Ain frewden geschray über das gefallen Bapstumb so yetz diser zeit durch Gottes wort vnd schwerdt überwunden ist.* N.p., n.d.

Schuler, Gervasius. *Ein christlicher trostspruch von der Aufferstehung am jüngsten tag.* N.p., 1543.

Schulin, Johann. *Kurtz Prognosticon Astrologicvm, Oder Practica Deutsch. Auff das Jar* . . . *M.D.LXXXV.* N.p., [1584?].

Schütz, Johann. *Newe Zeitung vnd Wunderpredig. Dadurch eine Arme einfoltige verachte Jungfraw* . . . *alle stende zur busse vnd besserung jres sündlichen lebens vermanet hat.* Erfurt, 1560.

Schwabe [Sueuus], Sigismund. *Arithmetica Historica. Die Löbliche Rechenkunst.* . . . Breslau, 1593.

————. *Cometen, Was sie für grosse Wunder vnd schreckliche ding zu bedeuten, vnd ankündigen pflegen.* . . . Görlitz, 1578.

————. *Speculum Mundi indurati. Spiegel der verstockten Welt. An den Zehen Egyptischen Plagen, Allen Menschen zur trewen Warnung furgestelt.* . . . Görlitz, 1582.

―――. *Spiegel des Jüngsten Gerichts.* Görlitz, 1585.

Scultetus, Abraham. *Evangelische Jubel Jahrs Predig.* Amberg, 1618.

Scultetus, Bartholomaeus. *Astronomische vnd natürliche Beschreibung von Des grossen vnd wunderbaren Cometen . . . 1577.* Görlitz, 1578.

―――. *Calendarivm Perpetvvm omnivm hvivs mvndi annorvm Christi directvs et extractvs . . . Almanach vñ Kirchenrechnung aller Jahr. . . .* Görlitz, 1574; another ed. 1580.

―――. *Von dem Römischen Calender. . . .* Görlitz, 1580.

[Secretis]. *De Secretis creationis. Von der heimligkeit der Schöpffung aller ding.* Strassburg, 1575.

Seidel, Moritz. *Trewhertzige Warnung an alle fromme Christen, dass sie sich auff schierkommenden Jüngsten Tag rüsten sollen. . . .* N.p., 1592.

Selnecker, Nicolas. *Der Prophet Daniel, vnd die Offenbarung Johannis.* N.p., 1567.

Sever[us], Paul[us]. *Practica, Newe Zeytunge, von der bedeutung, die da folgen werden, auss den obgemelten Constellation vnd der Finsternissen, von wegen jetzt vnserer schweren Sünden.* Nuremberg, [c. 1560].

―――. *Prophezeyung vnnd Weissagung, von dem M.D.LX. Jar, Biss auff das M.D.LXX. Jar werendt. . . .* N.p., [c. 1560].

Sleidanus, Ioannes. *De quatuor summis imperiis lib. III.* Strassburg, 1556.

Spanheim, Wigand. *Deutung vnnd Spiegel dess 1588 Jahrs vnd dieser letzten trübseligen Zeit. . . .* Zurich, 1588.

Specker, Melchior. *Von der Herrlichen Zükunfft Jesu Christi, zum Jüngsten Gericht. Vnd was im selben vnnd darnach geschehen werde. . . .* Strassburg, 1555.

Spindler, Joh. *Tuba novissima Dei. Frag vnd Antwort.* Frankfurt a.M., 1626.

Staiger, Johannes. *Ein Schön Newes Lied, von der Weltlauff vorm Jüngsten Tag.* Ulm, [c. 1590].

Stathmion, Christopher. *Practica . . . biss Jar, M.D.LXXXV.* Nuremberg, 1584.

Stifel, Michael. *Arithmetica integra . . . cum praefatione Philippi Melanchthonis.* Nuremberg, 1544.

―――. *Bruder Michael Styfel Augustiner von Esslingen, Von der Christförmigen rechtgegrunden leer Doctoris Martini Luthers, ain überauss schönkünstlich Lied, sampt seyner nebenausslegung. In Bruder Veyten Thon.* Augsburg, 1522.

―――. *Deutsche Arithmetica.* Nuremberg, 1545.

―――. *Ein Rechenbüchlein Vom End Christi. Apocalypsis in Apocalypsin.* Wittenberg, 1532.

―――. *Ein sehr Wunderbarliche wortrechnung. . . .* N.p., 1553.

Stiller, Caspar. *Geistliche Practica Astrologica. Oder Kirchen-Calender. . . .* Leipzig, 1620.

Stilsov, Johann. ΟΥΡΑΝΟΠΠΙΤΙΑ. *Das ist: Kurtze Erörterung dess Zweiffels, ob der Himmel von Ptolomaei Zeit an biss hieher sich . . . gesencket haben könne. . . .* Erfurt, 1631.

Strigenitz, Gregor. *Laqveus Aucupis, Das ist, Sechs Adventspredigten Vom Fallstricke. . . .* Leipzig, 1614.

Studion, Simon. "Naometria, seu Nuda, et prima libri intus, et foris scripti per claven Davidis, et calamum Virgae similem apertio. . . ." Manuscript, Württembergische Landesbibliothek, Stuttgart.

Stumpf, Johannes. *Vom Jüngsten Tag vnnd der Zukunfft vnsers Herren Jesu Christi, auch von dem Antichristen, vnnd den Zeichen vor dem letzten Tag.* . . . Zurich, n.d.

Taurer, Ambrosius. *Bericht von mancherley schrecklichen Wunderzeichen die vns vom nahen Ende der Welt predigen.* Halle, 1592.

———. *Der Geistliche, Uberflüssig gnugsam ausschlagende Feigenbaum. Das ist . . . warnung, das der Jüngste tag nahe ist.* . . . N.p., 1594.

———. *Von der Grundsuppe der Welt.* Eisleben, 1588.

Termopedius, Adelbert. *Vom Anti-Christ auss Prophetischen vnd Apostolischen Schrifften, darinnen . . . ein gewisser Tag der Zukunfft Christi benennet wird.* N.p., 1598.

Teting, Nic. *Ein kurtze Sermon Vom Reich Gottes.* . . . N.p., 1625.

[Teutsch]. *Teutsch Astronomei. Von Art, eygenschafften, vnd wirckung.* . . . Frankfurt a.M., 1545.

[Teutschen]. *Der Teutschen Planet, Das ist: Nothwendige Betrachtung Der frembden Kriegswaffen in Teutschland.* . . . N.p., 1639.

[Teutscher]. *Teutscher Nation Newer Post-Reuter, Welcher Berichtet Von dem Zustand . . . des Menschlichen Leibes vnd Lebens Zufallen.* . . . N.p., 1639.

Theobald, Zacharias. *M. Zachariae Theobaldi Einfältiges Bedencken, Was von dem Bergfall zu halten, welcher sich in vnserer Nachtbarschafft . . . begeben.* . . . Nuremberg, 1625.

Thurneisser, Leonhardt. *Alter vnd newer corrigirter Allmanach vnd Schreib Kalender . . . auf dz Schaltjahr M.D.LXXXIIII.* Berlin, [c. 1583]. Thurneisser issued many such annual works.

———. *Astrologisch Prognosticon . . . 1594.* [Frankfurt a.M.?], 1594.

———. *Impletio, oder Erfüllung der verheissung.* . . . Nuremberg, 1581.

Tilner, Jacob. *Chronologische Zeit Rechnung, vnd gewisse Beweisung . . . das die Welt . . . vergehen, vnd der liebe Jüngste Tag jnnerhalb 44. Jahren . . . kommen werde.* [Halle?], 1613.

Timann, Johann. *Etliche warhafftige weissagungen, vnd fürneme spruche . . . Hern Doctor Martini Luthers, des dritten Helie.* . . . Magdeburg, 1552.

Tripet, Maximilian. *Prognosticon. Auff das Jar . . . M.D.XCV.* Augsburg, 1594.

Ursinus, Adam. *Kurtze Beschreibunge der . . . vnnatürlichen Wunderzeichen am Himmel, im 1568, 69 vnd 70. Jhare.* . . . Erfurt, 1570.

———. *Prognosticatio. Auff das M.D.LXXI. Jhar.* . . . Erfurt, [c. 1570].

Ursinus, Georg. *Warhafftige, Vnd Gründtliche beschreibung, aller Finsternissen . . . Conjunctiones vnd Oppositiones . . . Von dem 1576. Jar an . . . bis . . . 1600. Jar.* Magdeburg, 1575.

———. *Zwo Practicken, Vom 1582. Jar, biss man schreiben wirdt 1600. Jar . . . Die Ander weret biss man schreiben wirdt 1588. Jar.* Augsburg, [c. 1580].

Ursinus, Theodorus. *Sonderliche Propheceyungen Vom heiligen Römi-*

schen vnd Teutschen vnd vom Türckischen Reiche. . . . [Nuremberg?], 1605.

Uttenhofer, Caspar. *Judicium de nupero cometa astrologo-historicum.* Nuremberg, 1619.

Utzinger, Alexandrus. *Process Des Jüngsten Gerichts.* . . . Schmalkalden, 1589.

Vaget, Bernhard. *Christliche vnd Richtige Erklärung, oder Ausslegung des Siebenden, Neundten, Eilfften vnd Zwölfften Capit. Danielis.* . . . Hamburg, 1595.

Van Dülmen, Richard, ed. *Johann Valentin Andreae: Fama Fraternitatis (1614), Confessio Fraternitatis (1615), Chymische Hochzeit: Christiani Rosencreutz Anno 1459 (1616).* Stuttgart, 1973.

Wagner, Johann [pseudonym: Johann Plaustrarius]. *Prognosticon, Oder Weissagung auff diese jetzige Zeit.* . . . N.p., 1621.

————. *Schrifftmesige Offenbahrung vnd erklärung etlicher geheimer Figuren, so in dem 1621. jahr zu Prag . . . gefunden worden.* N.p., 1621.

————. *Wunder- vnd Figürliche Offenbahrung: Das ist: I. Vergleichung der Welt Anfang vnd Ende.* . . . N.p., 1620.

Waldner, Wolffgang. *Bericht Etlicher furnemsten Stücke, den Jüngsten tage, vnd was darauff folgen wirdt, betreffend.* . . . Nuremberg, 1567.

————. *Newe Zeyttung. Einer wunderbarlichen Historien.* . . . Nuremberg, 1558.

Walther, Georg. *Prophezeiungen D. Martini Lutheri. Zur erinnerung vnd anreitzung zur Christlichen Busse.* . . . Wittenberg, 1559.

Warner, Johann. *Beschreibung etzlicher Visionen, Welche ihm sind von Gott, wegen des Zustandes der Lutherischen Kirchen . . . gezeiget worden.* . . . N.p., 1638.

[Warnung]. *Trewhertzige Warnung an des Heiligen Römischen Reichs Adeler, vnnd Teutscher Nation Liebhabende Patrioten.* . . . N.p., 1619.

Wehe, S. *Expositio Famae Sidereae novae Faulhaberianae, Das ist Statliche Aussputzung dess . . . Faulhaberischen Ausssschreibens.* Ulm, [c. 1619].

[Weigel, Valentin?]. *"Astrology Theologized." The Spiritual Hermeneutics of Astrology and Holy Writ,* ed. Anna Bonus Kingsford. London, 1886.

————. *Der güldene Griff, Alle Dinge ohne Irrthumb zu erkennen.* Hall, 1613.

Weinrich, Martin. *De ortu monstrorum commentarius.* N.p., 1595.

Weiss, Nicolaus. *Practica auff Zehen Jar . . . biss auff das 1588. Jar werende.* . . . N.p., 1578.

————. *Prognosticon Astrologicvm. Von dem 1572. bis auff das 1588. Jar wehrende.* . . . Vienna, [c. 1571]; other eds. Dresden, 1572, and Frankfurt a.M., 1573.

————. *Prognosticon: Von dem 1575. Jahr an, werende bis in das 1580. Jar.* . . . N.p., [c. 1575].

[Weissagung]. *Geistreiche Weissagung, von dem Grossen Wunderstern . . . 1572 . . . dessen Allermeiste Würckungen in diesem 1632. Jahr sich ereygnen.* N.p., 1632.

[Weyssagungen]. *Weyssagungen Dess Göttlichen Propheten Joachimi gewesten Abbts zu Hor in Calabria, von dem künfftigen Zustand der gantzen Welt.* . . . N.p., 1633.

Wigand, Joh. *Predigt . . . von den letzten Tagen vnd veränderung der Welt.* Jena, 1571.

Wilhelm, Balthasar. *Practica oder Prenostication auff tzuokunfftig tzythe, auss der heyligen schrifft getzogenn.* N.p., [c. 1524].

Wilhelm, Hieronymus. *Prognosticon oder Practica, auff das M.D.LXXI. Jar. . . .* N.p., [c. 1570].

Winand, Heinrich. *Annae Revolvtiones. Aus rechter natürlicher Kunst der Astrology von dem Jare 1593. an, biss an das ende des 1606. werende Pronostication. . . .* Magdeburg, 1593.

―――. *Consilivm Olympicvm. Reichstag der Sieben Firmamentischen Fürsten . . . auff das Jar M.D.LXXXX.* Magdeburg, [c. 1589].

―――. *Menstrvae Revolutiones. Der XII Monaten . . . M.D.XCIIII.* Magdeburg, [c. 1593].

Winckelmann, Johann. *Commentarius in Apocalypsin.* Frankfurt a.M., 1590.

Winckler, Nicholas Eberhard. *Practica . . . auff . . . M.DC.VI.* Nuremberg, [c. 1605]. Many similar works by this author appeared in the early seventeenth century.

Winckler, Nicolaus. *Bedencken Von Künfftiger verenderung Weltlicher Policey, vnd Ende der Welt, auss heyliger Göttlicher Schrifft vnnd Patribus, auch auss dem Lauff der Natur. . . .* Augsburg, [c. 1582].

―――. *Practica auff das Jar . . . M.D.LXXXIIII.* Augsburg, [c. 1583]. Winckler published a similar work for almost every year in the 1570s and 1580s.

[Wittenberg faculty]. *Auszführliche vnnd Gründliche Wiederlegung Des Deutzschen Arianischen Catechismi Welcher zu Rackaw in Polen anno 1608 gedruckt. . . .* Wittenberg, 1620.

Wolf, Johann. *Lectiones memorabiles et reconditae.* Frankfurt a.M., 1671; first ed. Lauingen, 1600.

Wolfhart, Barthol. *Vom jüngsten Tage.* N.p., 1563.

Wolther, Johann. *Aureum Johannis Woltheri Peinensis Saxonis: Das Ist: Gulden Arch, Darinn der wahre Verstand vnd Einhalt der wichtigen Geheimnussen, Wörter vnd Zahlen . . . gefunden wird. . . .* Rostock, 1623.

―――. *Chronologia Oder Zeit vnd Jahrrechnung. . . .* Königsberg, 1611.

―――. *Geistreiche vnd wolgegründte Ausslegung vber die heimliche Offenbahrung Johannis Evangelistae, vnd das zwölffte Capitel Danielis. . . .* Rostock, 1629.

[Wunder]. *Christliche Gedancken, worfür man, dass Wunder vnd Zeichen . . . dieses 1630. Jahrs . . . erschienen* Nuremberg, [c. 1630].

[Wunder-buch]. *Göttliches Wunder-Buch, Darinnen auffgezeichnet vnd geschrieben stehen I. Himlische Offenbahrungen vnd Gesichte . . . II. Propheceyungen. . . .* N.p., 1630.

[Wunder-Sterns]. *Eigendliche Anmerckungen, Des im . . . 1664sten Jahres erschienenen . . . Wunder-Sterns.* N.p., [c. 1665].

[Wunderzeichen]. *Ein gar wunderbarlich vnd seltzam wunderzeichen vnnd verenderung der Sonnen. . . .* N.p., 1572.

[Zeichen]. *Gründtliche vnd warhaftige Bericht, von dem Erschrecklichen vnd Wunderbarlichen Zeichen . . . zwischen Eissleben vnd Mansfelt. . . .* Erfurt, [c. 1561].
———. *Sechs vnnd dreissig Zeichen vor dem Jüngsten Tag, so vorher lauffen.* N.p., 1592.
[Zeittung]. *Newe Zeittung Vom schröcklichen Erdbidm . . . dess 1590. Jars, zu Wien in Oesterreich geschehen. . . .* N.p., 1591.
———. *Warhafftige Neuwe Zeittung. . . .* Augsburg, 1564.
[Zeitung]. *Klägliche newe Zeitung.* Eisleben, n.d.
———. *Newe Zeitung: Eine Warhafftige Historia, so sich am heiligen Ostertage dieses L.xxxj. Jahrs . . . begeben vnd zugetragen.* Schweinfurt, 1581. A report by two pastors, Johann Reinhard and Eberhard Döberlein.
———. *Newe Zeitung vnd Wunderpredig. Dadurch eine Arme einfeltige verachte Jungfraw. . . .* See under Schütz, Johann.
———. *Waarhaffte Zeitung von einem Newen Propheten. . . .* Erfurt, 1626.
[Zeitungen]. *Vier wahre Zeitungen.* Erfurt, 1625.
———. *Zwo warhafftigen newe Zeitungen . . . Sampt Einer Christlichen, hochnothwendigen erinnerung an alle Christenmenschen, zu diesen letzten betrübten zeiten. . . .* Rotenburg, 1623.
[Zeychen]. *Im M.D.Liii. Jar den xi. Junij, ist dis gesicht, oder zeychen . . . gesehen worden. . . .* Nuremberg, 1554.
[Zeyttung]. *Newe Zeyttung. Einer wunderbarlichen Historien von Zweyen Meidlein, so in jrer Kranckheyt seltzam ding reden. Sambt einer . . . Erinnerung D. Martini Lutheri. . . .* N.p., n.d.
[Zeytung]. *Newe Zeytung. Von einem erschröcklichen Gesicht vnd Wunderzeichen . . . von den Hochgelerten der löblichen Vniversitet Wittenberg, am Himel gesehen. . . .* [Wittenberg?, c. 1562].
———. *Newe Zeytung, Von dem Grausamen . . . jamer . . . inn der gewaltigen statt Venedig . . . Sampt einer trewen warnung an das Teutsche Landt.* Frankfurt, 1570.
Ziegler, Christopher. *Iubilaeus Evangelicus, Evangelisch Jubel Jahr, Das ist: Lutherisch Frewden- vnd DankFest. . . .* Leipzig, 1617.
Ziegler [Ciegler], Georg. *Weltspiegel, Darin gehandelt wird, von der Welt Leben, Wesen, vnd Vnbeständigkeit.* Lüneburg, 1637.
[Zustand]. *Elender, betrübter Zustand. Das ist: Genawe Ausrechnungen . . . Vom Kriege . . . Todt . . . Pestilentz . . . Hungersnoth. . . .* N.p., 1630.
Zwingli, Ulrich. *Commentary on True and False Religion.* Trans. S. M. Jackson. Philadelphia, 1929.
———. *Huldreich Zwinglis sämtliche Werke,* in *Corpus reformatorum,* vol. 88ff. Berlin, Leipzig, and Zurich, 1905–.

Secondary Sources

Alexander, Paul J. *The Byzantine Apocalyptic Tradition.* Berkeley, 1985.
Allen, Don Cameron. *The Star-Crossed Renaissance.* New York, 1966.

Althaus, Paul. *Die letzten Dinge: Lehrbuch der Eschatologie.* Gütersloh, 1933.
————. "Luthers Gedanken über die letzten Dinge," *Luther-Jahrbuch* 23 (1941), 9–34.
————. "Luthers Wort vom Ende und Ziel der Geschichte," *Luther Mitteilungen der Luthergesellschaft* (1958), pp. 98–105.
Andreas, Willy. *Deutschland vor der Reformation: Eine Zeitenwende.* Stuttgart and Berlin, 1932.
Arnold, Gottfried. *Histoire und Beschreibung der Mystischen Theologie.* Frankfurt a.M., 1703; reprinted Bad Cannstatt, 1969.
————. *Unpartheyische Kirchen und Ketzerhistorie.* Frankfurt a.M., 1699.
Asendorf, Ulrich. *Eschatologie bei Luther.* Göttingen, 1967.
Auerbach, Erich. *Mimesis: The Representation of Reality in Western Literature.* Princeton, 1953.
Bainton, Roland H. "The Joachimite Prophecy: Osiander and Sachs," in Bainton, *Studies on the Reformation,* pp. 62–66. Boston, 1963.
————. *The Reformation of the Sixteenth Century.* Boston, 1952.
Baker, J. Wayne. *Heinrich Bullinger and the Covenant: The Other Reformed Tradition.* Athens, Ohio, 1980.
Ball, Bryan W. *A Great Expectation: Eschatological Thought in English Protestantism to 1660.* Leiden, 1975.
Barkun, Michael. *Disaster and the Millennium.* New Haven, 1974.
Bauckham, Richard, ed. *Tudor Apocalypse.* Oxford, 1978.
Baur, Ferdinand Christian. *Die christliche Gnosis, oder die christliche Religionsphilosophie in ihrer geschichtlichen Entwicklung.* Tübingen, 1835; reprinted Darmstadt, 1967.
Beck, Hermann. *Die Erbauungsliteratur der evangelischen Kirche Deutschlands: Erster Teil.* Erlangen, 1883.
Beer, Theobald. *Der fröhliche Wechsel und Streit. Grundzüge der Theologie Martin Luthers.* Einsiedeln, 1980.
Beisser, Friedrich. *Claritas scripturae bei Martin Luther.* Göttingen, 1966. Forschungen zur Kirchen- und Dogmengeschichte, no. 18.
Benz, Ernst. *Endzeiterwartung zwischen Ost und West: Studien zur christlichen Eschatologie.* Freiburg, 1973.
Berner, Felix. *Gustav Adolph: Der Löwe aus Mitternacht.* Stuttgart, 1982.
Beste, Wilhelm. *Die bedeutendsten Kanzelredner der lutherschen Kirche des Reformationszeitalters in Biographien und einer Auswahl ihrer Predigten.* Leipzig, 1856.
Bezold, Friedrich von. "Astrologische Geschichtskonstruction im Mittelalter," in *Aus Mittelalter und Renaissance. Kulturgeschichtliche Studien,* pp. 165–95. Munich and Berlin, 1918.
Bizer, Ernst. *Frühorthodoxie und Rationalismus.* Zurich, 1963.
Blau, J. L. *The Christian Interpretation of the Cabala in the Renaissance.* New York, 1944.
Bloch, Ernst. *Das Prinzip Hoffnung.* 2 vols. Frankfurt a.M., 1959.
Blumenberg, Hans. *Die kopernikanische Wende.* Frankfurt a.M., 1964.
Bohnstedt, John W. "The Infidel Scourge of God: The Turkish Menace as Seen by German Pamphleteers of the Reformation Era," *Transactions of the American Philosophical Society,* n.s., 58, part 9 (Dec. 1968).

Boll, Franz, Carl Bezold, and Wilhelm Gundel. *Sternglaube und Sterndeu-tung: Die Geschichte und das Wesen der Astrologie.* Darmstadt, 1966.
Bornkamm, Heinrich. *Luthers geistige Welt.* Gütersloh, 1960.
———. *Mystik, Spiritualismus und die Anfänge des Pietismus in Luther-tum.* Giessen, 1926.
———. "Renaissancemystik, Luther und Böhme," *Luther-Jahrbuch* 9 (1927), 156–97.
Bossuet, W. *The Antichrist Legend: A Chapter in Christian and Jewish Folklore.* London, 1896.
Bossy, John. *Christianity in the West 1400–1700.* Oxford and New York, 1985.
Boyle, Marjorie O'Rourke. *Rhetoric and Reform: Erasmus' Civil Dispute with Luther.* Cambridge and London, 1983.
———. "Stoic Luther: Paradoxical Sin and Necessity," *Archive for Refor-mation History* 73 (1982), 69–93.
Burke, Peter. *Popular Culture in Early Modern Europe.* New York, 1978.
———. *The Renaissance Sense of the Past.* New York, 1969.
Burr, George L. "The Year 1000 and the Antecedents of the Crusades," *American Historical Review* 6 (Apr. 1901), 429–39.
Büsser, Fritz. "Der Prophet-Gedanken zu Zwinglis Theologie," *Zwingliana* 13 (1969), 7–18.
Butler, E. M. *The Fortunes of Faust.* Cambridge, 1952.
———. *The Myth of the Magus.* Cambridge, 1948.
Caroti, Stefano. "Comete, portenti, causalità naturale e escatologia in Fi-lippo Melantone," in Zambelli, ed., *Scienze, credenze occulte, livelli di cultura,* pp. 393–426. Florence, 1982.
Charles, R. H. *Eschatology.* London, 1913.
Chrisman, Miriam. *Lay Culture, Learned Culture: Books and Social Change in Strasbourg, 1480–1599.* New Haven and London, 1982.
Christianson, Paul. *Reformers and Babylon: English Apocalyptic Visions from the Reformation to the Eve of the Civil War.* Toronto, 1978.
Clasen, Claus-Peter. *The Palatinate in European History 1555–1618.* Ox-ford, 1963.
Clemen, Otto. *Luther und die Volksfrömmigkeit seiner Zeit.* Dresden and Leipzig, 1938.
Cohn, Norman. *The Pursuit of the Millennium: Revolutionary Millenari-ans and Mystical Anarchists of the Middle Ages.* New York, 1961.
Crouzet, Denis. "La Représentation du temps à l'époque de la Ligue," *Re-vue historique* 270, no. 2 (1983), 297–388.
Cullmann, O. *Christ and Time.* London, 1951.
Czerny, Albin. "Der Humanist und Historiograph Kaiser Maximilians I. Joseph Grünpeck," *Archiv für österreichische Geschichte* 73 (1888), 315–64.
Davis, Natalie Zemon. "From Popular Religion to Religious Cultures," in Steven E. Ozment, ed., *Reformation Europe: A Guide to Research,* pp. 321–41. St. Louis, Mo., 1982.
Dillenberger, John. *Protestant Thought and Natural Science.* New York, 1960.

Döllinger, J. *Die Reformation, ihre innere Entwicklung und ihre Wir-kungen im Umfänge des Lutherischen Bekenntnisses.* Regensburg, 1846, 1848; reprinted Frankfurt a.M., 1962.

Duchhardt, Heinz. *Protestantisches Kaisertum und altes Reich.* Wiesbaden, 1977.

Easton, Stewart C. *Roger Bacon and His Search for a Universal Science: A Reconsideration of the Life and Work of Roger Bacon in the Light of His Own Stated Purposes.* New York, 1952.

Ebeling, Gerhard. *Luther: An Introduction to His Thought.* Philadelphia, 1970.

Edwards, Mark U., Jr. *Luther's Last Battles: Politics and Polemics, 1531–46.* Ithaca and London, 1983.

Eisenstein, Elizabeth L. "The Advent of Printing and the Problem of the Renaissance," *Past and Present* 45 (1969), 19–89.

———. *The Printing Press as an Agent of Change: Communications and Cultural Transformations in Early-Modern Europe.* Cambridge, 1979.

Elert, Werner. *Morphologie des Luthertums.* 2 vols. Munich, 1965.

Eliade, Mircea. *Cosmos and History: The Myth of the Eternal Return.* New York, 1954.

Emmerson, Richard Kenneth. *Antichrist in the Middle Ages: A Study of Medieval Apocalypticism, Art, and Literature.* Seattle, 1981.

Evans, R. J. W. *The Making of the Habsburg Monarchy 1550–1700: An Interpretation.* Oxford, 1979.

———. *Rudolf II and His World.* Oxford, 1973.

Fausel, Heinrich. *D. Martin Luther: Leben und Werk 1522 bis 1546.* Munich and Hamburg, 1966.

Febvre, Lucien, and Henri-Jean Martin. *L'Apparition du livre.* Paris, 1958.

Ferguson, A. B. *Clio Unbound: Perception of the Social and Cultural Past in Renaissance England.* Durham, N.C., 1979.

Festinger, Leon, Henry W. Riecken, and Stanley Schachter. *When Prophecy Fails.* Minneapolis, 1956.

Firth, Katharine R. *The Apocalyptic Tradition in Reformation Britain 1530–1645.* Oxford, 1979.

Focillon, Henri. *The Year 1000.* New York, 1969.

Frick, Karl R. H. *Licht und Finsternis: Gnostisch-theosophische und freimaurerisch-okkulte Geheimgesellschaften bis an die Wende zum 20. Jahrhundert.* Graz, 1975.

Friedrich, Johann. *Astrologie und Reformation. Oder Die Astrologen als Prediger der Reformation und Urheber des Bauernkrieges. Ein Beitrag zur Reformationsgeschichte.* Munich, 1864.

Froom, Leroy Edwin. *The Prophetic Faith of Our Fathers.* 4 vols. Washington, D.C., 1946–54.

Gawthrop, Richard, and Gerald Strauss. "Protestantism and Literacy in Early Modern Germany," *Past and Present* 104 (1984), 31–55.

Gilbert, Neal. *Renaissance Concepts of Method.* New York, 1960.

Goldammer, Kurt. "Paracelsische Eschatologie: Zum Verständnis der Anthropologie und Kosmologie Hohenheims," *Nova acta paracelsica* 5 (1948), 45–85; 6 (1952), 68–102.

354 Bibliography

Grafton, Anthony. *Joseph Scaliger: A Study in the History of Classical Scholarship. Vol. 1, Textual Criticism and Exegesis.* Oxford, 1983.

Grant, R. M. *Gnosticism and Early Christianity.* New York and London, 1966.

Grundmann, Herbert. *Studien über Joachim von Floris.* Leipzig and Berlin, 1927.

Haase, Roland. *Das Problem des Chiliasmus und der dreissigjährige Krieg.* Leipzig, 1933.

Haber, Francis C. *The Age of the World: Moses to Darwin.* Baltimore: 1959.

Haeusler, Martin. *Das Ende der Geschichte in der mittelalterlichen Weltchronistik.* Cologne, 1980.

Harbison, Craig. *The Last Judgment in Sixteenth-Century Northern Europe: A Study of the Relation Between Art and the Reformation.* New York and London, 1976.

Hartfelder, Karl. "Der Aberglaube Ph. Melanchthons," *Historische Taschenbuch,* ser. 8, 6 (1889), 237ff.

———. *Philipp Melanchthon als Praeceptor Germaniae.* Berlin, 1889.

Haydn, Hiram. *The Counter-Renaissance.* New York, 1950.

Headley, John M. *Luther's View of Church History.* New Haven, 1963.

Heist, William. *The Fifteen Signs before Doomsday.* East Lansing, Mich., 1952.

Hellman, Clarisse Doris. *The Comet of 1577: Its Place in the History of Astronomy.* New York, 1944.

Hendrix, Scott. *Luther and the Papacy: Stages in a Reformation Conflict.* Philadelphia, 1981.

Hillerdal, Gunnar. "Prophetische Züge in Luthers Geschichtsdeutung," *Studia Theologica* 7 (1953), 105–24.

Hirsch, E. *Die Reich-Gottes-Begriffe des neueren europäischen Denkens.* Göttingen, 1921.

———. *Die Theologie des Andreas Osiander und ihre geschichtlichen Voraussetzungen.* Göttingen, 1919.

Hofmann, Hans-Ulrich. *Luther und die Johannes-Apokalypse.* Tübingen, 1982.

Holl, Karl. "Die Kulturbedeutung der Reformation," in *Gesammelte Aufsätze zur Kirchengeschichte,* vol. 1. Tübingen, 1948. Translated by Karl and Barbara Hertz as *The Cultural Significance of the Reformation.* Cleveland, 1959.

———. "Martin Luther on Luther," trans. by H. C. Erik Midelfort, in Jaroslav Pelikan, ed., *Interpreters of Luther: Essays in Honor of Wilhelm Pauck,* pp. 9–34. Philadelphia, 1968.

Hossbach, Wilhelm. *Johann Valentin Andreae und sein Zeitalter.* Berlin, 1819.

Huppert, George. *The Idea of Perfect History: Historical Erudition and Historical Philosophy in Renaissance France.* Urbana, Ill., 1970.

Hutton, Sarah. "Aspects of the Concept of Time in Elizabethan and Jacobean England." Dissertation, Warburg Institute, Universty of London, 1979.

Imerti, Arthur D. "Editor's Introduction: The Making of a Heretic," in Giordano Bruno, *The Expulsion of the Triumphant Beast*, pp. 1–20. New Brunswick, 1964.

Janssen, Johannes. *A History of the German People at the Close of the Middle Ages*. 16 vols. London, 1900–1912.

Joachimsen, Paul. *Geschichtsauffassung und Geschichtsschreibung in Deutschland unter dem Einfluss des Humanismus*. Leipzig, 1910.

Jonas, Hans. *The Gnostic Religion: The Message of the Alien God and the Beginnings of Christianity*. Boston, 1958.

Kaltenbrunner, F. "Die Polemik über die Gregorianische Kalender Reform," *Sitzungsberichte der . . . Kais. Akad. Wiss.* 87 (Vienna, 1877).

Kaminsky, Howard. "Chiliasm and the Hussite Revolution," *Church History* 26 (1957), 43–71.

Kampers, Franz. *Die deutsche Kaiseridee in Prophetie und Sage*. Munich, 1896.

Kantzenbach, Friedrich Wilhelm. *Orthodoxie und Pietismus*. Gütersloh, 1966.

Kästner, A. G. *Geschichte der Mathematik*. Göttingen, 1796–1800.

Keller, Carl-A. "Das Problem des Bösen in Apokalyptik und Gnostik," in Martin Krause, ed., *Gnosis and Gnosticism: Papers Read at the Seventh International Conference on Patristic Studies*, pp. 70–90. Leiden, 1977.

Kelley, Donald R. *Foundations of Modern Historical Scholarship: Language, Law, and History in the French Renaissance*. New York and London, 1970.

Kermode, Frank. *The Sense of an Ending: Studies in the Theory of Fiction*. London, 1966.

Klein, Thomas. *Der Kampf um die zweite Reformation in Kursachsen 1586–91*. Cologne and Graz, 1962.

Klempt, Adalbert. *Die Säkularisierung der universalhistorischen Auffassung: Zum Wandel des Geschichtsdenkens im 16. und 17. Jahrhundert*. Göttingen, 1960.

Koepp, Wilhelm. *Johann Arndt: Eine Untersuchung über die Mystik im Luthertum*. Berlin, 1912.

Kolb, Robert. "Dynamics of Party Conflict in the Saxon Late Reformation: Gnesio-Lutherans vs. Philippists," *The Journal of Modern History* 49, no. 3 (Sept. 1977), 1289–1305.

———. *Nikolaus von Amsdorf (1483–1565): Popular Polemics in the Preservation of Luther's Legacy*. Nieuwkoop, 1978.

Korn, Dietrich. *Das Thema des jüngsten Tages in der deutschen Literatur des 17. Jahrhunderts*. Tübingen, 1957.

Koselleck, Reinhart. "Vergangene Zukunft der frühen Neuzeit," in Hans Barion et al., eds., *Epirrhosis: Festgabe für Carl Schmitt*. Berlin, 1968.

Kurtze, Dietrich. *Johannes Lichtenberger. Eine Studie zur Geschichte der Prophetie und Astrologie*. Lübeck, 1960.

———. "Prophecy and History: Lichtenberger's Forecasts of Events to Come. . . ; Their Reception and Diffusion," *Journal of the Warburg and Courtauld Institutes* 21 (1958), 63–85.

Lerner, Robert. "The Black Death and Western European Eschatological

Mentalities," *American Historical Review* 86, no. 3 (June 1981), 533–52.

———. "Medieval Prophecy and Religious Dissent," *Past and Present* 72 (Aug. 1976), 3ff.

———. *The Powers of Prophecy: The Cedar of Lebanon Vision from the Mongol Onslaught to the Dawn of the Enlightenment.* Berkeley, 1983.

———. "Refreshment of the Saints: The Time After Antichrist as a Station for Earthly Progress in Medieval Thought," *Traditio* 32 (1976), 97–144.

Leube, Hans. *Kalvinismus und Luthertum im Zeitalter der Orthodoxie.* Leipzig, 1928.

———. *Orthodoxie und Pietismus: Gesammelte Studien.* Bielefeld, 1975.

List, Günther. *Chiliastische Utopie und radikale Reformation: Die Erneuerung der Idee vom tausendjährigen Reich im 16. Jahrhundert.* Munich, 1973.

Locher, Gottfried W. "Huldrych Zwingli's Concept of History," in Locher, *Zwingli's Thought: New Perspectives*, pp. 95–120. Leiden, 1981.

Logan, A. H. B., and A. J. M. Wedderburn. *The New Testament and Gnosis: Essays in Honour of Robert McL. Wilson.* Edinburgh, 1983.

Löwith, Karl. *Meaning in History.* Chicago, 1949.

MacRae, George. "Apocalyptic Eschatology in Gnosticism," in David Hellholm, ed., *Apocalypticism in the Mediterranean World and the Near East*, pp. 317–25. Tübingen, 1983.

Martin, James Perry. *The Last Judgment in Protestant Theology from Orthodoxy to Ritschl.* Grand Rapids, 1963.

Martin, Peter. *Martin Luther und die Bilder zur Apokalypse.* Hamburg, 1983.

Mau, Rudolf. "Luthers Stellung zu den Türken," in Helmar Junghans, ed., *Leben und Werk Martin Luthers von 1526 bis 1546: Festgabe zu seinem 500. Geburtstag*, vol. 1, pp. 647–62. Berlin, 1983.

Maurer, Wilhelm. *Melanchthon-Studien.* Gütersloh, 1964.

Maurice, K., and O. Mayr, eds. *The Clockwork Universe: German Clocks and Automata, 1550–1650.* New York, 1980.

McGinn, Bernard. *Visions of the End: Apocalyptic Traditions in the Middle Ages.* New York, 1979.

McGinn, Bernard, ed. *Apocalyptic Spirituality: Treatises and Letters of Lactantius, Adso of Montier-en-Der, Joachim of Fiore, the Franciscan Spirituals, Savonarola.* New York, 1979.

Meinhold, Peter. *Geschichte der kirchlichen Historiographie.* Munich, 1967.

Modalsi, Ole. "Luther über die letzten Dinge," in Helmar Junghans, ed., *Leben und Werk Martin Luthers von 1526 bis 1546: Festgabe zu seinem 500. Geburtstag*, vol. 1, pp. 331–45. Berlin, 1983.

Moeller, Bernd. *Imperial Cities and the Reformation: Three Essays*, trans. H. C. Erik Midelfort and Mark U. Edwards. Philadelphia, 1972.

Möller, Wilhelm Ernst. *Andreas Osiander: Leben und ausgewählte Schriften.* Nieuwkoop, 1965.

Mommsen, Theodor E. "St. Augustine and the Christian Idea of Progress:

The Background of the City of God," *Journal of the History of Ideas* 12 (1951), 346–74.

Montgomery, John Warwick. *Cross and Crucible: Johann Valentin Andreae (1586–1654), Phoenix of the Theologians.* The Hague, 1973.

Moran, Gerard T. "Conceptions of Time in Early Modern France: An Approach to the History of Collective Mentalities," *The Sixteenth Century Journal* 12, no. 4 (Winter 1981), pp. 3–19.

Nauert, Charles G., Jr. *Agrippa and the Crisis of Renaissance Thought.* Urbana, 1965.

Nolan, Barbara. *The Gothic Visionary Perspective.* Princeton, 1977.

Oberman, Heiko A. *Luther: Mensch zwischen Gott und Teufel.* Berlin, 1982.

Ong, Walter. *The Presence of the Word: Some Prolegomena for Cultural and Religious History.* New Haven, 1967.

Otto, Rudolf. *Kingdom of God and the Son of Man.* London, 1943.

Ozment, Steven E. *Mysticism and Dissent: Religious Ideology and Social Protest in the Sixteenth Century.* New Haven, 1973.

———. *The Reformation in the Cities.* New Haven, 1975.

Park, Katharine, and Lorraine J. Daston. "Unnatural Conceptions: The Study of Monsters in Sixteenth- and Seventeenth-Century France and England," *Past and Present* 92 (Aug. 1981), 20–54.

Patrides, C. A. *The Grand Design of God: The Literary Form of the Christian View of History.* London and Toronto, 1972.

Patrides, C. A., and Joseph A. Wittreich, Jr., eds. *The Apocalypse in English Renaissance Thought and Literature.* Ithaca, 1984.

Pauck, Wilhelm. *Das Reich Gottes auf Erden: Utopie und Wircklichkeit.* Berlin and Leipzig, 1928.

Pelikan, Jaroslav. *From Luther to Kierkegaard.* St. Louis, 1950.

Petry, Ray C. *Christian Eschatology and Social Thought.* New York, 1956.

Peuch, Henri-Charles. "La Gnose et le temps," *Eranos-Jahrbuch* 20 (1951), 68ff.

Peuckert, Will-Erich. *Die grosse Wende: Das apokalyptische Saeculum und Luther.* 2 vols. Darmstadt, 1966.

———. *Pansophie: Ein Versuch zur Geschichte der weissen und schwartzen Magie.* Berlin, 1956.

———. *Pansophie, zweiter Teil: Gabalia: Ein Versuch zur Geschichte der Magia naturalis im 16. bis 18. Jahrhundert.* Berlin, 1967.

———. *Pansophie, dritter Teil: Das Rosenkreutz.* Berlin, 1973.

———. *Die Rosenkreutzer: Geschichte einer Reformation.* Jena, 1928.

Pflanz, Hans-Henning. *Geschichte und Eschatologie bei Martin Luther.* Stuttgart, 1939.

Phelan, John Leddy. *The Millennial Kingdom of the Franciscans in the New World: A Study of the Writings of Geronimo de Mendieta (1525–1604).* Berkeley and Los Angeles, 1970. First published in 1956.

Pieper, Joseph. *The End of Time.* London, 1954.

Pocock, J. G. A. *Politics, Language, and Time.* London, 1972.

Preus, Robert D. *The Theology of Post-Reformation Lutheranism.* St. Louis, Mo., 1970.

Preuss, Hans. *Apokalyptische und prophetische Frömmigkeit seit dem Ausgange des Mittelalters.* Berlin, 1907.
———. *Martin Luther: Der Deutsche.* Gütersloh, 1934.
———. *Martin Luther: Der Prophet.* Gütersloh, 1933.
———. *Die Vorstellungen vom Antichrist im späteren Mittelalter, bei Luther und in der konfessionellen Polemik.* Leipzig, 1906.
Quanbeck, Warren A. "Luther and Apocalyptic," in Vilmos Vajta, ed., *Luther and Melanchthon in the History and Theology of the Reformation.* Philadelphia, n.d.
Quinones, R. D. *The Renaissance Discovery of Time.* Cambridge, Mass., 1972.
Quistorp, Heinrich. *Calvin's Doctrine of the Last Things.* Richmond, Va., 1955.
Rabb, Theodore K. *The Struggle for Stability in Early Modern Europe.* New York, 1975.
Reeves, Marjorie. *The Influence of Prophecy in the Later Middle Ages: A Study in Joachimism.* Oxford, 1969.
———. *Joachim of Fiore and the Prophetic Future.* London, 1976.
Reeves, Marjorie, and Morton Bloomfield. "The Penetration of Joachimism into Northern Europe," *Speculum* 29 (1954), 772–93.
Rich, Arthur. *Die Anfänge der Theologie Huldrych Zwingli.* Zurich, 1949.
Richter, Aemilius Ludwig, ed. *Die evangelischen Kirchenordnungen des 16. Jahrhunderts.* 2 vols. Weimar, 1846.
Rohr, J. "Die Prophetie im letzten Jahrhundert vor der Reformation," *Historisches Jahrbuch* 19 (1898), 29–56, 447–66.
Rothkrug, Lionel. *Religious Practices and Collective Perceptions: Hidden Homologies in the Renaissance and Reformation. Historical Reflections* 7, no. 1 (Spring 1980).
Rowland, Christopher. *The Open Heaven.* London, 1982.
Rudolph, Kurt. *Gnosis: The Nature and History of Gnosticism.* New York, 1983.
Russell, Paul. "'Your sons and your daughters shall prophesy . . .' (Joel 2: 28): Common People and the Future of the Reformation in the Pamphlet Literature of Southwestern Germany to 1525," *Archive for Reformation History* 74 (1983), 122–39.
Sabean, David Warren. *Power in the Blood: Popular Culture and Village Discourse in Early Modern Germany.* Cambridge, 1984.
Sarton, George. *An Introduction to the History of Science.* Baltimore, 1927.
Scheible, Heinz, ed. *Die Anfänge der reformatorischen Geschichtsschreibung: Melanchthon, Sleidan, Flacius und die Magdeburger Zenturien.* Gütersloh, 1966.
Schenda, Rudolf. "Die deutschen Prodigiensammlungen des 16. und 17. Jahrhunderts," *Archiv für Geschichte des Buchwesens* 4 (Frankfurt a.M., 1963).
Schilling, Heinz. "Job Fincel und die Zeichen der Endzeit," in Wolfgang Brückner, ed., *Volkserzählung und Reformation: Ein Handbuch zur Tradierung und Funktion von Erzählstoffen und Erzählliteratur im Protestantismus.* Berlin, 1974.

Schmithals, Walter. *The Apocalyptic Movement: Introduction and Inter-pretation.* Nashville and New York, 1975.

Schoeps, Hans Joachim. *Philosemitismus im Barock.* Tübingen, 1952.

Schöffler, Herbert. *Deutsches Geistesleben.* Göttingen, 1956.

Scholtz, Harald. *Evangelischer Utopismus bei Johann Valentin Andreae: Ein geistiges Vorspiel zum Pietismus.* Stuttgart, 1957. *Darstellungen aus der württembergischen Geschichte,* vol. 42.

Schönstadt, Hans-Jürgen. *Antichrist, Weltheilsgeschehen und Gottes Werk-zeug. Römische Kirche, Reformation und Luther im Spiegel des Refor-mationsjubilaeums 1617.* Wiesbaden, 1978.

Schulze, Winfried. *Reich und Türkengefahr im späten 16. Jahrhundert.* Munich, 1978.

Scribner, Robert. *For the Sake of Simple Folk: Popular Propaganda for the German Reformation.* Cambridge, 1981.

————. "Incombustible Luther: The Image of the Reformer in Early Mod-ern Germany," *Past and Present,* no. 10 (Feb. 1986), 36–68.

Seebass, Gottfried. *Das reformatorische Werk des Andreas Osiander.* Nu-remberg, 1967.

Senn, Matthias. *Die Wickiana.* Zürich, 1975.

Southern, R. W. "Aspects of the European Tradition of Historical Writing," *Transactions of the Royal Historical Society,* ser. 5, 20–23 (London, 1970–73).

Spieker, Christian Wilhelm. *Lebensgeschichte des Andreas Musculus.* Frankfurt a.O., 1858; reprinted Nieuwkoop, 1964.

Staats, Reinhart. "Luthers Geburtsjahr 1484 und das Geburtsjahr der evangelischen Kirche 1519," *Bibliothek und Wissenschaft* 18 (1984), 61–84.

Staehelin, Ernst. *Die Verkündigung des Reiches Gottes in der Kirche Jesu Christi. Zeugnisse aus allen Jahrhunderten und allen Konfessionen,* 4 vols. Basel, 1957.

Strauss, Gerald. *Luther's House of Learning: Indoctrination of the Young in the German Reformation.* Baltimore and London, 1978.

————. *Manifestations of Discontent in Germany on the Eve of the Ref-ormation.* Bloomington, Ind., 1971.

————. "The Mental World of a Saxon Pastor," in Peter Newman Brooks, ed., *Reformation Principle and Practice: Essays in Honour of Arthur Geoffrey Dickens,* pp. 157–70. London, 1980.

Stupperich, Martin. "Das Augsburger Interim als apokalyptisches Ge-schehnis nach den Königsberger Schriften Andreas Osianders," *Archive for Reformation History* 64 (1973), 225–45.

Stupperich, Robert. *Der unbekannte Melanchthon. Wirken und Denken des Praeceptor Germaniae in neuer Sicht.* Stuttgart, 1961.

Taubes, Jacob. *Abendländische Eschatologie.* Bern, 1947.

Tholuck, August. *Lebenszeugung der Lutherischen Kirche aus allen Staen-den vor und waehrend der Zeit des dreissigjaehrigen Krieges.* Berlin, 1859.

Thomas, Keith Vivian. *Religion and the Decline of Magic.* London, 1971.

Thorndike, Lynn. *A History of Magic and Experimental Science.* New York, 1923–58.

Tonkin, John. *The Church and the Secular Order in Reformation Thought.* New York, 1971.

Toon, Peter, ed. *Puritans, the Millennium and the Future of Israel: Puritan Eschatology 1600 to 1660.* Cambridge and London, 1970.

Torrance, T. F. *Kingdom and Church: A Study in the Theology of the Reformation.* Fair Lawn, N.J., 1956.

Troeltsch, Ernst. *The Social Teaching of the Christian Churches.* New York, 1949.

Trompf, G. W. *The Idea of Historical Recurrence in Western Thought: From Antiquity to the Reformation.* Berkeley, 1979.

Trunz, Erich. "Der deutsche Späthumanismus um 1600 als Standeskultur," in Richard Alewyn, ed., *Deutsche Barockforschung: Dokumentation einer Epoche,* pp. 147–81. Cologne and Berlin, 1965.

Tuveson, Ernest Lee. *Millennium and Utopia: A Study in the Background of the Idea of Progress.* Berkeley, 1949.

Vasiliev, A. "Medieval Ideas of the End of the World: West and East," *Byzantion* 16 (1942–43), 462–502.

Verheus, Simon Leendert. *Zeugnis und Gericht. Kirchengeschichtliche Betrachtungen bei Sebastian Franck und Matthias Flacius.* Nieuwkoop, 1971.

Voegelin, Eric. *The New Science of Politics.* Chicago, 1952.

Volz, Hans. *Die Lutherpredigten des Johannes Mathesius: Kritische Untersuchungen zur Geschichtsschreibung im Zeitalter der Reformation.* Leipzig, 1930.

Wadstein, Ernst. "Die eschatologische Ideengruppe: Antichrist, Weltsabbat, Weltende, und Weltgericht in den Hauptmomenten ihrer christlich-mittelalterlichen Gesamtentwicklung," *Zeitschrift für wissenschaftliche Theologie* 38 (1895), 538–616; 39 (1896), 251, 544ff.

Waite, A. E. *The Brotherhood of the Rosy Cross.* New Hyde Park, N.Y., 1961.

Walch, Johann Georg. *Historische und theologische Einleitung in die Religions-Streitigkeiten, welche sonderlich ausser der evangelisch-Lutherischen Kirche entstanden.* Jena, 1733–36.

Walker, D. P. *The Ancient Theology: Studies in Christian Platonism from the 15th to the 18th Century.* Ithaca, 1972.

Wallmann, Johannes. "Zwischen Reformation und Pietismus: Reich Gottes und Chiliasmus in der Lutherischen Orthodoxie," in Eberhard Jüngel, Johannes Wallmann, and Wilfrid Werbeck, eds., *Verifikationen: Festschrift für Gerhard Ebeling zum 70. Geburtstag,* pp. 187–205. Tübingen, 1982.

Warburg, Aby. *Heidnisch-antike Weissagung in Wort und Bild zu Luthers Zeiten.* Heidelberg, 1920. Reprinted in *Gesammelte Schriften,* vol. 2, pp. 487–558. Nendeln, 1969.

Watts, Pauline Moffitt. *Nicholas Cusanus: A Fifteenth-Century Vision of Man.* Leiden, 1982.

———. "Prophecy and Discovery: On the Spiritual Origins of Christopher Columbus's 'Enterprise of the Indies,'" *American Historical Review* 90, no. 1 (Feb. 1985), 73–102.

Weber, Bruno. *Erschröckliche und warhafftige Wunderzeichen, 1543–1586.* 2 vols. Zurich, 1971–72.

Weller, Emil. *Die ersten Deutschen Zeitungen 1505–99.* Tübingen, 1872; reprinted Hildesheim, 1962.

———. *Die falschen und fingierten Druckorte.* 2 vols. Leipzig, 1864; reprinted Hildesheim, 1960–61.

———. *Lexicon pseudonymorum.* Regensburg, 1886; reprinted Hildesheim, 1963.

Williams, Ann. *Prophecy and Millenarianism: Essays in Honour of Marjorie Reeves.* Harlow, 1980.

Williams, George H. *The Radical Reformation.* Philadelphia, 1962.

Williams, Glanmore. *Reformation Views of Church History.* London, 1970.

Wind, Edgar. *Pagan Mysteries in the Renaissance.* New Haven, 1958.

Wolgast, Eike. *Die Wittenberger Theologie und die Politik der evangelischen Stände.* Gütersloh, 1977.

Wollgast, Siegfried. *Der deutsche Pantheismus im 16. Jahrhundert: Sebastian Franck und seine Wirkungen auf die Entwicklung der pantheistischen Philosophie in Deutschland.* Berlin, 1972.

Yates, Frances. *Giordano Bruno and the Hermetic Tradition.* Chicago, 1964.

———. "A Great Magus," review of Peter J. French, *John Dee: The World of an Elizabethan Magus,* in Yates, *Ideas and Ideals in the North European Renaissance.* London and Boston, 1984.

———. *The Rosicrucian Enlightenment.* London, 1972.

Zambelli, Paola. "Fine del mondo o inizio della propaganda? Astrologia, filosofia della storia e propaganda politico-religiosa nel dibattito sulla congiunzione del 1524," in Zambelli, *Scienze, credenze occulte, livelli di cultura,* pp. 291–368. Florence, 1982.

———, ed. *'Astrologi hallucinati': Stars and the End of the World in Luther's Time.* Berlin and New York, 1986.

Zeeden, Ernst Walter. *Martin Luther und die Reformation im Urteil des deutschen Luthertums.* 2 vols. Freiburg, 1950.

Zimmermann, Albert, ed. *Mensura. Mass, Zahl, Zahlensymbolik im Mittelalter. Miscellanea Mediaevalia,* 16, pt. 1/2 (Berlin and New York, 1983–84).

Zinner, Ernst. *Geschichte und Bibliographie der astronomischen Literatur in Deutschland zur Zeit der Renaissance.* Stuttgart, 1964.

✑ Index

Library of Congress Cataloging-in-Publication Data

Barnes, Robin Bruce, 1951—
    Apocalypticism in the wake of the Lutheran Reformation: prophecy
and gnosis / Robin Bruce Barnes.
        p.   cm.
    Bibliography: p.
    Includes index.
    ISBN 0-8047-1405-3 (alk. paper)
    1. Eschatology—History of doctrines—16th century.   2. Lutheran
Church—Doctrines—History—16th century.   3. Bible—Prophecies—
History—16th century.   4. Gnosticism—History—16th century.
I. Title.   II. Title: Prophecy and gnosis.
BT819.5.B35   1988
236'.09'031—dc19   87-24138
                                                              CIP